SAT® READING:
Natural & Social Science

TEST PREP

50+ GRAPHS

ADVANCED PRACTICE SERIES

500+ QUESTIONS

READING COMPREHENSION FOR NATURAL AND SOCIAL SCIENCE PASSAGES

- Featuring High Complexity Science Topics
- Intense Focus on Graph Questions
- Time-Saving Advice, Proven Strategies

2000+ ANSWER EXPLANATIONS

Authors
Arianna Astuni, Co-Founder IES Test Prep
Khalid Khashoggi, Co-Founder IES Test Prep

Editorial
Christopher Carbonell, Editorial Director
Patrick Kennedy, Executive Editor
Megan Caldwell, Senior Editor

Design
Christopher Carbonell

Contributors
Arianna Astuni
Christopher Carbonell
Josephine Giaimo
Sigourney Hunter
Patrick Kennedy
Khalid Khashoggi
Astha Lakhankar
Jo Landau
Rajvi Patel
Cassidy Yong

Published by IES Publications
www.IESpublications.co
© IES Publications, 2019

ON BEHALF OF
Integrated Educational Services, Inc.
355 Main Street
Metuchen, NJ 08840
www.iestestprep.com

All rights reserved. No part of this book may be reproduced in any form, or incorporated into any information retrieval system, electronic or mechanical, without written permission of the copyright owner.

We would like to thank the IES Publications team as well as the teachers and students at IES Test Prep who have contributed to the creation of this book.

The SAT® is a registered trademark of the College Board, which was not involved in the production of, and does not endorse, this product.

ISBN-13: 9781674034188
QUESTIONS OR COMMENTS? Visit us at iestestprep.com

TABLE OF CONTENTS

Introduction **6-10**

Chapter One **11**

Chapter 1.1 (Wax Worms) 12-15

Chapter 1.2 (Blushing) 16-19

Chapter 1.3 (Video Games) 20-23

Chapter 1.4 (Thyroid Misdiagnosis) 24-26

Chapter 1.5 (Pluto's Surface) 27-30

Chapter 1.6 (Facebook Class) 31-33

Chapter 1.7 (Sea Lions) 34-36

Chapter 1.8 (Pain Coping) 37-40

Chapter 1.9 (Dark Patterns) 41-43

Chapter 1.10 (Voter Turnout) 44-47

Answer Key and Explanations 48-74

Chapter Two **75**

Chapter 2.1 (Stress Eating) 76-78

Chapter 2.2 (Rodenticide) 79-81

Chapter 2.3 (Generation Gap) 82-85

Chapter 2.4 (Gravitational Waves) 86-89

Chapter 2.5 (Data Fail) 90-93

Chapter 2.6 (Korean Pine) 94-97

Chapter 2.7 (DNA & Diet) 98-101

Chapter 2.8 (Nothing is Certain) 102-104

Chapter 2.9 (Antibiotic Combinations) 105-107

Chapter 2.10 (Alzheimer's Diet) 108-110

Answer Key and Explanations 111-137

Chapter 3 138

Chapter 3.1 (Chronic Bronchitis) 139-141

Chapter 3.2 (Bioluminescence) 142-144

Chapter 3.3 (School Start Times) 145-148

Chapter 3.4 (Talent vs. Luck) 149-151

Chapter 3.5 (Climate Change) 152-154

Chapter 3.6 (Greenland Shark) 155-158

Chapter 3.7 (Drowsy Driving) 159-162

Chapter 3.8 (Pluto's Classification) 163-166

Chapter 3.9 (Diabetic Lifestyle) 167-169

Chapter 3.10 (Cooperative Economics) 170-173

Answer Key and Explanations 174-200

Chapter 4 201

Chapter 4.1 (Coralline Algae) 202-204

Chapter 4.2 (Saccadic Movements) 205-207

Chapter 4.3 (Taste Perception) 208-210

Chapter 4.4 (End of Men) 211-214

Chapter 4.5 (Myth of ADD) 215-218

Chapter 4.6 (Crown of Thorns) 219-222

Chapter 4.7 (Redefining Health) 223-226

Chapter 4.8 (Wildfires) 227-229

Chapter 4.9 (*Wolbachia*) 230-232

Chapter 4.10 (Incredible Genes) 233-236

Answer Key and Explanations 237-266

Chapter 5 ... .267

- Chapter 5.1 (Rogue Waves) ... 268-270
- Chapter 5.2 (Preventing Alzheimer's) ... 271-274
- Chapter 5.3 (Carbonados) ... 275-277
- Chapter 5.4 (Marangoni Effect) ... 278-281
- Chapter 5.5 (Algae Biofuels) ... 282-284
- Chapter 5.6 (Ebola Vaccine) ... 285-288
- Chapter 5.7 (Africanized Bees) ... 289-292
- Chapter 5.8 (Behavioral Addiction) ... 293-295
- Chapter 5.9 (Microbiome of Rice) ... 296-298
- Chapter 5.10 (Flu Vaccine) ... 299-302
- Answer Key and Explanations ... 303-332

Dear student,

Ever since the SAT was updated in 2016, elements of the redesigned test have evolved and changed gradually over time. As I receive feedback from my students as they take their official tests, it is clear that these evolutions will continue to occur, but one way to always be prepared is to "Control the Test."

I created this book because I consistently have students who struggle specifically with Natural and Social Science passages. For some, the topics are not interesting or are perhaps too complex to understand. For others, synthesizing graphic data with the passage's ideas can be challenging. Regardless of your desired area of improvement, mastering your approach to these passages is imperative, since they account for THREE of the five passages on any given SAT Reading section.

It is my firm belief that, through isolated and repeated practice, students can identify their mistakes, and with discipline, work to correct those mistakes and improve their scores. Start slow and do a few passages, and look for patterns. Which types of questions are you getting wrong? Why are you getting them wrong? What did you miss? Take note of these ideas as you practice your first sections. Then, before you begin your next set of passages, examine your notes and try to find a pattern. Knowing this pattern is the key to your improvement so that you can learn to avoid the same traps and pitfalls as you continue to practice. Identifying your pattern takes time, but every student has one!

Enclosed you will find 50 passages, over 500 questions, and over 50 graphics that will help you with your targeted work in Natural and Social Science passages.

Always remember, "Accuracy is NOT intelligence; it's discipline!"

Wishing you the best of luck,

Arianna Astuni

INTRODUCTION

The purpose of this book is to provide repeated and isolated practice on the Natural and Social Science passages found in the SAT Reading section. Unlike the other SAT Reading passages, Natural and Social Science passages can feature informational graphics (bar graphs, pie charts, maps, etc...) that present data relative to the main ideas of the passage. These sections test a student's ability to synthesize the data from these graphics to the information presented in the passage. However, it should be noted that not all passages will feature an informational graphic.

The Natural and Social Science passages do NOT test a student's prior knowledge about a particular subject or topic. All the information needed to answer the questions can be found in the passage and its accompanying graphic (should there be one).

PASSAGE FORMAT

While Natural Science and Social Science passages may seem challenging to many, having a brief understanding of the general format of these passages can prove useful for reading and analyzing the text.

By way of illustration, these passages first introduce an overarching main idea that often presents an issue or a problem. Generally, the author will have a stance on this issue or problem, or in some cases, may only wish to examine the main idea from an informational viewpoint. Next, an overview of a study (or sometimes several studies) and research relative to the main idea is examined by the author. Sometimes the research and study (or studies) are detailed at length, while in other instances, only a general overview of this information is provided. The results of the study and research are then evaluated to determine the overall implications based on the author's stance.

While there may be some slight variances in the above format, this is generally what students can expect on the Natural and Social Science passages.

TOPICS

Below are examples of topics that may be found in these passages:

Natural Science

- Zoology/ Organisms
- Human Body/ Medicine
- Environment/ Ecology
- Astronomy/ Planetary Science
- Molecular Science
- Chemistry
- Physics
- Evolution Theory

Social Science

- Human Behavior
- Psychology
- Sociology
- Technology
- Economics
- Geography

GRAPHICS

Of the Natural and Social Science passages, generally two will feature an informational graphic. These graphics can vary from simple tables and bar graphs to more complex forms such as scatter plots and topographical maps. Regardless of the complexity of this content, understanding how to read and interpret the graph elements will always prove useful.

ALWAYS check for (or circle) the following on each graphic:

- Graph / Chart Title
- Axis Label / Title
- Units of Measurement (e.g., x-axis units, y-axis units)
- Legend
- Trend Lines
- Special Notations (i.e., graphic description)

The above are general graphic elements to always note, but each individual graphic may offer additional elements that may relate to the passage's ideas.

The student's job is to interpret the data in the graphic and to synthesize that data with the passage's ideas to answer up to three (or possibly more) questions for that passage. This data will often present similarities to the passage's ideas, research, or study.

Note: In some cases, the graphic's data may appear to be connected to the passage's ideas, but may not be fully relevant. It is important to also note the **<u>DIFFERENCES</u>** between the graphic's information and the passage's ideas as well!

HOW TO USE THIS BOOK

Each chapter provides ten passages with ten or more questions per passage. That's approximately 100 or more questions per chapter, with samples of all question types: Main Idea, Word in Context, Command of Evidence, Line References, and Graph Synthesis.

Most passages (but not all) have supplementary graphics with corresponding questions. Practice noting and circling the elements of each graphic. Occasionally, a single long comprehension passage may have two graphics or a double long comprehension passage may have one or more graphics. Regardless, it is necessary to analyze in some way the data and information in the graph(s).

Within each chapter, the topics will vary passage by passage to test the student's ability to **switch between different topics** that the student could see on a real SAT. (Please see potential topics on previous pages.)

At the end of each chapter, an answer key is provided for quick reference. Following the answer key, a comprehensive answer-explanation section is included for more detailed analysis and evaluation.

Chapter One

Questions 1-11 are based on the following passage and supplementary material.

1.1
Adapted from a research study published in *Current Biology*, "Polyethylene bio-degradation by caterpillars of the wax moth Galleria mellonella" by Paolo Bombelli, Christopher J. Howe, and Federica Bertocchini.

As the human population continues to increase exponentially, soaring above 9 billion in 2017, so does our waste. A 2013 study found that Americans alone generate 254 million tons of trash per year, with each individual generating about 4.4 pounds of waste per day. These staggering statistics leave us wondering: how can we minimize our damage to the planet even while our population continues to grow?

Recycling and composting have helped reduce our carbon footprint (a measure of the amount of carbon dioxide and other carbon compounds that are emitted as an effect of fossil fuel consumption), but they're only blips on the radar when it comes to the total amount of trash that's thrown away every year. The diligence it takes to find recycling and compost centers, coupled with lax regulations and the general indifference of the public, have made it difficult for these methods to be effective on their own in combating waste. In addition, certain materials are unable to be recycled and maintain a looming presence in our ecological system. Many types of plastics take up to 400 years to fully break down, and with over a trillion plastic bags used per year, they simply accumulate much faster than they can decompose.

The lasting omnipresence of these bags has become a global problem: they've seeped into rivers and oceans, even making their way to remote parts of the Arctic to be perpetually trapped by ocean currents and eaten by unwitting wildlife.

One of the worst culprits is Polyethylene Terephthalate (PET or PETE), a plastic used primarily for disposable packaging. It's used to contain everything from ketchup to shampoo, and is extremely popular with consumers because of its resistance to breakage. There's a catch, however: PET's durability, convenient as it may be, presents a problem when it's time to take out the trash. Biodegradation normally occurs when bacteria transform organic waste (such as wood, food scraps, or leaves) into soil. However, bacteria is not naturally attracted to plastic materials. As a consequence, petroleum-based products such as PET can be broken down into smaller pieces but never fully degrade. Once PET is left in a landfill or dumped into the ocean, it may remain there forever.

As of now, the only sure way to break down plastic is through photodegradation, a process utilizing UV rays in lieu of bacteria to cleave polymer bonds in molecular chains. This is not an ideal solution: photodegradation is only effective on waste that has been exposed to sunlight, and will not impact the huge amount of waste in the oceans or underground that is shielded from the sun.

Another proposed solution was to completely revamp the way products currently on the market are packaged. Polylactic acid (PLA), a plant-based hydrobiodegradable plastic derived from corn, was thought to be an appealing alternative to PET-manufactured products. PLA decomposes into water and carbon dioxide four times faster than do PET-based plastics floating in the ocean. Scientists have found, though, that while PLA efficiently breaks down in commercial composting facilities at high temperatures, it does not fare as well in an uncontrolled environment. If buried in a landfill, a PLA plastic bag may remain intact for as long as one made from oil or natural gas.

The most promising solution thus far comes from an unexpected source: nature itself. Common plastic-eating caterpillars known as wax worms were discovered at the home of Federica Bertocchini, a researcher at the Spanish National Research Council, in one of her beehives. "In cleaning the beehives, I put the worms in a plastic bag," she explains. "After a short while, they had escaped, and the plastic bag was full of holes." She immediately began wondering what had happened to the parts of the bag that were chewed away and, with the help of fellow researchers Paolo Bombelli and Chris Howe, hypothesized that the digestive ability of these creatures had developed to accommodate manufactured polymer breakdown due to the similarity between the polymers' chemical structure and that of beeswax. The researchers then confirmed that the worms' digestion process was breaking the polyethylene chemical bonds and converting them to ethylene glycol, which degrades on its own within a few weeks.

Compared to other methods of breaking down polyethylene, wax worms are clearly superior. Corrosives such as nitric acid take months to complete degradation of PET; on the other hand, 100 wax worms can biodegrade 92 milligrams of polyethylene in just 12 hours. As of now, there are no immediate plans to use the worms themselves for mass plastic waste disposal. Instead, scientists like Bertocchini and her team hope to examine the mechanism of the worms' catabolic process and replicate it in a lab. They

postulate that one molecule is solely responsible for the worms' extraordinary ability, and aim to isolate it through further experiments. If such a molecule exists and is found, we may have finally found a lasting
100 solution for a once-unsolvable problem.

Figure 1

Percentage of Waste in Landfills, Sorted by Type

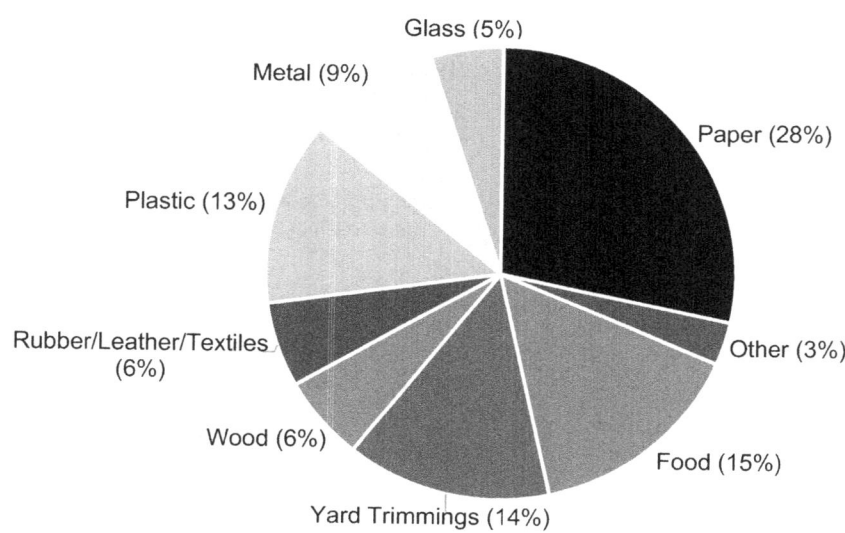

Figure 2

Estimated Breakdown Times of the Most Common Types of Plastic

Plastic	Time (Years)
PET -E-	5 to 10
HDPE	Centuries
PVC	∞
LDPE	500 to 1000
PP	Millennia
PS	< 50

1

Which statement best describes the developmental pattern of the passage?

A) A problem is introduced, several alternatives are evaluated, and a potential solution is proposed.
B) A study is described, its implications are analyzed, and an alternative method is promoted.
C) A practice is explained, its flaws are demonstrated, and further action is urged.
D) An argument is presented, its assumptions are refuted, and a consensus is reached.

2

According to the author, recycling as a practice has not gained much support from the public mostly because

A) it lessens our carbon footprint.
B) certain materials cannot be recycled.
C) of the infrequent placement of recycling centers.
D) of a lack of knowledge about recycling practices.

3

As used in line 20, "looming" most nearly means

A) towering.
B) persisting.
C) impending.
D) emerging.

4

Which statement best explains why PET cannot fully decay?

A) It becomes trapped by ocean currents.
B) It is extremely resistant to breakage.
C) It does not attract biodegrading bacteria.
D) It only breaks down at high temperatures.

5

Which choice provides the best evidence for the answer to the previous question?

A) Lines 35-37 ("There's…trash")
B) Lines 39-40 ("However,…materials")
C) Lines 41-44 ("As a…degrade")
D) Lines 61-63 ("that…environment")

6

Bertocchini and her team suggest that wax worms are capable of breaking down plastics because

A) they have recently adapted to include plastic bags as a food source.
B) they can transform plastics into easily biodegradable matter.
C) their normal food source shares properties with plastics.
D) they possess a unique molecular structure that allows them to digest inorganic material.

7

Which choice provides the best evidence for the answer to the previous question?

A) Lines 71-74 ("I put…holes")
B) Lines 78-81 ("The digestive…beeswax.")
C) Lines 81-85 ("The researchers…weeks")
D) Lines 95-98 ("They postulate…experiments")

8

As used in line 94, "mechanism" most nearly means

A) workings.
B) apparatus.
C) purpose.
D) system.

9

According to the author, which statement expresses a valid relationship between biodegradation and photodegradation?

A) Both are mechanisms of breaking down waste, but only photodegradation exploits UV rays.
B) Both are mechanisms of breaking down waste, but only biodegradation exploits UV rays.
C) Both are mechanisms of breaking down waste, but only biodegradation is a solution to the current problem.
D) Both are mechanisms of breaking down waste, but only photodegradation is a solution to the current problem.

10

Based on figure 1, which percentages correlate to the author's description of organic waste?

A) 13%, 14%, 15%
B) 5%, 9%, 27%
C) 3%, 6%, 14%
D) 6%, 14%, 15%

11

Which of the following statements from the passage is supported by figure 2?

A) Lines 3-6 ("A 2013…day")
B) Lines 21-24 ("Many…decompose")
C) Lines 30-32 ("One of…packaging")
D) Lines 64-65 ("If buried…gas")

Questions 1-11 are based on the following passage and supplementary material.
1.2
Adapted from "The Remedial Value of Blushing in the Context of Transgressions and Mishaps" by C. Dijk, P. J. de Jong, & M. L. Peters, a chapter which explores the way that humans interpret blushing in others and seeks to determine whether blushing has any cultural merit.

Imagine this: you're in a very loud and crowded room, trying to have a conversation with your friend, who is sitting next to you. In order for your friend to hear you, you must raise your voice. Perhaps you are merely talking about the weather, or maybe about a piece of toilet paper stuck on the foot of someone nearby. Without any obvious prompting, the room falls silent. You are mid-sentence, full volume. Everyone turns and stares directly at you.

Are your cheeks burning? If so, you are a remarkably sympathetic person! You are also experiencing something that is unique to the quintessentially social human species: blushing.

The fact that only humans blush is one of several reasons that this automatic, uncontrollable trait is so fascinating. Another is that, while we understand how it works on an anatomical and physiological level, we don't quite understand why certain circumstances would affect our nervous systems in such a way. Indeed, we know enough about the anatomy and physiology of a blush that it is possible for people who are chronic blushers to have a surgery to suppress this reaction. However, the psychological triggers of this phenomenon remain a partial mystery. Many studies of blushing have found—perhaps unsurprisingly to many chronic blushers—that most incidents are correlated with keen self-consciousness. It is worth probing further into blushing precisely because we don't entirely understand something that has a social function.

In 2009, a study was published in the scientific journal *Emotion* that tested the hypothesis that blushing can actually improve how someone is viewed after committing a transgression or having a social blunder. In order to do so, authors Dijk, de Jong, and Peters ran two separate experiments in which they recorded how participants viewed models who had supposedly done something that warranted shame or embarrassment. The key, though, was that some of the models would be blushing, and others would not.

The models themselves (24 in total) appeared in photos with a neutral expression, a neutral expression with a blush, an emotional expression, or an emotional expression with a blush. These photos were then presented to participants after they had read a story about an incident. The type of incident depended on whether the participant was in the transgression experiment or in the social mishap experiment. Both experiments had four versions: each of the 12 stories in a given experiment would be paired with one of the four expressions, and no model would appear twice in the same version. Participants were randomly assigned one of the versions.

After reading a story and viewing the photo, participants were asked a series of questions. Those specific to the transgression experiment were "How trustworthy do you find this person?" and "To what extent do you have the impression that this person is ashamed?" In the mishap experiment, participants were asked "Do you find this person socially skillful?" and "To what extent do you have the impression that this person is embarrassed?" Both experiments included the questions "How sympathetic do you find this person?" and "What is your general impression?" Participants rated the models on a scale of 0-100 for how sympathetic, trustworthy, embarrassed, ashamed, or socially skillful they seemed.

In the transgression experiment, the participants both judged the models more positively and viewed them as slightly more ashamed of their actions if they were blushing, regardless of whether they had a neutral or emotional expression. Interestingly, models with a neutral expression and a blush scored similarly to those who expressed emotion but without a blush. The mishap experiment also showed that blushing was significant to how the model was judged. In both experiments, models with emotional expressions and a blush were viewed the most positively.

These results show that expressing emotion and blushing can affect perception on their own, but are most potent together. Perhaps the most telling fact is that only 2 out of all 128 participants thought that the experiment had anything to do with blushing. It isn't possible to conclude anything certain from that, but it does suggest that blushing affects us on a subtle, perhaps unconscious, level. In 2011, a similar study was run at University of California, Berkeley that seemed to corroborate these results. The authors of this study found that those who blushed when relating an embarrassing incident were perceived as more trustworthy.

If we want to better understand blushing, future research could delve into differing cultural perceptions; such studies must, of course, include diverse

95 participants. For the present, though, these studies may be useful in reassuring chronic blushers that, as embarrassing as it may feel, frequent blushing can have a positive effect.

Figure 1

Respondents' Perceptions of Blushing Model as a Factor of Facial Expression

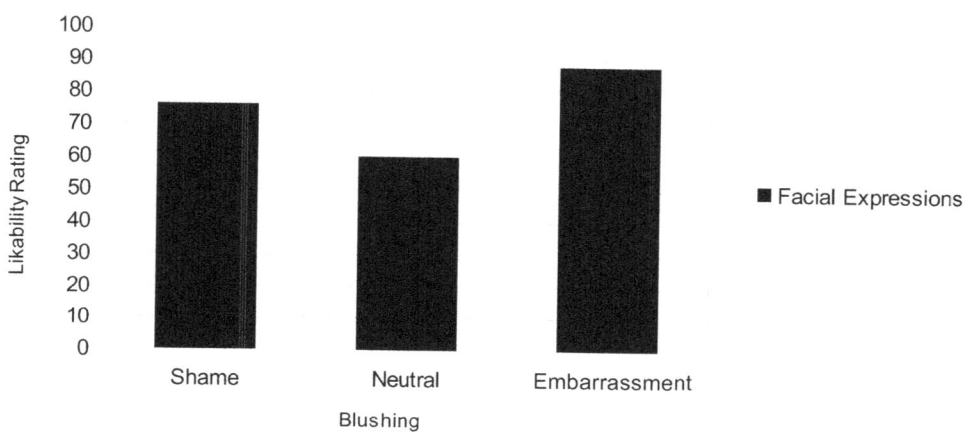

Figure 2

Respondents' Perceptions of Non-Blushing Model as a Factor of Facial Expression

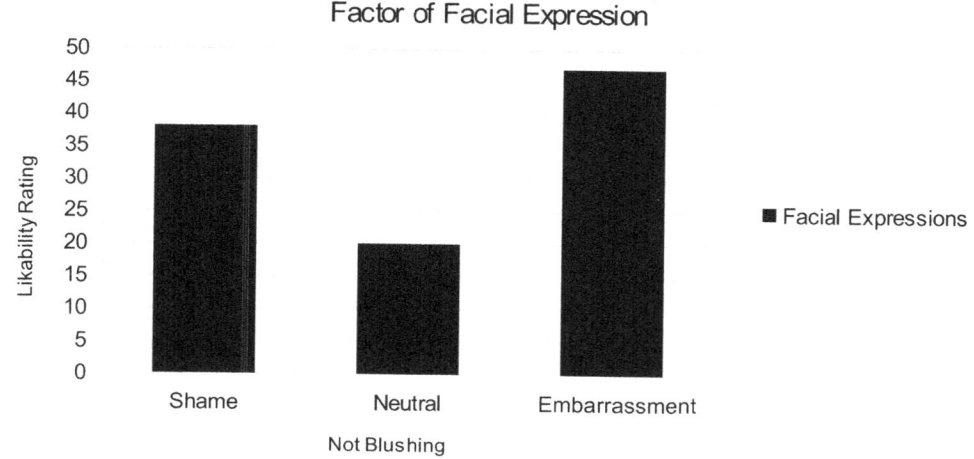

1

Which of the following experiments would NOT be likely to yield useful information about the social or psychological functions of blushing?

A) An experiment that examined whether blushing reactions were interpreted similarly by speakers of different languages.
B) An experiment that compared the relationship between blushing and shame in humans to the same relationship between factors among different mammal species.
C) An experiment that is designed to determine whether the intensity of a blushing reaction can be linked to the number of people present in an awkward situation.
D) An experiment that compares the frequency of blushing reactions among people who self-identify as introverts and people who self-identify as extroverts.

2

Which choice provides the best evidence for the answer to the previous question?

A) Lines 7-9 ("Without . . . you")
B) Lines 14-16 ("The fact . . . fascinating")
C) Lines 24-27 ("Many . . . self-consciousness")
D) Lines 27-30 ("It is . . . function")

3

Which of the following statements is supported by the author's discussion of "chronic blushers" in the third paragraph (lines 14-30)?

A) The psychological factors involved in blushing were at one point catalogued using a system that has since been revealed to be deficient.
B) The examination of processes similar to chronic blushing in animals can help researchers understand the functions of blushing in humans.
C) The label "chronic blusher" does not describe an untreatable problem, since a procedure exists that can counteract this form of blushing.
D) The resolution of mysteries surrounding the mechanics of blushing may shed light on larger and more complex inquiries into brain chemistry.

4

As used in line 27, "correlated with" most nearly means

A) indistinguishable from.
B) accompanied by.
C) likely to conform to.
D) aided by.

5

Both the transgression experiment and the social mishap experiment were designed to determine

A) whether the participants preferred expressions of shame or expressions of embarrassment.
B) the ethical values of the participants.
C) the participants' overall reactions to the models.
D) how closely the participants resembled the models.

6

As described in the passage, the 2009 study that appeared in *Emotion* was structured so that

A) the participants could discuss and revise their previous ideas about the social role of blushing.
B) the participants were given a choice of questions to answer for any given test subject.
C) the participants in the study were not fully aware of at least one of the study's key premises.
D) the participants were sorted into two test groups on the basis of initial reactions to transgressions and mishaps.

7

Which choice provides the best evidence for the answer to the previous question?

A) Lines 46-48 ("The type . . . experiment")
B) Lines 54-55 ("After . . . questions")
C) Lines 65-67 ("Participants . . . seemed")
D) Lines 81-83 ("Perhaps . . . blushing")

8

As used in line 85, "subtle" most nearly means

A) carefully refined.
B) mostly unimportant.
C) difficult to discern.
D) cleverly articulated.

9

Taken together, the two figures mainly support the conclusion that

A) blushing increased the likability rating of the respondents who exhibited shame, embarrassment, and neutral facial expressions.
B) blushing had no effect on the likability rating of the model for the neutral or embarrassment facial expression.
C) blushing increased the likability rating of the model for shame, neutral, and embarrassment facial expressions.
D) blushing decreased the likability rating of the model for the neutral facial expression.

10

The experiment referenced in figures 1 and 2 resembles the experiment described in the passage in that both experiments

A) did not yield any conclusive information regarding the perception of blushing.
B) measure likability ratings using the same numerical scale.
C) rely on the models' self-reporting in order to gather data.
D) examined the facial muscles used in smiling.

11

A student claims that the graphs support the passage's statements about the study performed by the "University of California, Berkeley" (line 87). The student's claim most likely relies on the assumption that

A) likability and neutrality are interchangeable qualities.
B) shame and embarrassment are interchangeable qualities.
C) trustworthiness and shame are interchangeable qualities.
D) likability and trustworthiness are interchangeable qualities.

Questions 1-11 are based on the following passage and supplementary material.
1.3
Adapted from "The Effects of Violent Video Game Habits on Adolescent Hostility, Aggressive Behaviors, and School Performance," a 2004 NCBI article by M.P. Vanderpump and a team of researchers at the Department of Medicine, Newcastle General Hospital, UK.

    In 21st century American society, video games are one of the favorite pastimes of children. In 2002, the average child in the US reportedly played video
Line games for 7 hours each week, with wide differences
5 among different ages and between boys and girls. Unfortunately for the millions of video game players, an increasing body of research links violent video games to aggressive behaviors, attitudes, and cognitions. Those who play video games, however,
10 would say they are cathartic expressions of aggression, thereby preventing violence rather than causing it—but opponents are not convinced. Can researchers document what is the long-presumed connection, if any, between these variables and video game
15 exposure?
    In 2004, researcher Douglas A. Gentile and others, using a General Aggression Model (GAM), looked at the possible connections between a number of variables and video game exposure. The GAM was
20 previously developed by Anderson and colleagues to help explain links between violent video gaming and aggressive behavior, attitude, and cognition. The GAM suggests specific results in relation to long-term exposure to violent content. For instance, it
25 postulates that repeated exposure to scenes of graphic violence may be desensitizing. So, over the long term, trait hostility may increase due to video game play. Additionally, violent game content may moderate or mediate the effect of violent games on one's aggressive
30 behavior, depending on other factors.
    The research team examined data from more than 600 8th and 9th graders from four schools in the Midwest, including urban private, suburban public, and rural public. Student data included anonymous
35 surveys, descriptive data about video game habits, school performance, demographic data, and measures of trait hostility. Students were told to include as video games any computer games, consoles including Nintendo, Gameboy, and other handheld devices, and
40 video arcades. Participants named their top three video games, rating them on how violent the games were. A video game violence exposure score was calculated for each subject. Then, subjects indicated how much violence they like in their games, using a 10-point
45 scale. Besides violent video game exposure, additional variables were the amount of video game play, trait hostility, parental limits, arguments with teachers, grades, and physical fights.
    The researchers found that, in general, youth
50 preferred a moderate amount of violence, with significant sex differences on this variable—boys preferred more violence than girls did. Most games that were rated among subjects' three favorite games fell into the category of having "some violence."
55 Parents for the most part were not involved in their children's video game playing, with few parents setting limits on the amount of game time. About one-fifth of the students got into arguments with teachers almost weekly or almost daily. About one-third had been in a
60 physical fight within the past year, with sex differences between boys and girls.
    After the results had been calculated, the study substantiated the initial predictions. First, it showed that violent video game content and amount of video
65 game play correlated positively with having a physical fight, getting into an argument with a teacher, and trait hostility—and correlated negatively with school grades. This means that the more time kids spend playing violent video games, the more likely they
70 are to have the aforementioned negative behaviors, and the less likely they are to have high grades. Second, parental limits correlated negatively with trait hostility and arguments with teachers—and correlated positively with school performance.
75   What this study tells us is that exposure to video games could very well be causing violent behaviors. The team finally nailed down definitely that when adolescents expose themselves to more video games, they generally become more hostile. Putting it simply,
80 students who were once not hostile, but have high exposure to violent video games, are more likely to exhibit violent behaviors as a result than even highly hostile students who play little to no violent video games (38% compared to 28%, respectively). Looking
85 at the data, it's not that there is 100 percent likelihood that students will become more violent after playing violent video games, but that there is a definitive rise in violence, which implies that parents should pay close attention to what their kids are doing in their free
90 time. The researchers conclude that "Clearly, media violence is not the sole cause of aggression. But it is likely that it is one of several causes leading to it."

Figure 1

Survey: Percentages of Video Game Preference Based on Favorite Genres For Boys and Girls

	Fantasy	Sports	Puzzles/ Trivia	Violent Strategy	Violent First-Person
Boys (325)	7%	39%	8%	13%	33%
Girls (275)	31%	6%	51%	6%	6%

Figure 2

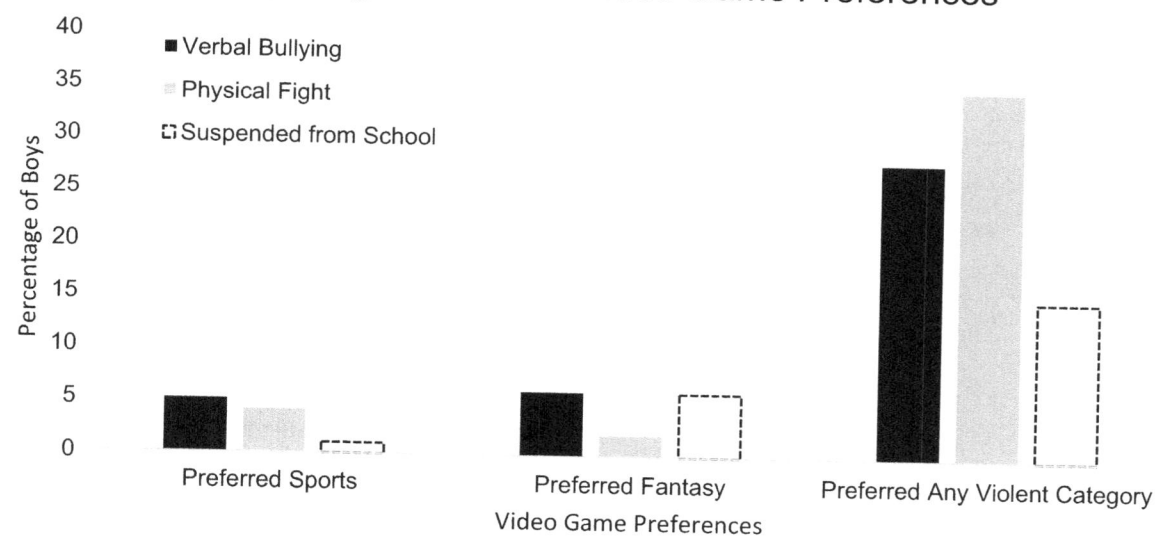

1

The main purpose of the passage is to present

A) research that was designed with the end goal of improving the mental health of young people.
B) an experiment that demonstrates that video games offer no cognitive or psychological benefits.
C) findings that relate to a debate over the repercussions of playing video games.
D) an argument in favor of designing less immersive and less violent video games.

2

Which choice best describes the overall structure of the first paragraph?

A) A broad trend is mentioned, different perspectives are discussed, and the possibility of validating a single perspective is raised.
B) A source of contention is raised, competing arguments are analyzed, and a compromise approach is presented as the most reasonable option.
C) A theory is introduced, a seemingly incompatible theory is outlined, and the original theory is shown to be more compelling.
D) A few historical developments are described, a crisis is explained in relation to these developments, and a possible solution is presented for further analysis.

3

As used in line 11, "preventing" most nearly means

A) precluding.
B) banning.
C) interrupting.
D) delaying.

4

The author explains that the General Aggression Model (GAM) described in the passage was

A) modified by Anderson and colleagues once its shortcomings became apparent.
B) developed in response to a perceived mental health crisis.
C) not exclusive to the 2004 research undertaken by Gentile and others.
D) relevant only to analysis of 8th and 9th graders.

5

As used in line 40, "named" most nearly means

A) stigmatized.
B) nominated.
C) designated.
D) appointed.

6

Which of the following measures would NOT clearly expand the scope of the study conducted by Douglas A. Gentile and affiliated researchers?

A) Surveying students from five different areas of the United States.
B) Surveying at least 10 schools in the Midwestern United States.
C) Surveying students from academic levels other than grades 8 and 9.
D) Surveying both boys and girls in terms of their video game preferences.

7

A woman allows her son to play video games with a moderate amount of violence, and the son is allowed to choose how many hours per week he plays. Which choice best indicates that the mother's approach may be hurting the son's grades?

A) Lines 55-57 ("Parents . . . time")
B) Lines 57-59 ("About . . . daily")
C) Lines 72-74 ("Second . . . performance")
D) Lines 79-84 ("Putting . . . respectively")

8

The author argues that the findings from the 2004 study of video gaming habits are

A) assumed to be indisputable.
B) constructive but not definitive.
C) intriguing despite methodological flaws.
D) destined to inspire further controversy.

9

Which choice provides the best evidence for the answer to the previous question?

A) Lines 45-48 ("Besides . . . fights")
B) Lines 59-61 ("About . . . girls")
C) Lines 77-79 ("The team . . . hostile")
D) Lines 84-90 ("Looking . . . time")

10

On the basis of figure 1, one notable disparity between the boys and the girls surveyed is that

A) puzzle and trivia video games are significantly less popular among the boys than among the girls.
B) fantasy video games are significantly more popular among the boys than among the girls.
C) the majority of the boys surveyed had never played a puzzle or trivia video game.
D) the majority of the girls surveyed had never played a violent video game of any sort.

11

Which of the following, if added to figure 2, would incorporate a new and relevant factor from the passage into this chart?

A) Data on the sports and extracurricular preferences of the students in each category.
B) Data on how many students in each category had an argument with a teacher at some point.
C) Data on how many students in each category were themselves the victims of bullying.
D) Data on whether the students in each category preferred relatively popular or relatively obscure video game series.

Questions 1-10 are based on the following passage and supplementary material.

1.4

The following passage is adapted from a 2012 article by Dana Trentini, "Is Your Thyroid Doctor Using the Old TSH Lab Standards?" in which the author provides a comprehensive description of thyroid disorders and their diagnosis criteria.

    Some people experience the myriad debilitating symptoms of a low-functioning thyroid, a condition known as hypothyroidism. Hypothyroidism manifests itself through such negative effects as weight gain, fatigue, depression, and impaired memory. Because of the clearly unwanted nature of the disorder, patients who suspect they have it typically ask their doctors to run the appropriate medical tests in an attempt to obtain a speedy diagnosis and treatment plan. However, such individuals—and their doctors—may not be aware of the importance of comprehensive, up-to-date testing. Changes in related diagnostic criteria have emerged in recent years, and the conflicting nature of the diagnostic criteria has led to some people with hypothyroid disease not being able to receive the proper diagnosis. The reality is that the diagnostic criteria for this increasingly widespread autoimmune disease continue to be complex and multi-faceted.

    The thyroid, a butterfly-shaped gland in the body, is susceptible to a number of autoimmune conditions—the most prevalent of which is low function. To render the diagnosis, doctors often opt for a thyroid stimulating hormone (TSH) test to determine current levels and perhaps include other tests, based on a blood sample. If the thyroid produces a low amount of thyroid hormone, the pituitary gland responds by increasing the amount of TSH in the body. Therefore, there is an inverse relationship between TSH levels and thyroid function. The lower the TSH level, the higher the level of thyroid functioning, as it produces thyroid hormone. Doctors usually work with an acceptable TSH range to determine a diagnosis.

    A 20-year study begun in the mid-1970s reported in 1995 that TSH levels of 2.0 mIU/L (milli-international units per liter) or higher were symptomatic of hypothyroidism. This study was conducted in the UK on close to 3,000 randomly selected adults. A second, larger study of more than 13,000 subjects was conducted between 1988 and 1994, but this one excluded subjects with conditions associated with thyroid disease. Its researchers proposed new acceptable TSH ranges of between 0.3 and 2.5 mIU/L. In 2002, the National Academy for Clinical Biochemistry evaluated the then available research data, and had recommended the same change in the TSH threshold, from 2.0 to 2.5 mIU/L, saying that "it is likely that the upper limit of the serum TSH reference range will be reduced to 2.5 mIU/L."

    The American Society of Clinical Endocrinologists (AACE) issued a statement in 2003 in support of changing the upper limit of the acceptable TSH range. They stated, "Now AACE encourages doctors to consider treatment for patients who test outside the boundaries of a narrower margin based on a target TSH level of 0.3 to 3.0." The same document cited a previous range of 0.5 to 5.0 mIU/L as a previously acceptable TSH range. The AACE acknowledged in the press release the possibility that patients with "mild thyroid disorder" may have gone untreated in the past, due to the use of TSH thresholds that, in effect, failed to properly identify patients with hypothyroidism.

    However, in 2012, the AACE, in conjunction with another organization, the American Thyroid Association, again reversed its recommendation, changing the upper limit of the range to 4.12 mIU/L, replacing the 3.0 mIU/L threshold identified in the earlier studies and press releases.

    As a result of these conflicting recommendations regarding acceptable TSH levels, and the ensuing consequences for thyroid patients, Dana Trentini states, "thyroid advocates and many integrative physicians are fighting to narrow that range." Dr. Weston Saunders and patient advocates like Mary Shomon suggest that subclinical symptoms that do not fit the current diagnostic criteria not be brushed aside or overlooked by doctors or patients. Shomon says patients must learn to advocate for themselves, and find another doctor, if their doctor will not listen to them. Shomon, like Trentini, recognizes that many of the various so-called acceptable TSH ranges fail to properly identify many who suffer from hypothyroidism.

    To solve the misdiagnosis issue, some doctors request a full thyroid panel in addition to the required TSH test, which provides a more comprehensive understanding of the patient's thyroid levels. A full thyroid panel helps to determine both proper diagnosis and an effective treatment plan. Trentini, a thyroid patient advocate who also blogs on the subject, says that "Many mainstream doctors do not run a full thyroid panel that should at least include Free T4, Free T3, Reverse T3, and thyroid antibodies. Unfortunately, TSH alone does not provide a complete picture." In the future, individuals who have the symptoms of any thyroid disorder need to be active in requesting that the proper diagnostic criteria be fulfilled.

| Acceptable TSH Range (mIU/L), Various Standards ||||
ORGANIZATION	YEAR	MINIMUM	MAXIMUM
NATIONAL ACADEMY FOR CLINICAL BIOCHEMISTRY	1996	0.1	1.9
AMERICAN SOCIETY OF CLINICAL ENDOCRINOLOGISTS	1997	0.25	2.25
AMERICAN THYROID ASSOCIATION	1997	0.125	3.875
NATIONAL ACADEMY FOR CLINICAL BIOCHEMISTRY	2001	0.5	4.5
AMERICAN SOCIETY OF CLINICAL ENDOCRINOLOGISTS	2003	0.3	2.7
AMERICAN SOCIETY OF CLINICAL ENDOCRINOLOGISTS	2012	0.4	3.85

1

Which choice best supports the claim in line 10 ("and their doctors")?

A) Lines 16-19 ("The reality...faceted")
B) Lines 32-33 ("Doctors...diagnosis")
C) Lines 75-78 ("suggest...patients")
D) Lines 89-94 ("Dana...picture")

2

As used in line 6, "unwanted" most nearly means

A) excessive.
B) detrimental.
C) inappropriate.
D) abandoned.

3

The information in second paragraph (lines 20-33) primarily serves to

A) provide background information necessary to understanding the study.
B) foreshadow difficulties that will later be encountered regarding the method of a study.
C) draw attention to a pattern in diagnosing a critical component of patients.
D) correct a misconception regarding the way that a key diagnosis is made.

4

It can be reasonably inferred from the sixth paragraph (lines 70-83) that the upper limit for an acceptable TSH range is

A) supported by a clear consensus between doctors and patients.
B) defined by doctors but should ultimately be defined by the patients.
C) still open to debate and likely to change again in the future.
D) recommended to remain at 4.12 mIU/L in order to solve the misdiagnosis issue.

5

Based on the passage, which individual would most likely be diagnosed with hypothyroidism in 2012 considering TSH level alone?

A) A patient whose TSH level is 0.7 mIU/L
B) A patient whose TSH level is 2.6 mIU/L
C) A patient whose TSH level is 3.2 mIU/L
D) A patient whose TSH level is 4.5 mIU/L

6

Which choice provides the best evidence in support of the idea advanced in lines 80-83 ("Shomon... hypothyroidism")

A) Lines 23-26 ("doctors...sample")
B) Lines 34-37 ("A 20-year...hypothyroidism")
C) Lines 67-69 ("changing...releases")
D) Lines 92-93 ("Unfortunately...picture")

7

Which of the following scenarios is most similar to the scenario presented in the passage?

A) Due to disagreements within the field, patients must go out of their way to receive the proper care needed.
B) Researchers have reached a mostly certain conclusion regarding a controversial area of health and medicine.
C) Future testing and consensus are required to determine whether an apparent ailment actually exists.
D) A study fails to come to a definitive conclusion regarding its subject and is left open to interpretation.

8

As used in line 76, "fit" most nearly means

A) adhere to.
B) settle for.
C) consist of.
D) cooperate with.

9

Based on the table, which of the following represents the lowest minimum for an acceptable TSH range?

A) The National Academy for Clinical Biochemistry in 1996
B) The American Society of Clinical Endocrinologists in 2003
C) The National Academy for Clinical Biochemistry in 2001
D) The American Society for Clinical Endocrinologists in 2012

10

Which information, if added to the table, would best support the claim in lines 84-87 ("To...levels")?

A) The currently agreed upon acceptable levels of thyroid antibodies
B) The currently accepted description for hypothyroidism
C) Acceptable levels of Free T4 & T3, Reverse T3, and thyroid antibodies
D) The number of patients diagnosed with hypothyroidism each year

Questions 1-11 are based on the following passage and supplementary material.
1.5
Adapted from "The Surface of Sputnik Planum, Pluto, Must Be Less Than 10 Million Years," a Public Library of Science article from 2016.

   As technology affords scientists the ability to peer further and further into space, they jump at the opportunity to search for exoplanets of all kinds. Each planet discovered has valuable information
5 to contribute to the fields of meteorology, geology, climatology, hydrology—the list goes on. An understanding of our neighbors in our own solar system also helps scientists to comprehend the composition of these exoplanets. They can use
10 observed phenomena of nearby celestial objects to gain insight into planets we may never reach in our lifetimes. The newest knowledge of our solar system comes from observations of Pluto. After pictures were taken of its surface, astronomers began working to
15 determine the age of Pluto's surface. The ages of any given planet's (or dwarf planet's) surface has more to do with geophysical processes than with the age of the planet itself. For instance, the Earth is a little over 4.5 billion years old, but a new island emerged from the
20 Pacific Ocean in 2015. Effectively determining the age of distant objects, though, requires a little more work on the part of astronomers.
   Two factors that astronomers can use are the number and depth of craters on a given surface,
25 because they show the frequency and intensity of impacts. If a celestial object is highly likely to experience impacts but there are very few craters, then astronomers must turn to the geophysical activity of the object itself. In the case of Mars, evidence of
30 asteroid impacts is often smoothed over by eruptions or landslides: depending on the size of the crater and its properties, it is possible for astronomers to use the time of the eruptions and landslides to estimate the age of a given area. In the case of Pluto, asteroid impacts
35 would occur as it crosses the Kuiper Belt, an asteroid belt similar to the one between Mars and Jupiter, but many times larger. Just as they do for Mars' estimates, astronomers use the time lapse of geophysical processes to estimate the age of Pluto's surface.
40   In 2015, Dr. David Trilling of the Department of Physics and Astronomy at Northern Arizona University, Flagstaff, used photos of the surface of Pluto to determine the maximum possible age of a section of the dwarf planet's surface, called Sputnik
45 Planum. Images of it were taken at two different resolutions, and researchers were surprised to find that in neither image resolution did craters appear; craters would have to be bigger than 2 kilometers to show up at the lower resolution, and a Kuiper Belt Object
50 (KBO) would have to be at least 100 km in diameter to leave a crater that size.
   In calculating the frequency of such an impact on Sputnik Planum, Trilling started with an established estimate of how many 100 km KBOs exist in one
55 square degree of the Kuiper Belt. He then calculated how long Pluto would take to cross the Kuiper Belt by using the volume and circumference of both orbits. By using both results, he concluded from this that Pluto was highly likely to be impacted by large KBOs during
60 its journey through the Kuiper Belt.
   The lack of large craters could usually be explained by familiar geophysical processes like those of Mars. But while Mars has a crust made mostly of volcanic basalt rock, Pluto has a surface comprised of
65 frozen nitrogen, and its geophysical activity involves freezing and melting—cryo-geophysical processes— similar to those observed on Ganymede, a moon of Jupiter; even then, Ganymede has frozen water. Trilling presents several cryo-geophysical scenarios
70 that could have erased the craters from Sputnik Planum. The first is viscous relaxation, which means that the tops of the craters were warmer than the bases, and the ridges melted, slowly filling in the craters. The second is convective overturn; essentially the opposite
75 of viscous relaxation, this process would mean that the bases of craters were warmer, thereby melting the tops over time. The third is cryovolcanism. In this scenario, the impact of the KBOs would create cracks in subsurface reservoirs, allowing melt to seep into the
80 craters. The potential time frame for any one of these to fill in a crater puts the estimate of Sputnik Planum's age at less than 10 million years old.
   However, this is a conservative estimate, to say the least. In fact, a more recent estimate based on new
85 images of Sputnik Planum puts the surface age at only around 180,000 years. If we plan on reconciling these greatly varying estimates, we need to know more about the actual surface of Pluto and the dwarf planet's relationship to the Kuiper Belt. Perhaps we
90 will—possibly from a Pluto Rover. But Trilling's methodology may yet be essential to understanding the surfaces of rocky exoplanets.

Figure 1

Chemical Composition of Pluto's Crust

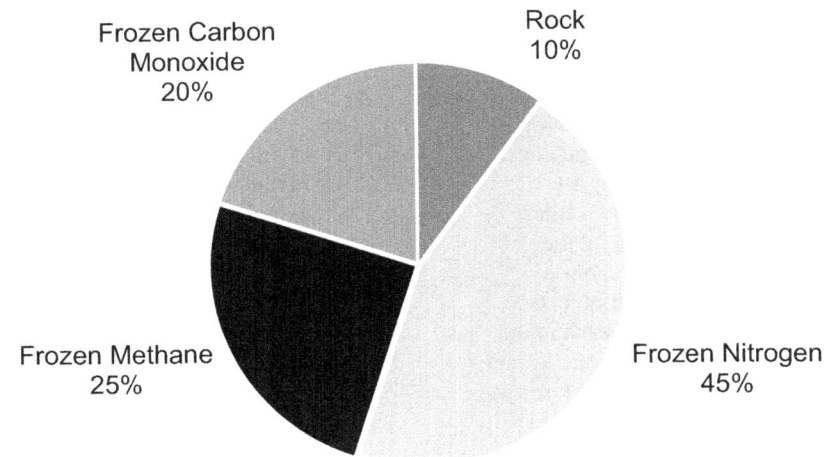

Figure 2

Chemical Composition of the Kuiper Belt

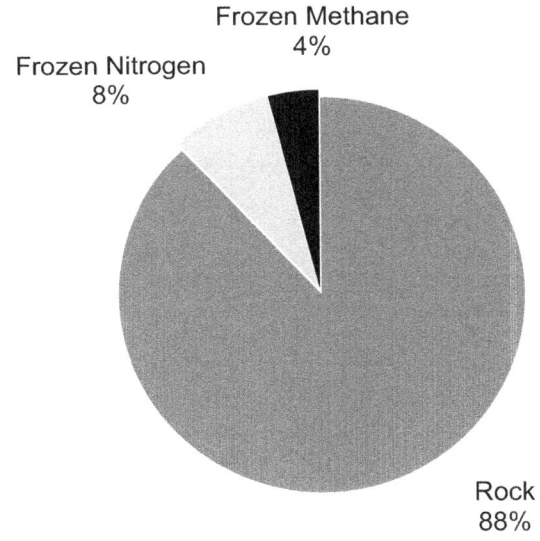

1

It can be inferred from the first paragraph of the passage that exoplanets

A) must exhibit some of the same conditions found on Earth in order to support life.
B) have inspired multi-disciplinary projects that draw together geologists and astronomers.
C) intrigue some of the same specialists who have recently mapped Pluto's surface.
D) are believed to be comparable to planets that are already known to astronomers.

2

Which of the following facts, if true, would CONTRADICT the author's ideas about the features that can be found on a planet's surface?

A) The number of craters present on a given planet has not been found to be proportional to a planet's size.
B) A planet that regularly passes through an asteroid belt can have an unexpectedly smooth surface due to geophysical activity.
C) Some dwarf planets have not experienced any changes in topography since they were first formed.
D) Portions of a given planet's surface that are of radically different ages can be adjacent to one another.

3

As used in line 11, "reach" most nearly means

A) make physical contact with.
B) manage to understand.
C) achieve harmony with.
D) attempt to possess.

4

Within the passage, the author mentions Mars primarily as a planet that

A) was the subject of early attempts to link crater impacts and surface aging.
B) provides a useful point of contrast for an analysis of Pluto.
C) has remained geologically stable for much longer than other planets of the same size.
D) is struck by asteroids almost as frequently as Pluto is.

5

Which choice provides the best evidence for the answer to the previous question?

A) Lines 26-29 ("If . . . itself")
B) Lines 29-34 ("In the . . . area")
C) Lines 61-63 ("The lack . . . Mars")
D) Lines 63-68 ("But . . . Jupiter")

6

The author indicates that viscous relaxation, convective overturn, and cryovolcanism are similar in that all of these processes

A) are seldom evident on planets with rocky surfaces.
B) yield similar age projections for Sputnik Planum.
C) cause pronounced cracking along a planet's surface.
D) result from subterranean warming on Pluto.

7

As used in line 80, "potential" most nearly means

A) plausible.
B) empowered.
C) promising.
D) expediting.

8

The author discusses Trilling's research in a manner that conveys

A) awareness of its theoretical brilliance despite anxiety about its reception.
B) appreciation of its applications but disregard of its precedents.
C) respect for its virtues along with awareness of its limitations.
D) fascination with its conclusions despite its questionable findings about exoplanets.

9

Which choice provides the best evidence for the answer to the previous question?

A) Lines 52-55 ("In calculating . . . Kuiper Belt")
B) Lines 69-71 ("Trilling . . . Sputnik Planum")
C) Lines 83-84 ("However . . . least")
D) Lines 90-92 ("But . . . exoplanets")

10

Which of the following substances, on the basis of figures, would NOT be indicative of an asteroid impact if found on Pluto's surface?

A) Rock
B) Frozen Nitrogen
C) Frozen Methane
D) Frozen Carbon Monoxide

11

Does the information present in figure 1 strengthen or weaken Trilling's arguments about Sputnik Planum?

A) Strengthen, because the chart indicates the presence of a significant amount of frozen matter that could have changed form to erase traces of craters.
B) Strengthen, because the chart supports Trilling's suggestion that Ganymede and Pluto are identical except for the presence of frozen water on Ganymede.
C) Weaken, because it is likely that the presence of rocky matter on Pluto would inhibit the geophysical processes described in Trilling's research.
D) Weaken, because the more significant portions of liquid matter than are indicated by the chart would be necessary in order to conceal crater impacts.

Questions 1-10 are based on the following passages and supplementary material.
1.6
Adapted from an article published on wired.com titled "Our Smart Phone Addiction Might Double as a Cure" by Simone Stozoff, an explanation of how smart phone apps came to be so addicting and how these addictive trends can be reversed in the same way that they came about.

Passage 1

In 2007, 75 students joined a research group at Stanford taught by behavioral psychologist BJ Fogg. The class, called the Persuasive Technology Lab, initially examined the role of technology in human
[5] action through questions such as, "How can you get people to stop smoking using SMS?" However, as platforms such as Facebook and the App Store became increasingly popular, Fogg's teachings began to shift to social media, prompting his students to use methods
[10] from behavioral psychology to create a paradigm of addiction.

The model Fogg created is deceptively simple: using the forces of motivation, trigger, and ability, it is able to tap into human vulnerabilities and capitalize
[15] on the need for continuous reinforcement. Imagine, for example, that you have just received a notification from Instagram indicating that a friend has tagged you in a photo. You're motivated to make sure you don't look ugly in photos, and triggered by the notification,
[20] you open the app. Your smartphone's swipe-to-view interface that takes you directly to the photo makes the process seamless, ensuring that you have the ability to constantly interact with the app. Multiply this process by 8 billion—the number of times Americans
[25] collectively check their smartphones per day—and you have a recipe for addiction.

"Fogg's Behavioral Model," as the process was later coined, was used by his students to tremendous success. The students who had walked into Fogg's
[30] class in September of 2007 walked out 10 weeks later with apps and programs that had amassed 16 million users and $1 million dollars in advertising revenue. They would go on to create and work for companies like Google, Uber, Instagram, and Facebook, all
[35] of which have implemented Fogg's techniques to perpetuate a cycle of continuous use.

Fogg is an unlikely face of a movement which has inspired such polarizing reactions. As a behavioral psychologist, he's taught classes on using behavior
[40] design to reconnect with nature and is often described by his students as committed to using technology as a force for good. Critics, however, say that his teachings have done more harm than good: companies such as Facebook have taken advantage of his model and
[45] have used it to foster addiction, not fulfillment. And in an era when the majority of apps are dependent on advertising to operate, this tactic is now seen by companies as simply a necessary strategy to survive.

Passage 2

In 2012, Tristan Harris gave a 144-slide
[50] presentation at Google called "A Call to Minimize Distraction & Respect Users' Attention." Harris, a prominent whistleblower of the tech industry and Google's first "design ethicist," revealed the extent to which social media design elements controlled and
[55] changed the way people interacted—and not for the better. The presentation went viral within the company; spurred by these results, Harris left Google in 2015 to found Time Well Spent, an organization that advocates for aligning the tech industry with societal well-being.

[60] "Never before has a handful of people working at a handful of tech companies been able to steer the thoughts and feelings of a billion people," he said in a recent talk at Stanford. "There are more users on Facebook than followers of Christianity. There are
[65] more people on YouTube than followers of Islam. I don't know a more urgent problem than this." Harris, a member of "The Facebook Class"—a group of students taught by behavioral psychologist BJ Fogg who went on to revolutionize the tech industry—along
[70] with former classmate Nir Eyal, is working to undo the harmful consequences of the method he had helped to implement.

Their efforts are finally starting to be recognized: France recently banned smartphones in public schools,
[75] and Facebook has redesigned its algorithm to promote content related to friends and family over that of viral videos and mindless consumption. Mark Zuckerberg, the founder and CEO of Facebook, wrote that in 2018 Facebook would prioritize "making sure the time spent
[80] on Facebook is time well spent," giving a clear nod to Harris's mission and acknowledging the need for ethics, even at the cost of advertising revenue.

Eyal sees this movement towards corporate mindfulness as a sign that things are moving in the
[85] right direction, writing in his new book *Indistractible* that people, as well as companies, can call on these advancements as inspiration to unplug from their cellphones and enjoy their lives in the real world. "People have the power to put this stuff away and
[90] they always have," he says. "But when we preach powerlessness, people believe that."

Harris, however, believes that companies are simply not doing enough. He refutes Eyal's claim that corporations are becoming more ethical by stating that
95 their interests are inherently intertwined with those of advertisers, causing them to seek profit above anything else. Even if we do our best to use our time on social media meaningfully, companies will always develop new ways to lure us back in. The only solution to this
100 complicated and manipulative system, then, would be to destroy the economic incentive that creates addiction in the first place.

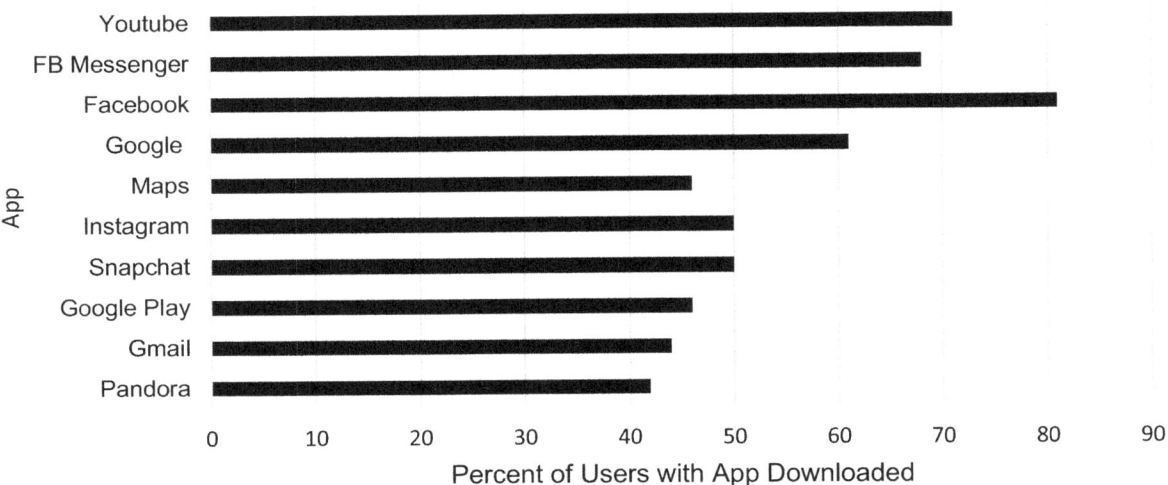

1

Which choice best reflects Fogg's perspective on his conception of behavioral design?

A) It can be used with technology as a positive influence.
B) It can be used to help curb addiction.
C) It is difficult to implement and relies on human vulnerabilities.
D) It is a necessary strategy for businesses to survive.

2

Which choice provides the best evidence for the answer to the previous question?

A) Lines 12-15 ("The model...reinforcement")
B) Lines 38-42 ("As a...good")
C) Lines 42-45 ("Critics...fulfillment")
D) Lines 45-48 ("And...survive")

3

As used in line 10, "paradigm" most nearly means

A) culture.
B) crisis.
C) pattern.
D) tendency.

4

As used in line 54, "controlled" most nearly means

A) shaped.
B) structured.
C) enticed.
D) dominated.

5

According to the author of Passage 2, why is Fogg's behavioral model unethical?

A) It is primarily used to increase dependency on social media applications, thereby keeping users addicted.
B) It creates a monetary incentive for social media companies to take full advantage of online advertising.
C) It distracts users from solving problems in their lives that would otherwise have been solved through religion.
D) It has a permanent negative impact on the self-esteem of social media users by depicting misleading images of perfection.

6

Which choice provides the best evidence for the answer to the previous question?

A) Lines 60-63 ("Never...Stanford")
B) Lines 63-64 ("There...Christianity")
C) Lines 83-88 ("Eyal...world")
D) Lines 97-99 ("Even...back in")

7

The relationship between the two passages is best described as

A) Passage 2 surveys the response of those who caused in a controversy in Passage 1.
B) Passage 2 provides context for an idea advanced in Passage 1.
C) Passage 2 refutes the methodology of the experiment depicted in Passage 1.
D) Passage 1 raises suspicions about a practice advanced in Passage 2.

8

Both authors would agree with which statement?

A) Apps have addictive properties.
B) Social media is unethical.
C) Fogg's model is ultimately harmful.
D) Fogg's model will be phased out in the future.

9

The last sentence of Passage 1 mainly serves to

A) provide justification for using Fogg's model.
B) advise companies to move away from current advertising norms.
C) solve Fogg's initial research methodology flaw.
D) provide an alternative to economic incentives.

10

Does the graph prove the idea presented in lines 43-45?

A) Yes, because over 80% of people use Facebook.
B) Yes, because it shows how applications foster addiction.
C) No, because it doesn't show the relationship between applications and addiction.
D) No, because it doesn't show how many applications use advertisements.

Questions 1-11 are based on the following passage and supplementary material.

1.7
Adapted from a 2017 PLOS ONE article by Erin Simmons, Elizabeth Bergeron, and John Florian titled "The Impact of Repetitive Long-duration Water Immersion on Vascular Function," in which the authors describe the impact of buoyancy and drag on underwater swimming speed.

Basal metabolic processes occur in all organisms and are essential to maintaining an internal balance, known as homeostasis, as well as a homeostatic relationship to the outside world. There are two different environments to which animals develop homeostasis: land, where animals breathe oxygen through the air via the lungs, and under water, where animals obtain oxygen by using their gills as a filtration system. Additionally, there are animals that live on land but feed themselves by hunting underwater for sustenance. One of these species, the sea lion, is a breath-hold diver, an animal that needs to dive great depths several times per day. Because of this, they have adapted a streamlined body shape ideal for making these dives as quickly as possible (holding your breath isn't exactly the most comfortable condition) and unique physiological qualities that allow for efficient use of oxygen. This economical oxygen use comes in handy when sea lions need to stay at extreme depths of water for long periods of time while hunting.

The mechanism that allows sea lions to have this special ability is facilitated by the hypothalamus and the adrenal gland, which respectively control homeostasis, and the process by which blood flow is directed throughout the body. We can think of this in terms of the "fight-or-flight" response in humans. When we are hyper-aroused, our adrenal gland sends adrenaline to the body, telling it to allow maximum blood flow to the heart, lungs, and brain, and minimal blood flow to all other organs. In the sea lion, the same result of maximum blood to the heart, lungs, and brain is needed while on a deep-sea dive, during which pressure from the external environment is constantly changing.

Just as these metabolic changes are essential to the livelihood of the sea lion during a deep sea dive, so too is the ability to swim as quickly as possible to and from its destination. To study what makes up the optimal condition for a sea lion to minimize travel time and therefore maximize time at the destination, researchers at the Atmosphere and Ocean Research Institute of the University of Tokyo designed an experiment using consenting sea lions as subjects. They designed their study around a mathematical model calculating optimal swim speed by accounting for propeller efficiency, aerobic efficiency, basal metabolic rate, drag, and buoyancy. Only the last two factors were varied in the experiment because previous research indicates that one or both is the key to maximizing speed underwater. Drag, the force generated by an object moving through a liquid, is the reason we move more slowly in water. It causes us to have a hard time running through the ocean, whereas we would not have such difficulty on land because the air does not have the same powerful drag. Buoyancy is the ability to float—think of a ball filled with air sitting on top of a pool. To the researchers in Tokyo, it seemed likely that buoyancy would not affect speed, but drag would.

In their experiment, the team set four conditions: a control, a condition that adds extra drag while not altering buoyancy, and two buoyancy conditions that don't alter drag (high buoyancy and low buoyancy). The subjects were three sea lions to which researchers attached a device to measure speed, as well as one that altered the sea lion's swimming ability for each of the three experimental conditions. Once equipped, the sea lions were allowed to carry on with their normal daily dives. At the end of the trials, the researchers collected data on swim speeds of the subjects, comparing all four conditions.

Unsurprisingly to the researchers, results proved that the sea lions swam at similar mean speeds for the control and two buoyancy conditions, but significantly more slowly for the added drag condition. Furthermore, the sea lions swam at speeds that matched the mathematical model used to predict optimal speeds, indicating proper accounting for basal metabolic state, aerobic fitness, and propellor speed, and that speed was simply a function of drag and not buoyancy.

Researchers do point out flaws in their study: sea lions do not dive to relatively deep depths when compared to other breath-hold divers, indicating that further research needs to be done to test how well the mathematical model holds up under those circumstances. Furthermore, as the sea lions were conducting dives as they normally would and were not interrupted, it was impossible for researchers to calculate the metabolic cost of each dive. If that data were to be added, it would provide valuable insight to the relationship of time, speed, and metabolic cost.

Statistics for Various Dive Depths (Adult Male Sea Lion)

Dive Depth (Meters)	Time Underwater During Descent (Minutes)	Percentage Increase in Adrenaline	Percentage Decrease in Lung Volume
50	0.5	2	0
100	1.05	4	0
150	1.55	5	0
200	2.15	9	0
250	2.55	15	10
300	3.25	20	12.5

1

The main purpose of the passage is to

A) pinpoint conceptual and procedural shortcomings in examinations of sea lion dives.
B) evaluate all factors that may help to explain an optimal sea lion dive.
C) suggest parallels between sea lion dives and dives performed by other mammals.
D) offer empirical evidence for a long-held idea about sea lion behavior.

2

It can be reasonably inferred from the passage that sea lions prey on organisms that

A) must be trapped and caught through high-speed pursuit.
B) are not themselves classified as predators.
C) cannot be easily found near the surface of the ocean.
D) have the same traits that can control blood flow.

3

Which choice provides the best evidence for the answer to the previous question?

A) Lines 4-9 ("There are . . . system")
B) Lines 9-11 ("Additionally . . . sustenance")
C) Lines 18-20 ("This economical . . . hunting")
D) Lines 30-34 ("In the . . . changing")

4

As used in lines 22 and 37, "ability" most nearly means

A) talent
B) capacity.
C) acquisition.
D) ingenuity.

5

As described in the passage, the results of the study performed by the University of Tokyo researchers were

A) somewhat expected.
B) thoroughly problematic.
C) gradually popularized.
D) noticeably counterintuitive.

6

Which of the following modifications to the experiment described in the passage would most clearly provide additional useful information about sea lion dives?

A) Observation of greater numbers of captive sea lions
B) Examination of fewer variables over a greater period of time
C) Comparison of a larger number of plausible mathematical models
D) Purposeful interruption of sea lion dives by the researchers

7

Which choice provides the best evidence for the answer to the previous question?

A) Lines 63-66 ("The subjects . . . conditions")
B) Lines 68-70 ("At the end . . . conditions")
C) Lines 75-77 ("Furthermore . . . speeds")
D) Lines 86-89 ("Furthermore . . . dive")

8

As used in line 80, "a function" most nearly means

A) an aptitude relevant to.
B) a measurement related to.
C) an objective derived from.
D) a process determined by.

9

On the basis of the data in the table, which of the following situations for the adult male sea lion under observation would NOT be plausible under any circumstances?

A) Lung volume decreases sharply at a depth of 150 meters.
B) The percentage increase in adrenaline almost doubles between 150 and 200 meters.
C) Adrenaline, as measured by a percentage, continues to increase beyond a depth of 300 meters.
D) Lung volume continues to decrease beyond a depth of 300 meters.

10

On the basis of the passage, increased blood flow correlates most directly with which of the quantities present in the table?

A) Increased adrenaline
B) Increased time underwater
C) Decreased lung volume
D) Decreased dive depth

11

Unlike the research conducted by the Atmosphere and Ocean Research Institute of Tokyo, the research documented in the table involved

A) sea lions that were monitored in the wild.
B) sea lions that were uniformly subjected to increased drag.
C) continuous measurements of underwater velocity for sea lions.
D) considerations of metabolic processes in sea lions.

Questions 1-10 are based on the following passage and supplementary material.
1.8
Adapted from a 2009 research article titled "Effects of cognitive pain coping strategies and locus of control on perception of cold pressor pain in healthy individuals: Experimental study" by Natasa Jokic-Begic, Dragutin Ivanec, and Dragana Markanovic at the University of Zagreb in Croatia.

Cognitive coping techniques can help to mask the physical experience of pain, new research from a university in Croatia has found. These findings could potentially be useful in the medical field for patients undergoing invasive procedures, such as those in dentistry or surgery, that are usually accompanied by noxious pain.

"Our study has important practical considerations," said Natasa Jokic-Begic, lead author of the study at Zagreb University's Department of Psychology. "Health professionals could teach the patients who are about to undergo a painful medical procedure how to use cognitive strategies that would help them cope with pain."

The perception of pain, also known as *nociception*, can be broken down into two parts: biological and psychological. Biological pain originates at the source of the stimulus, and manifests itself as an unpleasant physical sensation; the stinging of a paper cut and the throbbing of a bruise are both examples of this phenomenon. Psychological pain, on the other hand, arises when the original stimulus sends electrical signals from the point of impact to the brain via the peripheral nervous system. This is then interpreted by us as "ouch!" In short, physical pain is inevitable and results from actual or potential tissue damage, whereas psychological pain is subjective and varies upon our perception of the pain's intensity.

Jokic-Begic and her colleagues selected 96 undergraduates from the university's psychology department and divided them into three groups. Each group was subjected to acute pain by undergoing the Cold Pressor Test, in which participants' hands are submerged in a bath of water that is maintained at 2 degrees Celsius. The participants were instructed to remove their hands from the water once the pain became unbearable.

The control group followed the standard procedure for the Cold Pressor Test without any modifications. The second group performed a "distraction task" while their hands were immersed. Participants were asked to list several nouns beginning with a specified letter, switching letters after every minute as instructed by the investigator. The third and final group was asked to choose and read one or more positive statements that either confronted or redefined the pain experienced. These statements had been written beforehand by the researchers, and included phrases such as "This hurts, but I have control" and "The water is pleasantly cool." Participants were allowed to say the statements out loud or silently, and were encouraged to come up with self-statements in addition to the ones provided.

The researchers found that the cognitive pain coping strategies as used on the second and third groups of participants had a significant influence on their tolerance of pain. Compared to the control group, the experimental groups lasted almost two minutes longer in the Cold Pressor Test, therefore showing that they were able to extend their pain tolerance threshold using psychological techniques. No difference in pain tolerance time was found between the two experimental groups, indicating that distraction and redefining statements were equally effective in pain suppression.

This is not to say that the participants in the experimental groups did not feel pain—far from it. At the end of the study, each group was asked to rate their pain on a scale of 0-10. The intensity of the pain did not vary, with members from all groups responding with a pain level of around 7. However, participants from experimental groups perceived the time their hands were submerged as much shorter than the participants in the control group did. This suggests that while all groups felt pain equally, members of the experimental groups had their attention diverted enough for their recognition of the pain to be delayed.

Though this study could represent a breakthrough in the field of pain management, Jokic-Begic is still not completely convinced. "There are some limitations to our study. First, the participants are psychology students. The fact that they were all young and healthy could have biased the results toward higher pain tolerance. In addition, the study was conducted under laboratory conditions . . . the participant's feeling of safety could have influenced pain tolerance time. Therefore, we recommend that future studies be based on a sample of the general population to obtain the variability in baseline pain tolerance."

Figure 1

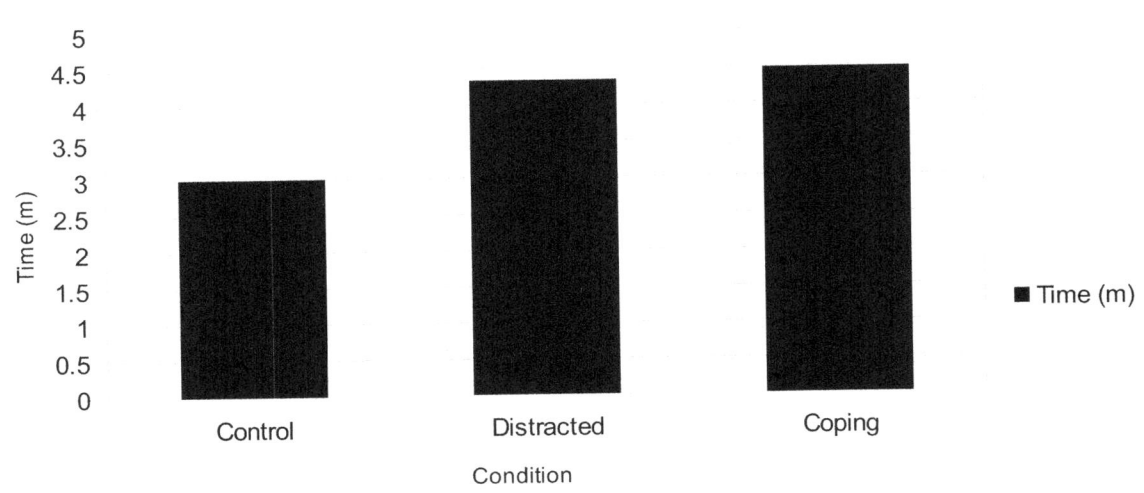

Average length of time that participants left their hands in a cold-pressor test across three conditions: control, a distraction task, or a coping task

Figure 2

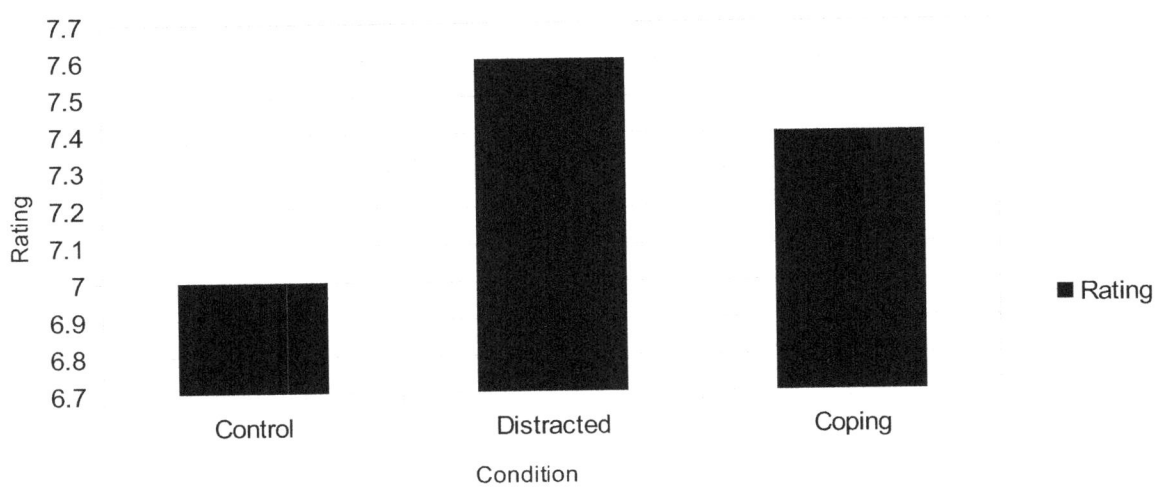

Average participant ratings of pain at the end of a cold-pressor test across three conditions: control, a distraction task, or a coping task.

1

It can be reasonably inferred that the purpose of quoting the study's author in lines 8-9 and 11-14 is to

A) lend credibility to a subject that is otherwise obscure.
B) demonstrate the study's applications in the real world.
C) describe an otherwise confusing method in simple terms.
D) elaborate on a previously mentioned medical technique.

2

As used in line 38, "standard" most nearly means

A) established.
B) common.
C) stereotypical.
D) basic.

3

Which of the following statements best exemplifies the author's description of the self-statements used in the experiment?

A) "The pain is beyond my own personal ability to alter."
B) "I am thoroughly enjoying the current experience."
C) "I wish to be anywhere but doing this experiment."
D) "The water should be much colder to be effective."

4

According to the passage, the chief finding was paradoxical in that

A) participants reported feeling some pain even though none should have been present.
B) participants in the control group felt less pain than did participants in the experimental group.
C) participants who listed nouns during the test reported the most enjoyment.
D) participants in the experimental groups reported equal pain to that of the control group's participants.

5

Which choice provides the best evidence for the answer to the previous question?

A) Lines 60-64 ("No difference...suppression")
B) Lines 65-66 ("This is...it")
C) Lines 70-74 ("However...did")
D) Lines 73-76 ("This suggests...delayed")

6

As used in line 76, "recognition" most nearly means

A) concession.
B) perception.
C) realization.
D) understanding.

7

Based on the study's findings, which of the following reasons explains why participants in the experimental group were able to tolerate more pain than the control group participants did?

A) Psychological pain was delayed because self-statements ultimately make the water feel warmer.
B) Psychological pain was delayed because self-statements temporarily redirected pain feelings.
C) Biological pain was delayed because self-statements ultimately make the water feel warmer.
D) Biological pain was delayed because self-statements temporarily redirected pain feelings.

8

Which choice provides the best evidence for the answer to the previous question?

A) Lines 53-56 ("The researchers...pain")
B) Lines 56-60 ("Compared to...Test")
C) Lines 65-70 ("This is...around 7")
D) Lines 70-76 ("However...delayed")

9

According to Figure 1, which technique was most successful at delaying onset of pain?

A) Control
B) Distract
C) Coping
D) All were equally successful.

10

According to Figure 2, what was the average pain rating for the condition that caused participants to experience the highest amount of pain during the experiment?

A) 4.2
B) 4.5
C) 7.6
D) 8

Questions 1-10 are based on the following passage.
1.9
Adapted from a 2017 New York Times article by Noam Schieber titled "How Uber Uses Psychological Tricks to Push Its Drivers' Buttons" describing the way that companies manipulate information to trick users into doing things that they otherwise wouldn't be interested in doing.

Dark patterns have been slowly creeping into our society, and this influx should alarm us. According to Harry Brignull, "dark patterns are tricks used in websites and apps that make you buy or sign up for things that you didn't mean to." The purpose of his site, *darkpatterns.org*, is to "spread awareness and to shame companies that use them." One example Brignull cites is a Condé Nast site offering a Wired magazine subscription that requests your payment to have the magazine mailed to your home. The site forces users to go through a complicated, six-step dance, opting in or out of a mine field of promotional offers, before finally completing the process. In a second example, to which Brignull gives the "evil genius" award, *Ryanair.com* takes advantage of the fact that most people who buy plane tickets online are not likely to read everything on the screen. Rather than giving users the option to select extra travel insurance, the unwary user "selects" to opt in automatically when selecting their country of origin from a drop-down list. Most users are unaware that they have been billed for the extra travel insurance.

Some companies undertake manipulative schemes and psychological tricks that fall outside Brignull's strict "dark pattern" definition, but these schemes are no less sinister. Consider the massive social experiment that rider-sharing service Uber has been conducting on its own drivers.

While the rise of Uber corresponds to the rise of the gig economy, Uber went further. It provided a series of incentives and "gamified" processes to entice drivers (who are independent contractors) into working longer hours and engaging in other Uber-related activities. Uber drew upon behavioral science research to manipulate drivers in a number of ways. As a result, the company was able to prod drivers into working during hours and at locations that were less than lucrative. Does Uber's practice of "pulling psychological levers" to control the behavior of others herald a brave new world of covert coercion?

It is not the only firm to employ such dubious tactics. Its main competitor, Lyft, engages in similar strategies, as do piecework giant Mechanical Turk and Postmates, a popular delivery service.

A 2017 *New York Times* article outlined the extent of Uber's dubious deeds, and clarified the distinction between past and present trends. Nudging buyers into selecting services and products using tricks is nothing new. "But extending these efforts to the workforce is potentially transformative," says the author. The kind of manipulation Uber engages in appears to be psychologically exploitative and has a direct impact on an individual's income—in this case, someone who is an independent contractor, not even an Uber employee.

For example, "Uber acknowledged that it had experimented with female personas to increase engagement with drivers," according to the Times article. Moreover, Uber's behavioral scientists noted that attrition rates among drivers dropped after they reached a 25-ride threshold. Uber put cheery-toned messages in place to encourage drivers to reach that threshold, a careful calculation rather than a benign word of encouragement on their part.

Taking advantage of drivers' understandable interest in reaching goals, Uber messages drivers with arbitrary dollar amounts and then tells them they were only a few dollars away from those goals, if only they were to keep driving. Of course, the "keep driving" button was already highlighted on the app display. In this way, drivers are lulled into working towards an elusive goal that is just beyond their grasp. As the psychologist Adam Alter writes in his book "Irresistible," this mental state has a name: the "ludic loop." The Uber app experience, for the driver, strongly resembles that of an addictive video game.

Like binge-watching on Netflix, some of the gamified features of the Uber app result in the loss of self-control and choice on the part of the driver. Do they end their shift or keep driving? Do they take a five-minute break or take the next rider who is already queued for them to pick up? Perhaps most notably, as Ms. Rosenblat and Luke Stark observed in an influential paper on these practices, Uber's app does not let drivers see where a passenger is.

According to a related article in Co.Design, "Uber was the first to layer all of these practices together in a strange new interactive symphony, which hit us deep in the stomach so that we'd sway to the beat." Even with the recent replacement of its CEO, Uber is expected to continue to employ behavioral research results to sculpt and fine-tune its drivers' motivations and behaviors. Other companies in the brave new world of the gig economy can be expected to implement similar dark patterns in the future.

1

The passage is primarily focused on

A) bringing light to an issue that has negative impacts on both employees and consumers.
B) exposing for the first time a problem that could become pervasive with popular companies.
C) implementing a new method of research that can prevent companies from manipulating consumers.
D) understanding and correcting one company's exploitative mechanisms for its employees.

2

The first paragraph (lines 1-22) introduces the subsequent discussion about Uber mainly by

A) detailing a study's results that are later proven to be false.
B) promoting a website that reveals the causes behind a corrupt business method.
C) citing an article that highlights the spread of misinformation.
D) explaining a practice that is illustrated with a few examples.

3

It can be reasonably inferred that the author of the passage would most strongly support a company that

A) rewards employees based on behavioral research results.
B) refrains from employing too many independent contractors.
C) encourages employees with attainable goals rather than with psychological tricks.
D) inspires employees to use company products in their daily lives.

4

Which choice provides the best evidence for the answer to the previous question?

A) Lines 8-10 ("a Condé...home")
B) Lines 30-34 ("It provided...activities.")
C) Lines 65-73 ("Uber messages...grasp")
D) Lines 89-92 ("Uber is...behaviors")

5

As used in line 23, "undertake" most nearly means

A) manage.
B) achieve.
C) employ.
D) assume.

6

Based on the passage, which of the following best describes the difference in the use of dark patterns between Ryanair.com and Uber?

A) Ryanair uses commonly accepted practices which are not harmful while Uber uses practices which degrade those affected.
B) Ryanair and Uber both use dark patterns in the same ways, which have negligible effects on those whom they reach.
C) Ryanair uses dark patterns to influence consumers while Uber uses dark patterns to influence employees.
D) Ryanair uses dark patterns in a primarily negative way while Uber uses dark patterns in a primarily harmless way.

7

Which choice provides the best evidence that the author would agree that Uber has used empirical methods to make its manipulative tactics effective?

A) Lines 26-28 ("Consider the... drivers")
B) Lines 29-30 (While the...further")
C) Lines 30-34 (It provided...activities")
D) Lines 34-35 (Uber drew...ways")

8

As used in line 47, "Nudging" most nearly means

A) forcing.
B) deceiving.
C) helping.
D) pushing.

42

9

Comparing Uber's tactic to a symphony in lines 85-88 primarily has which effect?

A) It causes the reader to realize the extent to which the tactics employed by Uber are rooted in manipulation.

B) It causes the reader to sympathize with Uber for needing to create an environment which would draw in customers.

C) It causes the reader to be become more likely to switch to using companies which do not employ deceit.

D) It causes the reader to have a deeper understanding of the similar methods involved in using Uber and composing music.

10

Based on the information in the passage, the author's stance on utilizing dark patterns is best represented as

A) a full endorsement because the tactics are shown to be effective.

B) a qualified endorsement because the tactics may only harm some people.

C) disagreement because the tactics rely on the psychological manipulation of people.

D) neutral because the passage was written from an informative perspective.

Questions 1-11 are based on the following passage and supplementary material.
1.10
Adapted from a 2017 *Washington Post* article by Mary Hui, "A political scientist has discovered a surprising way to increase voter turnout. It starts in childhood" that uses previously collected data to describe a novel method to get Americans interested in voting.

According to a 2018 *Washington Post* article, nearly half of the US voting age population did not cast a ballot in the 2016 presidential election. This statistic puts the US far behind nearly every other democratic nation in terms of voter turnout. There are many explanations for why that happens. For example, maybe young people don't have the foresight to care about changes that will come as a result of electing new and possibly different individuals to public office. Or maybe they might not know how to find their polling station, or believe the process to be too convoluted. What we need is not to look back and ask why, but to look forward and ask how can this problem be solved in the future.

Quick fixes have been suggested to address this problem: automatic voter registration, getting rid of laws requiring voter ID, making Election Day a national holiday, and holding elections on the weekend. None of these solutions seems to fit the needs of all citizens, however, and as a result they have not been implemented to any success. In a recently published study, political scientist John Holbein, assistant professor at Brigham Young University, offers a unique solution: teaching children social skills.

Holbein's research attempted to answer two related questions. First, assuming that efforts that target adults have small effects, would focusing on children be more effective? Second, is there a relationship between voter participation and social skills? Holbein explains the reason that these are important questions, saying, "voting is a foundational act of democracy," making implementing this mantra into children's minds appear to be a good first priority. He further suggests that inequalities in both voting and policies tend to go hand in hand.

The notion advanced by Holbein that childhood interventions can improve adult outcomes is hardly new, and the impact of these interventions has been studied for decades. In the early 1990s, a project called "Fast Track" was one of the first to demonstrate the impact of childhood interventions. This study set its focus on high-risk children in four different communities, looking at factors such as the utilization of general and mental health services (between the ages of 12 and 20), arrests, and reduced delinquency rates. Published in 2015, that research delineated the effects of treatment. Improvements in social and self-regulation skills from ages 6 to 11 led to the greatest reduction in crime committed during adolescence. Improvements in problem solving, emotion regulation, and prosocial behavior were also noted as greatly beneficial.

To determine whether these data correlated to greater civic engagement as well, Holbein conducted his own research, building on 20 years of data from Fast Track. His program began in 1992 and included 891 children. Half of the children were put into the "treatment" group, and the other half were placed in the "control" group. Children in the first group got special social skills training, which included communication and emotional understanding, as well as social problem-solving, self-control, and friendship.

When Holbein matched the Fast Track participant data and his own study's data to state voting records, he noticed that those receiving the training were much more likely to have voted. The rate of voting in the treatment group was 6.6 percent higher than that of the control group. Accounting for factors such as socioeconomic status, age, gender, and race, this number rose to 7.3 percent.

Holbein offers several explanations as to how social skills may lead to increases in political participation. One's ability to empathize can lead to recognizing social problems, resulting in a greater motivation to participate in politics. In addition, social skills such as emotional regulation, self-control, and grit can help people overcome various barriers in the voting process such as registering, scheduling time to travel, locating the polling place, and learning about the issues and the candidates.

He also suggests that his findings have important implications for public policy.

Most importantly, he notes that current civics education classes are usually dry and boring; they lack the necessary ingredients to create a compelling story and an active and engaged citizen. Instead, Holbein recommends a school program to promote general social skills. The best way to nurture such skills is to involve children in volunteering programs. In particular, he suggests ones that provide civic experiences that are hands-on and that increase personal self-control and empathy. In turn, he says, these experiences are likely to result in higher political participation later in life.

Although the low rate of US voter participation is "really dismal and depressing," Holbein does not describe the situation as "all gloom and doom." He remains optimistic, saying that "one of the things that comes out of my study is that it doesn't have to be that way." He recommends that the process begin early; this is compelling evidence that social skill programs can have a tremendous impact on whether children grow up to be heavily engaged participants in the democratic process.

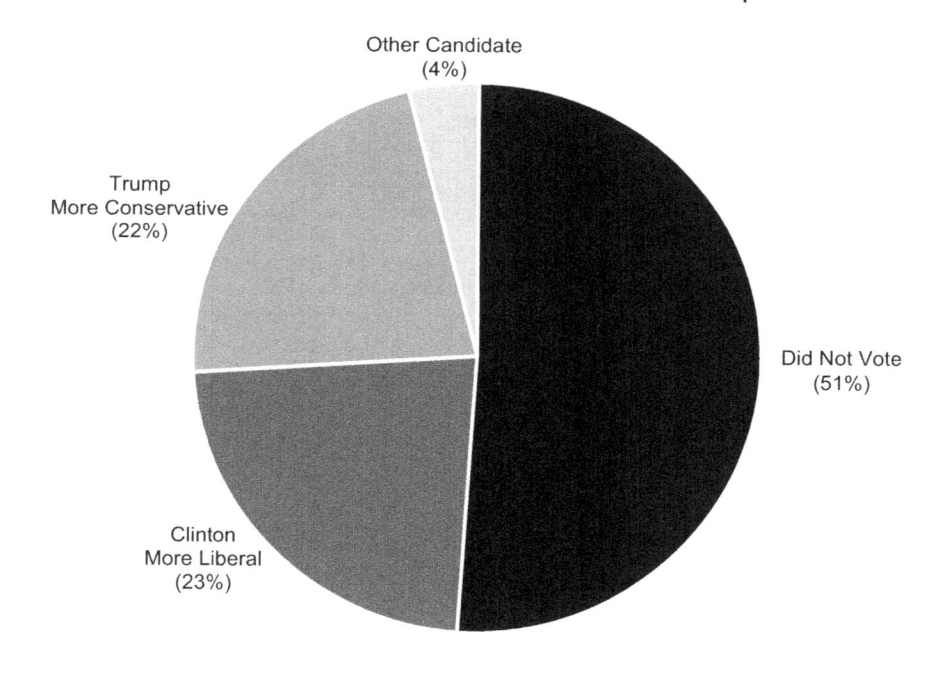

Figure 1

2016 U.S. Presidential Election Participation

- Other Candidate (4%)
- Trump More Conservative (22%)
- Clinton More Liberal (23%)
- Did Not Vote (51%)

Figure 2
2017 French Presidential Runoff Participation

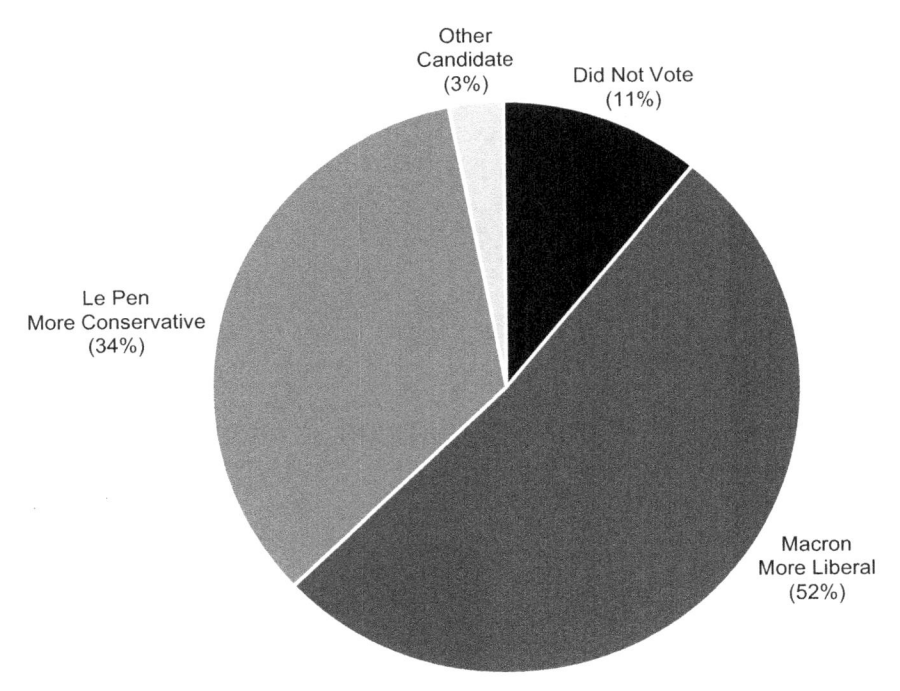

- Other Candidate (3%)
- Did Not Vote (11%)
- Le Pen More Conservative (34%)
- Macron More Liberal (52%)

1

As described in the passage as a whole, how does Holbein's study relate to the "statistic" (line 4) described in the first paragraph?

A) His research was designed to assess the statistic through analysis of official reports and long-term demographic data.
B) His research primarily examines whether the statistic is influenced by factors such as gender, ethnicity, and income.
C) His research could prove that social skills training at an early age may lead to an increased probability of voting.
D) His research did not initially account for the statistic but was modified to link this new information to public policy.

2

Which choice provides the best evidence for the answer to the previous question?

A) Lines 29-33 ("Holbein . . . priority")
B) Lines 36-39 ("The notion . . . decades")
C) Lines 56-59 ("His program . . . group")
D) Lines 63-66 ("When . . . voted")

3

It can be reasonably inferred from the passage that the author sees low voter participation in the United States as

A) a well-documented dilemma that should be addressed proactively.
B) an unprecedented situation that has not been satisfactorily explained.
C) an inevitable condition that is similar to other trends in society.
D) a situation that hinges mainly on the choices made by young adults.

4

As used in line 27, "small" most nearly means

A) previously indiscernible.
B) relatively minor.
C) prohibitively subtle.
D) clearly unimportant.

5

Which of the following statements, if true, would contradict the findings of the "Fast Track" project?

A) Adolescents who commit crimes exhibit problem solving skills that are superior to those of their peers.
B) Emotional regulation training among adults aged 25 to 30 does not effectively result in crime reduction.
C) Adolescents who are trained in prosocial behavior will gravitate mostly to one another when forming friendships.
D) Many high-risk children live in areas where mental health services have not been adequately funded.

6

The author calls attention to the "several explanations" (line 71) linked to Holbein's work in order to

A) shift the passage towards a more informal and accessible approach.
B) suggest that Holbein is interested in performing future studies.
C) introduce a few realistic interpretations of Holbein's data.
D) question the thoroughness of Holbein's work.

7

On the basis of the passage, Holbein would most likely fault the "Quick fixes" (line 15) for voter participation problems for

A) promoting voter participation in a manner that might weaken voters' personal empathy.
B) neglecting a set of findings that call attention to new difficulties in increasing turnout.
C) not clearly offering educational and civic opportunities that rely on the participation of young people.
D) attempting to change an existing system in ways most likely to disorient voters.

8

Which choice provides the best evidence for the answer to the previous question?

A) Lines 50-52 ("Improvements . . . beneficial")
B) Lines 73-75 ("One's ability . . . politics")
C) Lines 81-82 ("He also . . . policy")
D) Lines 87-89 ("Holbein . . . programs")

9

As used in line 75, "motivation" most nearly means

A) background.
B) agitation.
C) agenda.
D) probability.

10

As presented in the figures, which pairing represents the highest percentages of voters for the 2016 U.S. election and the 2017 French election, respectively?

A) Trump voters (U.S.) and Le Pen voters (France)
B) Clinton voters (U.S.) and Le Pen voters (France)
C) Clinton voters (U.S.) and Marcon voters (France)
D) Trump voters (U.S.) and Marcon voters (France)

11

What additional information, if considered alongside figures 1 and 2, would provide the best support for the claims in lines 3-5 ("This . . . turnout")?

A) Various measurements that indicate the relative health of the French and American economies
B) Information that clarifies the ideological preferences of non-voters in the United States and Europe
C) Voter turnout statistics from nations on various continents that held free elections from 2016 to the present
D) Rankings that evaluate the transparency and efficiency of elections in a variety of developed nations

STOP

Answer Key: CHAPTER ONE

SAT

1.01	1.02	1.03	1.04	1.05
1. A	1. B	1. C	1. D	1. D
2. C	2. B	2. A	2. B	2. C
3. B	3. C	3. A	3. A	3. A
4. C	4. B	4. C	4. C	4. B
5. C	5. C	5. C	5. D	5. D
6. C	6. C	6. D	6. D	6. D
7. B	7. D	7. C	7. A	7. A
8. A	8. C	8. B	8. A	8. C
9. A	9. C	9. D	9. A	9. D
10. D	10. B	10. A	10. C	10. D
11. B	11. D	11. B		11. A

1.06	1.07	1.08	1.09	1.10
1. A	1. D	1. B	1. A	1. C
2. B	2. C	2. A	2. D	2. D
3. C	3. C	3. B	3. C	3. A
4. A	4. B	4. D	4. C	4. B
5. A	5. A	5. D	5. C	5. A
6. B	6. D	6. B	6. C	6. C
7. A	7. D	7. B	7. D	7. C
8. A	8. B	8. D	8. D	8. D
9. A	9. A	9. C	9. A	9. D
10. C	10. A	10. C	10. C	10. C
	11. D			11. C

Answer Explanations

Chapter One

Chapter 1.1 | Wax Worms

1) CORRECT ANSWER: A
After explaining the environmental threats posed by waste (lines 1-29), the authors outline flawed plans for breaking down and eliminating plastic-based waste (lines 30-65) before explaining the potential solution suggested by the activity of wax worms. A properly reflects this content, while B wrongly indicates that the research devoted to wax worms is introduced EARLY in the passage. C and D both wrongly assume that the authors are preoccupied with a single concept or method, when in fact DIFFERENT methods for addressing a problem are analyzed before a desirable method is explained.

2) CORRECT ANSWER: C
In lines 15-19, the author explains that "the diligence it takes to find recycling and compost centers" can be directly linked to public "indifference," so that C is the best answer. A raises a possibly desirable environmental outcome, NOT an explicit liability in terms of recycling procedures. B misconstrues research content related to the difficulty of breaking down plastics to offer a faulty statement about the motives of the public, while D confuses one problem related to decision-making (lack of knowledge) for the problem that the passage actually raises (lack of interest even if knowledge IS present).

3) CORRECT ANSWER: B
The word "looming" refers to the presence of materials that are "unable to be recycled" (line 20) and that thus represent a problem that continues or persists. B is thus appropriate, while A refers to a physical trait (not to the severity of a problem). C indicates that the problem will occur later (not that it is a present liability) and D indicates that the problem is evolving or changing (not that it continues to be a known threat).

4) CORRECT ANSWER: C
In lines 41-44, the author references a "consequence" (namely, the fact that bacteria are not attracted to plastics) that explains why PET does not decay. This content supports C as the best answer. A and B refer to properties or traits of PET that do NOT directly relate to the question of why PET does not decay, while D is contradicted by the idea present in lines 41-44, since bacteria that can survive at non-extreme temperatures apparently could break down PET if these bacteria were attracted to the substance.

5) CORRECT ANSWER: C
See above for analysis of the correct line reference. A indicates that PET is durable but does NOT directly cite a factor that explains why this substance does not decay. B provides background information but does not, in the manner of C, directly discuss PET as a specific substance. D offers a discussion of PLA, not PET, and thus addresses the wrong topic.

6) CORRECT ANSWER: C
In lines 78-81, the authors indicate that the researchers saw a similarity between plastics and a "beeswax" food source as an explanation for why wax worms could break down plastics. This content supports C and contradicts A, since the wax worms adapted to break down beeswax and could COINCIDENTALLY break down plastics. B refers to a desired environmental outcome (not to an explanation of an organism's behavior) and D refers to a possibility raised in lines 98-100, not to a VERIFIED fact.

7) CORRECT ANSWER: B
See above for analysis of the correct line reference. A offers the observations made by one researcher but does not present an underlying reason for how wax worms break down plastics. C indicates that wax worms can break down plastics but does not explain WHY such activity is possible, while D presents a possible explanation instead of definite information that explains how wax worms operate.

8) CORRECT ANSWER: A
The word "mechanism" is used in reference to part of a biological "process" (line 95) that has been traced to wax worms. A would properly refer to a biological function. B wrongly raises a context of human implements or machinery, while C and D indicate that the biological process of how wax worms break down ingested substances is something that the worms think about or meticulously structure, NOT a biological function or trait.

9) CORRECT ANSWER: A
While the author defines biodegradation as related to bacteria (lines 37-39), the author then connects photodegradation to UV rays (lines 45-48); however, both processes involve breaking down waste products. A properly reflects this content, while B wrongly aligns the use of UV rays with biodegradation. C and D are contradicted by the fact that the author sees NEITHER option as a solution to the problem of plastic waste and instead raises the possibility that processes linked to wax worms could provide a solution.

10) CORRECT ANSWER: D
In lines 38-39, the author calls attention to various materials that are classified as organic waste; as considered in the graph, wood (6%), yard trimmings (including leaves, 14%), and food (15%) are forms of this type of waste. D thus presents the correct percentages. A, B, and C all bring in percentages that refer to non-organic categories (or to the "Other" category, which could include non-organic waste since its components are not specified) and should thus be eliminated.

11) CORRECT ANSWER: B
The chart indicates that plastics take varying amounts of time to break down, with some decomposing in five years and others not decomposing at ANY point. B properly calls attention to the fact that plastics can resist decomposition for centuries and is thus correct. A refers to trash generally (NOT to plastics specifically), C refers to only ONE type of plastic and does not clearly reference its lifespan, and D similarly references one type of plastic and does not clearly present a measure of lifespan.

Chapter 1.2 | Blushing

1) CORRECT ANSWER: B
In lines 14-16, the author explains that "only humans blush" and that this uniqueness is one factor that makes blushing fascinating. Thus, a comparison between blushing in humans and in other animals (which CANNOT blush) would be useless, so that B is the best choice. All other experiments WOULD interest the author; A and D are both contradicted by the fact that the author of the passage promotes further research on blushing among "diverse participants" (lines 94-95) such as those described in these hypothetical experiments. C is contradicted by the author's interest in the social circumstances related to blushing, as described in the first paragraph.

2) CORRECT ANSWER: B
See above for analysis of the correct line reference. A describes a social scenario that DOES interest the author, C presents a valid link between blushing and self-consciousness, and D indicates that blushing (though not fully understood) does have a social function. These line references can be used to ELIMINATE answers to the previous question that call attention to the social and psychological aspects of blushing in humans alone, since the author of the passage is clearly interested in such topics.

3) CORRECT ANSWER: C
In describing chronic blushers, the author indicates that such individuals can undergo "a surgery to suppress this reaction" (lines 22-23). This content directly supports C as the best answer. A is inaccurate because the author is interested in precisely explaining the nature and functioning of blushing but does NOT explain firm categories for psychological factors while doing so. B is contradicted by the idea that "only humans blush" (line 14, making examination of animals useless), while D distorts the discussion of the nervous system in the relevant line references; greater knowledge of the workings of the brain may clarify why people blush, but knowledge of blushing would NOT necessarily solve larger problems in terms of brain chemistry.

4) CORRECT ANSWER: B
The phrase "correlated with" is meant to describe the relationship between blushing and self-consciousness, which are factors that the author of the passage sees as meaningfully linked. B properly indicates a relationship between two factors that go together, while A would wrongly mean that the factors are confused with one another. Eliminate this answer, then eliminate C and D as answers that would best describe people cooperating, NOT factors that occur together.

5) CORRECT ANSWER: C
In lines 36-37, the author indicates that the purpose of each of the "two separate experiments" (transgression and social mishap) was to determine "how participants viewed models." This evidence supports C and makes A problematic; this trap answer seems to reference possible emotions that the test subjects could feel, but focuses on the issue of PREFERENCE instead of the true goal of determining RESPONSE to information. B (ethics) and D (identification) both raise broad issues that are not directly mentioned in the passage as research goals and that (at best) might be evaluated had the experiment been designed differently.

6) CORRECT ANSWER: C
In lines 81-83, the author explains that only "2 out of all 128 participants" in the relevant study actually discerned that the study was about blushing; thus, important information about the true nature of the study was not disclosed to the participants. C is an appropriate choice. A distorts an actual implication of the passage (that researchers would revise previous ideas about blushing as a result of new findings, NOT that study participants would). B and D both misconstrue the fact that the research described in the passage tested two separate concepts (transgressions and mishaps) for the idea that sorting based on these categories took place at an intermediate stage of the experiment.

7) CORRECT ANSWER: D
See above for analysis of the correct line reference. A indicates that study participants were pre-sorted into two groups, B indicates that participants responded to information by answering questions, and C indicates that participants rated models in terms of different criteria. None of these line references align with answers to the previous question, though make sure not to mis-align A with Question 6 D, which raises a similar topic but wrongly states that ALL participants were exposed to both aggression and mishap models.

8) CORRECT ANSWER: C
The word "subtle" refers to blushing effects that are present but require careful discernment, because such effects may be active on an "unconscious" (line 86) level. C properly reflects this content. A refers to sophistication or production (NOT to observation of effects), B is wrongly negative towards effects that (though hard to see) ARE important, and D best describes expression or personality.

9) CORRECT ANSWER: C
The two figures show the effect of blushing on the likability rating of models with shame, neutral, and embarrassment facial expressions. When compared, the likability ratings of the blushing model were consistently higher than the likability ratings of the non-blushing model, for all expressions. B is incorrect because there is a measured effect for blushing on likability for all expressions. D is incorrect because blushing is seen as increasing the likability, not decreasing it. A is incorrect because it refers to the likability rating of the respondents as opposed to that of the model, which C correctly mentions.

10) CORRECT ANSWER: B
While the participants in the study assigned ratings "on a scale of 0-100" (line 65) when responding to models, the figures do not present any likability ratings over 100, with 100 as the upper limit of the higher ratings in Figure 1. B properly reflects this resemblance, while A and C draw faulty assumptions about the multiple "Respondents" in the figures (since the figures only provide overall likability ratings, not details about how the ratings were collected or reported). D similarly refers to a detail that is at times considered in the passage (the number of participants) but NOT presented explicitly in terms of the figures.

11) CORRECT ANSWER: D
The University of California study described in the passage determined that blushing people can be perceived as more "trustworthy" (line 91), while the graph indicates that blushing people are perceived as more likable. Thus, the student is most likely relying on an assumed similarity (increase with blushing) between trustworthiness and likability. Choose D and eliminate A and B as answers that do not mention trustworthiness, the central concern of the University of California study. C wrongly indicates that shame is a desired quality, when in fact the figures indicate that blushing is linked to better results (and further indicate that people who exhibit embarrassment may be preferable to people who exhibit shame in any case).

Chapter 1.3 | Video Games

1) CORRECT ANSWER: C
After explaining the role of video games in society, the author describes research that considered "a number of variables and video game exposure" (lines 18-19) and presents the conclusion that video games relate to, but do not fully explain, trends in terms of violence (lines 84-92). This content supports C, while A (improvement) and B (argument against benefits) attribute the wrong PURPOSES to the research (which was designed mainly to record trends in video game usage). D presents a recommendation that may address the problem of violence but that is NOT considered by the author, who mainly provides an informative discussion of video game research.

2) CORRECT ANSWER: A
The author begins the relevant paragraph by explaining that video games are "one of the favorite pastimes of children" (line 2), then explains that video games may be linked to "aggressive" (line 8) tendencies; the author then concludes with a question about whether researchers can validate a

link between video games and aggression (lines 12-15). A properly reflects this content, while B and C both neglect the fact that the author ends the paragraph on a questioning or uncertain note. D wrongly describes a possibly negative connection (video games and aggression) as a definite crisis and wrongly references a definite solution instead of a question that MAY lead to a solution.

3) CORRECT ANSWER: A
The word "preventing" is contrasted with the word "causing" (line 11) in the context of a discussion of whether video games relate to aggression. Thus, a context of fully going against or precluding an outcome would be appropriate. Choose A for these reasons. B refers to official or regulatory action (NOT to an everyday outcome), while C and D would better refer to action that it suspended for a time but is not FULLY ruled out.

4) CORRECT ANSWER: C
The author explains that the GAM was used by Gentile and his collaborators but was "previously developed" (line 20) by other researchers; C properly indicates that Gentile's project was not the only research inquiry to make use of the GAM. A and B offer faulty statements about the GAM, which was in fact developed by Anderson and colleagues but was NOT seen as defective or crisis-oriented (since the GAM is mostly described as a useful way of understanding common trends). D references a feature of Gentile's experiment in terms of age group (lines 31-32), NOT a feature exclusive to the GAM that Gentile's team ALSO employed.

5) CORRECT ANSWER: C
The word "named" refers to the activity of participants in a study, who responded with information about "top" (line 40) video game choices and relevant violence ratings. C fits this context of giving or designating specific choices. A would wrongly indicate that the participants DISLIKED or rejected the "top" choices; B and D both refer to positive actions that involve giving people responsibilities, NOT providing information.

6) CORRECT ANSWER: D
In lines 31-34, the author explains that the relevant study only took account of "8th and 9th graders from four schools in the Midwest." The study could be expanded in terms of geographical scope (eliminating A), number of schools (eliminating B), and grade level (eliminating C). Because both boys and girls were considered (lines 49-52), the consideration of both genders would NOT expand the scope of the study; D is thus the best answer.

7) CORRECT ANSWER: C
In lines 72-74, the author indicates that "parental limits" on video game play align with lower aggression and higher academic performance. C thus relates to the fact that, by avoiding limits, the woman in the prompt may be following an approach that harms her son's grades. A and B raise topics relevant to video game habits and responses among students but do NOT explain these issues in terms of academic performance. D connects video games to problems in terms of aggression, NOT to problems in terms of grades or academics.

8) CORRECT ANSWER: B
In lines 84-90, the author argues that there is not a "100 percent likelihood that students will become more violent" as a result of video game exposure; this sense that some of the major factors considered in the relevant research are NOT definitively connected supports B as the best choice and can be used to eliminate A. While the author does not see the research as answering all possible questions about the link between video games and violence, the author does not find the research fundamentally problematic or divisive. C and D can thus be eliminated as overly negative.

9) CORRECT ANSWER: D
See above for analysis of the correct line reference. A and B present specific findings from the research described in the passage, not an OVERALL assessment of the research as required by the previous question. C points to ONE of the convincing findings of the research, but does not clearly indicate whether the research as a whole was completely valid (in support of Question 8 A) or somewhat inconclusive (in support of Question 8 B).

10) CORRECT ANSWER: A
Figure 1 indicates that the girls had preferences for puzzle and trivia video games (51%) that surpassed the preference for these video games (8%) exhibited by the boys. A properly reflects this content, while B presents the REVERSE of the actual situation (higher popularity among girls) for fantasy video games. C and D introduce the wrong issue, since the table is meant to indicate which genres the boys and girls preferred, NOT which genres or how many genres the boys and girls had played.

11) CORRECT ANSWER: B
The graph displays the association between boys' different video game preferences (sports, fantasy, and violence-based) and their negative behavior (including categories like verbal bullying, physical fighting, and

school suspension). The main trend that the graph supports is that boys with a preference for violent video games are more likely to engage in the listed negative behaviors. The most relevant factor to add to this graph is then arguments with teachers (B), another negative behavior that has already been mentioned in the passage as being correlated to a preference for violent video games. A, C, and D are incorrect as they do not seem to propose the same correlation between violent video games and negative behavior that B does.

Chapter 1.4 | Thyroid Misdiagnosis

1) CORRECT ANSWER: D
In the relevant portion of the passage, the author indicates that doctors "may not be aware" (lines 10-11) that comprehensive and up-to-date testing is important. D properly indicates that some doctors to not engage in comprehensive thyroid testing and thus supports the earlier claim with evidence from a quoted source, Dana Trentini. A does not directly mention doctors, B wrongly mentions a POSITIVE step taken by doctors, and C indicates that doctors may overlook problematic evidence, NOT necessarily that doctors avoid the earlier stage of comprehensive testing.

2) CORRECT ANSWER: B
The word "unwanted" refers to the nature of a "disorder" (line 6) and thus should take a strongly negative medical context indicating a problem or a danger. B is appropriate, while A indicates an overly large amount (NOT the fact that a disorder is a problem) and C indicates that the disorder goes against rules or expectations (NOT simply that it is a health danger). D is illogical in context, since the disorder is being studied and therefore has not been "abandoned."

3) CORRECT ANSWER: A
The relevant paragraph refers to low thyroid function and explains how doctors "render the diagnosis" (line 23) of this state by observing specific chemical TSH proportions. Because the passage as a whole deals with research involving thyroid function and TSH levels, this paragraph provides context; choose A and eliminate B and D as wrongly assuming negative tones for this mostly informative content. C wrongly focuses on a pattern (not on ONE method of diagnosis).

4) CORRECT ANSWER: C
The sixth paragraph (lines 70-83) focuses on various differing recommendations by different organizations about acceptable TSH levels and how patient advocates are pushing to rectify these inconsistencies. A

is incorrect because it states that there is a consensus about the acceptable TSH level, while the paragraph supports the opposite conclusion. B is incorrect because the passage does not support a particular side (patients or doctors) on the issue and thus, B cannot be assumed. Similarly, D is incorrect because the passage does not advocate for a specific level to be standardized but recognizes the existence of the debate over the issue. C is correct as it identifies that the issue is still unresolved and might be privy to further change (as indicated by the mentioned push of thyroid patient advocates).

5) CORRECT ANSWER: D
According to the passage (lines 64-69), in 2012, the American Thyroid Association made 4.12 mIU/L the standard upper limit for healthy TSH levels, while keeping 0.3 as the standard lower limit (line 56). Thus, having any levels below 0.3 mIU/L or above 4.12 mIU/L would be considered a symptom of hypothyroidism in 2012. D is the correct answer because it is the only answer choice that mentions a patient with a TSH level above 4.12 mIU/L, thus making it more likely that the patient would be diagnosed with hypothyroidism.

6) CORRECT ANSWER: D
In lines 80-83, the author references two researchers who maintain that within-range TSH measurements do not reliably account for hypothyroidism. D properly indicates that relying on TSH alone is problematic and thus continues the earlier claim. A describes an experimental method (NOT a problem), B presents the premises of a study and is not clearly negative, and C describes a change in criteria (NOT an issue in faulty diagnosis).

7) CORRECT ANSWER: A
The passage as a whole indicates that thorough thyroid testing is available though is not always provided by doctors, so that patients must (logically) take initiative and request such comprehensive measures. This content supports A, while the debate over TSH levels renders B ("mostly certain") problematic. C introduces a logical trap; problems such as hypothyroidism DO exist but still face some debate over assessment. D wrongly refers to a single study, when in fact the passage draws on various sources to explain the difficult status of studying and treating hypothyroidism.

8) CORRECT ANSWER: A
The word "fit" refers to symptoms that, in this context, may be "brushed aside or overlooked" (line 77). To "not fit" in this manner would be to NOT be overlooked, or to be considered valid or relevant. Such symptoms

would thus follow or "adhere" to specific criteria, so that A is correct. B (indicating calm or compromise) and D would both better refer to actions taken by people, while C misstates the relationship between the symptoms (which are explained by criteria but are not physically made up of criteria) and the logic behind them.

9) CORRECT ANSWER: A
A is the correct answer because its minimum range value 0.1 mIU/L is lower than those of all other answer choices—B, C, and D (0.3 mIU/L, 0.5 mIU/L, and 0.4 mIU/L, respectively).

10) CORRECT ANSWER: C
In lines 84-87, the author calls attention to the importance of a "full thyroid panel" as an important accompaniment for TSH testing in assessing a patient's thyroid levels. Such a panel includes consideration of factors listed in lines 91-93 and referenced directly in C as well. Choose this answer and eliminate A as an answer that calls attention to ONLY ONE factor considered under a full thyroid panel. B and D both relate to larger issues in the understanding and prevalence of hypothyroidism but do NOT reference either the full thyroid panel itself or any of its specific components.

Chapter 1.5 | Pluto's Surface

1) CORRECT ANSWER: D
The first paragraph directly states that "an understanding of our neighbors in our solar system" (lines 7-8) could facilitate comprehension of exoplanets. Choose D and eliminate A, since Earth is NOT singled out for analysis; in fact, Pluto seems to be a more significant topic. Eliminate B as similarly premised on a faulty inference, since the POSSIBILITY of multidisciplinary work is raised (lines 5-6) but ACTUAL specific projects are not named. C wrongly connects topics that are in fact present: both exoplanets and of Pluto are of possible research interest, but it is not clear that the SAME specialists have focused on both topics.

2) CORRECT ANSWER: C
The passage indicates that Pluto is a dwarf planet (line 44) and describes a study that traces geological changes and asteroid impacts; these topics are linked to the idea that ANY dwarf planet's age can be traced through analysis of such changes (lines 15-18). Choose C as a answer that contradicts this information by indicating a lack of change. A deals with a direct correlation (planet size and craters, not planet AGE and craters) that the author does not deal with as a main topic; B seems to raise an unlikely

possibility based on lines 34-39 but NOT a point that the author directly argues to be impossible. D is in fact SUPPORTED by lines 15-20 and should be dismissed for this reason.

3) CORRECT ANSWER: A
The word "reach" refers to the physical action of humans moving towards planets which are, in fact, impossible to get to physically and must be "observed" (line 10) in some distant respects instead. Choose A as properly reflecting a context of movement or contact. B refers to comprehension (a possible theme of the passage, but inappropriate to the more basic focus here on movement), C is overly positive and indicates emotion, and D indicates conquest rather than simple movement and exploration.

4) CORRECT ANSWER: B
In lines 63-68, the author indicates that Mars has a crust made of "volcanic basalt rock" and presents a contrast to Pluto, which is notable for freezing and melting processes. B reflects this contrast and indicates that C and D are problematic, since Mars is compared to planets of DIFFERENT size (Pluto and Jupiter) throughout the passage. A distorts an actual point from the second paragraph of the passage; Mars has been studied in terms of asteroid impacts, but whether these are the first "early" attempts to use this process or represent a more recent development (the more likely case from the context) is not addressed at length.

5) CORRECT ANSWER: D
See above for analysis of the correct line reference. A presents a general idea about celestial objects (NOT about Mars in particular), B indicates that Mars exhibits asteroid impacts that have been smoothed over (an idea that does NOT align with an answer to the previous question), and C represents a possible explanation (using Mars) for observations relevant to Pluto. Make sure not to wrongly use C as evidence for Question 4 B, since C represents a faulty analogy, NOT a direct point of contrast.

6) CORRECT ANSWER: D
The relevant processes are explained in detail in lines 71-82, and are introduced as possibilities that "could have erased the craters" (line 70) from one area of Pluto. Warming and melting are central to all three processes, so that D is the best choice. Note that the processes are mainly discussed in the context of Pluto (eliminating A as too broad) and ELIMINATE rough features such as craters (contradicting C). The author is mainly interested in how the processes could erase craters and in the time that it would take for a crater to be erased, not in the OVERALL age projection, at the relevant point in the passage, so that B is out of scope.

7) CORRECT ANSWER: A
The word "potential" is used to describe a time frame that would yield an "estimate of Sputnik Planum's age" (lines 81-82); this context of possibility and likelihood justifies A as acceptable. B (power or initiative), C (overly positive and often indicating a personal quality), and D (indicating making a process easier) all raise contexts inappropriate to determining the age of a region of a planet.

8) CORRECT ANSWER: C
In lines 90-92, the author indicates that Trilling's method of research "may yet be essential," indicating appreciation for the research but not certitude regarding its outcomes. C is appropriate while A ("anxiety") is overly negative, B ("precedents") falsely attributes a negative tone to earlier work, and D ("questionable") wrongly indicates that the author sees the research as fundamentally problematic, NOT as useful but susceptible to practical limitations.

9) CORRECT ANSWER: D
See above for analysis of the correct line reference. A and B describe points of Trilling's method, while C explains that some of Trilling's work may yield a conservative estimate. While the line references are relevant to Trilling, the false answers do NOT directly indicate the author's attitude in the manner of D and should all be eliminated for this reason.

10) CORRECT ANSWER: D
The Kuiper's Belt asteroids are composed of rock (A), frozen nitrogen (B), and frozen methane (C), so that an impact from an asteroid WOULD logically leave one or all of these substances on Pluto's surface. However, ONLY Pluto is composed in part of frozen carbon monoxide, so that D properly references a substance that would not indicate an asteroid impact.

11) CORRECT ANSWER: A
In the later paragraphs of the passage, Trilling is connected to "several cryo-geophysical scenarios" (line 69) that would require warming and melting on Pluto; figure 1 indicates that there is a significant amount of frozen material (which could be melted) on Pluto to fit the scenarios. A is an appropriate choice, while the fact that the figures omit ANY direct reference to Ganymede should be used to eliminate B as inaccurate. C and D are fundamentally flawed, because Trilling never indicates exactly how much rocky matter or liquid matter is needed for the scenarios; the presence of matter that could melt is mostly a baseline requirement for the possibilities that Trilling envisions.

Chapter 1.6 | Facebook Class

1) CORRECT ANSWER: A
In lines 38-42, the author points out that Fogg regards behavioral design as a way to "reconnect with nature," a positive objective in the context of the author's broader discussion of problematic responses to technology. A is thus appropriate, while B raises a possible problem (technology addiction) that though of interest to the author is NOT linked to Fogg's own goals. C is wrongly negative on Fogg's approach to behavioral design, while D raises a topic that interests the author (use of technology by businesses) but is NOT as clearly of interest to Fogg.

2) CORRECT ANSWER: B
See above for analysis of the correct line reference. A offers the author's own assessment of Fogg's work, C presents the perspective of Fogg's critics, and D raises the issue of technology use by companies. Though all of these items of evidence occur in the context of a discussion of Fogg, none of these answers reference Fogg's OWN perspective as required by the previous question.

3) CORRECT ANSWER: C
The word "paradigm" is used in the context of a discussion of "methods" (line 9) and of a resulting "model" (line 12) as these factors relate to addiction behavior. Thus, the context of explaining addiction as a widespread occurrence would indicate that the "paradigm" involves habits or patterns. C is appropriate. A relates to social achievements (NOT negative addiction), B would indicate that the paradigm (which should relate to useful information) is ITSELF a problem, and D refers to individual habits that would be modeled more BROADLY using the complete paradigm.

4) CORRECT ANSWER: A
The word "controlled" is directly linked to the word "changed" (line 55) in a discussion of human interactions; a context that calls attention to an influential shift, as in A, would be appropriate. B refers to a formal or extremely orderly method (NOT to reactions), while C refers to a positive reaction when in fact the author indicates that technology-related changes are troubling. D would indicate that the changes in behavior are the MOST important factors in human life, a conclusion that is not raised in the passage even though these changes are in fact important.

5) CORRECT ANSWER: A
In lines 63-64, the author indicates that Facebook has amassed "more

users" than Christianity has amassed followers; in context, the company has done so by manipulating human behavior to exploit addictive patterns. A is appropriate, while C offers a misreading of the same lines (since Christianity is presented for the sake of comparison in terms of group size, NOT directly mentioned as a superior means of solving problems). B (advertising) and D (images of perfection) raise problems with social media that, though possibly the subject of recent debates OUTSIDE the passage, do not directly interest the author.

6) CORRECT ANSWER: B
See above for analysis of the correct line reference. A points out that tech companies have overwhelming and disproportionate power (a negative that does NOT directly align with an answer to the previous question). C and D both present measures that may be taken AGAINST unethical responses to technology but do not clearly explain WHY features of Fogg's model (such as dependency) are problematic.

7) CORRECT ANSWER: A
While Passage 1 explains Fogg's "teachings" (line 8) and "model" (line 12) as passed on to his students, Passage 2 shows how members of Fogg's "Facebook Class" (line 67) are calling attention to problems related to the premises and the technologies that they themselves helped to spread. A reflects this relationship, while B neglects the negative tone of Passage 2 and D wrongly assumes that Passage 1 functions as a negative response to Passage 2 (not the other way around). C locates the wrong object of criticism (the outcomes of a model as applied to behavior, NOT the soundness of a methodology or experiment) and should be eliminated for this reason.

8) CORRECT ANSWER: A
While the author of Passage 1 mentions the mechanism behind app "addiction" in lines 18-26, the author of Passage 2 explains that technology can result in negative and habit-forming changes for its users in lines 49-59. This content supports A, while B and C are problematic in relation to the balanced approach that Passage 1 takes towards Fogg and his legacy. D wrongly indicates that Fogg's model will become irrelevant or obsolete, when in fact the deep-rooted problems linked to this model indicate that it will REMAIN important in the future.

9) CORRECT ANSWER: A
In the final sentence of Passage 1, the author calls attention to a "necessary strategy to survive" (line 48) that companies have adopted and that is linked to Fogg's ideas about online activity. A properly indicates that

Fogg's model, from the perspective of companies, CAN serve a productive purpose. Choose this answer and eliminate both B and D, which wrongly assume that the author is providing advice or recommendations, NOT facts about the behavior of companies. C wrongly criticizes Fogg's methodology, when in fact the sentence avoids any direct criticisms and the criticisms that DO appear in the passage relate to the behavioral problems that can be linked to Fogg's ideas.

10) CORRECT ANSWER: C
While lines 43-45 indicate that ideas such as Fogg's have helped companies to "foster addiction" to technology, the graph indicates the prevalence of various technologies but does NOT explicitly raise the issue of addictive behavior. Thus, the graph neglects a major factor considered within the passage; choose C and eliminate both A and B as automatically flawed in their reasoning. D wrongly raises an issue (advertising) that interests the author of Passage 1 but is NOT directly mentioned in the required line reference.

Chapter 1.7 | Sea Lions

1) CORRECT ANSWER: D
C is incorrect because dives by mammals other than sea lions were not mentioned and comprehensively discussed, and therefore were not compared to sea lion dives. A is incorrect because, while there were flaws pointed out in the study mentioned in the passage, the shortcomings of general sea lion dive examinations were not the main points of the passage. B is incorrect because not all factors of the optimal sea lion dive were evaluated, just drag and buoyancy in regards to speed. D is correct because the passage focuses on how a conducted study ("empirical evidence") proved the idea that drag affects sea lion speed ("long-held idea").

2) CORRECT ANSWER: C
B and D are incorrect because the passage gives no information about how the prey of the sea lions behaves, including whether prey organisms themselves are predators or have physiological traits related to the sea lions. A is incorrect because it cannot be assumed that the prey needs to be trapped in order to be caught. C is correct because the passage directly states that sea lions hunt at extreme depths of water, which indicates that the sea lion's prey cannot be found near the surface.

3) CORRECT ANSWER: C
See above for analysis of the correct line reference. A does not directly mention sea lions or sea lion prey, while B mentions that sea lions hunt underwater but does NOT provide evidence for Question 2 C because it is not specified here that sea lions hunt far beneath the surface. D indicates that sea lions perform deep-sea dives, but NOT that they do so in order to find prey, an idea that is only explicit in C.

4) CORRECT ANSWER: B
The word "ability" refers to an element of how sea lions swim that is enabled by a "mechanism" (line 21) and is important to the "livelihood" (line 36) of sea lions. B is appropriate as a word that calls attention to something that may be done for the sake of survival. A and C both refer not to biological traits or capacities but to behaviors that are learned, while D (indicating exceptional cleverness) introduces a faulty context for a discussion of survival-based and expected action.

5) CORRECT ANSWER: A
The results of the study are described in lines 71-80, a discussion introduced by the word "Unsurprisingly" and based on an expected relationship between drag and speed. A is thus appropriate, while the same content contradicts B and D. C calls attention to an issue (popularity or publicity) that distracts from the author's actual emphasis on whether the results were valid and on how the researchers (NOT the public) responded.

6) CORRECT ANSWER: D
In lines 86-89, the author indicates that the sea lion dives were not interrupted and that metabolic cost was thus impossible to calculate; interruption, if introduced in a future experiment, would thus provide information about metabolic cost. D is an appropriate choice. A, C, and D all indicate measures that OFTEN improve faulty experiments by increasing the quality of available data, but do not address omissions or shortcomings that are SPECIFICALLY traced to the experiment described in the passage.

7) CORRECT ANSWER: D
See above for analysis of the correct line reference. A indicates that three sea lions were studied but NOT that this set of test subjects was too small to be useful. B indicates that four conditions were assessed, while C indicates that a mathematical model was generally valid. None of these answers reference factors that would require further investigation in the manner of the reference to "metabolic cost" in D.

8) CORRECT ANSWER: B
The phrase "a function" refers to how speed related to specific factors that would increase or decrease speed, so that B properly calls attention to the context of measurement and causation. Choose this answer and eliminate A (which references skills but NOT scientific measurement) and C (which is also out of context in its reference to goals or motives). D wrongly refers to "speed" as a process that might have multiple parts, NOT as a single factor being assessed, and is thus illogical.

9) CORRECT ANSWER: A
The table indicates that lung volume for an adult male sea lion does not decrease AT ALL between 0 and 200 meters, so that A would implausibly assume a lung volume decrease within this range. B accurately describes a percentage increase from 5 to 9 (roughly double), while C accurately indicates that adrenaline MAY plausibly increase beyond 300 meters and thus continue the trend observed in the table. D similarly indicates that the trend for lung volume (greater decreases with greater depth) MAY plausibly continue beyond the depths present in the table.

10) CORRECT ANSWER: A
In lines 21-34, the author indicates that increases in adrenaline production lead to increases in blood flow, so that A is the best answer. B, C, and D all describe dive-related conditions that MAY require increased blood flow for the sake of survival, but that are not presented by the author as observing a direct cause-and-effect relationship such as that between adrenaline and blood flow.

11) CORRECT ANSWER: D
In lines 81-91, the author indicates that the researchers described in the passage could not study factors such as "metabolic cost" due to the limitations of the study; however, the table addresses adrenaline production, which the passage refers to as one of a group of "metabolic changes" (line 35). This content supports D, while the table does NOT clearly indicate where the sea lions were monitored (eliminating A), how much drag each sea lion experienced (eliminating B), or sea lion velocity (eliminating C). The only factors that are EXPLICITLY considered are dive depth, descent time, adrenaline production, and lung volume.

Chapter 1.8 | Pain Coping

1) CORRECT ANSWER: B
In the relevant lines, the author of the study discussed in the passage notes the "important practical implications" and potentially useful "cognitive

strategies" linked to her work. Thus, this specialist calls attention to practical or real-world implications; choose B and eliminate both A and C as wrongly criticizing the study, which is here presented in a thoroughly positive manner. D refers mainly to medical techniques ("dentistry and surgery" as mentioned in line 6), yet the author of the study is concerned mainly with a therapeutic measure that would ACCOMPANY these techniques.

2) CORRECT ANSWER: A
The word "standard" refers to a procedure that was followed "without any modifications" (line 39) in an experiment involving pain responses; this procedure would naturally be contrasted with the modified procedure that interested the researchers. A properly references a procedure that was in place for comparison or established before the experiment. B, C, and D all characterize (or criticize) the procedure as simplistic or well-known, when in fact the procedure was simply a comparative element of an experimental process.

3) CORRECT ANSWER: B
The author explains that the "self-statements" involved pleasant or at least positive references involving the water or the participants themselves (lines 47-52). B properly introduces a new positive self-statement, while A and C are both strongly negative. D indicates that the water is not cold enough to cause pain, a statement that could construe the experiment as ineffective and thus does not fit the positive tone of the provided self-statements.

4) CORRECT ANSWER: D
In lines 73-76, the author indicates that "all groups felt pain equally" even though (in context) the members of the experimental group kept their hands submerged longer and might have felt MORE pain had their attention not been diverted. This information supports D and directly contradicts B. Both A and C wrongly indicate that the experiment did NOT involve pain (either because pain was absent or because the participants enjoyed the experiment) and thus are contradicted by the design of the experiment as described in the passage.

5) CORRECT ANSWER: D
See above for analysis of the correct line reference. A compares two experimental groups (NOT an experimental and a control group as required by some of the answers to the previous question). B indicates that the participants in the experimental group did feel pain; while this answer does not align with an answer to the previous question, it DOES indicate

that Question 4 C is problematic. C references submersion times, NOT pain responses, and thus does not directly address the factor considered in most of the answers to the previous question.

6) CORRECT ANSWER: B
The word "recognition" is used in reference to a "delayed" (line 76) reaction linked to diverted "attention" (line 75); a context of response or perception as in B is appropriate. A wrongly refers to argumentation (admitting a point), while C and D both refer to a general context of knowledge or enlightenment, NOT to the more immediate context of observation and response.

7) CORRECT ANSWER: B
In lines 70-76, the author links the "diverted attention" (explained by verbal tasks, including the self-statements described in lines 47-52) of the experimental groups to delayed pain responses. B properly reflects this content, while A attributes the wrong pain-mitigating reaction (water feeling warmer, NOT distraction) to the self-statements. C and D both wrongly indicate that biological pain was delayed, when in fact the author notes that "all groups felt pain equally" (line 74) or experienced similar biological pain.

8) CORRECT ANSWER: D
See above for analysis of the correct line reference. A indicates that the experimental groups experienced distinctive pain tolerance patterns but does not indicate why, exactly, the coping strategies were effective. B and C similarly record experimental findings that suggest that the experimental groups witnessed reductions in psychological pain but do so without explaining the central factor (distraction) that made such responses possible.

9) CORRECT ANSWER: C
In figure 1, the "Coping" group members left their hands submerged for 4.5 minutes, slightly longer than the "Distracted" group members did and significantly longer than the "Control" group members did. C properly refers to the "Coping" group; eliminate A and B as representing lower-duration groups and D as wrongly indicating an equality across groups.

10) CORRECT ANSWER: C
In figure 2, the "Distracted" group experienced the highest average pain rating at 7.6, with the "Control" group at 7.0 and the "Coping" group at 7.4. Choose C; eliminate A and B as answers that appear to wrongly refer to the FIRST figure and D as an answer that refers to a value that exceeds the highest bar measurement present in either figure.

Chapter 1.9 | Dark Patterns

1) CORRECT ANSWER: A
After introducing the concept of "dark patterns" (lines 3-5) and explaining how these tactics can have negative effects on consumers, the author considers how companies such as Uber use similar tactics to undermine the "self-control and choice" (line 78) of workers. A properly reflects this significant content, while B both wrongly states that this passage is the first discussion of a problem that has ALREADY been diagnosed and is ALREADY used by major companies. C focuses on prevention, when in fact the author is mainly interested in explaining the extent of a problem. D distorts the content of the passage; the author uses Uber as a primary example, but not as the ONLY company that the passage considers in explaining broad trends.

2) CORRECT ANSWER: D
In the first paragraph, the author explains the nature of "dark patterns" (lines 3-5) and considers how consumers can be manipulated through the presence of such patterns. Later in the passage (lines 23-28), the author explains that Uber manipulates its workforce using dark pattern devices. D reflects this content, while A misconstrues the author's discussion of an expert (Harry Brignull) as a discussion of a formal study (a topic that the first paragraph avoids). B and C both appear to focus on specific sources such as Brignull's site, but these answers do NOT capture the idea of defining a term that is essential to the paragraph.

3) CORRECT ANSWER: C
Throughout the passage, the author consistently condemns companies' use of "manipulative schemes and psychological tricks" (lines 23-24) based on behavioral research to hurt both consumers and employees. Lines 65-73 explain how Uber manipulates drivers "into working towards an elusive goal that is just beyond their grasp" rather than encouraging them to pursue reasonable goals. Taken together, the main idea and specific line reference indicate that C is correct and that the author supports companies that give their employees straightforward objectives rather than unattainable ones. A is incorrect as the author only mentions instances in which a company's use of behavioral research (the basis of psychological tricks) hurts employees and doesn't reward them. B is incorrect because the author never comes out against a company's employment of independent contractors, simply its treatment of them. D is incorrect because the author does not mention employees using their company's products in their lives.

4) CORRECT ANSWER: C
See above for analysis of the correct line reference. A is incorrect because it focuses on the effect of dark patterns on consumers rather than the employees mentioned in the answer choices for question 3. B and D focus on Uber's use of psychology to further its business but are not specific enough in mentioning the elusivity of the goals that companies like Uber persuade their employees to take on.

5) CORRECT ANSWER: C
The word "undertake" is used to explain the "schemes" (line 23) and "tricks" (line 24) that are attributed to or used by companies to achieve specific results. C properly calls attention to a context of use, while A (context of coordinating people) and D (context of thought and ideas) raise faulty themes that do not directly fit the sentence. B is a trap answer that refers to the wrong stage of the process, since the companies employ the schemes to achieve results rather than seeking to achieve the schemes THEMSELVES as the end goals.

6) CORRECT ANSWER: C
While the Ryanair dark patterns relate directly to "people who buy plane tickets online" (line 16), the Uber dark patterns relate to "drivers" (line 35) who can be manipulated in the course of working for the company. This content supports C, while the author's willingness to point out the problematic nature of the dark patterns used by BOTH companies can be used to eliminate A and D as overly positive. B indicates that the two companies are fundamentally similar in the use of dark patterns (when in fact the companies use dark patterns differently) and is thus contradicted by the passage.

7) CORRECT ANSWER: D
In lines 34-35, the author indicates that, in successfully manipulating drivers, Uber relied on "behavioral science" that would naturally have empirical elements. D thus fits the requirements of the prompt. A (which broadly references a social experiment but does NOT clearly suggest actual scientific methods), B, and C all describe Uber's activities WITHOUT referencing the topic of empirical content that the question requires.

8) CORRECT ANSWER: D
The word "Nudging" is used to explain how customers can be led to make specific choices as a result of the use of "tricks" (line 48). D properly indicates that the buyer is being manipulated, while A (theme of physical exertion) and B (theme of dishonesty) raise negatives that are too strong

for the context of leading a buyer to a choice. C raises an overly positive tone when in fact the author calls attention to the negative aspects of manipulative methods in the passage.

9) CORRECT ANSWER: A
In the comparison between Uber and a symphony in lines 85-88, a source quoted by the author notes that Uber combined manipulative "practices" so that individuals would "sway to the beat." A references the proper themes of manipulation and strong response, while B is contradicted by the fact that the author critiques Uber's methods as problematic throughout the passage. C wrongly references other companies (a topic mentioned LATER but not in the comparison in lines 85-88), while D wrongly focuses on composing music ITSELF as an activity, not as a piece of imagery that primarily explains how Uber operates.

10) CORRECT ANSWER: C
In explaining the use of dark patterns, the author argues that the prevalence of such patterns should "alarm" (line 2) observers; moreover, the author indicates that Uber's use of dark patterns is suspicious or troubling by referencing the company's "dubious tactics" (lines 41-42) and "dubious deeds" (line 46). This strongly negative stance supports C and can be used to eliminate positive answers such as A and B as inaccurate. While D properly indicates that the passage provides important background information, this answer neglects the author's clear bias and should be eliminated for this reason.

Chapter 1.10 | Voter Turnout

1) CORRECT ANSWER: C
The relevant "statistic" concerns how much of the voting-age population in the United States "did not cast a ballot in the 2016 presidential election" (lines 3-4). As explained in lines 63-66, Holbein linked likelihood of voting to "training" in social skills; C properly reflects this content. A is problematic because Holbein's study was initiated in 1992, decades BEFORE the statistic emerged. B cites the wrong set of factors for Holbein's study (which primarily considered social skills), while D wrongly indicates that Holbein modified his study to account for the statistic, when in fact he accounted for social factors WITHOUT clearly deviating from the original design of his project.

2) CORRECT ANSWER: D
See above for analysis of the correct line reference. A indicates the importance of voting in the context of Holbein's work, but does not clearly reference social skills training in a manner that would support Question 1 C. B refers to childhood intervention but does NOT directly raise the topic of voting tendencies, while C explains how Holbein's study functioned but does not offer FINDINGS in terms of voting tendencies that would be relevant to the "statistic."

3) CORRECT ANSWER: A
In the first paragraph of the passage, the author references voting tendencies in the United States, which have been subjected to "multiple explanations," and explains that relatively low voter turnout is a "problem" that should "be solved in the future" (lines 1-15). This content directly supports A, while B wrongly indicates that the situation has NOT been investigated and C wrongly indicates that voting trends cannot be corrected (when in fact the author sees corrective action as possible). D distorts the author's discussion of Holbein's study (which focuses on children) to offer criticism of young adults (who may not be voting but are NOT clearly responsible for the fact that nearly half of eligible voters in the U.S. did not cast ballots in the 2016 presidential election).

4) CORRECT ANSWER: B
The word "small" refers to adult-centered efforts that are contrasted with "effective" (line 28) child-centered efforts; thus, something "small" in this context would not be especially effective or may only have minor usefulness. B is appropriate, while A wrongly indicates that outcomes were hard to detect (NOT that a problematic outcome was clearly detected). C calls attention to the irrelevant context of subtlety or sophistication, while D wrongly indicates that a finding is unimportant (when in fact the finding that adult-centered efforts were problematic IS an important fact to the author).

5) CORRECT ANSWER: A
In discussing the "Fast Track" study of children, the author links various skills, including effective problem solving, to "reduction in crime" (lines 46-52); the idea that problem solving and crime are likely to accompany one another would thus contradict the findings. Choose A and eliminate B as wrongly focusing on "adults" instead of on the child subjects considered in the "Fast Track" study. C rightly refers to children and behavior but wrongly introduces the topic of friendship, NOT the actual "Fast Track" topic of crime; D considers childhood behaviors in the context of funding, a consideration that is NOT explicitly linked to the "Fast Track" study.

6) CORRECT ANSWER: C
After explaining the "several explanations" linked to Holbein's work, the author indicates that Holbein's findings may "have important implications for public policy" (lines 81-82). This idea of providing explanations to then set up a discussion of practical applications supports C, while the discussion of the explanations does not change the mostly formal tone of the passage (eliminating A) or introduce a strong negative (eliminating D). B is a trap answer that distorts the actual importance of the explanations; Holbein is interested in APPLYING his fundings, not in STUDYING tendencies in a modified version now that he has gathered valid information.

7) CORRECT ANSWER: C
In lines 87-89, the author indicates that Holbein favors programs that promote "social skills" and volunteering for children as a response to flaws in voter participation; however, the "Quick fixes" (line 15) cited by the author target voting-age adults. Holbein would thus most likely fault the programs for targeting the wrong age group. Choose C and eliminate A because, while the "quick fixes" do not seem likely to increase empathy in a long-term way, Holbein never links DECREASED empathy to voting initiatives. Other answers can be eliminated because the quick fixes themselves are never discussed in relation to the research background of those proposing the fixes (eliminating B) or the emotions of the voters (beyond basic disengagement, eliminating D).

8) CORRECT ANSWER: D
See above for analysis of the correct line reference. A describes research that was NOT performed by Holbein himself and is thus not relevant to the previous question. B raises the idea of empathy but should NOT be taken as evidence for Question 7 A; while Holbein is interested in fostering empathy, it is not clear that the "quick fixes" for voter turnout problems have actually DECREASED empathy (despite the other practical flaws of the proposed "fixes"). C indicates that Holbein's findings have practical implications but does not specify those implications in a manner that, as in D, allows for assessment of the "quick fixes."

9) CORRECT ANSWER: D
The word "motivation" refers to the situation of people notable for "recognizing" (line 74) social problems and for consequently taking action in politics; people who become aware of problems would logically be more likely to take practical measures. D calls attention to the correct context of a probable response. A refers to formative traits or upbringing, NOT to a context of likely action. B introduces a faulty negative tone and

C indicates a highly formal and orderly course of action, not a direct and increasingly likely response.

10) CORRECT ANSWER: C
This question can be answered by determining the highest percentage of voters in each election (2016 U.S. election and 2017 French election) and then finding an answer choice that includes both of these percentages. The highest percentage of voters (non-voters not considered) in the 2016 US election are voters that voted for Hillary Clinton with 23%. The highest percentage of voters (non-voters not considered) in the 2017 French election are voters that voted for Emmanuel Macron with 52%. C is correct because it is the only answer choice that includes both Clinton and Macron.

11) CORRECT ANSWER: C
The claim present in lines 3-5 is that the U.S. is "behind nearly every other democratic nation in terms of voter turnout." Thus, assessment of figure 1 (the 2016 U.S. presidential election) alongside voting statistics for "free elections" from around the world in 2016 would enable direct assessment of the author's statement. Choose C and eliminate A as continuing the comparison of France and the U.S. as considered in the two present figures, NOT as considering the required information from the passage. B and D would consider additional countries as required by the content from the passage, but would not directly address the issue of voter TURNOUT (as opposed to ideological preferences and election ethics, respectively) in any clear way.

Chapter Two

Questions 1-10 are based on the following passage and supplementary material.

2.1
Adapted from a *Journal of Neuroscience* research article by L. Xu and colleagues, "High-fat Diet Mediates Anxiolytic-like Behaviors in a Time-dependent Manner Through the Regulation of SIRT1 in the Brain," in which the scientists explore the ability of high-fat diets to alter our feelings of anxiety over time.

What do ice cream, pizza, and donuts have in common? If your mind went to 3AM on a night before a big deadline, you're not alone. According to the American Psychological Association (APA), 38% of American adults report having engaged in unhealthy eating behaviors as a response to stress. For nearly half of these people, stress eating has become a routine: 49% of adults who stress eat do so on at least a weekly basis. While it's clear that stress eating is a common occurrence, knowledge about the mechanisms that make it so effective is much more elusive. Furthermore, with so many Americans engaging in stress eating to cope with the strains of daily life, it has become even more important to understand the implications of sustaining such an unhealthy habit.

New research has found that eating high-fat foods, such as those commonly consumed during stress eating, actually has a strong anxiolytic, or anxiety-reducing, effect. Neurobiologists from the Southern Medical University in Guangzhou, China recently conducted a study to observe the effects that different diets can have on mood. Inspired by a previous finding that linked the enzyme SIRT1 to major depressive disorder, the scientists sought to further explore the relationship between SIRT1 and other psychological afflictions.

The study was comprised of four groups of mice, organized by both type and duration of diet. Group 1 was fed a high fat diet (defined as 60% kcal fat) and sustained the diet for four weeks, while Group 2 was fed a high fat diet for twelve weeks. Groups 3 and 4 were fed standard diets (10% kcal fat) and sustained the diets for four and twelve weeks, respectively. The effects of these diets were measured in a series of behavioral tests. In one such test, mice were placed in an open field, where their movements around the area were tracked. More movement and exploratory activity indicated a sense of comfort, while refusal to move from the center of the space was a sign of anxiety and stress.

The results were surprising: reduced anxiety was found in mice who had been fed high-fat diets. These mice expressed lowered levels of SIRT1 compared to the control groups and thus were more engaged during the test trials performed. The positive effects were fleeting, however; Group 2, which ate a high-fat diet for twelve weeks, did not exhibit anxiolytic effects by the end of their trials. Their performance on the open-field test was actually comparable to that of the control groups, thus showing that they were unable to reap the benefits of a high-fat diet in the long term. Moreover, their diet seemed to have an adverse effect on their movements: even when mice in the group conveyed a desire to explore, they were hindered due to their rapid weight gain.

From this study, it is evident that fatty foods work with our brain to lower levels of anxiety, but that our bodies quickly adapt to the change in diet, causing the initial changes in our brain to be reverted. Furthermore, eating foods high in unwanted substances have adverse effects on our weight, which can lead to other negative long-term effects like depression. So while it may seem like a good idea to binge while you're feeling stressed, it might work against you as a long-term coping strategy.

But how certain can we be about the results of this study? This research was conducted using mice, which share many genetic traits with humans but are ultimately very different. Therefore, a mitigation of SIRT1 may have completely divergent consequences in humans. In addition, the human diet is much more complex than that of mice, with many more nutritional nuances that were not addressed in the study. The type of fat alone can have vastly differing effects on one's condition: trans fats and saturated fats have been shown to be the most harmful, while polyunsaturated fats and monounsaturated fats can, in fact, benefit both the mind and body. To build on this research, a future study should consider measuring the outcome of diet manipulation in humans, taking the type of fat consumed into consideration. Only with this additional information can we truly determine the effects of diet on our mental and physical health.

Changes in Perceived Anxiety in Study Participants over a 12-Year Period

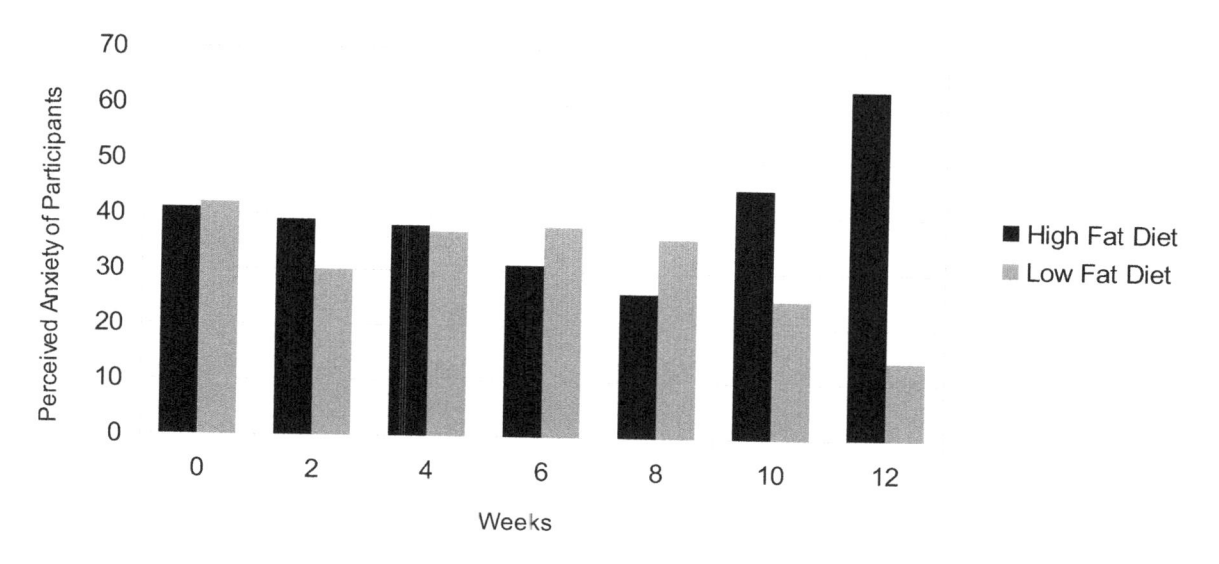

Bar chart showing Perceived Anxiety of Participants (y-axis, 0-70) over Weeks (x-axis: 0, 2, 4, 6, 8, 10, 12) comparing High Fat Diet (black) and Low Fat Diet (gray).

1

The second paragraph primarily serves to

A) reveal the physiological process behind a phenomenon.
B) introduce a problem that is explored through a study.
C) outline a hypothesis which will be undermined by an experiment.
D) explain the long-term psychological consequences of stress eating.

2

As used in line 15, "implications" most nearly means

A) influence.
B) repercussions.
C) significance.
D) consequences.

3

In conducting the experiment, the researchers were most concerned with observing the

A) psychological effects of weight gain in mice.
B) psychological effects of high-fat diets in mice.
C) physiological effects of weight gain in mice.
D) physiological effects of high-fat diets in mice.

4

In designing the experiment, the researchers assumed that

A) anxiety is different in mice than it is in humans.
B) the effects of a high fat diet would not last.
C) the effects of SIRT1 on mice are comparable to those of humans.
D) a diet of 60% kcal fat would increase the presence of SIRT1.

5

As used in line 26, "afflictions" most nearly means

A) anomalies.
B) mindset.
C) condition.
D) ailment.

6

Which finding, if accurate, would undermine the researcher's claims about anxiety in mice?

A) Mice exhibit a naturally higher SIRT1 level than do humans.
B) Symptoms of anxiety in mice are different than they are in humans.
C) The movement of mice is not linked to stress levels.
D) Mice naturally gravitate towards low fat foods when foraging for food.

7

The author's ultimate perspective on the study's results is

A) wholehearted agreement, because it shows that a high-fat diet is unhealthy.
B) reluctant approval, because a high-fat diet was effective in the short term.
C) qualified skepticism, because the findings do not necessarily apply to the intended population.
D) complete outrage, because stress eating should not be condoned even as a temporary solution.

8

Which choice provides the best evidence for the answer to the previous question?

A) Lines 12-15 ("Furthermore...habit")
B) Lines 45-48 ("The positive...trials")
C) Lines 62-65 ("So while...strategy")
D) Lines 66-69 ("But how...different")

9

Which lines exemplify the trends seen in the graph?

A) Lines 45-48 ("The positive...trials")
B) Lines 48-51 ("Their performance...long term")
C) Lines 52-55 ("Moreover...weight gain")
D) Lines 56-59 ("From...reverted")

10

Which claim CANNOT be answered by the information on the graph?

A) Consuming a low fat diet has more anxiolytic benefits than a high fat diet.
B) Eating fatty foods has an adverse effect on weight gain in the long term.
C) Eating a high fat diet has short-term anxiolytic benefits but not in the long term.
D) Within the first two weeks, high-fat diets produced a strong anxiolytic effect.

Questions 1-11 are based on the following passage and supplementary material.
2.2
Adapted from a 2013 Audubon Society Magazine article, "Poisons Used to Kill Rodents Have Safer Alternatives," by Ted Williams. In the article, the author describes the threat that second generation rodenticides pose on the environment.

Many raptors* in the US today are victims of what is known as "second generation anticoagulant rodenticides," according the Audubon Society's magazine in 2013. Such poisons, found in such brand names as Havoc, Talon, Generation, Hot Shot, and d-Con, are being used by homeowners, farmers, and exterminators due to the consuming hatred that many people have for mice and rats. According to the article, "the general attitude among the public is, 'if a little poison's good, a lot's better.' But even a little second-generation rodenticide kills non-target wildlife." If people do not start becoming more judicious with their use of rat poison, birds, humans, and other wildlife will certainly pay a grave price.

Second-generation rodenticides, which are used because they're known to be much stronger and deadlier to animals than first-generation rodenticides, do have legitimate uses—for example, if you have an island that is infested with rats and you want to restore its ecosystem. Meanwhile, mostly low-income children and many birds and mammals continue to be poisoned. Pro-raptor efforts such as RATS ("Raptors Are The Solution"), the Hungry Owl Project, and San Francisco's "Don't Take the Bait" consumer campaign are offering education and alternatives to these poisons.

Many people remain oblivious to the dangers associated with the widespread use of the second-generation rodenticides. It's generally better to use first-generation poisons first, so you have a backup, whereas if you use your strongest choice first, you have no backup. All a person has to do with a first-generation bait is leave it out for a week and it's just as efficient as a second generation. In contrast, second-generation rodenticides kill slowly, but by the time the rodent expires it contains multiple lethal doses and is deadly to other organisms while the poison is in its system.

As overuse by consumers is becoming a larger threat to the environment, the EPA declared second-generation rodenticides too dangerous for public use, ordering their removal from the general market. However, courts allowed 3 large manufacturers to defy the order, and many stores still have large stocks of these chemicals. At Tufts Cummings School of Veterinary Medicine, clinical assistant professor Maureen Murray has many birds who, as a result of this poisoning, do not have enough red blood cells to deliver oxygen to their bodies.

According to a study by the EPA conducted from 1999 to 2003, at least 25,549 children who were under the age of 6 had eaten enough rodenticide to show symptoms of poisoning. Each year, 15,000 calls to the Centers for Disease Control (CDC) come in from parents whose children have eaten a rodenticide. Since rodents often distribute baits around the home and property, measures to place bait where a child cannot get it often fail.

As of the time this study was conducted, New York and California had been the only two states to have looked at the problem of rodenticide poisoning. In the state of California, these poisons showed up in 78 percent of mountain lions, 79 percent of fishers, 92 percent of San Diego County raptors, and 84 percent of San Joaquin kit foxes. In New York state, they were found in 81 percent of great horned owls and 49 percent of a dozen different species of necropsied raptors.

After researching these harmful chemicals, New York City's local Audubon Society asked the public to refrain from using Brodifacoum and Difethialone—the most toxic second-generation rodenticides that are poisonous to birds. They also ask people not to use them during nesting season, or only as a last resort. But the organization's director, Glenn Phillips, stopped short of demanding a total ban, arguing that New York City has a "huge rat problem." The best solution, it appears, is to use second-generation rodenticides in moderation, and to attempt to keep them away from vulnerable groups like children and pets.

*A bird of prey (such as an owl or a falcon) that hunts on rodents and other small animals

Comparison of Lethal Doses per Animal of First Generation Rodenticide to d-Con Rodenticide

Animal (full-grown adult male of each species)	Lethal Dose (grams ingested) of 1st Generation Rodenticide	Lethal Dose (grams ingested) of d-Con rodenticide
Field Mouse	2.5	3.0
Chipmunk	2.5	3.5
Squirrel	6.5	8.5
Rat	7.0	8.0
Groundhog	22.5	20.5
American Kestrel (Falcon)	6.5	5.0
Barn Owl	8.0	6.0
Great Gray Owl	12.5	16.5
Great Horned Owl	20.0	15.5
Human	145.0	165.0

1

The main purpose of the passage is to

A) discourage readers from engaging in pest control.
B) advocate the implementation of an alternative method.
C) bring awareness to an ongoing health crisis.
D) promote the protection of a specific species.

2

Which choice best supports the idea that certain populations are at a higher risk than others are?

A) Lines 1-3 ("Many...rodenticides")
B) Lines 20-22 ("mostly...poisoned")
C) Lines 27-30 ("people...first")
D) Lines 36-38 ("it contains...system")

3

Based on the context of the passage, the general public's use of second-generation rodenticide would be best characterized as

A) overzealous.
B) judicious.
C) warranted.
D) unprecedented.

4

Which choice provides the best evidence for the answer to the previous question?

A) Lines 9-10 ("the general...better")
B) Lines 15-18 ("second-generation...uses")
C) Lines 27-29 ("Many people...rodenticides")
D) Lines 51-53 ("at least...poisoning")

5

As used in lines 30 and 32, "backup" most nearly means

A) desperate resort.
B) viable alternative.
C) essential support.
D) willing substitute.

6

Which species is NOT cited in the passage as having consumed rodenticide inadvertently?

A) Children under 6
B) Foxes
C) Squirrels
D) Mountain lions

7

The primary purpose of the 6th paragraph (lines 59-65) is to

A) provide support for the claim that overuse of rodenticides has detrimental effects on unintended targets.
B) argue that the only way to stop people from using second-generation rodenticides is to show them the effects.
C) dispute the widely-held belief that rodenticides have negative consequences only on small children, rodents, and birds.
D) discuss the effects that rodenticides have in California and New York, and conclude that these areas are most strongly affected.

8

As used in line 62, "showed up" most nearly means

A) made appearances.
B) randomly emerged.
C) asserted themselves.
D) were detected.

9

Which choice provides the best evidence for the claim that second-generation rodenticide should only be used as a secondary method to kill animals?

A) Lines 10-11 ("But even...wildlife")
B) Lines 18-20 ("For example...ecosystem")
C) Lines 29-32 ("It's generally...backup")
D) Lines 34-38 ("In contrast...system")

10

Based on the table and the information in the passage, which of the following raptors has a higher lethal dosage of d-Con rodenticide compared to the lethal dosage of first generation rodenticide?

A) Great Gray Owl
B) Groundhog
C) Great Horned Owl
D) American Kestrel (Falcon)

11

Does the information in the table provide support for the main idea of the passage?

A) Yes, because it shows that raptors require a lesser lethal dose of second-generation rodenticide than of first-generation rodenticide.
B) Yes, because in many species second-generation rodenticides require a larger lethal dose than do first-generation.
C) No, because it fails to show how the effects of second-generation rodenticides can be far-reaching.
D) No, because it is impossible to tell whether rats are the cause of the common presence of second-generation rodenticides.

Questions 1-11 are based on the following passage and supplementary material.
2.3
Adapted from a 2013 Business Insider article, "18–29-Year-Olds Use Their Phones Totally Different From Older People," by Jay Yarow.

Humans are tribal creatures. We have been so since the first hunter-gatherer groups banded together as a means of protection and identity, and one only has to look at our loyalties to groups from political [5] parties to sports teams to know that this still persists in modern society. But how does this tendency to "stay to one's own"—the very core of tribalism—manifest in our use of technology? Cell phones, in particular, were created as a means of connecting us to others around [10] the world. But several studies examining the usage of cell phones among different cohorts, or generations, have found that instead of bridging the gap between generations, phones have reinforced the tribal barriers that separate age groups.

[15] Several groups of researchers have noted the trend and have sought to find whether there is truth in the stereotypes regarding different cohorts' usage of cell phones. They focused particularly on the cell phone habits of two prominent generations: Baby Boomers [20] (born in the 1940's–1960's) and Millennials (born in the 1980's–1990's). Baby Boomers have gained a reputation among younger generations for being "technologically illiterate," whereas Millennials are frequently criticized for their apparent attachment to, [25] or borderline obsession with, to their phones.

The studies compiled data from several different databases, including the Pew Research Center's research on the topic of cell phone use. The data included information describing both the amount of [30] time spent on mobile devices and the type of content perused during that time. The researchers then compared the findings between the two generations. Millennials were found to spend 3.1 hours per day on their smartphones, while Baby Boomers were [35] noticeably less active, spending only 1.2 hours, or about ⅔ less time, on their phones per day. Millennials are also more likely to use their phones as sources of entertainment: 50% use applications to find restaurants, and 71% use their mobile phones to read the news. [40] Comparatively, only 25% and 41% of their older counterparts use their phones in the same respective ways.

The researchers also found interesting patterns in the use of SMS (texting) and OTT ("over the top": [45] audio, video, and other media that are delivered via the Internet) that furthered the distinction between the two generations. SMS, or traditional texting, is popular among Boomers, with over 90% of them using the service as their primary mode of communication. [50] On the other hand, Millennials use SMS at a rate of 79%, but are more likely to use OTT platforms such as Facebook Messenger, Snapchat, and Google Hangouts.

What could be causing these striking differences and how do they affect these groups' perceptions [55] of one another? For one, Boomers and Millennials were raised in completely different technological environments. In the 1950s, when most Boomers were children, the prominent forms of media were television and the radio. This preference still stands today, as [60] the researchers found that Boomers watch TV, read newspapers, and listen to the radio for 4.3 hours per day in addition to using their cell phones. In contrast, Millennials, who came of age in the 80's and 90's and therefore had access to devices such as computers [65] and MP3 players, quickly took to smartphones as they had been immersed in similar technologies since childhood.

As smartphones have become more integrated into daily life and have begun to act as essential [70] tools in communication, Boomers are consequently feeling "left behind." Skeptical attitudes regarding new technology and a steep learning curve in acquiring the skills needed to use smartphones have further perpetuated the divide between Boomers and [75] Millennials. As a result, Boomers have grown to reject assimilation into more tech-savvy communities, which can lead to grave consequences. Because of their limited technological knowledge, for example, Boomers are more likely to fall for phishing scams and [80] fake news that Millennials can easily detect and avoid.

Understanding these trends is the first step in reconciling the two generations' misperceptions of each other. Ashton Applewhite, author of the book, *This Chair Rocks: A Manifesto Against Ageism*, [85] suggests that self-awareness can help Baby Boomers reconnect with members of other generations, advising that Boomers make a conscious effort to push back against generational stereotypes. She recommends using the Internet, mixing things up with friends of [90] all ages, and asking for help from younger people as strategies to maintaining an open worldview: "keeping up with new technology helps people connect across geography and generations—always a good thing." Though she sympathizes with those who would rather [95] hear the voices of their grandchildren than receive a text from them, Applewhite also hopes that her friend's grandchildren will offer to teach her to text, and that she will take them up on the offer.

Figure 1

Cell Phone Activities of Baby Boomers

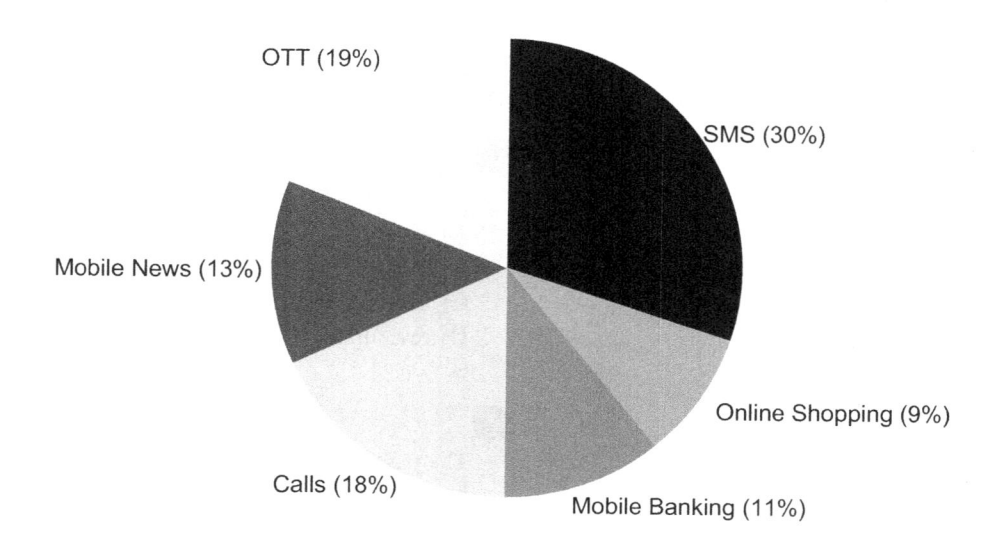

- OTT (19%)
- SMS (30%)
- Mobile News (13%)
- Online Shopping (9%)
- Calls (18%)
- Mobile Banking (11%)

Figure 2

Cell Phone Activities of Millenials

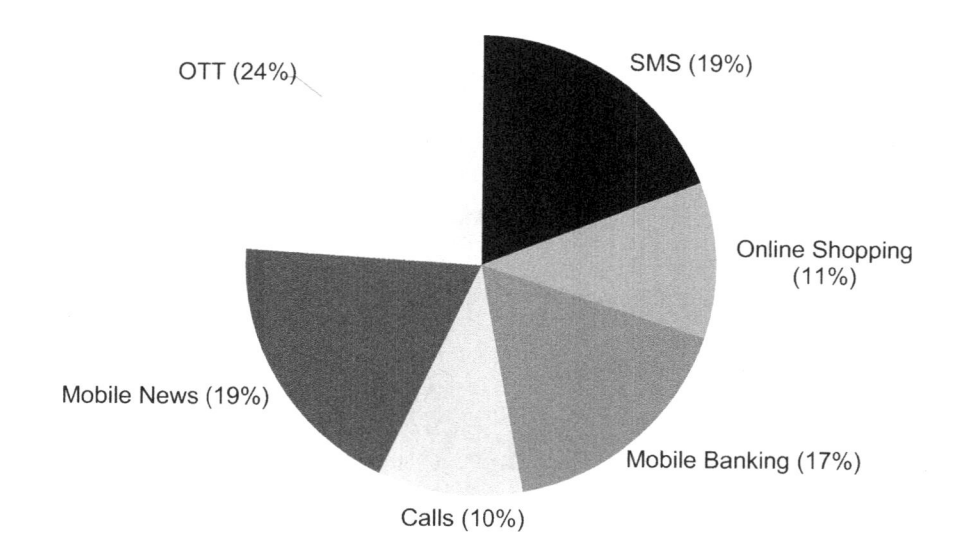

- OTT (24%)
- SMS (19%)
- Online Shopping (11%)
- Mobile News (19%)
- Mobile Banking (17%)
- Calls (10%)

1

The first paragraph of the passage serves mainly to

A) explain how the findings detailed in the passage can relate to a variety of problems.
B) introduce a historical fact that is widely believed to be a misconception.
C) assert a connection between a particular technology and a universal tendency.
D) demonstrate how technology usage has promoted intergenerational conflict.

2

Which choice provides the most effective support for the claim that cell phones have reinforced the "tribal barriers" (line 13) described early in the passage?

A) Lines 33-36 ("Millennials . . . day")
B) Lines 47-52 ("SMS . . . Google Hangouts")
C) Lines 55-57 ("For one . . . environments")
D) Lines 71-75 ("Skeptical . . . Millennials")

3

The author's purpose in noting that Baby Boomers can be described as "technologically illiterate" (line 23) and "left behind" (line 71) is to

A) criticize Millennials for making hasty and counterproductive judgments.
B) indicate that self-consciousness will prompt Baby Boomers to change their tendencies.
C) pinpoint negative perceptions of a generation's technology-related habits.
D) urge a single generation to improve its communication skills.

4

Which of the following best fits the passage's definition of an OTT Internet platform?

A) A program that flags calls from unfamiliar cell phone numbers by playing a personalized ringtone
B) A messaging service that can provide automatic translation of simple greetings and phrases
C) An app that can vary the fonts and background colors of e-mails to different recipients
D) A website that allows its users to record and upload spoken readings of original poetry

5

As used in line 53, "striking" most nearly means

A) surprising.
B) heavy-handed.
C) evident.
D) disturbing.

6

As used in line 65, "took to" most nearly means

A) approached.
B) promoted.
C) adopted.
D) revitalized.

7

The passage indicates that the habits that Millennials have formed as a result of technology usage are

A) discerning.
B) frivolous.
C) self-defeating.
D) unchanging.

8

Which choice provides the best evidence for the answer to the previous question

A) Lines 36-39 ("Millennials . . . news")
B) Lines 63-67 ("Millennials . . . childhood")
C) Lines 77-80 ("Because . . . avoid")
D) Lines 88-93 ("She . . . thing")

9

On the basis of the charts, a Millennial who uses a cell phone for 3 hours each day and a Baby Boomer who uses a cell phone for 3 hours each day would be most likely to spend similar amounts of time

A) reading online news.
B) shopping online.
C) making or receiving calls.
D) sending texts.

10

How does the information provided in the two figures relate to the ideas set forward by Ashton Applewhite?

A) The figures indicate that Applewhite's recommendations about texting have changed the OTT habits of some Baby Boomers.
B) The figures indicate that Baby Boomers may be following Applewhite's warnings about online financial platforms and online news.
C) The figures indicate that some Baby Boomers may be following Applewhite's recommendations about texting and Internet usage.
D) The figures indicate that Applewhite correctly predicted an increase in the number of Baby Boomers using online communication platforms.

11

Which of the following is considered in the passage but NOT in the figures?

A) The use of online news platforms by Millennials
B) The use of OTT platforms by Millennials
C) The use of online banking platforms by Millennials
D) The average hours of daily cell phone usage by Millennials

Questions 1-11 are based on the following passage and supplementary material.

2.4
Adapted from "This Year's Neutron Star Collision Unlocks Cosmic Mystery" by Emily Conover, a 2018 Science News article in which the author explains the results of the first ever mass-witness of two neutron stars colliding and hypothesizes about what information can be extracted from the event.

Line
    Scientists have discovered that neutron stars could be the source of heavy metals, as indicated in recently published research. They claim that these
5 heavy metals were formed when two super-dense, super-small stars—called neutron stars, the product of two ultra dense stars colliding—smashed together. On August 17, 2017, astronomers detected these two stars merging in galaxy NGC 4993, more than 130 million light-years away. In this case, the collision of the two
10 massive stars occurred at a velocity of 1/3 of the speed of light, creating gravitational waves. The waves from such a crash, which astronomers say happens only once every 100,000 years, were picked up by scientific instruments on Earth, making scientists able to witness
15 the event for themselves—and the scientific event has been heralded as one of the biggest of 2017.
    What's much more interesting than two stars colliding in the night, though, is that this crash possibly resulted in the creation of enormous gold, platinum
20 and silver stores. There is new evidence of a strong link between these heavy metals and dark matter, but at this point it's equally as unlikely as it is likely. The proposal is that during a collision, a black hole settles in the middle of the involved star (or stars).
25 Once inside, the black hole eats up the center of the star, like white blood cells killing intruders in our immune system. As a result, the star begins to spin more quickly, resulting in some of its contents flying out—specifically heavy metals, which would have a
30 hard time holding their place in the star as a result of such speeds.
    The same scientists who were awarded a Nobel Prize for discovering gravitational waves announced that they had detected the collision first, and they
35 alerted astronomers world-wide. As a result, as many as fifteen percent of all scientists pointed their telescopes at the sky in unison to record the unprecedented observations, detecting gamma rays, X-rays, radio waves, and visible light—waves
40 predicted by Einstein's theory of relativity. The waves compressed and stretched spacetime and they moved outwards like ripples.
    What made this event so unusual was that while the waves were created 130 million years ago, they
45 arrived at Earth at the very moment when astronomers finally had the equipment to detect them. The highly-sensitive instruments register shifts in spacetime that are smaller than a proton. Observatories located in Louisiana and Washington in the US and in Pisa, Italy
50 noticed the waves and were able to use triangulation to locate the source. Only two seconds later, a high-energy burst of light was recorded by gamma-ray telescopes.
    In the ensuing days, radio waves, X-rays, and
55 visible, infrared and ultraviolet light were all captured by telescopes. Outstripping all previous astronomical finds, the event resulted in many papers announcing results and ruling out hundreds of theories providing alternatives to dark energy, which has been a somewhat
60 perplexing explanation that most astronomers commonly offered as to why the universe is expanding at an accelerated rate.
    The rate at which the universe is expanding has puzzled astronomers for years, but these observations
65 finally gave researchers an opportunity to take new measurements of that acceleration. Previous data obtained from watching neutron stars said that the universe was expanding at 73 kilometers per second for each parsec (a standardized space distance of about
70 3.26 light years). Measurements using ancient light offer an expansion rate of 67 km/s per megaparsec. It turns out that this new measurement is 70 km/s per megaparsec, midway between the other two readings. This finding provides valuable insight, but in order to
75 resolve the impasse additional neutron stars will have to be observed. Scientists hope that this event is just the first of many and that they will be able to gain more information from future collisions, like what makes up neutron stars and what do they have to do with dark
80 matter.
    Duncan Brown, a member of the research collaboration and astronomer at Syracuse University, says, "we're going to be puzzling over the observations we've made with gravitational waves and with light
85 for years to come." As a result of the complexity of the universe, the discovery is probably going to have a larger impact on human understanding than on understanding gravitational waves. Still, it's not every day that we get to see two stars collide, given how vast
90 the universe is, which makes this discovery so exciting to many. And with the Internet making the world much more connected in terms of information sharing, this exhilarating event—and events like it in the future—

will captivate a larger audience than has ever been possible. Interestingly, as technology makes the world smaller, it subsequently makes the observable universe bigger.

The Universe's Rate of Expansion

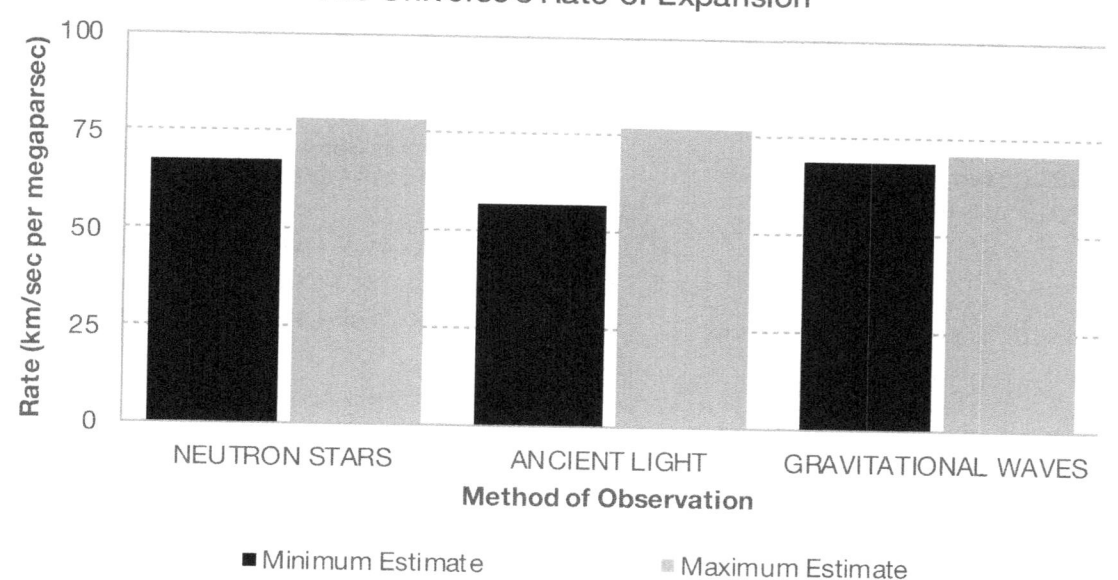

1

Early in the passage, the author explains that the "heavy metals" that could have resulted from a collision of two stars

A) can destabilize a star's rotation when generated in large quantities.
B) may offer a new understanding of an unconfirmed connection.
C) form rapidly during the collision but are just as quickly destroyed.
D) are typically prized for their beauty and utility on Earth.

2

Which choice provides the best evidence for the answer to the previous question?

A) Lines 3-6 ("They claim . . . together")
B) Lines 17-20 ("What's . . . stores")
C) Lines 20-22 ("There is . . . likely")
D) Lines 27-31 ("As a result . . . speeds")

3

As used in line 18, "crash" most nearly means

A) debacle.
B) harm.
C) conflict.
D) encounter.

4

The comparison that the author introduces in lines 26-27 primarily serves to

A) suggest a new line of inquiry that will combine two seemingly disparate scientific fields.
B) pinpoint a conceptual difficulty that has been addressed satisfactorily in the recent past.
C) illustrate a process through a comparison to a fairly common occurrence.
D) create a visual image that is meant to elicit strong emotions.

5

As used in line 37, "in unison" most nearly means

A) at the same moment.
B) with similar intent.
C) in close cooperation.
D) to show allegiance.

6

According to the author of the passage, the detection of gravitational waves was in part dependent on

A) a fortunate coincidence.
B) a systematic collaboration.
C) a theoretical breakthrough.
D) a media initiative.

7

Which choice provides the best evidence for the answer to the previous question?

A) Lines 35-40 ("As a result . . . relativity")
B) Lines 43-46 ("What . . . them")
C) Lines 48-51 ("Observatories . . . source")
D) Lines 56-62 ("Outstripping . . . rate")

8

When discussing the rate of expansion of the universe, the author calls attention to an "impasse" (line 75) in order to indicate that

A) the presence of dark matter appears to account for divergences in expansion estimates.
B) seemingly extreme expansion estimates have been proven unusually reliable.
C) new research is unlikely to yield a consensus in the face of valid yet competing expansion estimates.
D) a newly-obtained expansion estimate should not be regarded as definitive.

9

The author's statement about "human understanding" in lines 85-88 ("As a . . . waves") is best understood to mean that

A) the principal outcomes of a the inquiry central to the passage are impossible to explain clearly to non-experts.
B) the study of gravitational waves offers the key to establishing relationships between seemingly disparate occurrences in the universe.
C) recent findings will be met with continued fascination even if they cannot be comprehensively explained.
D) future analysis of gravitational waves will be facilitated mainly by advances in communications technology.

10

Which of the following quantities present in the graph represents the lowest rate of expansion?

A) Neutron Stars, minimum estimate
B) Neutron Stars, maximum estimate
C) Ancient Light, minimum estimate
D) Gravitational Waves, maximum estimate

11

In relation to the passage's discussion of the expansion of the universe (line 63), the graph primarily supports the author's claim that the Gravitational Waves method

A) offers rate values located between the values derived from other methods.
B) is considerably more accurate than any other widely-accepted method.
C) results in minimum and maximum values that are almost identical.
D) improves upon methods that make use of visual observation.

Questions 1-10 are based on the following passage and supplementary material.
2.5
Adapted from the 2016 *New York Times* article "How Data Failed Us in Calling an Election" by Steve Lohr and Natasha Singer in which the authors make the claim that over-reliance on data to make predictions is harming more than helping.

Imagine scrolling through your inbox and looking through the emails from companies you've subscribed to. How many of those companies would you guess have used predictive analytics to gage your interests and sell you products?

If you answered all of them, you're probably right. Predictive analytics, a trendy field of statistics, has pervaded all aspects of modern life from economics to politics to advertising. This technology utilizes artificial intelligence that tracks previous interactions to predict the likelihood of future occurrences. Information about these past actions can be acquired through data mining, in which patterns are extracted from large data sets. This data is often bought and sold among companies without our knowledge: Microsoft, for example, bought business social media platform LinkedIn for $26 billion dollars primarily to access its database of over 400 million profiles. So each time you like something on Facebook or click on a link in an email, you can be sure that predictive analytics is recording your actions for future use.

Predictive analytics can be useful for companies that want to maximize profits and efficiency, or for consumers seeking a tailor-made and seamless shopping experience. But the technology is not without its limitations. In an attempt to predict the number of future flu outbreaks, Google Flu Trends did not take into account human error, and grossly overstated the number of cases in the 2012-2013 flu season. More humorously, Microsoft's "Cleverbot" was intended to "learn conversational understanding" through data mining of online conversations. However, it began to generate offensive racial comments, and was pulled shortly thereafter. Because predictive analytics sacrifices nuance for accuracy, it ultimately falls short of both.

Regardless of these mishaps, people still had faith in the power of data, and it was only after Donald Trump's unexpected win in the 2016 U.S. presidential election that the techniques behind predictive analytics were questioned. All major vote forecasters had predicted that Hillary Clinton, Trump's opponent, would win in a landslide, citing 70-99% chances of her victory. In an attempt to understand this anomaly, journalists contacted the major polling companies that had made predictions of Clinton's success. Amanda Cox, editor of The Upshot, and Sam Wang, of the Princeton Election Consortium, were surprised at the failure of their platforms to predict an accurate outcome, blaming faulty data sourcing such as inaccurate representation in polls and surveys. According to Wang, "state polls were off in a way that has not been seen in previous presidential election years." He further speculated that people might have changed their minds in the election booth, causing discrepancies between their answers to the polls and their votes in the election itself.

Data scientists, on the other hand, were not at all surprised. Erik Brynjolfsson, a professor at MIT, cited misunderstanding of the nature of probability analytics as a primary factor in the 2016 election results. "Data science is a tool that is not necessarily going to give you answers, but probabilities." Even if Clinton had had a 99% chance of winning the election, the 1% outcome was still a possibility. In addition, election models only accounted for data in a limited time frame, usually dating back two decades. When that data set is expanded to include earlier decades, the predictions change drastically.

Dr. Pradeep Mutalik, a research scientist at the Yale Center for Medical Informatics, had calculated that the vote models used prior to the election would be off by 15-20 percent, comparing election modeling to weather forecasting: "even with the best models, it is difficult to predict the weather more than 10 days out because there are so many small changes that can cause big changes. In mathematics, this is known as chaos." Brynjolfsson concurred, stating that the results of the election were "not really a shock to data science and statistics. It's how it works."

After the failure of predictive analytics to determine the outcome of one of America's most important events, it might seem like a good idea to let go of the technology completely. However, a better solution entails changing our approach to interpreting the data, rather than relying blindly on it. Instead of treating predicted outcomes as certain, it would be wiser to remember that they are just that: probabilistic predictions. Furthermore, we must accept that the decisions that ultimately drive the results of elections are psychological, not logical. In the case of elections, then, it would be best to follow the advice of Thomas E. Mann, an election expert at the Brookings Institution, a research group in Washington, D.C.: "if

95 we could go back to the world of reporting being about the candidates and the parties and the issues at stake instead of the incessant coverage of every blip in the polls, we would all be better off. They are addictive, and it takes the eye off the ball."

Figure 1
Predictive Measures: Likelihood of Election for Hillary Clinton (HRC) or Donald Trump (DJT) based on Election Polling

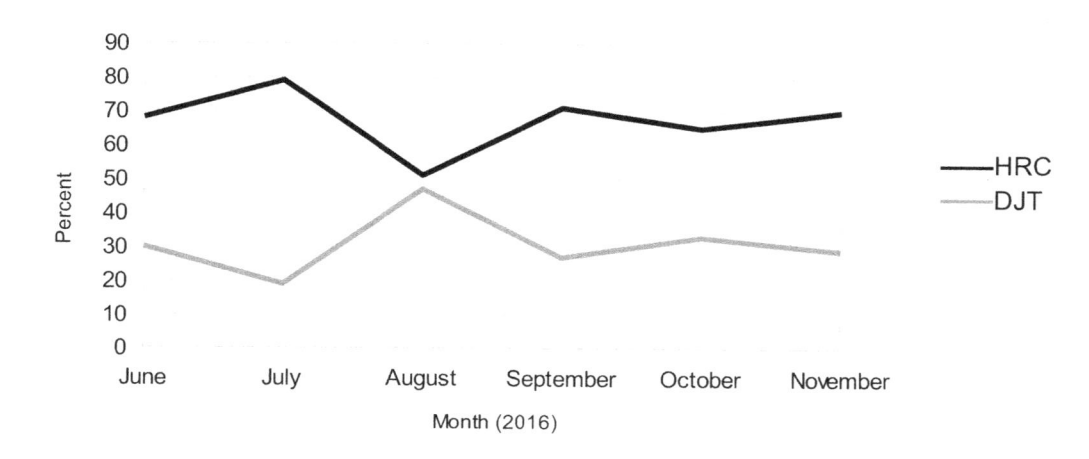

Figure 2

Election Year	Democratic Candidate with Likelihood of Election	Republican Candidate with Likelihood of Election	Elected Candidate
1992	Clinton **49%**	Bush **37%**	Clinton
1996	Clinton **52%**	Dole **41%**	Clinton
2000	Gore **48%**	Bush **46%**	Bush
2004	Kerry **48%**	Bush **51%**	Bush
2008	Obama **53%**	McCain **46%**	Obama
2012	Obama **49%**	Romney **46%**	Obama

U.S. Presidential Election Polling Prediction with Actual Election Result

1

Which choice best describes the overall structure of the passage?

A) An overview of a tool, a list of its shortcomings, and an explanation of why the tool failed to meet expectations.
B) A description of a hypothesis, an analysis of its misapplications, and the promotion of a potential solution.
C) An introduction to a technology, a list of its uses, and speculation on its performance in a specific situation.
D) An explanation of a method, a consideration of its advantages and disadvantages, and a definitive conclusion.

2

As used in line 13, "extracted" most nearly means

A) removed.
B) selected.
C) determined.
D) predicted.

3

Throughout the passage, the author claims that predictive analytics is

A) dangerous, because it presents an invasion of our privacy.
B) limited, because the data that it requires are insufficient.
C) ineffective, because its calculations are inaccurate.
D) misleading, because its results are wrongly interpreted as definite.

4

The author would most likely agree with which claim regarding the results of the 2016 election?

A) The number of people who would have voted for Clinton was overstated in polls.
B) Many voters were swayed by emotion rather than by the policies of the candidates.
C) Those who expressed support for Clinton ultimately decided to vote for Trump.
D) Clinton was defeated because she only considered data from within the past two decades.

5

Which choice provides the best evidence for the answer to the previous question?

A) Lines 26-29 ("In a...season")
B) Lines 54-57 ("He further...itself")
C) Lines 65-67 ("In addition...decades")
D) Lines 89-91 ("Furthermore...logical")

6

As used in line 38, "power" most nearly means

A) influence.
B) authority.
C) reliability.
D) advantage.

7

Based on the passage, which individual would not be surprised by the results of the 2016 election?

A) Erik Brynjolfsson
B) Amanda Cox
C) Thomas E. Mann
D) Sam Wang

8

Which choice provides the best evidence for the answer to the previous question?

A) Lines 52-54 ("state polls...years")
B) Lines 74-78 ("even with...chaos")
C) Lines 78-80 ("Brynjolfsson...works")
D) Lines 94-99 ("if we...ball")

9

Which data point from figure 1 best supports the author's claim that Donald Trump's victory in the 2016 election was unexpected?

A) In November 2016, Clinton's likelihood of election was about 40 points higher than Trump's.
B) In July 2016, Clinton had a 60% higher chance of being elected than Trump did.
C) Trump's likelihood of election fell 15 points from August to September.
D) In July 2016, Trump's likelihood of election hit an all-time low of 18%.

10

Which data point from figure 2 is most analogous to the situation described in the passage?

A) Obama won both 2008 and 2012 elections, regardless of the decrease in his likelihood of election.
B) In 2000, Gore lost to Bush, whose likelihood of election was predicted as being 2 points lower.
C) In 1996, Dole won the election, despite the fact that his likelihood of being elected was 11 points lower than Clinton's.
D) In 2004, Kerry lost to Bush, whose likelihood of being elected was barely over 50%.

Questions 1-11 are based on the following passage and supplementary material.

2.6
Adapted from "Response of Korean Pine's Functional Traits to Geography and Climate," a 2017 Public Library of Science article by Yichen Dong and Yanhong Liu.

It is no secret that there is an ongoing scramble to protect endangered species, but it might come as a surprise to some that trees are among the targets for
Line preservation. In fact, some people go to great lengths to
5 prevent local trees from getting cut down; for instance, the so-called "tree massacre" events of Sheffield, 2015, (during which a company was engaged by the city to cut down many old, healthy trees) prove that saving trees can even be a flashpoint for government officials
10 and their constituents.

Humans seeking to remove trees for their own personal benefit are not the only culprit of tree extinction, however: climate change and nature itself also play major roles. In cases of widespread
15 disease afflicting entire populations, such as fungus chipping away at Torreya numbers in Florida, solutions have centered on cross-breeding individual trees to create a more resilient species, or on raising them carefully in nurseries. While the Torreya, and other
20 species in extreme peril of extinction, may need to be rehabilitated away from its natural environment, many experts are looking at ways to promote the growth of trees *in situ*, or while the tree is alive and in its natural habitat. Doing so requires that the trees and their
25 characteristics be monitored during growth seasons in order to evaluate how they adapt.

One of the first studies to do so took place from June to August of 2015, targeting the Korea Pine as its subject. At 8 different sites around Northeastern China,
30 between 10 and 20 individual trees were chosen as representatives for all trees of each particular region. The traits of the trees necessary to their survival—also known as functional traits—were measured and sampled, and then analyzed against environmental
35 factors that fell into one of three broad categories: geography, temperature, or moisture. However, since human interaction was minimal in the regions, there were no weather stations from which to record climate; instead, a verified climate equation was used.
40 Measured functional traits included density, thickness, and dryness of leaves, root length, and the phosphorus and nitrogen content of both the leaves and the roots. These were compared to the geographic factors of latitude (how far north or south the tree was
45 located), longitude (how far east or west the tree was), and altitude. Temperature factors included mean for the whole year, mean for the growth season, and mean for the coldest month. Moisture factors similarly employed means for precipitation of the whole year and the
50 growth season, as well as the potential for moisture to return to the atmosphere from both the land and plants, known as *evapotranspiration*.

By the end of August, several significant relationships were established. So many, in fact, that
55 the only environmental factors that showed negligible or unclear correlations were longitude and mean annual temperature. Both latitude and altitude showed a remarkable connection to all functional traits: as either increased—that is, the further north or the higher
60 the elevation—so too did the dryness of the leaves and the nitrogen content of the leaves and the roots. In the same way, a decrease in leaf density, leaf thickness, root length, and phosphorus content in both leaves and roots coincide with increases in latitude and altitude.
65 Furthermore, precipitation showed a correlation to every functional trait except for the density of the leaves, meaning that with more precipitation, the aforementioned traits become more favorable to living conditions for the trees.
70 At first blush, it may seem obvious that trees will be more lush if the climate is warmer and wetter, but the specific findings on the nitrogen and phosphorus content have a broader implication. These two elements are essential to the growth and function of
75 plants, and their interplay over latitude and altitude is quite telling of the adaptation strategies of the Korean Pine. In terrestrial plants, nitrogen is used for amino acids, nucleic acids, and chlorophyll; phosphorus is used to form nucleotides, which help with energy
80 storage in cells and the construction of DNA and RNA—it also tends to move very quickly through the systems of both plants and animals. The decreasing phosphorus content in the Korean Pine demonstrates that the species tends to reduce energy consumption
85 while respiring (storing and making use of nutrients already present in the plant) the further north it is. The increase of nitrogen in leaves indicates that the Korean Pine also has longer-lasting leaves in more northern sites. These two factors show that the Korean
90 Pine tends to adopt a slow-growth strategy in colder climates.

Overall, the results show that it is quite possible to predetermine the best places to regenerate populations of Korean Pine, and may even have implications for
95 targeted nutrient treatment in the soil. However, this could pose risks: over-use of nitrogen and phosphorus

can be downright toxic to aquatic ecosystems. As a result, caution would be necessary in such cases. The researchers stress that it is now another tool in the efforts to preserve endangered trees, but that it cannot yet be applied to an entire ecosystem. Looking to the future, the ability of researchers in the Korean Pine experiment to implement a safe method with which to study trees *in situ* is promising for staving off endangerment and extinction.

Korean Pine, 30 Trees Per Region from 8 Locations in Northeastern China

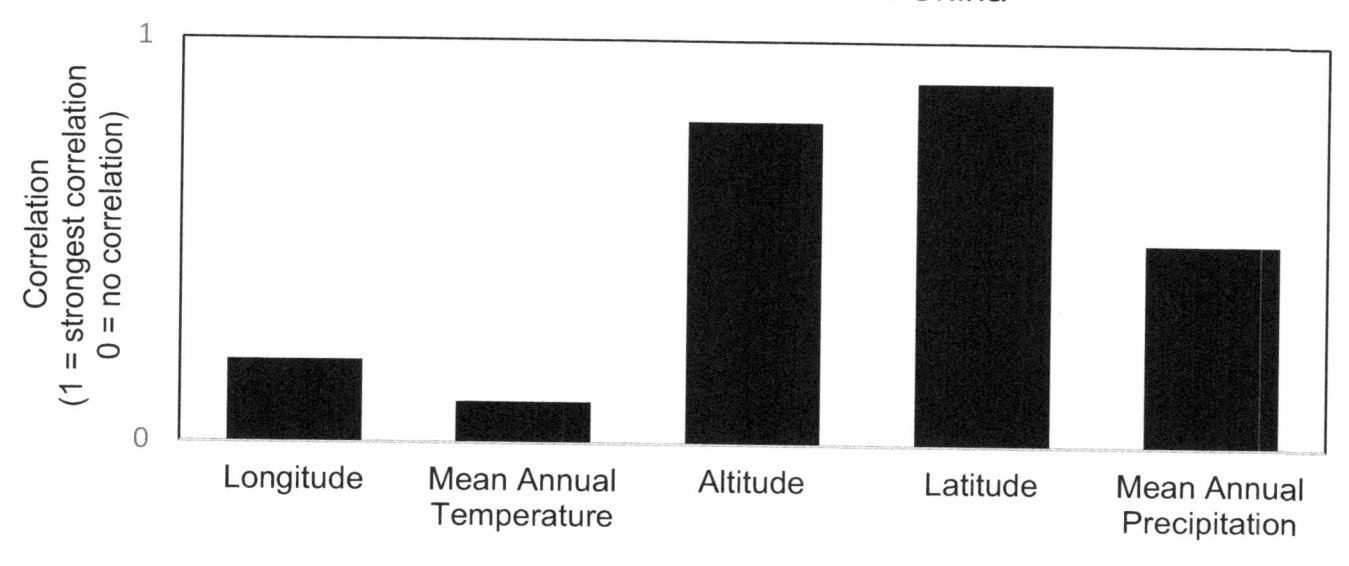

A bar chart showing correlation (1 = strongest correlation, 0 = no correlation) for five variables:
- Longitude: low
- Mean Annual Temperature: very low
- Altitude: high
- Latitude: highest
- Mean Annual Precipitation: moderate

1

The author mentions "some" (line 3) and "some people" (line 4) in order to establish a contrast between

A) those who consciously hinder plant preservation research and those who are actively involved.
B) those who may be unaware of tree conservation efforts and those who are central to such efforts.
C) those who are uninterested in plant biology and those who are working to expand the scope of the discipline.
D) those who participated in a research endeavor and those who challenged its primary conclusions.

2

The author suggests that the study centering on the Korean Pine was

A) mostly unprecedented in its non-invasive approach to biological study.
B) created in direct response to a crisis that is most pronounced in Asian countries.
C) premised on fieldwork of a type that was discouraged by earlier researchers.
D) to some extent reliant on mathematical modeling in place of direct observation.

3

Which choice provides the best evidence for the answer to the previous question?

A) Lines 19-24 ("While . . . habitat")
B) Lines 24-26 ("Doing . . . adapt")
C) Lines 27-31 ("One . . . region")
D) Lines 36-39 ("However . . . used")

4

The passage lists all of the following as dangers to trees EXCEPT

A) the activities of humans.
B) disease.
C) climate change.
D) nesting and tunneling by animals.

5

Which of the following findings would indicate that the Korean Pine observations recorded in the passage can be observed among coniferous trees in general?

A) Coniferous trees of a single species vary in root length depending on such factors as longitude and mean annual temperature.
B) Coniferous trees at high altitudes have a different root length than do trees of the same species at lower altitudes.
C) Coniferous trees experience variations in leaf density as a result of changes in annual precipitation levels.
D) Coniferous trees of the same species experience different lifespans depending on variations in longitude.

6

As used in line 58, "remarkable" most nearly means

A) severe.
B) unquestionable.
C) gifted.
D) well-known.

7

The author characterizes the research findings presented in the passage as

A) more interesting for theoretical than for practical reasons.
B) conclusive though displeasing to those who hope to preserve trees.
C) in accordance with expected logic but still significant.
D) suggestive of the need for a larger and more comprehensive study.

8

Which choice provides the best evidence for the answer to the previous question?

A) Lines 70-73 ("At first . . . implication")
B) Lines 87-91 ("The increase . . . climates")
C) Lines 92-95 ("Overall . . . soil")
D) Lines 98-101 ("The researchers . . . ecosystem")

9

As used in line 99, "stress" most nearly means

A) emphasize.
B) ruminate.
C) pressure.
D) exaggerate.

10

A team of scientists would like to design a further experiment to investigate a factor related to the Korean Pine that yields neither a strong nor a weak correlation. On the basis of the chart, the scientists would be most likely to investigate

A) mean annual temperature.
B) mean annual precipitation.
C) latitude.
D) longitude.

11

One significant difference between the study considered in the chart and the study considered in the passage is that the study in the chart

A) yielded information on different environmental factors.
B) was conducted at a different date.
C) considered a larger number of trees.
D) involved a larger number of sites.

Questions 1-11 are based on the following passage and supplementary material.

2.7
Adapted from a 2018 *LA Times* article by Melissa Healy titled "Your DNA Won't Determine the Best Way to Help You Lose Weight," in which the author describes the best method for losing weight while debunking the notion that we are somehow genetically programmed to lose weight more efficiently in one way or another.

    In our current age of information, dieting can seem impossible. It's almost that we know too much about the influencers of weight loss—gut bacteria, diet type, diet length, stressors, DNA, and personality
5 can each play a roll. So, how do we figure out which information to use when determining the best method to lose weight? A recent study says we should forget all of the things we currently know about dieting, and focus on the basics: eating less and sticking to whole
10 foods.
    In the study, researchers split 632 overweight or obese people into three groups based on DNA: sensitive to fat, sensitive to carbohydrates, or sensitive to neither. Participants were then told to eat
15 either low-carbohydrate or low fat, based on their predetermined genetics; half of the "neither" group went to each dieting condition. At the end of the study, the researchers recorded how much weight was lost by participants of all groups, and found
20 surprisingly similar numbers regardless of participants' sensitivities. The low-carb group lost 13 pounds and the low-fat group lost 11.5 pounds, on average.
    Not surprisingly, in both groups, some people lost no weight or gained weight during the process. This
25 is a result we often see in the real world of dieting—a person sets out to lose weight and becomes disengaged with the diet and therefore ends up losing no weight or binge-eating out of frustration. What was surprising, though, was that nothing about the participants' DNA
30 testing predicted who would win at dieting and who would lose, even in a controlled experimental setting.
    The researchers did everything they could to make the diets successful. They told participants not to count calories (a part of dieting known to cause aversion),
35 held group meetings to keep everyone on track, and even encouraged the dieters to enjoy their food. Furthermore, the study included several helpful tips for dieting in general, including preparing food at home, eating more vegetables and less processed food, and
40 directed participants to never let themselves to get too hungry (or too full).

    Still, nothing the researchers attempted during the study predicted weight loss, although it's possible that psychological issues caused stress which led to
45 increased eating, especially of high-fat and high-sugar foods. So, what can be made of this seemingly "null" result? Interestingly, it's the failure of the experiment that gives it its significance. By not finding a good predictor of "diet success" in DNA, the researchers
50 provided support for aforementioned idea that it's time to go back to the basics with dieting.
    Research methods have a major flaw when it comes to human studies: by controlling out "extraneous variables," or those that help isolate an
55 independent variable, results are less reflective of the real world. Any time a researcher controls for a factor to ultimately make participants more similar, the resulting study lacks in diversity. And while this is optimal for determining cause and effect relationships,
60 it is quite sub-optimal for approximating life-like conditions. As life has diversity, so too should experiments, but that in itself poses a catch-22. If research studies are made more like extra-laboratory conditions, the outcomes are less certain due to the
65 independent variables that the study intends to test. On the other hand, if research studies are more controlled and less life-like, they test the independent-dependent variable relationship, but approximate life much less.
    In the case of dieting, the solution is probably
70 simply to take the parsimonious route. While it is important to consider each individual on a case-to-case basis rather than to assume we're all the same, it is equally important to follow the golden rules of dieting: eat more vegetables and less sugar and processed
75 food, while maintaining a regime of not overeating or starving yourself.

Chart 1

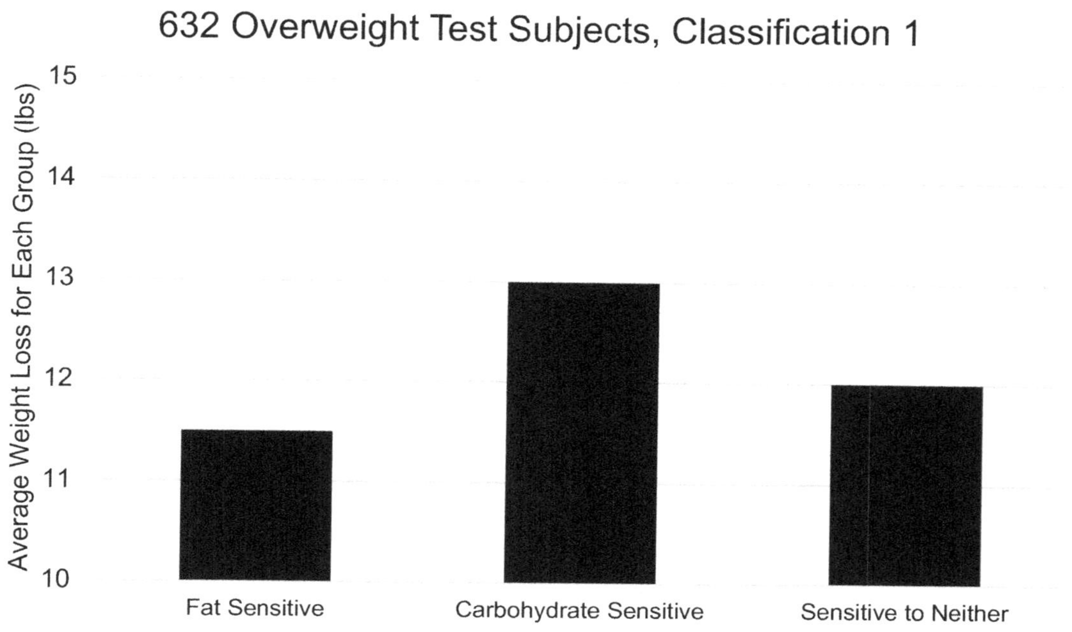
632 Overweight Test Subjects, Classification 1
Average Weight Loss for Each Group (lbs)
15
14
13
12
11
10
Fat Sensitive
Carbohydrate Sensitive
Sensitive to Neither

Chart 2

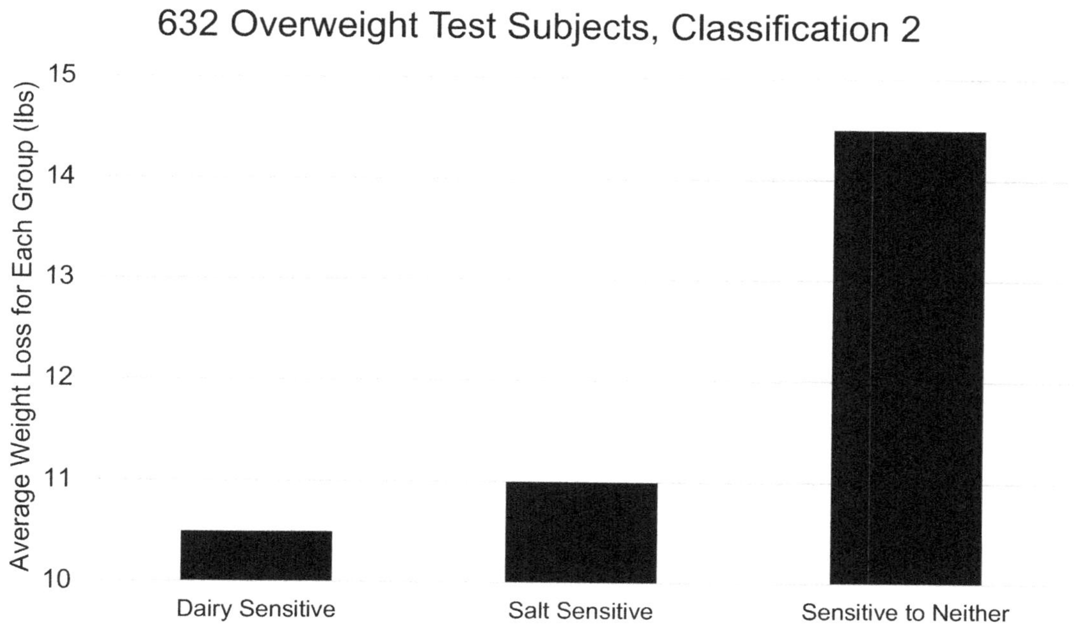
632 Overweight Test Subjects, Classification 2
Average Weight Loss for Each Group (lbs)
15
14
13
12
11
10
Dairy Sensitive
Salt Sensitive
Sensitive to Neither

1

The main purpose of the passage is to

A) suggest that current dietary classifications cause more harm than good when taken seriously by researchers.
B) demonstrate that there is scientific support for the efficacy of simple and straightforward ideas about dieting.
C) create a systematic series of distinctions between low-fat and low-carbohydrate diets.
D) document the methodological flaws in a research project in order to arrive at new dietary recommendations.

2

As used in line 3, "influencers of" most nearly means

A) inspirations behind.
B) factors related to.
C) principles involved in.
D) advocates for.

3

The questions posed by the author in lines 5-7 and lines 46-47 both serve the purpose of

A) anticipating decisive answers on the part of the passage's author.
B) referencing popular perspectives for the sake of skeptical examination.
C) inspiring critical reflection among the members of the passage's audience.
D) presenting new insights in a manner meant to surprise the reader.

4

Within the passage, the author characterizes the "real world of dieting" (line 25) as

A) premised on seemingly separate concepts that in fact describe the same few occurrences.
B) accurately reflected in certain outcomes of recent research.
C) easier to understand in practice than in theory.
D) impossible to replicate using even a highly detailed experimental procedure.

5

Which of the following choices best indicates that the author attributed a useful purpose to the study described in the passage?

A) Lines 17-21 ("At the . . . sensitivities")
B) Lines 32-33 ("The researchers . . . successful")
C) Lines 37-41 ("Furthermore . . . full")
D) Lines 47-48 ("Interestingly . . . significance")

6

As used in line 40, "directed" most nearly means

A) advised.
B) organized.
C) compelled.
D) supervised.

7

According to the author, one problem inherent in research on dieting is that

A) participants may engage in non-dieting activities that lead to weight loss even when advised not to do so.
B) both the participants and the researchers involved may have incentives to report inaccurate dieting results.
C) socioeconomic factors play a greater role in dieting preferences than most researchers acknowledge.
D) effectively replicating the conditions of the real world in a diet study can make the study itself difficult to work with.

8

Which choice provides the best evidence for the answer to the previous question?

A) Lines 42-46 ("Still . . . foods")
B) Lines 48-51 ("By not . . . dieting")
C) Lines 62-65 ("If research . . . test")
D) Lines 69-70 ("In the . . . route")

9

Taken together, the two charts indicate that fat-sensitive test subjects

A) lost half as much weight, on average, as did the carbohydrate-sensitive test subjects.
B) lost slightly more weight, on average, than did the salt-sensitive test subjects.
C) had significantly higher body masses than did the dairy-sensitive test subjects.
D) had slightly lower body masses than did the salt-sensitive test subjects.

10

Could the two charts present data from the same group of 632 test subjects?

A) Yes, because the classification system for diet sensitivity changes fundamentally from one chart to the next.
B) Yes, because each chart indicates that the average amount of weight lost in the group was 13 pounds per subject.
C) No, because the maximum average weight loss per group in the second chart exceeds the maximum average per group for the first chart.
D) No, because the average weight loss of the subjects in the "sensitive to neither" category is significantly different for the two charts.

11

Which of the following statistical pairings from the charts would NOT fit the author's concept of "surprisingly similar numbers" (line 20)?

A) Fat Sensitive and Sensitive to Neither (Chart 1)
B) Carbohydrate Sensitive and Sensitive to Neither (Chart 1)
C) Dairy Sensitive and Salt Sensitive (Chart 2)
D) Salt Sensitive and Sensitive to Neither (Chart 2)

Questions 1-10 are based on the following passage and supplementary material.

2.8
Adapted from an article published in the National Institute of Health's Journal of General Internal Medicine, "A Web-based Generalist–Specialist System to Improve Scheduling of Outpatient Specialty Consultations in an Academic Center" by Michael Weiner, Geroges El Hoyek, and colleagues.

For many, going to the doctor's office is tedious: scheduling an appointment requires more effort than we are used to in today's technologically advanced world, and the bureaucratic process is time consuming. Indeed, these factors make this seemingly simple task a daunting one. What causes this is almost a mystifying idea for the millennials: the healthcare industry still runs on paper. Although many hospitals and doctor's offices are now using Electronic Medical Records (EMR), it turns out that less than 10 percent of hospitals report being able to exchange patient records using their digital systems. Instead, they are relying on faxes to exchange patient information and to send referrals to other doctors. Unfortunately, this means that about half of the medical-related faxes that are sent never make it to their intended destination.

According to researchers, this is mostly due to the "lack of timeliness" and "delays in completion" within current referral systems. Under the current system, referrals—or recommendations your doctor makes for the care he thinks you require that is out of his area of expertise—are likely to be lost by way of simple human error: busy office workers can forget to refill fax machines and can easily misplace an inconspicuous piece of paper. When such mishandling occurs, it can be hard to track or even identify.

This lack of communication between health systems, and the complexities of those communications, is of concern to patients and health care professionals alike. It's important to be able to get a patient to an appointment, not just for the health of the patient, but for a health care system to be reputable for the sake of revenue generation. The reputations of hospitals, insurance companies, and medical device and pharmaceutical companies depend upon patients getting to doctors as efficiently as possible. In this way, the health care system can be described as a tightly-knit ecosystem: everyone will suffer whenever any part of the communication chain breaks down.

According to a paper published in the Journal of General Internal Medicine, unreceived specialist referrals pose a major risk: they often translate into medical errors. Some referrals never arrive at their destination because of failures in technology or in processing. Researchers attempted to determine whether the move from a paper-based referral to an online system with automated track features would lead to an increase in the scheduling of appointments among the patients who were referred. They hoped to minimize the cumbersome process, therefore increasing the number of appointments and making the process run much more smoothly and efficiently.

The study was designed as part of a staggered implementation of a project designed to improve levels of quality, comparing a control group, consisting of referrals made via faxes, to an intervention group, consisting of referrals made via the internet. In the intervention group, generalists and specialists shared the referral application, which provided automated notifications to the specialty offices, as well as enhanced communications. Researchers compared scheduling both before and after implementation, as well as the time elapsed between the referral and the appointment.

Among the 40,487 referrals that occurred, only 54% resulted in specialty visits among the control group. In contrast, 83% resulted in specialty visits among the intervention group. Furthermore, median time to an appointment dropped from 168 days to 78 days when the intervention was implemented. The researchers then found that referrals under the intervention condition were "more than twice as likely to have scheduled visits."

The researchers suggest that by making the referral system more efficient, improvements in quality of both care and costs can occur. Similar approaches in other aspects of the medical industry, such as electronic messaging systems, have been reported as useful in facilitating communications between primary and secondary care. Such online systems are almost three times as likely to lead to a visit being scheduled, implying that this health care technology may be able to nearly eradicate the problem of failed scheduling. As a result, the researchers anticipate shorter waiting times and greater efficiency and accuracy for appointments in the future.

United States Hospitals Using Online Referral Systems and Patients Scheduling Second Appointments Based on Referrals

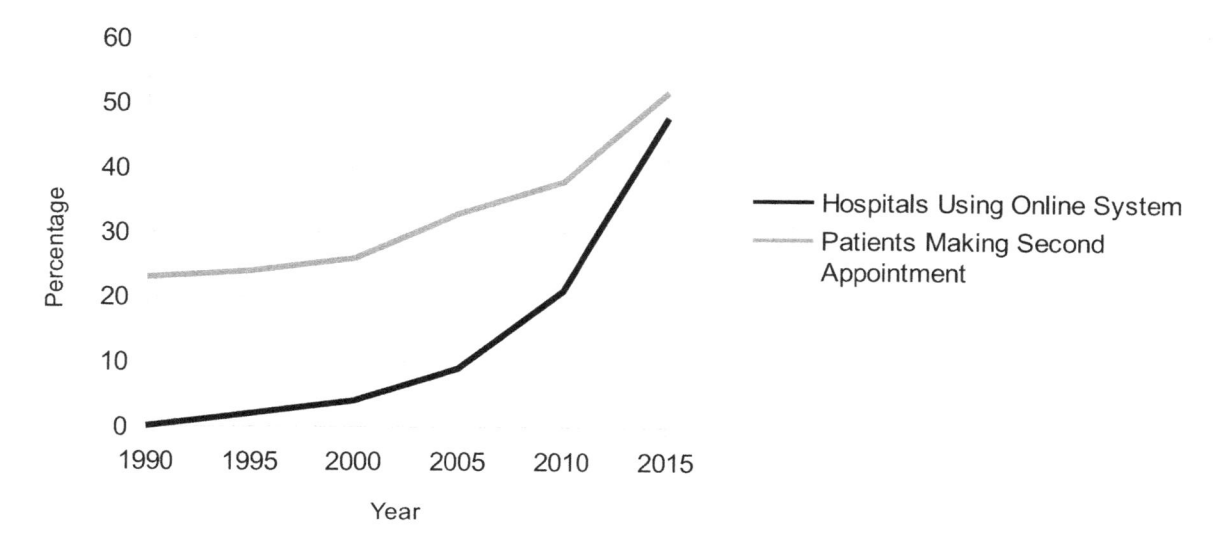

— Hospitals Using Online System
— Patients Making Second Appointment

1

The author references a "tightly-knit ecosystem" (lines 36-37) most likely to

A) emphasize the strength of the bonds within a community.
B) explain the reason that lack of communication is not important.
C) highlight the importance of a seemingly insignificant process.
D) imply that all departments of a field are responsible for a problem.

2

The main focus of the passage shifts from

A) a description of a surprising phenomenon to an explanation of the consequential negative effects.
B) a suggestion to update a practice to the reasons that a specific entity will benefit from these changes.
C) an earnest call for change in an industry to a study that details how that change will ultimately be beneficial.
D) an overview of problems in current practices to a review of a study aimed at possible solutions to those problems.

3

As used in line 26, "identify" most nearly means

A) remember.
B) notice.
C) analyze.
D) label.

4

In discussing the hospitals' inability to exchange referrals efficiently, the author is primarily concerned about the

A) economic consequences it poses.
B) patient concerns it causes.
C) environmental issues it creates.
D) ethical problems it raises.

5

Which choice provides the best evidence for the answer to the previous question?

A) Lines 3-5 ("the bureaucratic...one")
B) Lines 14-16 ("Unfortunately...destination")
C) Lines 27-30 ("This lack...alike")
D) Lines 30-33 ("It's important...generation")

6

As used in line 42, "translate into" most nearly means

A) exacerbate.
B) transform into.
C) reveal.
D) lead to.

7

Which of the following conclusions about hospital and and patient behavior changes is suggested by both the passage and the chart?

A) Referral systems have become increasingly sophisticated and efficient over time.
B) Increased appointments have encouraged hospitals to implement online systems.
C) Patients are more likely to make appointments when online systems are available.
D) Online systems have promoted mutually beneficial patient-doctor relationships.

8

Which choice provides the best evidence for the answer to the previous question?

A) Lines 49-52 ("They hoped...appointments")
B) Lines 71-73 ("The researchers...visits")
C) Lines 74-76 ("The researchers...occur")
D) Lines 84-86 ("the researchers...future")

9

It can be reasonably inferred from the passage and the graph that patients are making more second appointments for their referrals because

A) they find it more timely and less monotonous to interact with doctors and therefore are likely to see them more frequently.
B) they find the process of signing up for appointments in all areas of health and medicine to be facilitated by online systems.
C) they can sign up for and schedule appointments via a process that is more streamlined and less prone to error.
D) they no longer have to go through the expensive and tedious process of using outdated methods to make doctor's office visits.

10

What information discussed in the passage is represented in the graph?

A) Lines 61-64 ("Researchers...appointment")
B) Lines 65-67 ("Among… group")
C) Lines 71-73 ("The researchers...visits")
D) Lines 74-76 ("The researchers...occur")

Questions 1-11 are based on the following passage.

2.9
Adapted from a 2015 NIH article, "Antibiotic Combinations May Combat MRSA Infections," by Dr. Harrison Wein. In this article, the author describes the reason for and process of producing new antibiotics.

Today, the public health problem of antibiotic resistance is growing. The microbes responsible for many bacterial infections have become increasingly
Line difficult to treat because they have adapted and
5 are becoming more resistant to even the most effective antibiotics. MRSA, or methicillin-resistant Staphylococcus aureus, has evolved into a serious public health concern. Now one of the most common infections that can be acquired in a hospital, MRSA
10 continues to develop new strains in the community and is able to cause severe infections in people who would be considered healthy otherwise.

As MRSA does not respond to methicillin and related antibiotics, this superbug is being increasingly
15 seen outside the hospital setting. MRSA is responsible for causing skin infections, and sometimes more serious illnesses, such as bloodstream infections or pneumonia. In 2014 alone, the Center for Disease Control (CDC) estimated that more than 11,000 deaths
20 and 80,000 aggressive infections in the US were due to MRSA.

In order to move forward, scientists have to look into the past of bacterial infections. Much early research was on the S. aureus infection, which was
25 treated with penicillins (specifically, compounds known as beta-lactams) as early as the 1940s. Beta-lactams prevent bacteria from reproducing and growing by interfering with the synthesis of cell walls, but bacteria soon emerged that are capable of
30 making enzymes that can break down beta-lactams. The subsequent second-generation penicillins, like methicillin, were resistant to these enzymes. Soon after the drug's induction, though, methicillin-resistant strains emerged. The resistant strains acquired genes
35 from other types of bacteria, letting them produce cell walls, even when beta-lactams were present. Researchers are working to create new types of antibiotics, specifically ones that can combat MRSA. However, reports of resistance to many of these
40 antibiotics already have been emerging.

An interesting new approach may come to the rescue of bemused researchers: combining multiple antibiotics has achieved success in initial tests. Dr. Gautam Dantas, located at Washington University
45 School of Medicine in St. Louis, led an NIH-funded team that tested an approach using multiple drugs to fight MRSA. They chose a number of drugs to study that not only were clinically approved but which also work in a synergistic way, meaning that the effect
50 of combining pharmaceuticals is stronger than the effect of any one drug on its own. Because they saw that resistant strains were producing cell walls, the team decided to target various aspects of the MRSA machinery that focuses on the synthesis of the cell
55 wall. The researchers chose from 3 separate subclasses of beta-lactam compounds including tazobactam, piperacillin, and meropenem.

The first drug was intended to combat a strain of MRSA that is extremely resistant to 23 different
60 antibiotics. The tazobacam-peperacillin-meropenem trio proved more effective than any of the three drugs by themselves or when paired in combating the strain, hence the aforementioned "synergy." The triple combination showed itself to be effective in the
65 laboratory against a group of strains that was taken from 72 other MRSA clinical cases.

Next, researchers tested the drug trio's ability to counteract developing resistance to MRSA. They exposed the bacteria to small does of these antibiotics
70 for 11 days. Afterwards, they observed no evolution of resistance. When the same three drugs were used individually or in pairs, the bacteria were able to develop resistance to all the drugs in 1 to 8 days, further proving that three drugs are better than one (or
75 two).

The team also tested the drug on MRSA-infected mice. All the mice treated with the tazobacam-peperacillin-meropenem trio combination survived for 6 days, and the infection was confirmed to have been
80 eliminated by testing blood that was taken from the mice. This result was comparable to that obtained with mice that had been treated with linezolid, a much more expensive drug that is used to treat resistant infections. Dantas, the lead researcher, observed that when the
85 three-drug combination is used, it appears to prevent MRSA resistance. He describes this combination as buying us some time, potentially a large amount of time, before the bacteria develops antibiotic resistance, as all bacteria do eventually.

90 As bacterial infections are on the rise, many healthcare professionals are concerned about what is going to be done to prevent this problem. "We rely on antibiotics to deliver modern health care," NIH senior investigator Dr. Julie Segre says. However, as drug-
95 resistant bacteria are on the rise, "we're running out

of new antibiotics to treat bacterial infections." Some of the more potent antibiotics just aren't working as well. While the trio of antibiotics seems promising, it is suggested that more research and testing is needed.
(100) Furthermore, it seems likely that, eventually, bacteria will evolve to become resistant to even this new, promising solution. Researchers need to determine what about the bacteria is making them so resistant and to combat it more aggressively if they wish to stop this
(105) problem once and for all.

1

The primary purpose of the passage is to

A) introduce a study that shows a multitude of ways that MRSA has become increasingly resistant to treatment over the years.
B) provide the overview, method, and results of a study that was the first of its kind in providing information about bacterial resistance.
C) describe the public health issue caused by bacterial resistance and provide one possible method of making antibacterial treatment more effective.
D) report findings from the CDC about the most prevalent bacterial infections and describe why they are no longer treatable.

2

It can be reasonably inferred from the passage that the author referenced the Center for Disease Control in lines 18-19 because

A) the CDC corroborates a claim mentioned earlier in the passage.
B) this inclusion adds empiricism to a thus far speculative report.
C) the information cited discredits the notion that MRSA causes a lot of deaths.
D) the statistics provided will be mentioned again later in the passage.

3

Which choice provides the best evidence for the answer to the previous question?

A) Lines 9-12 ("MRSA continues...otherwise")
B) Lines 13-15 ("As MRSA...setting")
C) Lines 22-26 ("In order...1940's")
D) Lines 39-40 ("However...emerging")

4

To combat the problem of antibiotic-resistant bacteria, researchers first attempted to

A) utilize the early generation of superbug-attacking antibiotics including methicillin.
B) develop a new generation of antibiotics that hinder the production of cell walls.
C) synthesize antibiotics from multiple sources that work together in a synergistic way.
D) make a breakthrough with beta-lactams, which had previously proven ineffective.

5

As used in line 28, "interfering" most nearly means

A) adjusting.
B) blockading.
C) restricting.
D) intervening.

6

According to the information in the passage, the term "resistant strains" in line 34 refers to bacterial infections that developed the ability

A) to evade researchers' attempts at making antibiotics less immune to beta-lactams.
B) to avoid detection by drugs at the level of the cell wall inside the human body.
C) to degrade beta-lactams by synthesizing their DNA with that of other bacteria.
D) to reproduce even in the presence of enzymes intended to prevent this ability.

7

Based on the passage as a whole, the primary purpose of paragraph 4 (lines 41-56) is

A) to introduce of a new study that directly solves a problem brought up in the previous paragraphs.
B) to interject optimism about finally solving the problem that bacterial infections have posed thus far.
C) to resolve a debate that has been plaguing areas of health and medicine since before antibiotics were first introduced.
D) to clarify the flaws in methodology that many of the previous studies have relied upon, causing them to ultimately fail.

8

As used in line 52, "producing" most nearly means

A) orchestrating.
B) sustaining.
C) constructing.
D) triggering.

9

It can be reasonably inferred from the passage that the author would react to lines 70-71 ("Afterwards, they... resistance") with

A) pessimism, because he has seen other similar solutions to antibiotic resistance fail in the past; therefore this one will ultimately fail as well.
B) optimism, because this marks the first time that researchers have achieved such a feat and the problem has most likely been solved for the last time.
C) ambivalence, because other such solutions have appeared groundbreaking in the past but ended up being thwarted by enterprising bacteria.
D) pride, because his team has solved a problem that many researchers have been trying to make a breakthrough in for many centuries.

10

Based on the author's description of the tazobacam-peperacillin-meropenem trio, a secondary benefit is that

A) the drug combination can be used in a smaller dose than any other antibacterial medication has been effective at in the past.
B) the effect of the drug trio is comparable to that of another, similar drug that has a much higher price point.
C) mice with bacterial infections that were treated with the drug survived almost a week and eventually became infection free.
D) in the future, it is likely that this combination of drugs will be able to be used effectively against other types of infections.

11

Which choice provides the best evidence for the answer to the previous question?

A) Lines 81-83 ("This result...infections")
B) Lines 86-89 ("He describes...eventually")
C) Lines 90-92 ("As bacterial...problem")
D) Lines 94-99 ("However, as...needed")

Questions 1-11 are based on the following passage and supplementary material.

2.10
Adapted from a 2006 National Institute of Health article by M.C. Morris, D.A. Evans, C.C. Tangeny, J.L. Bienias, and R.S. Wilson, titled "Associations of Vegetable and Fruit Consumption with Age-Related Cognitive Change."

For over 100 years, scientists have been attempting to better understand one of the most mysterious disorders of the mind in the world: Alzheimer's Disease. First discovered in 1906 by a doctor of the same name, Alzheimer's disease is characterized by a progressive loss of memory, leading ultimately to death. At its conception, the disease was understood only in terms of its phenotypical—non-genetic—symptoms: cognitive decline, confusion, loss of memory, and paranoia. The first Alzheimer's patient died soon after her symptoms were discerned and—upon autopsy—it was discovered that her brain showed severe shrinkage, as well as abnormal deposits in what was left of its mass, compared to the brain of an individual not plagued with Alzheimer's now-hallmark symptoms.

With the introduction of innovative brain scanning techniques that can, while a patient is alive, provide a still image of the brain or reveal brain chemical or electrical processes in real time, researchers now have a better understanding of what an Alzheimer's-affected brain looks like from inception of the disorder throughout its entire progression. What has been found is similar to the shrinkage and deposits originally discovered by Dr. Alzheimer, but further exploration also shows abnormal transmission of neurotransmitters in the brain and possible biological markers of the disease.

One of the possible biological markers is a protein called 'tau.' In a normally functioning brain, tau poses no threat. But in an Alzheimer's-affected brain, tau begins to act abnormally, and becomes tangled up, possibly explaining the abnormal deposits Dr. Alzheimer discovered. A second hypothesis is that proteins called amyloids are disrupting neuronal connections by getting in the way of the synapse, or space through which neurons send communication back and forth. As neighboring neurons are blocked by amyloid, therefore being blocked from communicating, they shorten in length and eventually stop sending information throughout the brain. Without effective communication among critical memory areas of the brain like the hippocampus, people become confused, and subsequently forgetful of important information that allows them to perform everyday functions like get to work. Both of these hypotheses have been studied in parallel for many years without either one being disproven, implying that they likely both play a part in causing the disorder.

Interestingly, neither tau nor amyloid researchers have yet been able to show exactly how their respective protein has caused the disorder, although both have proved some connection between their research and the Alzheimer's genotype, or genetic markers. Because of this, and because of how devastating and prevalent the disorder is, it is paramount to find some underlying mechanism by which to at the very least hold off its onset. To do this, scientists are turning to dietary possibilities, the first of which is called the MIND (Mediterranean intervention for neurodegenerative disorders diet). To follow this diet, one must follow a strict regimen of eating more leafy greens, vegetables, nuts, berries, legumes, whole grains, fish, poultry, and olive oil—while eating less red meat, butter, cheese, fried food, and sweets. The diet is still in its early days of testing, but it has been shown to fight inflammation, one of the symptoms coupled with cognitive decline.

In the future, researchers hope to be able to use this diet as an early intervention for people who are at-risk for developing Alzheimer's disease. If individuals who have known instances of Alzheimer's in their family begin modifying their eating habits based on this diet as early as their 40th birthday, it is possible that they can prevent either tau or amyloid or both from attacking their neurons and disrupting vital connections. While this seems to be working with patients who have adopted the MIND diet, the scientific community is still far from proving the direct connection that would link it to Alzheimer's prevention. There is yet much to be learned about genetic causes of the disorder, but this information could prove to be a crucial factor in linking the competing hypotheses and ultimately solving the puzzle.

Buildup	Process	Atrophy	Process
Tau Protein	Destroy Nerve Cells	Hippocampus	Learning and Memory
Amyloid Proteins	Spread Tau	Cortex	Higher Cognitive Functions
Vertricles	Shrink Interior Brain Matter	Myelin	Make Transmissions Faster
Plaques	Block Cell Firing/Connection	—	—

1

What is the central claim of the passage?

A) There is still much research to be done on Alzheimer's disease, particularly on the causes of the disease.
B) Research must be done in order to find out the exact relationship that tau and amyloid proteins have with Alzheimer's disease.
C) Until researchers identify what causes Alzheimer's, scientists should find ways to delay its effects through methods like the MIND diet.
D) With new technologies like brain scanning techniques, researchers can eventually determine a permanent solution to Alzheimer's.

2

Based on the passage, which of the following do researchers wish to discover regarding Alzheimer's Disease?

A) The physical symptoms of the brain that come along with the loss of memory
B) Brain scanning methods that can reveal the brain of a living person
C) Possible proteins and other biological markers that are connected to the disease
D) Methods that might mitigate or slow down the symptoms of Alzheimer's

3

Which choice provides the best evidence for the answer to the previous question?

A) Lines 1-4 ("For over...Disease")
B) Lines 7-10 ("At its...paranoia")
C) Lines 50-53 ("Interestingly...genotype")
D) Lines 54-57 ("Because of...onset")

4

As used in line 7, "conception" most nearly means

A) discovery.
B) understanding.
C) creation.
D) origination.

5

According to the passage, which of the following is a symptom of Alzheimer's disease?

A) Several close family members who have had Alzheimer's Disease
B) Possession of the proteins tau and amyloid along with other biological markers
C) Abnormality in protein deposits and transmissions of neurotransmitters
D) Successful application of the MIND diet starting from the early 40s

6

Which choice provides the best evidence for the answer to the previous question?

A) Lines 7-10 ("At its...paranoia")
B) Lines 23-28 ("What has...disease")
C) Lines 46-49 ("Both of...disorder")
D) Lines 58-61 ("To do...diet")

7

As used in line 19, "still" most nearly means

A) motionless.
B) quiet.
C) continued.
D) smooth.

8

The primary function of the fourth paragraph (lines 50-68) is to

A) show how baffled researchers still are by Alzheimer's.
B) introduce the MIND diet and explain why it is necessary.
C) discuss research on the MIND diet and its connection to Alzheimer's.
D) analyze two sides of a debate on whether tau or amyloid causes Alzheimer's

9

Which of the following foods should be avoided by someone on the MIND diet?

A) Legumes
B) Dairy products overall
C) Olive oil
D) Cheese

10

According to the figure, which of the following is responsible for blocking cell firing?

A) Tau protein
B) Amyloid protein
C) Vertricles
D) Plaques

11

Which of the following choices best identifies a point of disagreement between the figure and the passage?

A) The passages states that the amyloid protein disrupts neural connections and the hippocampus while the figure shows that the amyloid protein disrupts the spread of tau and the condition of the cortex.
B) The passages states that tau begins to act abnormally in Alzheimer patients, leading to abnormal deposits, while the figure shows that tau disrupts nerve cells which can affect memory.
C) The passages states that only tau and amyloid proteins might be the causes of Alzheimer's, while the figure shows ventricles and plaques as other reasonable explanations.
D) The passages states that loss of memory is the primary symptom of Alzheimer's and thus that the proteins that cause it must affect memory, while the figure shows that other symptoms include cognitive decline.

STOP

Answer Key: CHAPTER TWO

SAT

2.01	2.02	2.03	2.04	2.05
1. A	1. C	1. C	1. B	1. A
2. D	2. B	2. D	2. C	2. C
3. B	3. A	3. C	3. D	3. D
4. C	4. A	4. D	4. C	4. B
5. C	5. B	5. C	5. B	5. D
6. C	6. C	6. C	6. A	6. C
7. C	7. A	7. A	7. B	7. A
8. D	8. D	8. C	8. D	8. C
9. A	9. C	9. B	9. C	9. A
10. B	10. A	10. C	10. C	10. B
	11. C	11. D	11. A	

2.06	2.07	2.08	2.09	2.10
1. B	1. B	1. C	1. C	1. C
2. D	2. B	2. A	2. A	2. D
3. D	3. A	3. B	3. B	3. D
4. D	4. B	4. A	4. B	4. A
5. B	5. D	5. D	5. C	5. C
6. B	6. A	6. D	6. D	6. B
7. C	7. D	7. C	7. A	7. A
8. A	8. C	8. B	8. C	8. C
9. A	9. B	9. C	9. C	9. D
10. B	10. A	10. D	10. B	10. D
11. C	11. D		11. A	11. B

Answer Explanations

Chapter Two

Chapter 2.1 | Stress Eating

1) CORRECT ANSWER: A
In the second paragraph, the author outlines "New research" (line 16) that is premised on the linkage between an enzyme and "major depressive disorder" (lines 23-24). A thus appropriately captures the idea that the author, while referencing a research project, is explaining a trend or occurrence. B is illogical because the dietary topic of interest to the researchers was outlined in a PREVIOUS paragraph, while C wrongly indicates that the researchers are rejecting (not building upon) an earlier finding. D references long-term effects that are only assessed in a LATER paragraph (lines 56-65).

2) CORRECT ANSWER: D
The word "implications" refers to the effect of "sustaining an unhealthy habit." A ("influence") is incorrect because it refers to producing an effect, rather than the effect itself. B ("repercussions") is incorrect because this word refers to an unintended or unwelcome effect and the context has not yet established whether the effect will be positive or negative. C ("significance") is incorrect because it refers to importance rather than the cause-and-effect relationship following "sustaining an unhealthy habit." D ("consequences") is correct because it directly refers to an effect.

3) CORRECT ANSWER: B
The authors directly state that the research discussed in the passage was designed to consider "the effects that different diets can have on mood" (lines 21-22). B thus properly indicates that dieting and psychology were the researchers' primary interests. Eliminate A and C as referencing a possible outcome (weight gain) of dieting rather than referencing dieting ITSELF. C and D can also be eliminated because these choices omit references to mental or psychological responses and focus ENTIRELY on physical reactions.

4) CORRECT ANSWER: C
The authors place a study that involved mice (lines 27-40) in the context of ideas about human stress as linked to dietary choices (lines 1-26), including ideas that interested the researchers who considered human SIRT1 reactions and who utilized mice for the relevant study. Thus, the passage indicates possible parallels that involve physiology in mice and in humans. This information supports C and makes A problematic. While B refers to a possible research finding (NOT to an element of research DESIGN), D presents a connection between SIRT1 and a test group (line 29) that is not justified by the passage, since the researchers wanted to DETERMINE the connection between SIRT1 and fat intake.

5) CORRECT ANSWER: C
The word "afflictions" is used in reference to psychological states such as "a major depressive disorder" (lines 23-24); such a diagnosed state or overall tendency could be properly described as a "condition." Choose C and eliminate A (context of an uncommon occurrence) and B (context of conscious mental training) as inappropriate to the authors' discussion. D would best refer to a physical illness or malady, not to a habit or tendency of thought.

6) CORRECT ANSWER: C
In lines 37-40, the authors present a direct link between movement levels and anxiety levels, with more movement indicating lower anxiety. The idea that movement and anxiety do NOT have a meaningful link would thus go against a major premise of the research considered in the passage. Choose C and eliminate A and B as factors that do NOT necessarily contradict the findings of the study; mice can provide some useful information even though (according to lines 66-74) humans and mice are very different. D references foraging behavior and dietary choices, topics which are not directly relevant to a research project meant to chart PRE-DETERMINED diets.

7) CORRECT ANSWER: C
In lines 66-79, the author raises the possibility that the results of the study are not "certain" on account of the differences between mice and humans. While the author does appreciate the study as a promising inquiry, the reservations here presented support C as the best answer. Eliminate A as overly positive and D as overly negative; B should also be eliminated as wrongly referencing a valid finding (NOT a drawback in methodology) as a source of objection.

8) CORRECT ANSWER: D
See above for analysis of the correct line reference. A wrongly references content that occurs BEFORE the research inquiry considered in the passage is introduced. B and C reference the findings of the study and suggest some practical implications, yet these choices (despite the seemingly appropriate topic) do NOT explain the author's viewpoint or perspective as required by the previous question.

9) CORRECT ANSWER: A
The graph indicates that, over a 12-week period, participants on a high-fat diet eventually rated higher in terms of anxiety than participants on a low-fat diet. This information aligns with lines 45-48, which similarly consider a 12-week timeframe and note the "fleeting" anxiety-reducing effects of a high-fat diet. Choose A and eliminate B, which is contradicted by the indication in the graph that a high-fat diet resulted in a long-term disadvantage (not comparable performance between high-fat and low-fat groups). C (movements) and D (brain responses) consider factors that are not directly assessed in the graph and should thus be eliminated.

10) CORRECT ANSWER: B
While the graph considers anxiety-reducing or "anxiolytic" effects, the graph does NOT (in contrast to the passage) at any point provide data related to weight gain or weight loss. B is thus an appropriate answer, while A, C, and D all appropriately consider the anxiety levels over time for different dietary groups.

Chapter 2.2 | Rodenticide

1) CORRECT ANSWER: C
The author calls attention to the problems that face "birds, humans, and other wildlife" (line 13) as a result of pesticide use and goes on to explain the persistence of such problems later in the passage. This content supports C and can be used to eliminate D, because the author is more interested in problems that face MULTIPLE species than in problems unique to a specific species. A is incorrect because the author supports modified and relatively safe pest control methods (lines 77-80), not the abandonment of pest control entirely, while B misconstrues such recommendations as the main content of the passage, not as a less-prioritized topic that proceeds from the passage's focus on a set of negative health conditions.

2) CORRECT ANSWER: B
In line 20-22, the author calls attention to specific groups that are "mostly" poisoned; the reasonable inference is that other groups (for instance, children who are NOT from low-income families) are less at risk. This content supports B. A calls attention to the risks that face raptors but does NOT indicate that other groups may not be at such high risk. C and D call attention to the problematic nature of rodenticides but do NOT distinguish specific groups affected by those rodenticides for the sake of comparison.

3) CORRECT ANSWER: A
In lines 1-3, the author notes that raptors are "victims" of second-generation rodenticide use; if the adoption of such rodenticides is a widespread problem, the public has thus been energetic yet destructive in its use of these chemicals. A, "overzealous" or over-energetic, thus is a sensible answer. B and C are both wrongly positive, while D establishes a comparison between past and present states that the relevant line reference (which is mostly devoted to present dangers) avoids entirely.

4) CORRECT ANSWER: A
See above for analysis of the correct line reference. B notes that the rodenticides are dangerous but NOT that their use is widespread, while C indicates that people are oblivious to the dangers of using rodenticides widely (but does not definitively state that the rodenticides ARE being used in an energetic and destructive manner). D describes the destructive effects of the rodenticides but NOT the public response.

5) CORRECT ANSWER: B
The word "backup" refers to something that could be used in place of relatively weak first-generation poisons; the idea is that the "strongest choice" (line 31) will not be used initially, enabling the poisons used to become stronger. B properly indicates that a second choice that is potent or "viable" is present. A introduces a faulty negative that describes emotion, C contradicts the idea of having a "choice" (since something "essential" would not leave room for replacement with other options), and D ("willing") introduces a term that best describes people, not items or alternatives.

6) CORRECT ANSWER: C
The author explains that children under 6 (lines 51-52, eliminating A), foxes (line 65, eliminating B), and mountain lions (lines 63, eliminating D) had all consumed rodenticide or exhibited rodenticide traces without being aware of the danger posed by the substance. Squirrels, mentioned in C, are not directly mentioned as accidentally harmed by rodenticide; the

passage's broad references to the wildlife that are thus endangered should NOT be taken as involving squirrels if they are not directly named.

7) CORRECT ANSWER: A
In the relevant paragraph, the author references the problem of rodenticide poisoning and explains that non-rodent animals exhibited rodenticide traces. This content supports A, while B presents a recommendation, NOT a body of facts. C references earlier content and assumes that the author is targeting specific groups with faulty beliefs rather than explaining a situation, while D distorts the use of geographical information in the passage. California and New York state provided instances of animals threatened by rodenticides, but are not compared to OTHER areas in a manner that suggests that animals in California and New York are most strongly affected.

8) CORRECT ANSWER: D
The phrase "showed up" refers to "poisons" (line 62) that were found to be present in animal species in the course of a scientific study. These poisons would thus be discovered or "detected' by researchers. D is appropriate while A refers to the action of a person or to a repeated event, NOT to evidence. B (randomness or luck) and C (assertion or strength of character) both introduce inappropriate contexts.

9) CORRECT ANSWER: C
C is the appropriate choice given that it directly states that first-generation rodenticides should be used first so that a backup option (second-generation rodenticides) is still available to use. A simply describes an effect of using second-generation rodenticide. B explains a possible reason that someone might want to use a second-generation rodenticide, while D describes the way in which second-generation rodenticides exterminate animals. A, B, and D do not pass judgement or explain whether to use second-generation rodenticide as a first or second option.

10) CORRECT ANSWER: A
Based on the information in the passage, "raptors*" (line 1) are defined as birds of prey such as owls or falcons. Using this information, only A, C, and D can be options as B does not fit the definition of a raptor. Based on the table, the correct answer's lethal dosage of d-Con rodenticide must be higher than the lethal dosage of its 1st generation rodenticide. A indicates a higher lethal dosage of d-Con rodenticide (16.5 grams) compared to that of 1st generation rodenticide (12.5 grams) and thus answers the question. C and D both indicate a higher lethal dosage of 1st generation rodenticide compared to that of d-Con rodenticide.

11) CORRECT ANSWER: C
The passage focuses on the use of 2nd generation rodenticides, their harmful effects on the environment, and the discouragement of their use. C correctly explains that the table offers no evidence to support the idea that 2nd generation rodenticides have become such a problem that there is a push for them to be regulated; the table simply lists and compares dosage amounts of rodenticides without mentioning said harmful effects. A and B mention differences in specific lethal dosage amounts of 1st and 2nd generation rodenticides which are not mentioned in the passage, making both answer choices incorrect. D is incorrect because the passage does not mention rats as a cause of the presence of 2nd generation rodenticides.

Chapter 2.3 | Generation Gap

1) CORRECT ANSWER: C
After explaining that "Humans are tribal creatures" (line 1), the author considers how tribal traits are made "manifest in our use of technology" (lines 8-9). This content supports C as properly indicating a connection between topics. While the possibility of conflict is mentioned, A (research findings) and D (demonstration of ideas) refer to content that only appears LATER in the passage when the author considers specific research. B wrongly indicates that the author is correcting flawed ideas, NOT presenting ideas that have effective and valid connections.

2) CORRECT ANSWER: D
In lines 71-75, the author explains that practices related to cell phone use have "perpetuated the divide" between two age groups, a fact that relates back to the concept of an age group as a "tribal" group in line 13. This content supports D, while A and B reference different age groups but NOT (despite possible differences in technology preferences) the idea that the groups remain separate or somewhat antagonistic. C indicates that two age groups were raised under different conditions but avoids the theme of a tribal "divide" that is much more explicit in D.

3) CORRECT ANSWER: C
The relevant phrases are used to explain the "reputation" (line 22) of Baby Boomers and to describe how Baby Boomers themselves are "feeling" (line 71), respectively. Thus, both of the negative phrases introduce perceptions, so that C is appropriate. A references Millennials (NOT Baby Boomers), while B and D distort the negative content of the passage to suggest positive changes that, though potentially useful, the author never explicitly considers.

4) CORRECT ANSWER: D
The author defines OTT content forms as "audio, video, and other media" (line 45) that can be delivered over the Internet and that, though sent by users, are NOT primarily based on texting. D properly references audio content that users would send, while A references audio content that is only of interest to a SINGLE user. B and C both reference content that is primarily text-based, and both answers should be eliminated for this reason.

5) CORRECT ANSWER: C
The word "striking" refers to specific "differences" (line 53), including the clear preference for SMS among Baby Boomers and contrasting preference for OTT among Millennials. Such a difference is obvious or evident, so that C is appropriate. A would wrongly indicate that the difference overturned assumptions (which the author does not present), NOT simply that the difference is clear. B and D both introduce inappropriately negative tones for a neutral description of differing habits.

6) CORRECT ANSWER: C
The phrase "took to" describes how Millennials, who have been "immersed" (line 66) in communication technologies, responded positively to smartphones. C properly reflects a context of technology preference and use. A would wrongly indicate that the Millennials physically confronted or moved towards the phones. B and D would, despite introducing positive tones, wrongly indicate that the Millennials actively hoped to popularize a technology, NOT simply that they found a technology useful.

7) CORRECT ANSWER: A
In lines 77-80, the author indicates that Millennials "can easily detect or avoid" problems in technology use that trouble Baby Boomers. This positive content supports A and can be used to eliminate negative answers such as B and C as fundamentally flawed. D distorts the content of the passage; while Millennials are treated as a group with key characteristics, the author does NOT argue that these characteristics will remain entirely constant over time.

8) CORRECT ANSWER: C
See above for analysis of the correct line reference. A indicates that Millennials use phones to find information, while B indicates that Millennials are natural technology users due to long-term technology exposure. These answers do NOT raise the only positive trait (discernment) considered in the previous question. D features

a recommendation for connection across generations, NOT a direct characterization of Millennials as a single group.

9) CORRECT ANSWER: B
In the charts, "Online Shopping" would take up a similar portion of time for three hours of cell phone usage for a Baby Boomer (9%) and a Millennial (11%). B is thus the best answer. A indicates an activity that would take up considerably more than three hours for a Millennial, while C (calls) and D (represented by SMS) represent activities that would take up considerably more of the same amount of time for a Baby Boomer.

10) CORRECT ANSWER: C
While Applewhite recommends "using the Internet" (line 89) for Baby Boomers, the charts indicate that Baby Boomers are using cell phones for Internet-based activities such as online shopping and may thus be following Applewhite's advice. This content supports C as accurate. A and D wrongly consider increases over time, when the charts simply compare the habits of Millennials and Baby Boomers at a SINGLE point in time. B considers warnings against online dangers, a factor that does not appear in the graphs despite the consideration of online news, and is thus out of scope.

11) CORRECT ANSWER: D
While the graphs consider "Mobile News" (eliminating A), "OTT" content (eliminating B), and "Mobile Banking" (eliminating C) for both Baby Boomers and Millennials, only the passage considers daily hours of smartphone use (lines 33-36). The graphs consider how such hours might be portioned out WITHOUT providing a number for daily hours for Millennials, so that D is the correct answer.

Chapter 2.4 | Gravitational Waves

1) CORRECT ANSWER: B
In lines 20-22, the author points out a possible but not verified connection between "heavy metals and dark matter," so that B properly reflects the author's ideas about heavy metals. A is inaccurate because the heavy metals are the products of violent movements involving stars but do not themselves CAUSE violent processes. C calls attention to the destruction of the metals, which do have a hard time staying in place (lines 29-31) but are not necessarily quickly destroyed. D offers a positive value judgment linked to the metals, which may in fact be beautiful or useful but are NOT described in this manner by the author.

2) CORRECT ANSWER: C
See above for analysis of the correct line reference. A and B indicate that a collision generated heavy metals but do NOT align with answers to the previous question, since choices such as Question 1 C wrongly emphasize the destruction of heavy metals. D explains that heavy metals can be dispersed after they form, NOT that such metals themselves destabilize stars as wrongly indicated in Question 1 A.

3) CORRECT ANSWER: D
The word "crash" refers to the action of "colliding" (line 18) stars; D would properly indicate that two physical bodies interact with or encounter one another. A and B wrongly introduce strong negative or critical tones when the author is mostly offering a neutral explanation of a physical process. C indicates incompatible ideas or antagonism between people, NOT a physical process involving large masses.

4) CORRECT ANSWER: C
The comparison in the relevant lines uses the imagery of white blood cells to explain how a "black hole eats up" (line 25) the center of a star; because the author cites "our" immune system, the author is using a common happening to explain an occurrence involving heavenly bodies. C is appropriate, while A and B neglect the idea of giving an analogy to wrongly indicate that the author is interested in medicine itself. D is problematic because, even though this answer indicates that the author is using imagery, the comparison is meant to explain a process rather than to call up emotions for the reader.

5) CORRECT ANSWER: B
The phrase "in unison" refers to an action performed by a considerable portion of "all scientists" (line 36) with the purpose of observing a feature of the universe. B properly captures the theme of purpose or intent, while A indicates that the actions were PERFECTLY simultaneous instead of similarly motivated at roughly the same time. C and D wrongly indicate friendship or partnership among scientists, when in fact the scientists simply responded to information that motivated common actions.

6) CORRECT ANSWER: A
In lines 43-46, the author explains that the detection of gravitational waves was possible because the waves arrived on Earth "at the very moment" when technology capable of observing the waves was available. This content supports the idea of a coincidence (technology and arrival) in A and can be used to eliminate C because practical (NOT theoretical) developments in observation explain how the waves were detected. B

and D distort the idea that various scientists were prompted to observe the gravitational waves at roughly the same time; this event was based on distributed specialized information, NOT collaboration or media intervention

7) CORRECT ANSWER: B
See above for analysis of the correct line reference. A and C indicate that various scientists observed the waves AFTER initial detection and thus does not fit the previous question. D refers to the reaction to the gravitational waves among scientists, not to the INITIAL detection of the waves or to the conditions that made such detection possible.

8) CORRECT ANSWER: D
In explaining the "impasse" that relates to the expansion rate of the universe, the author indicates that "additional neutron stars will have to be observed" (lines 75-76). Thus, more data must be considered in assessing the expansion rate of the universe, so that D is an effective answer. The author does mention dark matter but as part of a DIFFERENT topic for analysis (eliminating A). Note also that the author provides different expansion estimates but does NOT indicate which ones are most reliable (eliminating B) and does NOT point out that consensus in terms of an expansion estimate cannot be reached (eliminating C); at most, the current estimates are incompatible but may EVENTUALLY be replaced.

9) CORRECT ANSWER: C
In the relevant lines, the author explains that "human understanding" will be more strongly impacted than understanding of "gravitational waves." This focus on human response is explained by the later idea that gravitational wave findings (though difficult to understand fully) will "captivate a larger audience" (line 94) over time. C properly reflects this content, while A wrongly indicates that the material described in the passage is fundamentally difficult or obscure (NOT that it is interesting material with a few difficult elements). B and D both omit any focus on public or non-specialist responses to gravitational wave findings and thus do not fit a major topic of interest to the author.

10) CORRECT ANSWER: C
In the graph, "Ancient Light, Minimum Estimate" (second dark bar) is the ABSOLUTE lowest quantity and is surpassed both by the other two minimum estimates and by all three maximum estimates. Choose C to reflect this information and eliminate A, B, and D as representing higher estimates.

11) CORRECT ANSWER: A
In comparing gravitational wave readings of the expansion rate of the universe to other readings, the author indicates that gravitational waves yield an estimate "midway between" (line 73) two other estimates. The graph similarly indicates that a gravitational wave estimate will occur midway between a neutron star (higher maximum) and ancient light (lower minimum, higher maximum) estimate. A is thus correct, while the author largely AVOIDS discussion of accuracy from method to method, so that B and D are problematic. Note also that C represents a fact presented in the graph but NOT considered in the passage (which avoids discussion of minimum and maximum estimates) and should thus be eliminated.

Chapter 2.5 | Data Fail

1) CORRECT ANSWER: A
After explaining the nature of "Predictive analytics, a trendy field of statistics" (line 7), the author continues on to provide examples of how predictive analytics proved flawed in effectively predicting outcomes, with particular focus on the modeling of the 2016 U.S. presidential election results. This movement from explanation to analysis of undesirable results supports A, while B and C wrongly assume that the author is presenting a theory or a hypothesis, NOT an overview of existing practices. D neglects the fact that the author's emphasis in the later stages of the passage becomes strongly negative (with correction of misconceptions as a possible focus) and should be eliminated for this reason.

2) CORRECT ANSWER: C
The word "extracted" refers to the manner in which "patterns" (line 13) can be yielded by large data sets; a context of information being analyzed or trends being determined is thus appropriate. Choose C and eliminate A as wrongly referring to a physical action. B indicates an inappropriate theme of preference or bias, while D indicates a stage that would occur only AFTER a pattern has been discerned through consideration of data.

3) CORRECT ANSWER: D
While the author calls attention to perceived failures of predictive analytics throughout the passage, in lines 70-80 the author calls attention to the fact that the models of predictive analytics are not truly EXPECTED to achieve complete accuracy under normal conditions. Thus, the belief that predictive analytics should perfectly anticipate the outcome of an event such as the 2016 U.S. presidential election is fundamentally misguided. D is the best answer, while A refers to a theme from the early paragraphs (lines 1-9) that the author does NOT directly present

in a negative light in terms of privacy. B criticizes the data provided for predictive analytics (when in fact the method of ANALYZING data seems to be flawed and misunderstood), while C wrongly indicates that predictive analytics is not useful (which it may in fact be despite its predictive flaws) simply because it is not perfectly accurate.

4) CORRECT ANSWER: B
In lines 89-91, the author indicates that decisions such as those behind the 2016 U.S. presidential election are "psychological, not logical." This information directly indicates that emotion (as opposed to behavior that can be easily modeled) may play a role in election choices; B is thus an appropriate answer. A is out of scope because the author does not explain exactly HOW the polls deviated from the ultimate vote count in terms of voter activity, while C distorts an actual yet broad idea from the passage (lines 54-57) to offer an inappropriately SPECIFIC statement about voter preferences. D mistakes a feature of data analytics use (lines 65-69) for a procedure used by Clinton (who is not directly linked to the lines in question).

5) CORRECT ANSWER: D
See above for analysis of the correct line reference. A refers to a project related to Google, NOT to the 2016 U.S. presidential election, while B refers to the possibility that voters changed their minds and C refers to the limited time frame of election models. Of these answers, only B explains a behavior linked to the 2016 U.S. presidential election, but (because it is not clear WHICH candidates voters switched their preferences to) this answer should not be mistaken for evidence for Question 4 C.

6) CORRECT ANSWER: C
The word "power" refers to a property or quality of data that people "had faith" (lines 37-38) in; the data itself was thus seen as valid or reliable. C is an appropriate choice, while A and B both better refer to attributes of people or organizations. D indicates a context of comparison (with one group or individual having an advantage over another) that is not supported by the actual context for the word.

7) CORRECT ANSWER: A
In lines 78-80, the author explains that Erik Brynjolfsson saw the results of the 2016 U.S. presidential election as "not really a shock," so that A properly references an individual who was NOT surprised by the election results. B and D reference individuals who (on the basis of lines 47-57) WERE surprised, while C references an individual who wants reporting to focus less on polling but does NOT argue that the election results were unsurprising (or surprising) in any clear way.

8) CORRECT ANSWER: C
See above for analysis of the correct line reference. A refers to an individual who found state polls problematic (and who might thus be surprised by the contradiction of an expected election result). B provides testimony from an individual who is NOT mentioned in the previous question, while D presents the opinion of an individual who wants political reporting to focus less on polls but does NOT weigh in on whether the results of the 2016 U.S. presidential election were surprising or not.

9) CORRECT ANSWER: A
Because likelihoods can fluctuate considerably over time, evidence from a timeframe close to the election (November) should be used when considering whether or not Trump's victory was expected. A references the fact that, according to the chart, the percent likelihood for Clinton's election was CONSIDERABLY higher in November than the percent likelihood for Trump's election. B, C, and D all reference timeframes (September and earlier) that are far from the election in comparison and that would thus be less relevant to predictions surrounding the FINAL outcome.

10) CORRECT ANSWER: B
The passage describes the 2016 U.S. presidential election, in which a major candidate with a lower predicted likelihood of being elected ultimately defeated a candidate with a higher predicted likelihood of being elected. B references the 2000 U.S. presidential election, in which the candidate with a lower likelihood similarly prevailed. Choose this answer; A and D both indicate cases in which the candidate with a higher likelihood prevailed, while C presents a scenario (Dole winning the 1996 election) that is contradicted by the table.

Chapter 2.6 | Korean Pine

1) CORRECT ANSWER: B
While the reference to "some" is meant to indicate people who are surprised by tree preservation efforts, the reference to "some people" indicates those who go to "great lengths" (line 4) to preserve trees. B properly indicates a contrast between those who are distant from the efforts and those who are directly involved. A misidentifies the "some" as opponents of tree preservation (not as people who are UNAWARE of such efforts), while D also misidentifies these individuals as directly involved in some respect. C raises the topic of "plant biology," a much broader discipline than tree preservation, and thus wrongly expands the scope of the passage beyond the actual topic.

2) CORRECT ANSWER: D
In lines 36-39, the author explains that, in the relevant study, "human interaction was minimal" while "a verified climate equation was used." This content directly indicates that the study favored mathematical modeling over direct observation. D is thus an appropriate choice, while the ABSENCE of fieldwork as a trait of the study indicates that C is a problematic answer. A confuses the idea that the study avoided direct observation with the idea that this non-invasive approach was new (a topic that the author does not clearly address), while B overstates the content of the opening paragraphs (lines 1-26), which indicate that trees are indeed in danger but NOT that Asia is a site of highest threat.

3) CORRECT ANSWER: D
See above for analysis of the correct line reference. A and B call attention to the possibility of rehabilitating threatened trees without removing them from their natural habitat, but these answers should NOT (since Asia is not clearly mentioned) be taken as justification for Question 2 B. C calls attention to a multi-region study of trees conducted in Asia, but the topic raised here (geographical scope) is not the direct focus of any answer to the previous question.

4) CORRECT ANSWER: D
In lines 11-19, the author indicates that humans, climate change, and disease ALL affect trees negatively. A, B, and C can thus be eliminated, while D raises a threat that is nowhere mentioned in the passage and should NOT be confused with the fact that non-animal organisms (such as fungi, lines 15-16) can harm trees.

5) CORRECT ANSWER: B
In lines 57-69, the author explains that "latitude and altitude" variations were connected to variations in root length for the trees observed in the study. Thus, B appropriately indicates that root length variation can be extended to other species. Choose this answer and use lines 53-69 to eliminate A (since longitude and annual mean temperature do NOT relate to any measured variations in the trees) and C (since leaf density specifically does not correlate in any to with changes in annual precipitation levels). D raises a factor (lifespan) that was not directly listed among the functional traits considered by the researchers and is thus beyond the scope of the passage.

6) CORRECT ANSWER: B
The word "remarkable" refers to the apparent and direct connection between specific traits and specific factors, which the author contrasts with the "negligible or unclear" (lines 55-56) connections in other instances.

B properly indicates that the connections were evident and verified. A introduces a negative that better refers to danger or to a strict personality, while C (aptitude) and D (reputation) raise faulty contexts despite introducing positive tones.

7) CORRECT ANSWER: C
In lines 70-73, the author indicates that the research findings considered in the passage have an "obvious" element yet offer "a broader implication" as well. C properly reflects this content, while the author's sense that the findings are practical and useful (lines 92-95) can be used to eliminate both A and B. D may seem to be justified by lines 101-105, but it is not clear whether a future project will be "larger and more comprehensive," ONLY that future research is possible.

8) CORRECT ANSWER: A
See above for analysis of the correct line reference. B indicates one finding linked to the relevant study but does not offer a general assessment that aligns with an answer to the previous question, while C offers a broadly positive assessment but raises a topic (possible usefulness) that does not in fact align with an answer to the previous question. D returns to the topic of usefulness and raises a possible negative (limited applicability) that does not align with the much stronger negatives raised in Question 7 B (displeasing outcome).

9) CORRECT ANSWER: A
The word "stress" is used in the context of recommendations made by researchers, who have developed a useful method but are aware that such a method "cannot yet be applied" (lines 100-101) comprehensively. This context of awareness and emphasis supports A as appropriate. B would better refer to private thought than to the actual context of declaration and acknowledgment, C would better refer to a physical exertion, and D introduces an inappropriate negative to suggest that the researchers may not be reliable.

10) CORRECT ANSWER: B
While the chart provides weak correlations (close to 0) for longitude and mean annual temperature, the same chart provides a strong correlation (close to 1) for latitude. Only mean annual precipitation has a middling correlation (close to 0.5). Eliminate A, C, and D on the basis of this evidence and choose B as the only appropriate answer.

11) CORRECT ANSWER: C
While the study described in the passage considered "between 10 and 20 individual trees" (line 30) at eight sites for between 80 and 160 trees total, the study reflected in the graph considered 30 trees per region in eight regions, or 240 trees total. Thus, C properly reflects a clear difference in the number of trees considered in each project. A is contradicted by the fact that the environmental factors considered in the graph are the same factors listed in lines 43-52, while B is out of scope because the date for the study considered in the graph is never given. D is contradicted by the fact that both the study considered in the passage and the study considered in the graph involved a total of eight sites.

Chapter 2.7 | DNA & Diet

1) CORRECT ANSWER: B
After describing a study that did not find especially predictable connections between weight loss and various factors, the author explains that it is apparently time to "go back to basics with dieting" (line 51) and offers guidance for doing so (lines 69-76). This content supports B and can be used to eliminate C, which focuses on classification rather than results and advice. A and D both misread the negative elements of the author's discussion: weight loss is difficult to align with specific factors, but this fact does not make classification harmful (eliminating A) or make the study in the passage (which was apparently well-designed but yielded an inconclusive result) itself problematic (eliminating D).

2) CORRECT ANSWER: B
The phrase "influencers of" refers to the various items listed by the author (lines 3-5) that play a role in "determining the best method to lose weight" (lines 6-7). Thus, the "influencers" would play a role in or be factors in possible weight loss. Choose B and eliminate A and D as describing positive roles that would normally be taken by humans, not influences ON humans. C refers to broad ideas or values, not to more specific elements of real life that cause possible results.

3) CORRECT ANSWER: A
While the question in lines 5-7 calls attention to the goal of figuring out the best possible weight loss method, the question in lines 45-46 calls attention to the result of a study centered on weight loss. In each case, the author provides direct and subsequent discussion (description of a study that addressed the goal indicated in the first question, analysis of the study's null result as indicated in the second question). Thus, A is an appropriate choice. Note that the questions are meant to move the author's

OWN analysis along and do not focus on the perspective of any other individual; B (popular perspectives), C (passage's audience), and D (the reader) thus misrepresent the emphasis of the questions.

4) CORRECT ANSWER: B
The author explains that one result of the study (unpredictable weight loss patterns as described in lines 23-24) can be seen in the real world; this connection between everyday outcomes and the research that is a key topic of the passage supports B as accurate. Notice that the author is focused on results at this point, NOT on the theories or concepts that explain the results; A and C thus raise inappropriate topics. Moreover, the author seeks to draw a parallel between the real world and an experiment, but does not indicate that the GOAL of the experiment was to replicate the real world, so that D raises a faulty point of debate in terms of the experiment's validity.

5) CORRECT ANSWER: D
In lines 47-48, the author indicates that the findings described in the passage have "significance" for a particular practical reason, namely that such diets indicate the need "to go back to the basics with dieting" (line 51). D thus presents appropriate content and references. A provides a research premise (NOT a practical application), while B indicates that the researchers worked to implement successful diets (not that the diets WERE successful or practical). C indicates that the study included dieting tips, but it is not clear from the line reference that these tips (despite the intentions of the researchers) were ultimately effective.

6) CORRECT ANSWER: A
The word "directed" occurs within a discussion of "helpful tips" (line 37) that were given to study participants. Thus, a context of instruction or advice is present, so that A is an appropriate answer. B and D refer to OTHER parts of the experiment that involved design and planning but are not directly relevant to a context of providing guidance. C would wrongly indicate that the participants were forced to follow a procedure, not that helpful but less overbearing tips were provided.

7) CORRECT ANSWER: D
In lines 62-65, the author explains that experiments that parallel life in terms of "diversity" will have "less certain" outcomes due to a realistically large number of variables. D properly reflects the idea that replicating the complexity of the real world in a study can lead to profound challenges. Keep in mind that the passage focuses largely on different dietary practices and diet configurations; A (non-dieting activities) and C (socioeconomic

factors) thus reference ideas that are largely out of scope. Also note that working with challenging evidence is a VERY different negative from falsifying evidence; B thus raises a theme of dishonesty inappropriate to the passage.

8) CORRECT ANSWER: C
See above for analysis of the correct line reference. A indicates a possible difficulty that the study encountered but does not provide a sufficiently decisive and general statement to support Question 7 D. B notes that the results of the experiment were problematic but does not explain WHY it was impossible to predict dieting success, while D provides a dietary recommendation but does not reference dieting-based research.

9) CORRECT ANSWER: B
While fat-sensitive test subjects lost over 11 pounds, salt-sensitive test subjects lost the lower quantity of exactly 11 pounds. This content supports B, while A overstates the weight loss (13 pounds) by carbohydrate-sensitive test subjects. Note also that body mass, though broadly relevant to the question of weight loss, is NOT explicitly considered in the graphs; thus, C and D are out of scope.

10) CORRECT ANSWER: A
Each chart considers 632 test subjects but relies on a different classification; it is logically possible, given this information, that the same test subjects were re-classified into entirely different categories at two different stages. A is thus appropriate, while B is incorrect because NEITHER chart considers the average weight loss for all 632 participants (ONLY the average weight loss in each sub-group). C is problematic because differences in maximum average weight loss could be explained by reconfiguring the same test subjects into new groups with higher or lower average figures. D uses faulty logic, since the "sensitive to neither" category involves insensitivity to DIFFERENT dietary components for Chart 1 and Chart 2.

11) CORRECT ANSWER: D
The phrase "surprisingly similar numbers" refers, roughly, to average weight loss of between 11.5 and 13 pounds. A and B indicate average weight losses in EXACTLY this range, while C indicates a difference between 10.5 and 11 pounds (so that the range is similar to the required 1.5-pound range mentioned in the passage). D indicates a difference between 14.5 and 11 pounds, so that this 3.5-pound difference does not indicate "surprisingly similar numbers" on the basis of the passage.

Chapter 2.8 | Nothing is Certain

1) CORRECT ANSWER: C
The reference to a "tightly-knit ecosystem" is meant to explain the current medical system, which relies in part on a "communication chain" (line 39) that can break down if any part is disrupted. In other words, even a single and seemingly insignificant flaw could be problematic; C is logically appropriate, while A and B both depict the medical "ecosystem" as either more secure or less sensitive than it actually is. D wrongly directs a negative tone towards ALL elements of the system in the case of a problem, not towards the ONE possible weak element that would be the true object of the author's critique.

2) CORRECT ANSWER: A
After explaining the problematic and "mystifying idea" (line 7) that modern healthcare remains reliant on paper documents, the author presents the results of a study, which itself indicates that paper-based as opposed to online referrals lead to problems with medical appointment scheduling. A properly reflects the author's explanation of a current problem and a study devoted to it. B wrongly focuses entirely on ideas from the FINAL stages of the passage by emphasizing updates and improvements, while C and D both misrepresent the structure of the author's discussion. The use of paper documents is revealed as problematic by the study cited by the author, NOT set out as automatically flawed compared to electronic documentation early in the passage.

3) CORRECT ANSWER: B
The word "identify" refers to something that it may be possible to "track" (line 26) in terms of flaws in medical documentation. This emphasis on details, documents, and observation makes B an appropriate answer. A wrongly indicates that something is being recollected (NOT that it is being observed initially as information), C indicates a more complex activity than simply noticing information, and D wrongly indicates that the information or documents that interest the author would be classified when more basic matters of attention and awareness are the author's real concerns.

4) CORRECT ANSWER: A
In lines 30-33, the author calls attention to the idea that flaws in the healthcare system may negatively affect reputation and "revenue generation." This focus on economic liabilities supports A, while it is not clear whether patients or the public in GENERAL would have cause for concern. B is thus flawed in its logic, while C and D raise issues that

(though common in real-world criticisms of business functioning) are not analyzed at length by the author and should NOT be mistaken for the passage's actual critique of inefficient messaging.

5) CORRECT ANSWER: D
See above for analysis of the correct line reference. A and B indicate that modern bureaucracy is daunting and inefficient but, despite these seemingly relevant criticisms, do NOT align with any answers to the previous question. C raises the issue of patient concerns and may seem to align with Question 4 B, but C is ultimately too narrow in scope because the author ALSO calls attention to the concerns of healthcare professionals as a primary issue.

6) CORRECT ANSWER: D
The phrase "translate into" is used to help explain how problems in communicating referrals connect to "medical errors" (line 43), so that the problems would logically result in risks. D captures the proper cause-and-effect relationship, while A (a negative word meaning "to make worse") does not capture this DIRECT meaning despite a seemingly relevant general tone. B and C would both best refer to physical actions and are thus inappropriate to the context.

7) CORRECT ANSWER: C
In lines 71-73, the authors of the passage indicate that online intervention in referral methods increases the likelihood of successful scheduling; the chart similarly indicates a correlation between the percentage of hospitals using online resources and the percentage of patients to successfully make appointments. C is thus an appropriate choice that reflects the usefulness of online systems. A (sophistication) and D (relationships) consider factors that are NOT directly assessed on the basis of the graph, while B indicates a cause-and-effect relationship that is not supported by the graph and that if anything wrongly REVERSES the idea that an online system improves the appointment-making process.

8) CORRECT ANSWER: B
See above for analysis of the correct line reference. A indicates a desired (NOT actual) outcome and is thus not fully relevant to a discussion of definitive data. C and D both reference future recommendations or possibilities and, for this reason, are also out of the scope of analysis that (for effective comparison between the passage and the chart) should rely almost entirely on present data.

9) CORRECT ANSWER: C
In lines 49-52, the authors note that the researchers saw paper-based medical scheduling as a potentially "cumbersome process"; the research findings and the idea that online medical scheduling is preferable, as discussed in the passage, both support this characterization. Thus, C properly reflects the idea that online scheduling is more accurate and efficient. A (doctors and interaction) and D (expenses) raise factors that the authors, who focus mainly on efficient communication through documents, do NOT in fact point to as highly problematic. B wrongly indicates that all areas of health (NOT simply the specialist referrals that mostly interest the authors) would benefit from online scheduling practices.

10) CORRECT ANSWER: D
In lines 74-76, the authors indicate that efficiency (understood in the passage as adoption of online communication) can improve outcomes; the chart considers how more prevalent adoption of technology can lead to one desired outcome in terms of scheduling second appointments. D thus indicates the positive relationship also indicated by the graph. A references research methods (NOT results), B references a control group which did NOT use online resources, and C references one data set, NOT changing trends over time as indicated by both D and the graph.

Chapter 2.9 | Antibiotic Combinations

1) CORRECT ANSWER: C
After explaining "the public health problem of antibiotic resistance" (lines 1-2) early in the passage, the author outlines an "interesting new approach" (line 41) that can target bacteria using a synergistic combination of antibiotics. This content supports C, while A and B both rightly focus on the topic of resistance but WRONGLY neglect the possible solution that is a major focus of the passage. D similarly raises a seemingly valid topic by mentioning bacterial infections but itself neglects the counter-measures cited by the author and takes on an overly negative tone.

2) CORRECT ANSWER: A
The author references the CDC in order to present figures on deaths and aggressive infections due to MRSA; this information supports the earlier claim that MRSA is a "serious public health concern" (lines 7-8). Choose A as appropriate, while B wrongly calls into question the validity of the author's earlier information (which, though general, is NOT meant to seem suspiciously broad in any way). C is contradicted by the fact that MRSA has caused several thousand deaths, while D is contradicted by the fact

that the statistics (though important to an understanding of the threat posed by MRSA) are never explicitly referenced a second time.

3) CORRECT ANSWER: B
In lines 18-19, the CDC estimates that there is an increasing number of deaths and infections due to MRSA. C is incorrect as it focuses on historical research on bacterial infections and doesn't refer to an increasing number of MRSA cases (as the CDC does). Similarly, D is incorrect because it focuses on a resistance to antibiotics rather than on an increase in MRSA cases. A, while indicating that MRSA "continues to make new strains in the community," doesn't directly refer to MRSA's increased presence. B does make this reference ("this superbug is being increasingly seen outside the hospital setting") and therefore, is correct.

4) CORRECT ANSWER: B
In preparing their study, the researchers described in the passage decided to target the process of "the synthesis of the cell wall" (lines 54-55) in MRSA; the goal of this early stage was to weaken resistant strains by affecting cell wall production. B is thus appropriate, while A refers to an antibiotic that MRSA has grown to resist (lines 33-34), NOT to a step in new research. C refers to an end result of the research, NOT to an early step, while D refers to a material that the bacteria considered in the study can effectively break down (lines 29-30) instead of to a possible way of weakening the bacteria.

5) CORRECT ANSWER: C
The word "interfering" refers to a measure taken against bacteria that at one point could not successfully create cell walls but that later became more "capable" of countering preventative measures. C properly indicates that the bacteria were kept from creating cell walls at one point. A and D do not sufficiently indicate that negative or limiting action was taken against the bacteria, while B wrongly refers to a physical action typically taken by large masses of people.

6) CORRECT ANSWER: D
The author explains that the resistant strains "acquired genes" (lines 34) from other types of bacteria and, as a group, survived antibacterial measures over time; if the bacteria were able to live on with genetic variations, they logically were able to reproduce. D is thus an appropriate choice. A improperly defines a beta-lactam (which is ITSELF antibiotic in nature), while B raises a topic (difficulty of detection) that should not be confused with the true danger posed by bacteria (resistance to antibiotics) as described in the passage. C distorts the content of the passage by

indicating that bacteria, which acquired genes from OTHER bacteria, instead acquired genes from beta-lactams.

7) CORRECT ANSWER: A
The relevant paragraph mainly describes an "interesting new approach" (line 41) to addressing the resistance developed by MRSA, the dangerous bacterial strain primarily considered in the earlier portions of the passage. A reflects this content while B introduces an overly positive tone; at this point, the author is setting out the premises of a study, NOT outlining the promising results that become of interest later in the passage. C indicates that researchers are faced with a challenge but wrongly calls attention to a distant historical period ("before antibiotics were first introduced), while D focuses on previous flawed studies instead of on the apparently sound present study that interests the author.

8) CORRECT ANSWER: C
The word "producing" refers to the physical synthesis of cell walls by resistant strains of MRSA. D incorrectly refers to the enactment of a process rather than the process itself (in this case, the creation of the cell wall). B is incorrect because it refers to maintaining something rather than creating it (as the resistant strains are evidently doing). A is more related to manipulating elements to work together rather than creating one new product (like a cell wall) and is thus, incorrect. C is appropriate because it refers directly to the physical creation of a cell wall.

9) CORRECT ANSWER: C
In lines 69-70, the author calls attention to the development of resistance by a bacterial strain, a process that has happened before in other contexts (lines 22-40) and that is an expected yet unfortunate occurrence. C properly indicates a mixed sentiment and refers to information presented previously, while A offers an overly negative prediction (when in fact the author sees the research as useful) and B neglects the fact that the author is calling attention to a negative result. D wrongly situates the author, who is mostly reporting on research performed by others, as a researcher involved in the study described in the passage.

10) CORRECT ANSWER: B
In lines 81-83, the author explains that the drug combination considered in the passage was comparable in effectiveness to "a much more expensive drug." This content directly supports B, while A raises a quantitative issue (dosage comparisons) that the passage does not directly consider. C offers a misdirected reading of evidence related to mice; the question calls for a "secondary benefit" related to the drug's intended recipients

(humans), while mice were used only as part of the testing process. D offers a misreading of statements about future testing for the MRSA drug combination (lines 98-105), a topic which should not be confused with the topic of new testing for OTHER antibacterial purposes.

11) CORRECT ANSWER: A
In reference to the previous question's correct answer, the evidence cited here must relate to the tazobactam-piperacillin-meropenem trio's similarity to a more expensive drug. B, C, and D all fail to reference any other drug and relevant similarities. A directly refers to the tazobactam-piperacillin-meropenem trio's results as comparable to results linked to linezolid.

Chapter 2.10 | Alzheimer's Diet

1) CORRECT ANSWER: C
After providing an overview of current knowledge of Alzheimer's Disease, the author indicates that researchers are still unable to explain how specific proteins "caused the disorder" (line 52) but points to the potential utility of the MIND diet as a form of "early intervention" (line 70). This content supports C, while A, B, and D all omit the dietary recommendations that are central to the passage and are problematic for this reason. D also indicates that researchers WILL definitely determine a permanent solution to Alzheimer's, NOT that such a solution is desirable but elusive.

2) CORRECT ANSWER: D
In lines 54-57, the author indicates the importance of finding the "underlying mechanism" that might "hold off the onset" of Alzheimer's. D properly indicates a desire to address the fundamentals of the disease; choose this answer and eliminate A and C as referencing factors that HAVE been discovered already in terms of Alzheimer's research. B distorts the passage's early discussion of the examination of a dead patient; the author does discuss brain scanning techniques but never indicates that these techniques are ONLY applicable to those who have died.

3) CORRECT ANSWER: D
See above for analysis of the correct line reference. A references the desire to better understand Alzheimer's but does not reference any SPECIFIC factors that remain unexplained, while B explains the symptoms of Alzheimer's but not the research linked to the disease. C calls attention to the difficulties encountered in explaining how specific proteins link to Alzheimer's, but these topics (proteins and indeterminacy) do not directly align with any answers to the previous question.

4) CORRECT ANSWER: A
The word "conception" is used in the context of Alzheimer's when this disease was "First discovered" (line 4), so that a context of early discovery is appropriate. Choose A and eliminate B as raising a theme that is broadly related (understanding and inquiry) but that does NOT fit the specific context of initial discovery. C and D both call attention to the emergence of Alzheimer's ITSELF in the human race, NOT to the discovery of this disease (which may have gone undiagnosed for a long period of time), and are problematic for this reason.

5) CORRECT ANSWER: C
In lines 23-28, the author notes that unusual brain "shrinkage and deposits" and "abnormal transmission of neurotransmitters" have been linked to Alzheimer's; C properly references these signs of the disease. A distorts the passage's emphasis on the possible (NOT definite) genetic factors involved in Alzheimer's, while B similarly treats factors that are of interest to researchers and have not been fully explained in terms of the disease as definite symptoms. D wrongly indicates that the MIND diet signals a disease, NOT that it is a means of addressing Alzheimer's, and should be eliminated as wrongly negative.

6) CORRECT ANSWER: B
See above for analysis of the correct line reference. A references Alzheimer's symptoms that, though valid as topics, are NOT referenced in any answer to the previous question. C references hypotheses linked to Alzheimer's, and D references a method that may prove effective against Alzheimer's; though both answers mention the disease, neither mentions a specific observed sign or symptom of Alzheimer's itself.

7) CORRECT ANSWER: A
The word "still" refers to a brain image that is contrasted with an image series that records "processes in real time" (line 20); thus, the contrasting "still" image does not feature movement. A properly reflects this context, while B wrongly refers to a context of sound. C and D would both effectively describe images that ARE moving and are thus inappropriate choices.

8) CORRECT ANSWER: C
In the relevant paragraph, the author points to difficulties in explaining the workings of Alzheimer's and suggests that, among "dietary possibilities," the MIND diet may be useful and instructive. C reflects this content, while A and D both neglect the crucial topic of the MIND diet. B does not

effectively reference the discussion of research, which is used to set up the discussion of the MIND diet, and is problematic for this reason.

9) CORRECT ANSWER: D
In line 65, the author directly points out that cheese is meant to be avoided under the MIND diet. Choose D and eliminate A and C as referencing food types that are ALLOWED (lines 63-64) under the MIND diet. B references dairy overall, when in fact it is not clear whether all dairy products are only a few (such as cheese and butter) are off-limits under the MIND diet, and is for this reason out of scope.

10) CORRECT ANSWER: D
The table directly indicates, under the "Process" column, that plaques are responsible for blocking cell firing. D is thus appropriate, while A, B, and C reference buildup types that align with entirely different processes in terms of both negative (second column) and positive (fourth column) effects.

11) CORRECT ANSWER: B
While the passage links tau to "abnormal deposits" (line 33), the table indicates that tau can destroy nerve cells but NOT that this protein is responsible for any sort of buildup of cells. B thus reflects a valid point of disagreement, while A misstates the role of amyloid proteins (which spread tau protein INSTEAD of disrupting tau movement) indicated by the table. C distorts the content of the passage (which indicates that tau and amyloid proteins are of interest to researchers, not that these are the ONLY possible fundamental factors involved in Alzheimer's). D distorts the content of the passage, since symptoms OTHER than memory loss are explained in lines 7-16.

Chapter Three

Questions 1-11 are based on the following passage and supplementary material.

3.1
Adapted from a 2018 NIH article by Laura Hooper and a team of researchers at the University of Washington, Division of Pulmonary and Critical Care Medicine, titled "Ambient Air Pollution and Chronic Bronchitis in a Cohort of U.S. Women."

Air pollution is a favorite topic of conversation among those who are concerned about the future of the environment and global warming, as carbon dioxide is both the leading air pollutant and the leading cause of rising temperatures. A second effect of air pollutants, though, is the impact they have on those who breathe them in. Bronchitis, a common clinical condition defined by chronic cough and mucus production, can be caused by the same viral culprits that give us the flu. There is also a second—less well known but infinitely more present—cause of bronchitis: breathing in particulate matter, more commonly known as air pollutants. A recent study by the National Institute of Health seeks to determine just how much of an effect everyday air pollution can have on both acute (short-term) and chronic (long-term) bronchitis.

While the relationship between short-term air pollution exposure and acute respiratory symptoms is well established, limited data suggest a relationship between long-term ambient pollution exposure and COPD (chronic obstructive pulmonary disorder), of which chronic bronchitis is a phenotype—a physical symptom that manifests itself as a result of contracting any of the disorders that fall under the umbrella of COPD such as bronchitis or emphysema.

There is a paucity of data on the possible relationship between classically defined chronic bronchitis and long-term exposure to particulate matter, pieces of dust that remain in the atmosphere as a result of gas fumes or dirt that are unknowingly ingested every day. To address these relationships in a larger study, using specific outcome definitions and advanced exposure assessments, the NIH investigated the association between residential exposure to small and large particulate matter, and both incident (newly diagnosed cases) and prevalent (previously occurring cases) chronic bronchitis in a nationwide cohort of more than 50,000 U.S. women.

Outcome Assessment Chronic bronchitis was defined according to the classical symptom-based definition of chronic cough productive of phlegm for at least 3 months out of a year for a minimum of 2 consecutive years. Participants were asked about the presence of cough and phlegm independently, and the duration of each symptom was specified using questions derived from the British Medical Research Council adult respiratory symptom standardized questionnaire. Women with cough and phlegm symptoms, both present for at least 3 months per year out of the previous 2 years, were considered to have chronic bronchitis.

At baseline, 1,351 (3.1%) women met symptom-based criteria for chronic bronchitis, whereas 4,698 (10.6%) participants reported ever having had a physician diagnosis of chronic bronchitis. Prevalent chronic cough was reported by 3,749 (8.5%) and chronic phlegm by 2,776 (6.3%) participants at baseline. No statistically significant associations were found between incident chronic bronchitis and any of the air pollution exposures. For prevalent chronic bronchitis, a statistically significant positive association was seen with large particulate matter. Similar magnitudes of association with prevalent chronic bronchitis were seen for nitrous oxide and small pieces of particulate matter, but were not statistically significant. Large particulate matter was also statistically significantly associated with chronic cough, chronic phlegm, and chronic cough or phlegm.

This is the largest study to investigate the association between classically defined chronic bronchitis and long-term ambient air pollution exposure using a validated national exposure model. The team did not find an association between incident chronic bronchitis and any of the air pollution measures. However, exposure to higher concentrations of large particulate matter was significantly associated with all prevalent outcomes: chronic bronchitis, chronic cough, chronic phlegm, and chronic cough plus phlegm. These findings were statistically robust. The researchers also found that nitrous oxide exposure was significantly associated with chronic cough and chronic cough or phlegm. Prior to this study, there had been no known association between large particulate matter and classically defined chronic bronchitis. These findings provide evidence that long-term ambient air pollution exposure, especially to large particulate matter, is a risk factor for chronic bronchitis and the chronic respiratory symptoms of cough and phlegm that define it.

Correlation Between Amount of Large Particulate Matter in the Air and Instances of Diagnosed Chronic Bronchitis for the Same Area

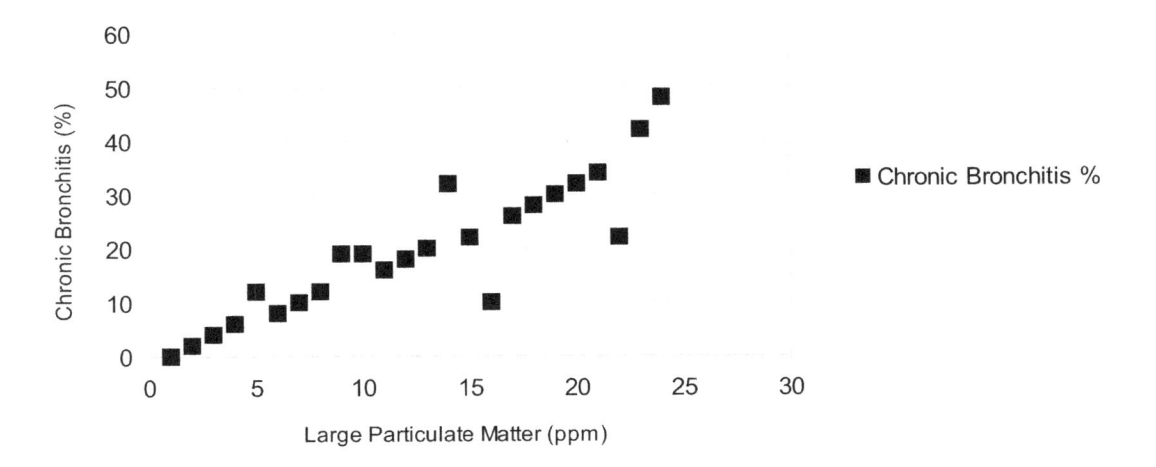

1

The author of the passage develops her discussion in the first three paragraphs (lines 1-38) by presenting

A) side comments that establish an approachable and candid tone towards pollutants.
B) recent reactions to an influential study on how health is impacted by pollutants.
C) definitions of terms and concepts that are central to research on pollutants.
D) common yet easily refuted misconceptions about the effects of pollutants.

2

As used in line 1, "favorite" most nearly means

A) widely respected.
B) deeply endearing.
C) heavily prioritized.
D) excessively indulged.

3

The "recent study" (line 13) that is described throughout the passage is notable for its

A) extensive and unprecedented scope.
B) comprehensive measurements of air pollution.
C) connection to a specific public health policy.
D) status as a synthesis of earlier inquiries.

4

Which choice provides the best evidence for the answer to the previous question?

A) Lines 26-31 ("There is . . . day")
B) Lines 43-48 ("Participants . . . questionnaire")
C) Lines 58-60 ("No statistically . . . exposures")
D) Lines 69-73 ("This is . . . model")

5

As used in line 37, "cohort" most nearly means

A) allegiance.
B) sampling.
C) following.
D) delegation.

6

According to the passage, prevalent chronic bronchitis is NOT statistically linked to

A) exposure to small particulate matter.
B) exposure to large particulate matter.
C) chronic phlegm.
D) chronic cough.

7

Which choice provides the best evidence for the answer to the previous question?

A) Lines 31-38 ("To address . . . women")
B) Lines 52-55 ("At baseline . . . bronchitis")
C) Lines 63-66 ("Similar . . . significant")
D) Lines 66-68 ("Large . . . phlegm")

8

According to criteria set forward in the passage, which of the following women would be considered to have chronic bronchitis at the time of writing?

A) A woman who has exhibited severe cough symptoms for every month of a single year.
B) A woman who has exhibited severe cough and phlegm symptoms for at least one month of each of the previous five years.
C) A woman who has exhibited severe cough and phlegm symptoms for four months a year for the previous three years
D) A woman who has experienced alternating cough and phlegm symptoms for all twelve months of the previous three years.

9

The author's description of the National Institute of Health findings as "statistically robust" (line 79) serves mainly to

A) resolve a point of contention that was raised without resolution earlier in the passage.
B) reinforce the sense that the study described in the passage is valid and significant.
C) imply that new therapeutic methods can be developed based on the study described in the passage.
D) suggest that the study that is the focal point of the passage should inspire future research.

10

Which of the following situations would NOT conform to the predominant trend indicated by the chart?

A) 10% risk of chronic bronchitis, exposure to 25 ppm large particulate matter
B) 10% risk of chronic bronchitis, exposure to 100 ppm small particulate matter
C) 40% risk of chronic bronchitis, exposure to 100 ppm large particulate matter
D) 60% risk of chronic bronchitis, exposure to 120 ppm large particulate matter

11

Which of the following conclusions about chronic bronchitis from the passage is also supported by the chart?

A) Greater exposure to large particulate matter is the main factor that is responsible for an increased incidence of chronic bronchitis.
B) Greater exposure to large particulate matter makes the symptoms of chronic bronchitis increasingly pronounced.
C) Greater exposure to large particulate matter generally correlates with increased incidence of chronic bronchitis.
D) Greater exposure to small particulate matter does not automatically increase the risk of contracting chronic bronchitis.

Questions 1-11 are based on the following passage and supplementary material.

3.2
Adapted from the 2010 article "Bioluminescence in the Sea," by Steven Haddock, Mark Moline, and James Case. The authors attempt to explain the various instances of bioluminescence and the mechanism that makes it possible.

On his travels, famed evolutionary biologist Charles Darwin was fascinated with the glowing light emitted by marine animals, illustratively describing it in his writing: "the vessel drove before her bows two billows of liquid phosphorus, and in her wake she was followed by a milky train." What he was referring to is the phenomenon of a plant or animal emitting light, known as bioluminescence. The chemical process occurs in many marine animals, both invertebrates and vertebrates. Sometimes, the animals chemically produce the light themselves, and in other cases the light is produced through a parasitic or symbiotic relationship with another organism, such as a bacterium. Scientists have explored the chemistry and evolution of bioluminescence in significant depth and found that bioluminescence is used functionally by a variety of organisms in nature, serving a number of purposes, including counterillumination, camouflage, attraction, defense, warning, communication, mimicry, and illumination.

These functions are as fascinating as they are diverse. Marine animals known as dinoflagellates may use bioluminescence as a defense: when they detect a predator, they shine. Sea-fireflies live in sand, emitting a dull glow, but when disturbed, they emit a cloud of shimmering blue light to confuse any predators. Railroad worms, in their larval stage, emit green light, which some scientists believe may serve a defensive role. When they mature, they become the only terrestrial organisms to emit red light—from their heads! Even more interestingly, some predatory deep-sea fish were discovered to have a black lining to their stomachs, so that if they have ingested a bioluminescent animal, larger predators cannot see what they have eaten.

The way bioluminescence is used by squid is of special interest, as many species utilize a bacterium symbiotically to manufacture their glow—and with 70 squid genera that are bioluminescent, there's a plethora of subjects to study. Squid use bioluminescence the same way that some squid use their ink, as a bacterial slurry or bioluminescent chemical mixture, expelling it to distract or repel. These creatures may go to great lengths when their survival is at stake: "the deep sea squid *Octopoteuthis deletron* may [shed] portions of its arms, which are luminous and continue to twitch and flash, thus distracting a predator while the animal flees," stated one researcher.

Squid have a light organ that is colonized by the bacteria almost immediately after the bacteria hatch. Nyholm and McFall-Ngai reported in 2004 that "the squid exhibit bioluminescence mainly on their ventral side, where it mimics the appearance of the moon and starlight to provide camouflage." This amazing phenomenon is known as counter-illumination concealment.

The process that makes this possible is called an exothermic reaction, which is used by bacteria to produce bioluminescence, as reported in 1998 by Wilson and Hastings. The energy released by the reaction becomes a photon, a particle representing a quantum of light or other electromagnetic radiation. In this process, the bacteria population must reach a specific density, known as a quorum, in order for the intensity of the light to be produced, and the specific density is determined by the expression of the gene of the bacteria, according to research by Rader and Nyholm in 2012.

The research further determined that a multi-step process which requires a large amount of energy is needed to produce photons. In addition, the process requires luciferins and enzymes as substrates, called luciferases. In 2005, Galperin found that the specific enzymes required for bioluminescence are located within the bacteria. When the gene that causes bioluminescence mutates slightly, it inhibits the ability of the bacteria to survive inside of the squid's light organ. Galperin also found in 2005 that there are adhesive mechanisms within the squid's light organ that are used by the epithelial cells so that the Vibrio Fischeri bacteria can attach to squid. Part of the amino acid sequence of the luciferase determines the color of the light that is emitted.

While seemingly unaware of the complex process required to afford them bioluminescence, these squid employ bioluminescence to defend against predators during their nocturnal activity. Both the bacteria and the squid benefit from producing this light, making it even more fascinating to researchers. Turning the energy into light emission by the bacteria, combined with the ability of the squid to take advantage of this opportunity, shows how ingenious these invertebrates truly are.

Bioluminescence Across Several Species

Species	Number of Ecotypes* that Use Bioluminescence	Primary Use
Jellyfish	>1000	Confuse or Repel Predators
Squid	>70	Distract or Repel Predators
Anglerfish	All	Attract Prey
Lanternfish	All	Mating
Firefly	All	Mating
Fungi	>700	Attract Insects (to colonize new areas)

*subspecies adapted to a particular set of environmental conditions

1

The main purpose of the passage is to

A) demonstrate that bioluminescence is too diverse in the forms it takes across organisms to suggest a single theory of development.
B) explain how differing speculations about the survival roles of bioluminescence were resolved by a series of related findings.
C) present various pieces of information about the functions and study of bioluminescence, with an eventual focus on a single species.
D) investigate an instance of bioluminescence that has led scientists to re-formulate the expected relationship between bioluminescence and symbiosis.

2

The first paragraph of the passage helps to introduce the discussion that follows by

A) setting out a traditional viewpoint that is later taken as a point of reference by present-day researchers.
B) providing a standard definition of bioluminescence that is expanded upon by the researchers mentioned later in the passage.
C) alluding to the possible drawbacks of bioluminescence with the goal of later arguing that these liabilities have been misunderstood.
D) referencing practical purposes for bioluminescence that are then illustrated through descriptions of specific organisms.

3

According to the passage, some animals have responded to bioluminescent organisms by

A) learning to distinguish different forms of prey based on the shade and intensity of emitted light.
B) avoiding bioluminescent organisms and preying on their non-bioluminescent counterparts.
C) developing anatomical feautres that minimize the danger of consuming bioluminescent prey.
D) emitting substances that keep prey organisms from using bioluminescent defenses.

4

Which choice provides the best evidence for the answer to the previous question?

A) Lines 24-27 ("Sea-fireflies . . . predators")
B) Lines 27-29 ("Railroad worms . . . role")
C) Lines 31-35 ("Even more . . . eaten")
D) Lines 40-43 ("Squid . . . repel")

5

As described in the passage, Nyholm is notable for

A) first postulating the existence of bioluminescent bacteria in a squid species.
B) contributing to multiple research studies involving bioluminescence in squid.
C) arriving at conclusions that became the direct motivation for Galperin's research.
D) providing an early yet rigorous definition of "counter-illumination concealment."

6

As used in line 60, "released" most nearly means

A) omitted.
B) generated.
C) communicated.
D) unburdened.

7

As used in line 79, "adhesive" most nearly means

A) congealing.
B) close-knit.
C) coherent.
D) connective.

8

Which of the following choices best indicates that the squid described in the final portions of the passage might not be able to produce photons on their own?

A) Lines 60-62 ("The energy . . . radiation")
B) Lines 69-71 ("The research . . . photons")
C) Lines 73-75 ("In 2005 . . . bacteria")
D) Lines 81-83 ("Fischeri bacteria . . . emitted")

9

In the final paragraph of the passage, the author uses the phrasing "take advantage" (line 91) and "ingenious" (line 92) primarily to indicate that the squid

A) exhibit consciousness of how their abilities set them apart from other animals.
B) can utilize bioluminescence to effectively raise their chances of survival.
C) developed their central defensive mechanism rapidly and efficiently.
D) provide various benefits to a specific species of bioluminescent bacteria.

10

Which of the following claims, if true, would NOT challenge or undermine the information presented in the table?

A) Sea creatures that exhibit bioluminescence do not use this ability to attract prey.
B) Bioluminescence has been observed in fewer than 50 of the known squid ecotypes.
C) Over 2000 different types of fungi exhibit some form of bioluminescence.
D) Organisms that inhabit land-based and water-based ecosystems never use bioluminescence for similar purposes.

11

Unlike the passage, the graph explicitly references the role of bioluminescence in

A) mating.
B) confusing predators.
C) hiding from predators.
D) attracting prey.

Questions 1-11 are based on the following passage and supplementary material.

3.3
Adapted from a 2017 article in Oxford University Press's *SLEEP* by a team of researchers at Duke-NUS Medical School in Singapore, "The Impact of Delaying School Start Time on Students' Well-Being in a Singapore High School."

A good night's sleep has more benefits than originally thought, and the definition of what constitutes a "good" sleep might be changing. Based
Line on a new study printed in Oxford University Press'
5 *SLEEP*, students perform better when they're well rested—but that's not a surprising find. The surprising result of the study is that the number of hours of sleep isn't the main determiner of how well-rested kids will be during the early morning hours—it's the time they
10 wake up that matters.

Based on data from the Center for Disease Control, the average school start time for US middle and high schools is 8:03 am, with times ranging from 7:40 to 8:23. Moreover, it has been this way for so long
15 that it's thought of as a cultural norm, and culturally accepted norms can be difficult to change. Take breakfast foods for example—if you wouldn't feel comfortable eating soup, salad, or any other typical lunch food during "normal breakfast hours," you are
20 certainly not alone. With the case of school start times, though, the implications of changing normal behavior are much larger than simply trading your Cheerios for a Waldorf salad. For students, the results could be life-changing.

25 With a plethora of data on circadian rhythms, researchers in the study set out to put theory into practice. It has long been known that children need over eight and a half hours of sleep per night, and that peak performance is at risk if they don't reach
30 this mark. Furthermore, the brain functions better or worse during certain hours of the day. For example, melatonin (the hormone that makes us feel tired at night) secretion ends around 7:30 am. After secretion of the hormone stops, it takes some time for its
35 presence to vacate the bloodstream, meaning that we will not feel alert immediately after the hormone stops flowing. For children attending school, then, it appears that pushing the start time to one that correlates with lowered levels of melatonin would be appropriate.

40 In the study, researchers adjusted start times for kids, pushing arrival times to 45 minutes later than usual, and measured the effect on sleep timing, sleepiness, and well-being (mood). Subjects were 15 year old Singaporean students, who normally begin
45 their school day at 7:30 am. After making the change to 8:15 start times, students reported getting an average 23 minutes more sleep per night, as well as lower levels of sleepiness and an improvement in overall well-being, and they maintained this beyond the initial
50 follow-up assessment. Additionally, students reported that they were getting at least 8 hours of sleep, which puts them much closer to the recommended amount.

Although this study did not use US children as its subjects, it has implications for students all over the
55 world. As hypothesized, the findings imply that there are clear-cut mental benefits for kids who have later class start times. By pushing sleeping hours to a time that syncs with young children's circadian rhythm, the researchers have finally proven a connection between
60 not just total sleep hours, but "proper" sleep hours and well-being. Furthermore, the benefits could reach further than their direct effects: parents wouldn't have to wake up so early to get their kids to school, making this a win-win situation. And school start times would
65 still be before the typical nine-to-five workday, giving parents time to get to work after they drop their kids off.

This study is far from perfect, however. Only 337 kids were studied, and they already had an earlier
70 start-time than kids in the US have. Beyond that, the 23 minutes more that participants were getting after the experiment dropped to 9 minutes 10 months after the experiment began. This is not to say that there were no positive long-term takeaways from the study. Seeing
75 a boost in positive moods and alertness as a result of sleeping longer implies that the number of hours of sleep wasn't the only benefit from the later school start times; kids' overall wellness was a less anticipated but nonetheless welcome secondary effect.

80 In the future, it would be beneficial to replicate the study in other countries, and to vary the start-time delays beyond 8:15 am. Additionally, researchers should extend the length of the study to at least a full school year so that the long-term benefits can be
85 assessed. Overall, the study's researchers are optimistic that "starting school later in East Asia is feasible and can have sustained benefits" and that the implications "argue strongly for disruption in practice and attitudes surrounding sleep and well-being." We should really
90 consider changing class start times for school children if that change will have a positive effect on their overall wellness and performance, while not showing any negative effects on the community.

Figure 1

Student Report on Sleep Timing, Sleepiness, and Mood with a Normal 7:30 AM Start Time

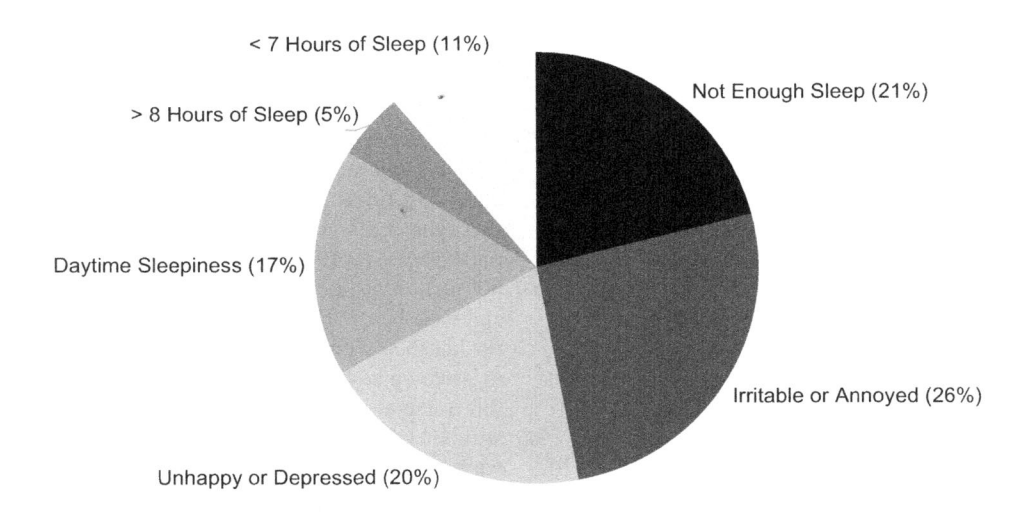

- < 7 Hours of Sleep (11%)
- > 8 Hours of Sleep (5%)
- Daytime Sleepiness (17%)
- Unhappy or Depressed (20%)
- Irritable or Annoyed (26%)
- Not Enough Sleep (21%)

Figure 2

Student Report on Sleep Timing, Sleepiness, and Mood with an Adjusted 8:30 AM Start Time

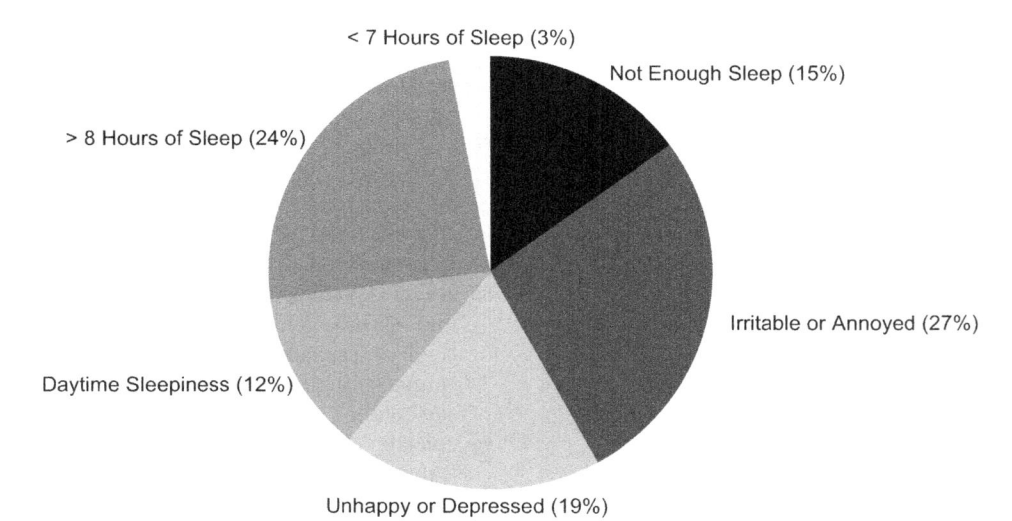

- < 7 Hours of Sleep (3%)
- > 8 Hours of Sleep (24%)
- Daytime Sleepiness (12%)
- Unhappy or Depressed (19%)
- Irritable or Annoyed (27%)
- Not Enough Sleep (15%)

1

What is the central claim of the passage?

A) Studies like the one conducted on the Singapore high school students are inapplicable in the United States.
B) Current school start times are a result of habit and a series of cultural norms rather than the result of research.
C) Research into circadian rhythms only looks into how many hours of sleep children need in a night but much more research is needed.
D) While further research should be conducted, there is evidence that later school start times would be beneficial for student performance and well-being.

2

As used in line 21, "implications" most nearly means

A) consequences.
B) decisions.
C) repercussions.
D) significance.

3

In the design of the study, the researchers assume that

A) students are getting more sleep each night because of the study itself.
B) cultural norms primarily dictate students' sleep schedules.
C) later start times are beneficial to both students and parents.
D) the fluctuation of melatonin is consistent among students.

4

Which choice provides the best evidence for the answer to the previous question?

A) Lines 14-16 ("Moreover, it...change")
B) Lines 37-39 ("For children...appropriate")
C) Lines 53-55 ("Although this...world")
D) Lines 64-67 ("And school...off")

5

As used in line 42, "measured" most nearly means

A) assessed.
B) observed.
C) evaluated.
D) considered.

6

Through the study, the researchers confirmed that

A) the more time children spend sleeping, the better their school performance.
B) optimizing sleep schedules to reflect circadian rhythms would improve students well-being.
C) children need to sleep past 7:30 AM in order to have the best student performance.
D) the production of melatonin is connected to a student's wakefulness in the morning.

7

Which of the following situations is analogous to the one in lines 70-73 ("Beyond that...began")?

A) Patients showed a more positive mood after six months of behavioral therapy compared to those who had undergone treatment for six weeks.
B) Patients prescribed to a new drug would experience increased tolerance to the point that the effects of the drug have become negligible.
C) Students taking a test at the end of their course exhibit improved scores from their diagnostic exam which had consisted of similar questions.
D) Participants in a weight loss study initially drastically lost weight but the weight loss begins to plateau after a couple of months.

8

Which choice best supports the conclusion that the results of the study analyzed in the passage may not translate to students in the United States?

A) Lines 68-70 ("This study...have")
B) Lines 70-73 ("Beyond that...began")
C) Lines 80-82 ("In the...8:15 AM")
D) Lines 82-85 ("Additionally...assessed")

9

Based on the figures, which of the following categories showed the greatest benefit from pushing back school start times?

A) More than 8 hours
B) Irritable and annoyed
C) Not enough sleep
D) Daytime sleepiness

10

Based on the figures, which of the following categories showed the lowest benefit from pushing back school start times?

A) Daytime sleepiness
B) Irritable or annoyed
C) More than 8 hours
D) Unhappy or depressed

11

Would the researchers (line 40) consider the information in the figures to be a perfect simulation of their study?

A) Yes, because the start times for both figures are the same as those in the study explained in the passage.
B) Yes, because the start time in figure 2 is pushed back by 60 minutes.
C) No, because the start time in figure 2 is later than the adjusted start time conducted in the study.
D) No, because the start time in figure 1 is earlier than the start time in the study.

Questions 1-10 are based on the following passage and supplementary material.

3.4
Adapted from a 2018 Cornell University Library article by A. Pluchino, A. E. Biondo, and A. Rapisarda titled "Talent vs Luck: the role of randomness in success and failure."

We learn from an early age that if we work hard, success will be ours. And this indeed sounds nice, but what if it's simply not true? Maybe the best idea won't
Line be the one that goes viral; maybe the person with the
5 most talent won't be the person who is selected for the job; maybe a high probability won't cause a desired outcome. If we know these "maybes" to be true, and I'm sure most of us can use anecdotal evidence to corroborate that, then what we should be studying is
10 *why* they're not true.

One current, prevalent method of "learning to be successful" is to ask someone who already has success—but there are inherent flaws in that logic. For one, no *good* research is based on outcome alone.
15 Any researcher will tell you that cause cannot precede effect if you want to understand how to get a result and replicate it. A second flaw is human nature: we remember things in a way that's shaded by our own current internal status. If I'm happy, I'm much more
20 likely to remember things as positive than as negative. Therefore, if I'm successful, I'm more likely to remember events in the past as leading to my success, rather than as just existing with no relation to my success.
25 To better understand these seemingly confounding ideas, researchers sought out a mathematical model that could predict likelihood of success, using luck and talent as variables. It seems intuitive that talent would be a better indicator of success—which in this study
30 is defined as acquisition of wealth—than luck. But unfortunately it doesn't appear to be that simple: what actually predicts success is a combination of talent and proper exploitation of luck (when it happens to come your way).

35 The study utilized a normally-distributed factor of talent, meaning that there was an "average" amount of talent which is plotted in the center of a curve, at fifty percent probability, and beyond that talent was symmetrically distributed above (higher than
40 fifty percent probability) and below (lower than fifty percent probability) average, while declining at such a rate that the distribution looks like an upside-down U that tapers off at the end—never truly hitting zero. This distribution was utilized because it approximates
45 talent in real life, and because random assignment of people to a place on the curve gives everyone a fair probability of being talented in the simulation.

In our lives, the most hoped-for outcome would be higher talent correlating to higher wealth. In this
50 scenario, wealth would be distributed along the same curve as talent, and would be superimposed over the talent curve to predict which people would accrue the most wealth. But because the scientists knew that was not true to a realistic model of wealth (in which 80
55 percent of the wealth is distributed among 20 percent of the population), they added the second factor: chance. Chance was added in hopes of approximating the same 80/20 wealth/population divide.

Luck, it turns out, is the X-factor in predicting
60 who will become wealthy and who will fare less well. By adding "lucky events" at the probability of completely random chance, the researchers approximated the way wealth is actually distributed in the world. Talent and luck, each on its own, were not
65 good indicators of success. However, once combined, they played a significant role in predicting who would be successful, but only when those who had chance opportunities took full advantage of them.

What does this mean in real life, especially when
70 we can't predict when lucky events will happen to us? One possible application lies in the field of laboratory research. Currently, research funds are usually distributed to the labs that have the most success, but that isn't at all logical, mathematically speaking.
75 In the mathematical model of probability, each probable event has its own, independent probability of occurring. For example, each time you flip a coin, the probability of heads is 1/2, or 50%, even when you've flipped that same coin and landed on heads ten
80 times prior. Based on this knowledge, research funds, or small business funds to make this research even more ecologically valid, should be equally distributed among all labs. The equal distribution of funds would increase the probability of *any* researchers that have a
85 serendipitous finding being able to exploit that finding and use it to its maximum potential. There certainly is a long way to go before funders can be convinced of this, but at least having mathematical proof should serve as a good start.

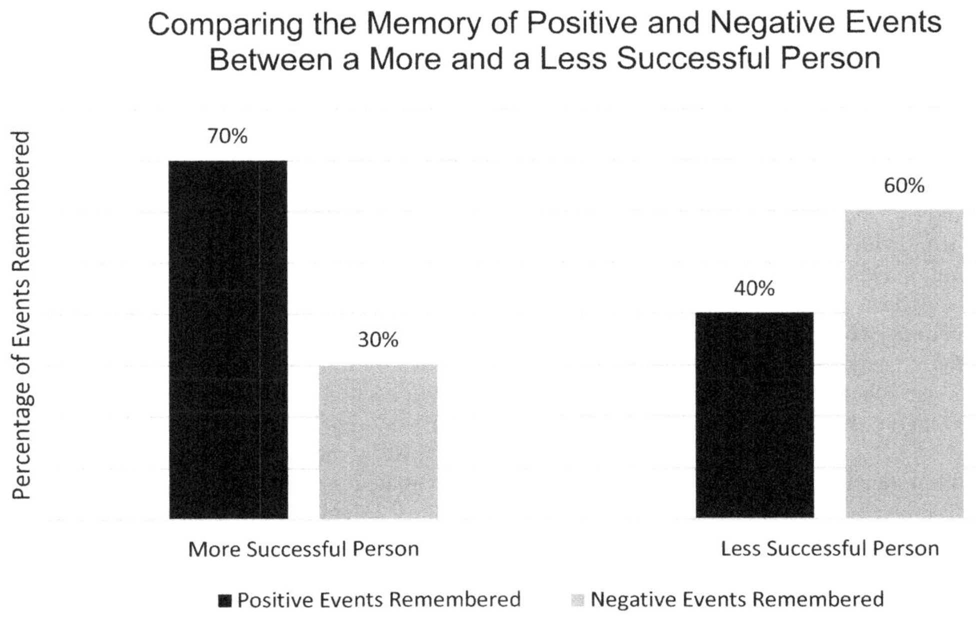

Comparing the Memory of Positive and Negative Events Between a More and a Less Successful Person

More Successful Person: Positive Events Remembered 70%, Negative Events Remembered 30%

Less Successful Person: Positive Events Remembered 40%, Negative Events Remembered 60%

(Y-axis: Percentage of Events Remembered)

■ Positive Events Remembered   ■ Negative Events Remembered

1

What is the central claim of the passage?

A) Those who are intelligent are less likely to be successful than those who are lucky.
B) Success can be attained through the skillful exploitation of random opportunities.
C) People tend to have a distorted view of the circumstances that lead to success.
D) Success is a complex phenomenon for which no one cause can be determined.

2

Which choice best supports the claims in lines 3-6 ("Maybe...job")?

A) Lines 45-47 ("random assignment...simulation")
B) Lines 59-61 ("Luck, it...well")
C) Lines 64-65 ("Talent...success")
D) Lines 69-70 ("What does...us")

3

The information in the second paragraph is primarily provided to

A) point out the faulty reasoning behind a common perspective.
B) explain a complex set of circumstances in relatable terms.
C) introduce a study that will be discussed later in the passage.
D) reveal the author's own thoughts on acquiring success.

4

As used in line 19, "internal" most nearly means

A) private.
B) subjective.
C) innate.
D) inherent.

5

Based on the passage, in which situation would a person have the greatest opportunity to be successful?

A) A wealthy tycoon who invests all of his money into an unstable stock market
B) A skilled pianist who takes advantage of an opportunity to play at a famous venue
C) A scientist who spends his life at a university researching his life's passion
D) A prospective employee who brings his self-proclaimed "lucky charm" to an interview

6

Which choice provides the best evidence for the answer to the previous question?

A) Lines 48-49 ("In our lives...wealth")
B) Lines 61-65 ("By adding...the world")
C) Lines 65-68 ("Once combined...them")
D) Lines 83-86 ("The equal...potential")

7

As used in line 85, "exploit" most nearly means

A) abuse.
B) apply.
C) profit from.
D) impose upon.

8

According to the author, what leads to the most success?

A) Talent and hard work together
B) Talent and luck separately
C) The accumulation of wealth
D) The exploitation of talent and luck

9

According to the passage, the author would view the information in the graph as

A) unreliable.
B) incorrect.
C) accurate.
D) crude.

10

Which information from the passage best represents the information provided by the graph?

A) Lines 11-13 ("One current...logic")
B) Lines 15-17 ("Any researcher...replicate it")
C) Lines 21-24 ("if I'm...success")
D) Lines 28-30 ("It seems...wealth")

Questions 1-11 are based on the following passage and supplementary material.
3.5
Adapted from the bestselling book by Al Gore, *An Inconvenient Sequel: Truth to Power*, in which Gore describes the issue of our changing climate and what people can do to prevent negative impacts in the future.

    A "hot" topic in the news lately has been escalating temperatures. Scientists have long been claiming that humans are causing this change and that we are moving rapidly towards the point of no return, [5] but does recent data support the notion of an escalating climate crisis? Must we change? To answer to this question, Al Gore would say, emphatically, "yes!"
    Former Vice President Al Gore is one of the most vocal proponents that climate change is real and that [10] we humans must change our ways now to preserve the earth for future generations. He has worked to combat this issue for the last decade, training others through the "Climate Reality Project," which addresses the growing threat posed by climate change. In his 2017 [15] book, *An Inconvenient Sequel* (a follow-up to *An Inconvenient Truth*, which became a major motion picture in 2008), Gore compiles recent findings that provide a compelling argument. As a result of his research, he believes that "one reason we've failed [20] to recognize the damage we're doing is that we've assumed it's fine to use our atmosphere as an open sewer."
    When Gore was in college in 1968, his professor, Roger Revell, showed him a graph of carbon dioxide [25] concentration over time, as measured at Hawaii's Mauna Loa Observatory. Then, the CO2 level was about 325 ppm (parts per million)—the pre-industrial level was only 280 ppm. When Gore's first book, *An Inconvenient Truth*, was published, the level had risen [30] to more than 382 ppm. In March of 2017, the CO2 had reached 409.5 ppm, an all-time high. According to many scientists, this is alarming, as a "safe" CO2 level for humanity is considered to be 350 ppm.
    In 2016, to study this phenomenon, scientists [35] collected data that ultimately showed a shift in summer temperatures over time. They used as a baseline summer temperature data collected between 1951 and 1980, compiled in a "normal distribution," or a frequency distribution that shows roughly the same [40] number of days on either end. In this original figure, there were roughly equal numbers of days with average temperatures. Plotting the data from subsequent years and showing these distributions alongside the baseline, the scientists found that the number of extremely [45] hot days has increased significantly—a noticeable shift towards the higher end of the temperature scale. Nowadays, extremely hot days cover 14.6 percent of the earth, whereas during the baseline period, they only covered 0.1 percent of the planet. This evidence [50] supports the view that the earth is indeed getting hotter. Compared to 30 years ago, extremely hot days are actually nearly 150 times more common than they used to be. Furthermore, NOAA has been tracking anomalies in the ocean and global land temperatures [55] between 1880 and 2016. Scientists discovered that 16 of the past 17 hottest years have occurred in the past 17 years alone, with 1998 as the sole exception. There is clearly an upward trend in temperatures: one sure way of determining that climate change is real.
    [60] In 2017, L. Cheng, K.E. Trenberth, et al, measured the change in global heat content since 1950. Their data showed exponential increases in such content. Why is this buildup of heat occurring in the oceans? Because 90 percent of all the heat energy trapped by [65] man-made global warming pollution goes into the ocean. This creates a perfect "storm" of a situation needed for major storms to occur: if the water's surface temperature is at least 80 degrees, any weather disturbance (such as a thunderstorm) allows convection [70] energy to easily be picked up and turn into Superstorm Sandy or Hurricane Harvey.
    Besides the first-order consequences of these changes, there are second-order consequences, such as disrupting the global cycle of water, which also occurs [75] as oceans continue to heat up. When the additional water vapor is added to the atmosphere, the result can be downpours that are record-breaking. When a complex system has many consequences and you change the system, all of the consequences change.
    [80] Now that our world is both wetter and warmer, storms are different. The increase of intense downpours, such as "rain bombs," is further evidence of second-order consequences. So is the increase of a variety of extreme weather events, including floods and [85] downpours like the ones experienced in Houston, TX. Because of these increases, what used to be a 500-year flood is on track to become an annual flood.
    Even the Insurance Information Institute agrees, sharing data showing increases in the number of [90] insurance claim events reported in recent years. The prediction is that extreme downpours by the end of the 21st century may increase by 400 percent. In another NOAA study, the link between fire, drought, and high temperatures was well established as yet another [95] second-order consequence. Rates of crop production,

food supplies, and diseases are all impacted due to the warmer temperatures. In summary, Gore warns, "predictions of our future can no longer be based on our past."

Average Global Temperature, 1880 to Present Day

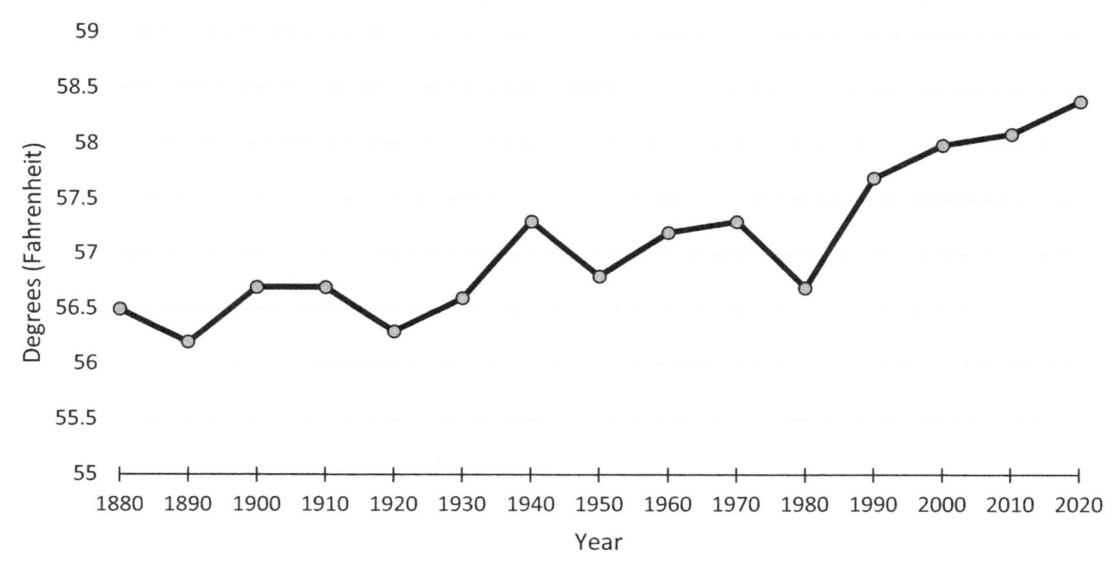

Source: NASA GISS. The above figure represents approximations.

1

The main purpose of the passage is to

A) explain a series of emerging threats and determine which of these dangers pose the greatest risks to contemporary civilization.
B) establish a consensus viewpoint on an ecological issue that has recently been open to dispute.
C) correct various misconceptions by presenting evidence from a set of authoritative sources.
D) call attention to various findings that suggest the magnitude and urgency of an environmental problem.

2

The author of the passage responds to Gore's ideas in a manner that could best be described as

A) amused.
B) ambivalent.
C) approving.
D) alarmed.

3

Which choice provides the best evidence for the answer to the previous question?

A) Lines 6-7 ("Must . . . yes!")
B) Lines 8-11 ("Former . . . generations")
C) Lines 14-18 ("In his . . . argument")
D) Lines 28-31 ("When Gore's . . . high")

4

As used in line 20, "recognize" most nearly means

A) vouch for.
B) comprehend.
C) welcome.
D) certify.

5

As used in line 32, "alarming" most nearly means

A) insulting.
B) intimidating.
C) worrying.
D) aggravating.

6

On the basis of the third paragraph (lines 23-33), it can be reasonably inferred that

A) worldwide CO2 levels can be measured most accurately in laboratory facilities in areas that are not heavily industrialized.
B) there is a direct correlation between increased temperature and increased CO2 levels.
C) the Earth's atmosphere has a maximum possible CO2 level.
D) a "safe" CO2 level once coexisted with industrial activity.

7

The passage indicates that one of the second-order consequences of global climate change is

A) a rapid and consistent increase in worldwide ocean temperatures.
B) dramatic increases in the frequency of extreme weather events.
C) increasingly disparate rain and weather patterns in seemingly similar regions.
D) dangerous flooding patterns in regions that were once arid.

8

Which choice provides the best evidence for the answer to the previous question?

A) Lines 72-75 ("Besides . . . heat up")
B) Lines 77-79 ("When . . . change")
C) Lines 81-83 ("The increase . . . consequences")
D) Lines 88-90 ("Even the . . . years")

9

The tone of Gore's quotation in the final paragraph of the passage can best described as that of

A) enthusiasm.
B) concern.
C) pessimism.
D) ambivalence.

10

According to the graph, the last time the average global temperature was lower than 57.0 degrees was approximately in

A) 1960.
B) 1970.
C) 1980.
D) 1990.

11

Which of the following information, if present in the graph, would be most useful in evaluating the ideas about global warming present in the passage?

A) The worldwide CO2 level in ppm as observed over the past 140 years
B) The devastation caused by floods and hurricanes as measured by loss of human life
C) The CO2 level in ppm as measured for a few different non-industrialized countries
D) The average worldwide ocean temperature as measured before 1950

Questions 1-11 are based on the following passages and supplementary material.

3.6
Passage 1 is adapted from a 2017 *The New Yorker* article by M. R. O'Connor, "The Strange and Gruesome Story of the Greenland Shark, the Longest Living Vertebrate on Earth." Passage 2 is adapted from a Live Science article by Mindy Weisberger titled "No, Scientists Haven't Found a 512-Year-Old Greenland Shark."

Passage 1

As far as living creatures go, age is always a factor of interest. Humans search for the coveted "fountain of youth," get botox, and attempt to do anything that allows them to appear and feel younger. Unfortunately
5   for humans, our lifespan has been increasing slightly but not enough to compete with that of non-human animals. We may live until 100 or just beyond, but certain species of tortoise and other sea creatures can live longer than 200 years. It is not always clear,
10 though, just which living animal is the oldest.
      Until recently, an Aldabra giant tortoise named Adwaita was considered to be the world's oldest living animal. It died at an estimated age of 255 years in March 2006 in Alipore Zoo, Kolkata, India. But on
15 December 14, 2017 Marine biologist Julien Nielsen discovered a Greenland shark estimated to be at least 272 years old—yet possibly over 512 years—making this specimen the oldest living vertebrate in the world. The discovery was made in the waters of the North
20 Atlantic by Danish scientist Jan Heinemeier, who at the time was completing his PhD thesis on Greenland sharks.
      Earlier this year Kim Praebel from the Arctic University of Norway, concluded that these sharks
25 could have a lifespan of up to 400 years; however, recent research has proven that the species could live to be even older. The method to determine the age of Greenland sharks was implemented just last year: a mathematical model that analyzes both the lens and
30 cornea of a shark, and links those to its body length (snout to caudal fin) to help researchers predict its age. The quantifiable data of this most recent specimen has led researchers to predict that the shark in question may have been born in 1505, predating even
35 Shakespeare.
      In the study, scientists determined the approximate ages of 28 genetically-related sharks using a radioactive dating method that analyzes carbon from their eye lenses. But determining the exact date of
40 any of these animals proved too difficult, as a result of carbon-14 levels in the ocean (which compete with those in the lens of the shark's cornea) and not knowing from where exactly the shark originated (which would help buffer out the clouding effects of
45 carbon-14 levels in the ocean). This means that the scientists have no choice but to use a wide timeline for the possible birthdate of the shark, making it probable that the organism is almost six centuries old.
      How could these animals live so long? According
50 to *The New Yorker*, the most likely explanation may be that their slow metabolisms in conjunction with the cold waters they inhabit contribute to the longevity of the species. The rate of anabolic and catabolic processes in part derives from the speed at which the
55 heart pumps blood throughout the body. Higher heart rates are correlated with lower lifespans because of the increased stressors on the organ. With each contraction the muscle walls and atrial valves wear down, just as tread on a tire erodes from increased mileage on the
60 road, eventually leading to organ failure. Animals with fast metabolisms and heart rates, such as mice, live shorter lives because their hearts need less time to fully circulate blood in their smaller bodies. And the less volume the heart needs to fill, the faster it can
65 pump. So, does this evidence make it highly probable that a currently-living shark is 500 years old? Not very likely. But is it plausible? Science says yes.

Passage 2

What is behind humanity's obsession with living forever? Do people even think about the consequences
70 of drastically increasing lifespan? Human cells evolved to be the way that they are through a slower-than-snail's-pace journey of millions of years, and although our cells do live longer than ever before, it would not be beneficial if they could live for 500 years.
75   This obsession parallels our fascination with long-living species. If other species can live for hundreds of years, naturally humans assume the same is true for them. In comes the Greenland shark, a species that has recently been in the news for its prospective 600-year
80 lifespan. When scientists tested a new method of dating these organisms, the best result they could come up with had a huge margin of error—something like three hundred years. That margin of error is longer than the lifespan the shark would have at the short end of the
85 spectrum, which is only 272 years.
      So why, if it doesn't seem plausible for the shark to be 600 years old, do newspaper articles put that age in the title? The simple answer is that news has to be sensational in order to interest readers. In the age of
90 information, there are so many news articles pumped

out into the mainstream every day that no one could possibly keep up. As a result, only the most extreme titles get "clicks," or views.

Going back to the shark experiment, what do
95 humans believe is the benefit to knowing that another species has lived over 500 years? That certainly doesn't mean that we can transpose the sharks' abilities onto our own. This creature lives at near-freezing temperatures, and in depths of up to 2,200
100 meters, causing a slowed heart rate and moving speeds. Biologists accredit this slowing of the heart to the reason that the shark can live for so long—one hypothesis is that the heart "expires" after a certain number of beats, making slowing heart rate down a
105 cause of longer lifespans. Knowing this, it doesn't seem possible that any humans would still be interested in switching lifespans with the Greenland shark.

Lifespans and Habitats of Oldest Known Species

Species	Lifespan (Yrs)	Habitat
Parrot	~80-100	Land
Tortoise	~190	Land, Water
Koi	~200	Fresh Water
Tuataras	~200	Land
Branterik Eel	~150	Fresh Water
Bonehead Whale	~245	Salt Water
Greenland Shark	~512	Salt Water
Bivalvic Mollusk	~509	Fresh Water
Aurelia Jellyfish	Infinite	Salt Water

1

According to Passage 1, in what respect does Aidwata the giant tortoise resemble the Greenland shark discovered by Julien Nielsen?

A) Neither animal has spent most of its life in captivity.
B) Neither animal's age has been calculated to an indisputable number of years.
C) Both animals were extensively studied by biologists interested in longevity.
D) Both animals have outlived the oldest living invertebrates by several decades.

2

The passage suggests that an animal with a relatively long lifespan would be most likely to have

A) a fast metabolism and a fast heart rate.
B) a fast metabolism and a slow heart rate.
C) a slow metabolism and a fast heart rate.
D) a slow metabolism and a slow heart rate.

3

Which choice provides the best evidence for the answer to the previous question?

A) Lines 45-48 ("This . . . old")
B) Lines 53-55 ("The rate . . . body")
C) Lines 55-57 ("Higher . . . organ")
D) Lines 60-63 ("Animals . . . bodies")

4

As used in line 59, "increased" most nearly means

A) burdensome.
B) further.
C) enhanced.
D) exaggerated.

5

Which of the following facts, if proven true, would NOT overturn one of the findings present in Passage 1?

A) Different ocean areas exhibit consistent amounts of carbon-14, and these amounts are too small to be statistically significant in carbon dating.
B) The world's oldest living invertebrate has been shown to have a maximum lifespan of just over 200 years.
C) There is no statistically significant relationship between the composition of a Greenland shark's cornea and the length of the shark's body.
D) The maximum margin of error in estimating the lifespan of a Greenland shark is just under 150 years.

6

As used in line 84, "short" most nearly means

A) sudden.
B) deficient.
C) conservative.
D) weak.

7

The author of Passage 2 characterizes the "benefit" (line 95) mentioned in the final paragraph of the passage as

A) enduring.
B) underestimated.
C) illusory.
D) fascinating.

8

Which choice best summarizes the relationship between the two passages?

A) Passage 2 investigates how non-specialists could respond to some of the facts presented in Passage 1.
B) Passage 2 argues that the findings celebrated in Passage 1 are ultimately insignificant.
C) Passage 2 questions the validity of an important piece of data from Passage 1.
D) Passage 2 decisively answers a series of questions that are given noncommittal answers in Passage 1.

9

Which topic, as it relates to the Greenland shark, is mentioned briefly in Passage 1 and conclusively analyzed in Passage 2?

A) The medical treatments that are being developed in order to reproduce the Greenland shark's longevity in humans
B) The historical events that overlap with the lifespan of a long-lived Greenland shark
C) The publicity that the issue of this animal's long lifespan has achieved
D) The comparison between the lifespan of the Greenland shark and the lifespans of other aquatic animal species

10

The author of Passage 2 would respond to the depiction of humans that occurs in the first paragraph of Passage 1 with

A) personal affront, but would acknowledge that the human quest for longevity has been taken to unhealthy extremes.
B) clear skepticism, but would accept the research cited throughout Passage 1 as in many ways illuminating.
C) general concurrence, but would point out that humans may not be aware of the implications of longevity.
D) vigorous disagreement, but would not question the earnestness of the opinions expressed in Passage 1.

11

Which choice indicates that table may overestimate the typical lifespan of one of the animals listed?

A) Lines 7-9 ("We may . . . 200 years")
B) Lines 86-88 ("So . . . title?")
C) Lines 98-101 ("This . . . speeds")
D) Lines 101-105 ("Biologists . . . lifespans")

Questions 1-11 are based on the following passage and supplementary material.

3.7
Adapted from a 2015 Huffington Post article titled "Here Are Tech's Big Ideas for Ending Drowsy Driving" by Joseph Erbentraut in which the author describes how and why drowsy driving needs to be addressed by the technology industry.

In October 2017, the National Highway Traffic Safety Administration released statistics on vehicle crashes from 2011 to 2015. More specifically, these statistics revealed that drowsy driving poses
5 a significant risk: out of 6,296,000 crashes, 90,000 involved drowsy driving. Furthermore, according to a CDC Morbidity and Mortality Report from 2013, a survey conducted from 2009 to 2010 indicated that 1 in 25 drivers had reported falling asleep at the
10 wheel in the prior 30 days. What this means is that drowsy driving is extremely common and extremely dangerous. Laws against it have helped in some areas, but individual detection and prevention are equally important in reducing the number of crashes involving
15 drowsy driving.

To start, many car manufacturers have been developing technologies that could alert drivers to impending collisions or abnormal driving behavior, such as drifting in the lanes. While this may help lessen
20 the number of accidents, there is certainly quite a ways to go: most of these technologies are available only in luxury or brand-new cars. Furthermore, it may be one thing for technology to detect driver or car behavior, but quite another to predict it.

25 An experiment was run at Aix-Marseilles University in France to test several factors commonly measured to determine drowsiness. The premise of the experiment was to feed independent variables about participating drivers into one of two artificial
30 neural networks (ANNs). One would determine whether the driver was drowsy, and the other would predict how soon the driver would become drowsy. The output of the ANNs would then be matched against the evaluations of video footage by two scorers.
35 However, because drowsiness occurs on a scale, the ANNs would be trained with participant information and driving time.

All 21 participants were questioned on susceptibility to motion sickness and drowsiness, age,
40 amount of sleep, driving frequency, and circadian type (essentially whether they were predisposed to prefer morning or evening). This information would then be used as participant information. Both ANNs would have access to information about driving performance,
45 physiological information, and behavioral data. Driving information—or car input—was based on 7 different factors, including position in lane and speed. For the physiological input, heart and respiration rates (and their variations) were measured. The behavioral
50 input included blink duration and frequency, percentage of eye closure, rapid eye movement between fixed points, and head rotation.

Participants were put in a driving simulator set in a room with a temperature of about 75° Fahrenheit.
55 The experiment was run just after lunch (right about the time you would want to take a nap), and lasted one hour and forty or fifty minutes. They would drive on a "highway" for about an hour and a half, during which they would encounter no traffic, except for a sudden
60 burst of 22 cars on the right of the highway. This was intended to alter the driver's drowsiness. They would then continue, turning off the highway to reach a city, and then drive through the city for about 5 minutes.

In all cases, the ANNs performed best if they
65 also had access to both driving time and participant information. Behavioral input also seemed to correlate to the top performances. Indeed, if driving time or participant information was not included, the behavioral input or combined input led to the best
70 results in the ANNs. In both detection and prediction, the car input by itself led to poor results. Ultimately, the researchers found that a comprehensive ANN can predict drowsiness around 5 minutes before it happens.

These results show that current technology
75 may be measuring some of the wrong—or simply insufficient—aspects of drowsy driving. For instance, technology that relies on lane drift or departure as indicators may not be accurately monitoring drowsiness: the driver may be distracted by a spilled
80 beverage or a rowdy child in the backseat. At best, the researchers conclude, car behavior by itself is more suited to detecting severe drowsiness, but likely would not be able to monitor it over a longer period of time. Moreover, while driving time was found to
85 be an important factor, it could never be used by itself to predict drowsiness: it would be unable to take into consideration any event that would wake up a driver.

In the future, it would be necessary to replicate this experiment before basing any new technology on
90 its findings. The participants were a fairly small group, and ranged from 20 to 27 years old. The experiment also took place in a controlled setting, so it would also be prudent to test the ANNs on people who are truly driving—perhaps not on busy streets, but maybe on a
95 closed course. The researchers themselves also suggest that, since it is difficult to measure the very things

they used for behavioral input in an actual car, there should in fact be a focus on developing models that use driving and physiological information.

Causes of Reported Drowsiness Percentage Breakdown

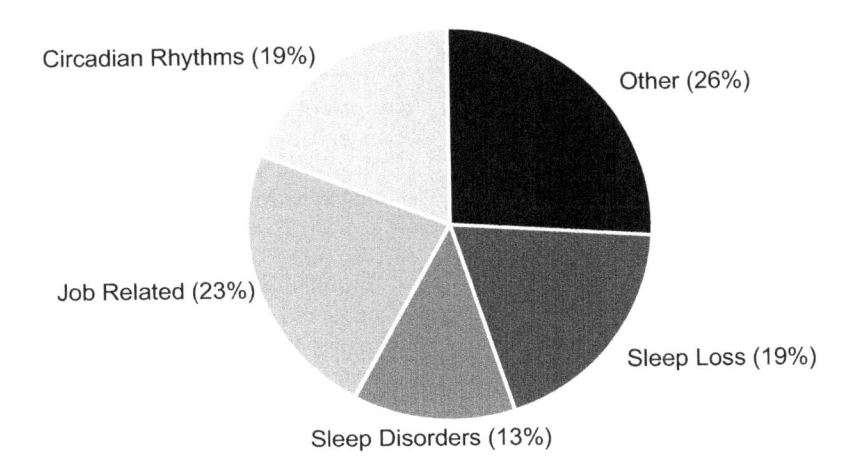

- Circadian Rhythms (19%)
- Other (26%)
- Sleep Loss (19%)
- Sleep Disorders (13%)
- Job Related (23%)

1

What is the central claim of the passage?

A) Physiological information is the best measurement with which to predict drowsy driving.
B) Car manufacturers have a responsibility to implement technology that can predict drowsy driving.
C) Preventative measures should be taken to reduce the number of accidents involving drowsy driving.
D) Technology used to prevent drowsy driving must be improved by becoming more comprehensive.

2

As presented in the passage, the researchers at Aix-Marseilles University primarily relied on which type of evidence?

A) Direct observation
B) Historical data
C) Expert testimony
D) Case studies

3

As used in line 27, "premise" most nearly means

A) purpose.
B) assumption.
C) basis.
D) method.

4

According to the results from the research, which would be the LEAST accurate predictors of drowsy driving?

A) Respiration rates and blink duration frequency
B) Rapid eye movement between fixed points and head rotation
C) Speed of vehicle and its position in lane
D) Percentage of eye closure and variations in heart rate

5

Which choice provides the best evidence for the answer to the previous question?

A) Lines 16-22 ("many car…new cars")
B) Lines 47-49 ("For the…measured")
C) Lines 57-61 ("They would…drowsiness")
D) Lines 70-71 ("In both…results")

6

As used in line 61, "alter" most nearly means

A) interrupt.
B) vary.
C) recalibrate.
D) amplify.

7

The passage indicates that current technologies aimed at preventing collisions on the road by alerting drivers may not be accurate indicators of drowsy driving because these technologies

A) are only available in high-end vehicles.
B) cannot distinguish between drowsiness and other factors that may lead to abnormal driving.
C) are created for safety but do not monitor speed.
D) use driving duration as a predictor of drowsiness.

8

Which choice provides the best evidence for the answer to the previous question?

A) Lines 21-22 ("most…cars")
B) Lines 46-48 ("Driving…speed")
C) Lines 77-80 ("technology that…backseat")
D) Lines 84-87 ("Moreover…driver")

9

The primary function of the seventh paragraph (lines 74-87) is to

A) summarize a study's findings.
B) analyze a study's results.
C) highlight the limits of a study.
D) outline a study's implications.

10

Do the data from the figure support the ideas presented in the passage?

A) Yes, because factors like sleep loss and circadian rhythms were used as participant information.
B) Yes, because 26% of drowsiness is caused by unknown factors.
C) No, because the graph indicates that physiological conditions are important factors in drowsy driving.
D) No, because the passage primarily deals with the possible predictors of drowsiness.

11

Based on the information in the figure, what was the most common predictor of drowsiness for the category with the highest percentage?

A) The percentage of eye closure and blink duration frequency
B) Other causes that led to drowsy driving that are unlisted
C) There is not enough information in the figure to yield a conclusion.
D) The duration of the drive and the vehicle's location in the lane

Questions 1-11 are based on the following passage and supplementary material.

3.8
The following passage is adapted from a 2016 *The Guardian* article by Andrew Anthony, "2006: A Space Oddity—The Great Pluto Debate," in which the author describes the rise and fall of Pluto's planetary status.

   In 2006, the International Astronomical Union (IAU) defined planets as celestial bodies that pass three tests, namely that they "are in orbit around the sun"; they have sufficient mass to assume "a nearly round shape," also called hydrostatic equilibrium; and they have "cleared the neighborhood" around their orbits. In contrast, dwarf planets pass only the first two tests.
   Because of the implementation of this definition, Pluto was suddenly demoted to dwarf status—not even a planet—in 2006, after enjoying 75 long years of planetary-status inclusion. This change has proven to be controversial: astronomers, planetary scientists, and the public alike are taking sides concerning Pluto's proper classification. What is the hard science that lies behind these events? Do scientists have an objective basis for their differences of opinion? Is the planet Pluto the victim of a shady conspiracy and personal vendetta, or merely the casualty of changes and advancements in the field? A May 2016 article published in *The Guardian* attempts to unravel the details of the possibly shady demotion of the ninth planet, which was discovered in 1930 by astronomer Clyde Tombaugh.
   After Tombaugh discovered Pluto, another astronomer named Brian Marsden reportedly set out to discredit him. According to the article, a planetary scientist named Stern reports that after Tombaugh died in 1997, "Marsden went on a jihad to diminish his reputation by removing Pluto from the list of planets." Marsden apparently found his opportunity at the 2006 meeting of the IAU in Prague, in which attendees agreed to have a vote to demote Pluto. Interestingly, the vote that determined Pluto's fate consisted of only 4% of the total attendance or about 400 members. Stern criticized the vote, saying that astronomers do not have the specialized scientific knowledge that planetary scientists have: "just as you shouldn't go to a podiatrist for brain surgery, you shouldn't go to an astronomer for expert advice on planetary science."
   Claiming their objectiveness, members of the IAU maintain that when they voted, they used three tests that evolved over years of committee discussions leading up to the 2006 vote. Of the tests it had to pass, Pluto failed the requirement that it "clear the neighborhood around its orbit," meaning that when a planet forms, it must achieve what is known as gravitational dominance, with no other bodies of similar size under its gravitational influence except for its satellites.
   Stern objects to the process and criteria used to demote Pluto at the IAU meeting. "Science isn't about voting," he says. "We don't vote on the theory of relativity. We don't vote on evolution. The image of scientists voting gives the public the impression that science is arbitrary." His objection to the third test is shared by Dr. Gerald van Belle, an astronomer who attended the IAU voting session. Of a planet clearing the neighborhood around its orbit, van Belle says, "I have yet to encounter a succinct mathematical definition of this concept." Van Belle calls the third test an "ill-defined, dynamic argument." Stern argues that Neptune does not even pass the third test and should also be demoted if this were the standard used to define all planetary objects.
   Meanwhile, other astronomers like Brown, a professor of planetary astronomy at CalTech, see things much differently. "Pluto," according to Brown, "is essentially this insignificant chunk of ice that really is of no consequence in the solar system." In this way, whether Pluto had passed the three tests or not, it would never be worthy in his eyes of planetary status. Brown is unapologetic in his stance, and has written a memoir entitled, "How I Killed Pluto, and How It Had It Coming."
   Both Brown and Stern accuse each other of personal involvement, holding less than scientifically defensible positions. Each argues that the other is being nostalgic for a simpler time. Stern compares planets to other geographical elements like rivers and mountains, saying we don't limit their number. Brown counters with the argument that we expect the number of planets to be "smallish." Meanwhile, van Belle offers the alternative criteria of hydrostatic equilibrium, that is, "big enough to be a ball," as sufficient to determine Pluto's status.
   In a 2008 press release published by the Planetary Science Institute based in Tucson, Arizona, scientists agreed to disagree. "We all have a conceptual image of a planet. Therefore, we need a term that encompasses all objects that orbit the Sun or other stars." Larry Lebofsky, who works there as Senior Education Specialist, thinks of this as a teachable moment for all scientists who wish to maintain objectivity in their respective fields. For the foreseeable future, everyone, including the scientists, has something to learn.

Planetary Objects and Their Statuses

Object Name	Size (Diameter)	Status
HR 2562b	30 X Jupiter	Exoplanet
Kepler-22b	2.5 X Earth	Exoplanet
Kepler-452b	1.5 X Earth	Dwarf
Ceres	591.8 mi	Dwarf
Pluto	1430 mi	Dwarf
Eris	1445 mi	Dwarf
Haumea	892.3 mi	Dwarf
Makemake	882 mi	Dwarf
Moon (Earth's)	1079 mi	Moon
Jupiter	43,441 mi	Planet
Earth	3959 mi	Planet

1

The main purpose of the passage is to

A) define a term central to the field of astronomy and use it to back up one individual's claim about a planet.
B) introduce a debate about a prominent topic in astronomy and detail the positions of several experts.
C) describe a long-standing argument between two scientists and the negative impact it has on their field.
D) come to a consensus about the proper definition of a term and reconcile diverging opinions on the matter.

2

Based on the passage, what question were all individuals described in the passage attempting to answer?

A) How can Pluto's orbit best be objectively defined?
B) What can change about Pluto to make it a planet?
C) Does Pluto fit the current definition of a planet?
D) Which criteria does Pluto have to fit to be a planet?

3

The primary purpose of lines 2-6 ("are in...neighborhood") is to

A) detail changes to a term that was initially defined in 1930.
B) provide a definition that is later debated among several specialists in the field of planetary science.
C) offer a new, objective description of an issue that has been aggressively argued for centuries.
D) outline an answer to a question that many astronomers have tried and failed to determine previously.

4

It can be reasonably inferred from the passage that which individual would agree with the IAU's definition of a planet?

A) Clyde Tombough
B) Brian Marsden
C) Gerald van Belle
D) Larry Lebofsky

5

The inclusion of the words "hard science" (line 14) and "objective basis" (line 16) have what effect on the tone of the second paragraph (lines 8-23)?

A) They interject a tone of skepticism towards the way that planetary scientists are addressing the issue of Pluto's status.
B) They bolster the objective stance taken by all parties within the passage regarding the primary definition of planets.
C) They bring clarity to an otherwise confusing topic that may be nearly impossible for many readers to understand.
D) They describe the issue of planetary classification in language that is particular to the topic.

6

Which of the following situations most closely reflects the idea of "gravitational dominance" (line 47) as described in the passage?

A) A celestial body has several much larger bodies of mass within its orbit.
B) An asteroid is in orbit with two other celestial bodies of twice its mass.
C) A celestial body has an orbit that contains no other bodies of any size.
D) An asteroid and several smaller satellites leave their orbit permanently.

7

As used in line 55, "arbitrary" most nearly means

A) subjective.
B) whimsical.
C) unnecessary.
D) undemocratic.

8

The difference between Marsden's and Brown's view of Pluto is that

A) Marsden believes that Pluto should be a planet while Brown believes that it should not.
B) Marsden and Brown both believe that Pluto's planetary status is beside the point.
C) Marsden believes that Pluto should not be a planet while Brown believes Pluto's status does not matter.
D) Marsden and Brown both believe that Pluto should not be a planet for different reasons.

9

As used in line 84, "sufficient" most nearly means

A) extra criteria.
B) fitting description.
C) enough data.
D) adequate evidence.

10

Based on both the passage and the figure, which view of Pluto's status is correct?

A) It should be viewed as a planet because it accurately fits the IAU's definition of one.
B) It should not be viewed as a planet because it does not achieve gravitational dominance.
C) There is not enough information to come to a consensus that all parties would agree on.
D) Its planetary status should no longer matter because of other, more important issues.

11

How many planetary objects in the figure are bigger than Earth in size?

A) 2
B) 3
C) 4
D) There is not enough information to determine the answer.

Questions 1-11 are based on the following passage.

3.9

The following passage was written with consent from Aimee Richardson, based on her unpublished research about website usability. In her research, she attempts to discern the best way to provide to users viable, trustworthy information on the website www.MyDoctorOnline.com.

When someone is newly diagnosed as prediabetic or diabetic, he or she are often at a loss about how to proceed. Such a diagnosis can be daunting, overwhelming, and confusing. Patients may have a variety of thoughts, feelings, and emotions, due in part to the plethora of seemingly contradictory advice they receive. How can they control this baffling illness so that it does not get any worse? What aspects of their current lifestyle can they change to improve their health? How effective are medical websites in providing patients with accurate and helpful information?

In an unpublished study, user experience researcher Aimee Richardson sought to discover how well the diabetes section of a medical website, www.MyDoctorOnline.com, supported the needs of those who are diagnosed as pre-diabetic. Her research sought to identify gaps in the website's ability to fulfill patient needs, exploring both specific content and site organization.

Subjects in the study had varied needs: some were younger, diagnosed years ago, and had developed strategies to keep their illness under control; others were older, newly diagnosed, and were overwhelmed by all the potential changes they'd need to make. Richardson sought to understand how one website might meet the needs of these different patients.

To test the effectiveness of the website, Richardson conducted her research using 3 different methodologies with five subjects: in-person interviews; a task-based usability study using the "think-aloud" protocol; and a desirability list (adjective test). In addition to these three methods, overall website satisfaction ratings on a 0-10 scale were collected.

Traditionally, in-person interviews are chosen as a research method when the aim is to obtain a sense of a person's goals, behaviors, needs, and mindset. Task-based studies seek to uncover issues that are functional in nature, and assess the value of information to the patient. Adjective tests are often used in conjunction with quantitative data and are often preferred because they can elicit candid, revealing patient responses.

Task-based studies were either open-ended and exploratory, meaning the respondent can choose any answer (not limited to a few options), or close-ended, meaning the respondent was prompted to choose an answer from a set list (i.e. "yes or no" or a scale of 1–10). The tasks were presented in such a way as not to "lead" the subject to give an answer that would be desirable for the findings the researcher aims to get. Moderators qualitatively gauged how much assistance subjects needed to complete each task. In one open-ended task, users were prompted to "explore the pre-diabetes website," during which they were asked to walk the moderator through their thought process. One of the close-ended tasks instructed subjects to look at the tools section of the site, and were told, "Let's say you wanted to walk more. How would you do this?" Related measures included *Time on Task* and *Number of Errors*, two typical measurements in any test that quantify data from the participant and make their data easily comparable to those of others.

The adjective test, or desirability list, that Richardson used was based on one created by Microsoft in 2002. In Microsoft's version, 120 different adjectives comprising a controlled vocabulary are presented to the subject after using the site, to gauge its aesthetic appeal. Users are asked to select the five adjectives that best describe the site. To counteract the positive bias that subjects typically display, 2/3 of the presented adjectives were negative, while the remaining 1/3 were positive. Examples of adjectives used in the Microsoft test include empowering, approachable, and disconnected. Richardson's modified version consisted of 15 adjectives, nine of which were negative and six of which were positive.

Richardson's findings suggested that the pre-diabetes section of the MyDoctorOnline.com website could be significantly improved by providing the exact content that patients were looking for. The website satisfaction rating of 6.5 out of 10 suggests that there is room for improvement. Regarding the use of the exercise tracking tool on the website, patients did not see any value in using it to graph their progress. On balance, patients indicated that the site was helpful and easy to use.

"Patients want to know what they can do right now to make a difference with small, actionable steps." They expected the website to provide motivation and support, offering realistic testimonials from other patients, and tips and strategies that other patients had used successfully. They asked for the option to connect with each other online through the website. "I'm not into groups, but I like hearing others' stories," said one subject. Patients suggested that the organization of content on the website could be improved, so they can find the information they are looking for quickly. Users had a great desire to know more (6.2 out of 7 points). Most patients did not understand that the most important change they could make was to lose weight: some thought exercise was most important, while others thought it was their diet.

Ultimately, the study's findings imply that medical websites such as MyDoctorOnline.com can be useful, so long as website owners conduct appropriate user experience research to identify and meet their patients' specific, varied needs. In order for these sites to be most beneficial, studies like Richardson's should be part of a preliminary process, incorporating users' advice and expectations into the final design of the site.

1

The main purpose of the passage is to

A) introduce a website that has the ability to be transformative in all areas of health and medicine.
B) detail important changes that should be made in the way diabetes is diagnosed and treated.
C) provide the results of a meta-analysis of several studies conducted on the same medical website.
D) describe a website that falls short and how it could be more effective in aiding a population.

2

The series of questions at the end of the first paragraph primarily has which effect?

A) To prompt the reader to evaluate the efficacy of a study
B) To propose several ways to look at a recent diagnosis
C) To reinforce a previously mentioned notion
D) To prepare the reader for the shortcomings of a hypothesis.

3

As used in line 18, "gaps" most nearly means

A) orifices.
B) drawbacks.
C) lapses.
D) vacuities.

4

The author believes which of the following to be the reason that users experience difficulties using www.MyDoctorOnline.com?

A) The study has not been published and therefore is inaccessible to patients.
B) The needs of patients are varied and therefore difficult to address at the same time.
C) The methodology of the study is extensive and therefore not relevant to everyone.
D) The website has not been able to reach patients due to a lack of advertising.

5

Which choice provides the best evidence for the answer to the previous question?

A) Lines 13-17 ("In an...pre-diabetic")
B) Lines 17-20 ("Her research.. organization")
C) Lines 21-25 ("Subjects in...make")
D) Lines 28-30 ("To test...interviews")

6

Which choice represents an implementation that Richardson used to ensure that the task-based studies would not "lead" (line 49) the subjects to respond in a manner desirable for the researcher?

A) She varied the moderators to ensure that the subjects would answer without bias.
B) She conducted in-person interviews with each person in order to better understand the subjects.
C) She employed multiple methods of data collection to vary the assessment of the subjects relative to their task.
D) She asked questions that she knew the subjects would enjoy responding to so that they would remain engaged.

7

As used in line 56, the phrase "close-ended questions" suggests that

A) the respondents can choose any answer they like.
B) the respondents are instructed to only answer yes or no.
C) the respondents are limited by preselected answer choices.
D) the respondents cannot answer these questions at all.

8

Based on the information in the passage, which choice best represents a closed-end task?

A) When asked how he feels about his math teacher, a student responds with the first idea that comes to mind.
B) After eating a sandwich, several participants agree on three words that best define their eating experience.
C) In an effort to obtain the most accurate ratings, a website expands its pre-chosen list from 5 items to 10.
D) Because it can be difficult for participants to think up answers on the spot, a test implements pre-selected answer choices.

9

If all of the following options present accepted definitions, which option most closely matches the design used by Richardson to conduct her experiment?

A) A case study design, which is conducted using a few subjects and evaluates them using a few different methods of assessment.
B) An experimental design, which tests a control versus an experimental variable and holds all other variables constant.
C) A correlational design, which compares the likelihood of occurrence of two variables but ignores causes.
D) A naturalistic design, in which a researcher attempts to observe people in their natural habitats without disturbing them.

10

Which change to the website is most similar to one recommended by the participants in the study?

A) Optimization of the site's usability by moving the most desirable tools to the top of the front page
B) Implementation of new tools on the site that have been requested by participants during the study
C) Adding more exercise graphs that will help to better track user's progress over longer periods of time
D) Changing the content of the adjective test so that it has more visual appeal and positive answer choices

11

Which of the following provides the best evidence for the answer to the previous question

A) Lines 63-72 ("The adjective...positive.")
B) Lines 77-80 ("Richerdson's...for.")
C) Lines 82-84 ("Regarding...progress.")
D) Lines 95-97 ("Patients... quickly.")

Questions 1-10 are based on the following passage and supplementary material.

3.10
Adapted from "High Status Males Invest More than High Status Females in Lower Status Same-sex Collaborators," a 2017 article from the Public Library of Science in which authors Henry Markovits, Evelyne Gauthier, Emilie Gagnon-St-Pierre, and Joyce Benenson describe the difference in sharing behaviors between the sexes.

One of the least favorable utterances for a child to hear is "you have to share." But what of adults? Do humans carry the reluctance to share beyond adolescence? And if so, how does that manifest itself when what's being shared isn't just a toy? Researchers at the University of Reading, United Kingdom, set out to answer these questions in a study published in PLOS ONE in 2017. Based on primate studies of the same nature, the team hypothesized that humans would be more likely to share a monetary reward with others who performed well if they were of a higher status than the "sharee," or person receiving the a portion of the "sharer's" reward. This has implications for careers: the first is that if you help your superior receive bonuses, he or she is likely to share them with you because you are perceived as competent. The second is that you are likely not expected to share your rewards in return because of your subordinate status.

The researchers utilized 44 male and 44 female Canadian undergraduate students, splitting them randomly into arbitrary high or low status positions. They were then broken up into three fictional collaborating groups: their coworker is either of higher, lower, or equal status. Furthermore, the fictional coworker always was assigned as being equally or more competent than the participant. In the first study, the reward was hypothetical, meaning the participant did not have any tangible money to share with the partner and received no actual reward for the job performed. At the end of the study, the team found that participants shared more money with the more competent, lower-status individuals; this means that monetary reward increased as a function of competence and status.

In a subsequent study, designed using real monetary rewards, the researchers sought to further their hypothesis by including claims regarding the difference between male and female sharing behavior. They believed that males would share more than females would, regardless of the sex of the partner. The experiment was set up the same as the first one, except that tangible money was used as an incentive. As expected, an interaction between sex and status was found, meaning that while the results mimicked study one (participants shared more with high-competence, low-status partners), males shared significantly more than females. Furthermore, there was an interaction between status and competence level, meaning that when participants were assigned to a higher status (furthering the status divide between the participant and his/her partner) they shared more, but when the competence level of the partner was low, this generous sharing behavior disappeared.

There are clear-cut real world implications here. When performing a job, often we cannot obtain a result on our own—for example, if a person writes a book, it is likely that he/she will need help editing the final product. Naturally, if a person provides assistance, that person will expect a reward. But prior to this study, it would not be understood what mechanisms underlie the sharing behavior, therefore giving no explanation as to why competent partners may sometimes be more highly rewarded than at other times. Now, based on the findings from the study, we can better understand how to collaborate for maximum productivity and therefore maximum reward.

As for why males share more than females, the researchers had a few hypotheses. First, males form large, stable groups of peers whom they largely view as equals, regardless of rank. In female-centric groups, the interactions are usually in unrelated, equally-ranked dyads (or two-person groups). Because of this, males see lower-status peers in a more positive light, and therefore are more likely to want them to succeed. Females, on the other hand, view rank as a competition and prefer to maintain their higher status, therefore wanting to keep lower-ranked peers below them. Furthermore, males are more inclined to behave in such a nature as to keep a group intact, whereas females, who were not part of a large group to begin with, have no such motivators.

In the future, it would be beneficial to expand beyond using just college students as participants, incorporating people who are already in the job sector. This could eliminate some of the hypothetical nature of the task, as it has been shown many times in the past that people have a tendency to report beliefs about themselves that are contradictory to their actions in a non-hypothetical situation.

Figure 1

Sharing Behavior of Men as a Factor of Both Status and Competence of Their Partners

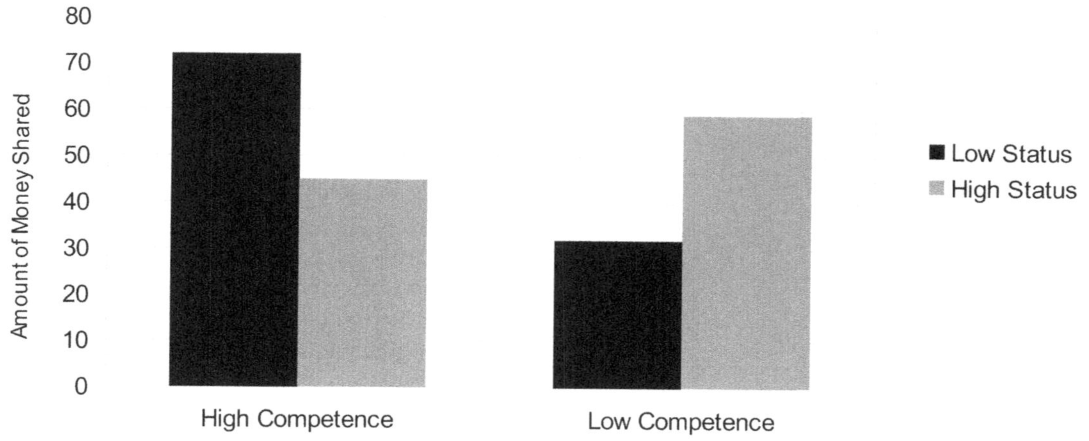
80
70
60
50
40
30
20
10
0
Amount of Money Shared
High Competence
Low Competence
Low Status
High Status

Figure 2

Sharing Behavior of Women as a Factor of Both Status and Competence of Their Partners

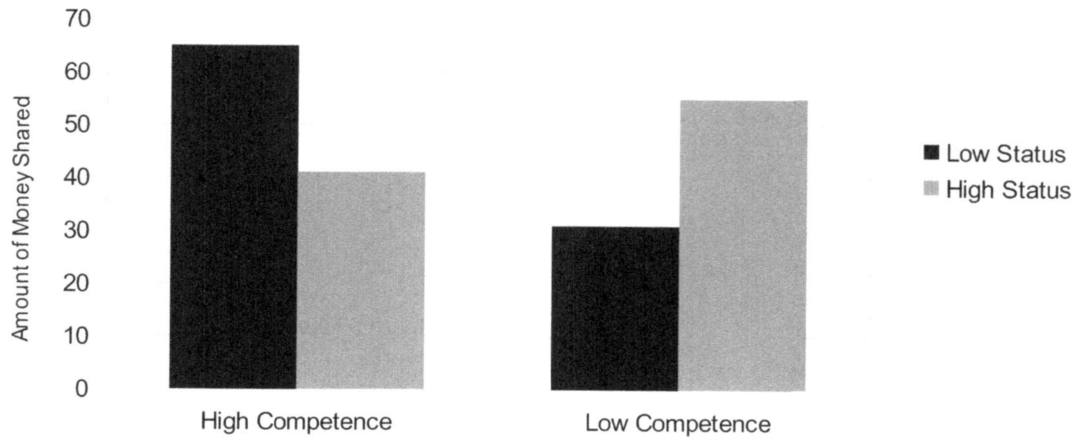
70
60
50
40
30
20
10
0
Amount of Money Shared
High Competence
Low Competence
Low Status
High Status

1

Over the course of the passage, the main focus shifts from a description of a hypothesis to

A) an application of the hypothesis to real life situations.
B) the details of a study's findings that expand on the hypothesis.
C) a comparison of two studies that test the hypothesis.
D) an explanation of the factors that substantiate the hypothesis.

2

As used in line 11, "status" most nearly means

A) stature.
B) worth.
C) condition.
D) regard.

3

Based on the results of the first study, in which situation would an individual be most likely to share?

A) A manager is nominated for a promotion by her subordinates after demonstrating her excellent leadership abilities on a project.
B) A CEO gives a generous year-end bonus to an employee who had consistently been a productive and hardworking team member.
C) A female prospective employee is offered a job at a prestigious tech company as part of an initiative to diversify the STEM industry.
D) A group of entrepreneurs splits profits equally among themselves after successfully opening and sustaining a new business venture.

4

Which choice provides the best evidence for the answer to the previous question?

A) Lines 16-18 ("The second...status")
B) Lines 24-26 ("Furthermore, the...participant")
C) Lines 30-32 ("At the...individuals")
D) Lines 36-38 ("the researchers...behavior")

5

As used in line 33, "as a function of" most nearly means

A) proportional to.
B) immediately following.
C) regardless of.
D) in addition to.

6

According to the author, the findings from the second study differed from those of the first study in what way?

A) While both studies examined sharing behavior, only the second study used real money as an incentive.
B) While competence and status were always factors in sharing behavior, the second study revealed a relationship between sex and sharing.
C) While both studies assigned competence levels to their participants, only the second study designated the sharee as less competent.
D) While participants always shared with high-competence partners, the second study showed that status also impacted sharing.

7

The author implies that males are more willing to share primarily because

A) males are more likely to have a higher status, while females are not.
B) males are more practical, while females are more selfish.
C) males are more group-oriented, while females are more competitive.
D) males are more trusting, while females are more suspicious of others' intentions.

8

Which choice provides the best evidence that the results of the experiments might not play out the same way in the real world?

A) Lines 51-53 ("but when...disappeared")
B) Lines 54-56 ("There are...own")
C) Lines 82-84 ("In the...sector")
D) Lines 87-89 ("people have...situation")

9

In figure 1, which combination of factors resulted in the smallest monetary reward shared?

A) High competence and low status
B) High competence and high status
C) Low competence and low status
D) Low competence and high status

10

In figure 2, which combination of factors resulted in the largest monetary reward shared?

A) High competence and low status
B) High competence and high status
C) Low competence and low status
D) Low competence and high status

STOP

Answer Key: CHAPTER THREE

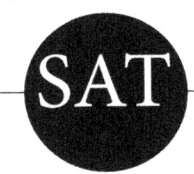

SAT

3.01	3.02	3.03	3.04	3.05
1. C	1. C	1. D	1. B	1. D
2. C	2. D	2. D	2. C	2. C
3. A	3. C	3. D	3. A	3. C
4. D	4. C	4. B	4. B	4. B
5. B	5. B	5. B	5. B	5. C
6. A	6. B	6. B	6. C	6. D
7. C	7. D	7. D	7. B	7. B
8. C	8. C	8. A	8. D	8. D
9. B	9. B	9. A	9. A	9. B
10. B	10. C	10. B	10. C	10. C
11. C	11. A	11. C		11. A

3.06	3.07	3.08	3.09	3.10
1. B	1. D	1. B	1. D	1. B
2. D	2. A	2. D	2. C	2. A
3. D	3. C	3. B	3. B	3. B
4. B	4. C	4. B	4. B	4. C
5. B	5. D	5. A	5. C	5. A
6. C	6. A	6. C	6. C	6. B
7. C	7. B	7. A	7. C	7. C
8. A	8. C	8. D	8. D	8. D
9. C	9. B	9. D	9. A	9. C
10. C	10. D	10. C	10. A	10. A
11. B	11. C	11. C	11. D	

Answer Explanations
Chapter Three

Chapter 3.1 | Chronic Bronchitis

1) CORRECT ANSWER: C
In the first three paragraphs, the author defines or explains terms such as bronchitis (line 7), particulate matter (line 12), and COPD (line 21), and also explains two variations of chronic bronchitis (lines 35-37). This content supports C and, as important material in a scientific and technical discussion, indicates that A ("approachable") is a problematic choice. B is contradicted by the absence of explanations or feedback other than the author's own, while D is problematic because the discussion is mostly informative and does NOT contain any clear negatives from other perspectives that would count as "misconceptions."

2) CORRECT ANSWER: C
The word "favorite" is used to refer to "Air pollution" (line 1), which is discussed by those who have environmental or global warming-related concerns; thus, these people would be preoccupied with "Air pollution" as an important threat. C is appropriate, while A and B introduce positives inappropriate to a dangerous force and a factor that causes concern. D (indulging or enabling) introduces a context appropriate to a person but NOT to an environmental threat.

3) CORRECT ANSWER: A
In lines 69-73, the author indicates that the study described throughout the passage is the "largest" research project of its type to investigate certain factors. A properly calls attention to the impressive scope of the study, while B OVERSTATES the actual content of the passage by indicating that the study is comprehensive (or explains everything) as opposed to rigorous and important. C (response to a single policy, NOT to be mistaken for the passage's emphasis on broad public health implications) and D (bringing together other inquiries, NOT to be mistaken for the passages emphasis on the consequential nature of the research) similarly distort some actual content from the passage.

4) CORRECT ANSWER: D
See above for analysis of the correct line reference. A indicates a lack of data but does NOT clearly reference the notable traits of the study that interests the author, B explains how data was gathered using a questionnaire, and C explains that there was NOT a correlation between bronchitis and air pollution by one experimental measure. Make sure not to wrongly assume that B, which references a standardized method, is evidence for Question 3 B, which references a more absolute "comprehensive" method.

5) CORRECT ANSWER: B
The word "cohort" is used to describe "50,000 U.S. women" (line 38) who make up a group that has been subjected to experimental study. Since these women are only those selected for the experiment and thus would not be ALL of the women in the United States, a usage indicating selection or sampling is appropriate. Choose B and eliminate A, C, and D as words that wrongly indicate that the women are COOPERATING for some set purpose, not that they were simply selected for study.

6) CORRECT ANSWER: A
In lines 58-60, the author notes that there is NOT a link between chronic bronchitis and air pollution, which the author links to small particulate matter in context (lines 63-66). This content supports A, while the same paragraph (lines 52-68) indicates that chronic bronchitis IS correlated with the factors named in false answers B, C, and D.

7) CORRECT ANSWER: C
See above for analysis of the correct line reference. A indicates the specific factors considered in an experiment but does NOT decisively indicate which ones do or do not correlate with chronic bronchitis. B notes the prevalence of chronic bronchitis but does not indicate which influences are or are not responsible, while D presents factors that both accompany one another and CAN indicate that chronic bronchitis has arisen.

8) CORRECT ANSWER: C
In lines 39-42, the author explains the criteria (cough, phlegm, and a three months per year for two consecutive years incidence) that indicate chronic bronchitis. C involves the necessary physical symptoms and meets both the month and the year criteria. A does not meet the two-year requirement, B does not meet the three-month requirement, and D does not meet the requirement that cough and phlegm must be simultaneously present, NOT alternating.

9) CORRECT ANSWER: B
The author uses the phrase "statistically robust" to describe findings in which one factor was "significantly associated" (line 76) with others or offered a clear relationship. B properly indicates that the findings are clear and valid, while A wrongly introduces a negative tone that assumes an earlier sense of conflict in the discussion. C and D both focus on later steps or developments, NOT on the author's actual issue of the validity of completed research.

10) CORRECT ANSWER: B
B is the only answer choice to reference "small particulate matter" when the chart only features data relating to large particulate matter. A, C, and D all address the chart's predominant trend regarding "large particulate matter."

11) CORRECT ANSWER: C
The chart relates exposure to large particulate matter to incidence of chronic bronchitis, and indicates that higher ppm exposure increases the percent of incidents in a sample of test subjects. C properly reflects the quantities being assessed and their overall relationship, while A draws a cause-and-effect relationship that would require assessment of factors OTHER than large particulate matter. B (symptoms) and D (small particulate matter) both consider factors mentioned in the passage but NOT in the chart.

Chapter 3.2 | Bioluminescence

1) CORRECT ANSWER: C
The passage begins with an overview of the phenomenon of bioluminescence (a subject that interests researchers), then presents several different research inquires tied to "The way bioluminescence is used by squid" (line 36). This content supports C and can be used to eliminate A and B, since these answers do not properly indicate the passage's eventual focus on a SINGLE animal species and relevant bacteria. D is a distortion of the actual aim of the passage, which is to present findings relevant to bioluminescence mechanisms, NOT to work with the fundamentally different biological issue of symbiosis.

2) CORRECT ANSWER: D
The first paragraph ends with a listing of the "purposes" (line 18) of bioluminescence, a topic that is continued with references to specific

species in lines 21-35 and with references to squid in the remainder of the passage. Choose D to reflect this content and eliminate C, since the advantages of bioluminescence are presented as varied while "drawbacks" are never considered. A ("point of reference") and B ("standard definition") both appear to be misreadings of the content linked to Charles Darwin, which presents an anecdote relevant to bioluminescence but NOT ideas that explicitly guide later research inquiries.

3) CORRECT ANSWER: C
In lines 31-35, the author explains that some fish have developed ways to keep recently-eaten bioluminescent prey from alerting predators—namely, other creatures that would then eat the fish. This idea of consuming prey without incurring further danger supports C. A and B may result from misreadings of lines 21-31, since these lines consider the role of bioluminescence in eliminating threats but not the subsequent adaptive RESPONSES of predators. D is a misreading of the mechanism explained in lines 31-35, since the fish that eat bioluminescent prey keep the prey from being seen but do not do so by emitting a new substance.

4) CORRECT ANSWER: C
See above for analysis of the correct line reference. A indicates that sea-fireflies can use bioluminescence to confuse predators, B indicates that railroad worms can use bioluminescence in a defensive manner, and D indicates that squid can use bioluminescence to repel danger. These answers all consider the role of bioluminescence among bioluminescent organisms THEMSELVES rather than considering in detail how non-bioluminescent organisms respond and should be eliminated for this reason.

5) CORRECT ANSWER: B
Nyholm is mentioned in the context of two separate research studies (line 51 and lines 67-68), a fact that directly supports B. Choose this answer and eliminate A as a misreading of the purpose of the second study (which was to trace a bacterium gene, NOT to determine the existence of bacteria). C is a misreading of the discussion of Galperin's work in lines 73-83, which is explained after the discussions of Nyholm's work but is never designated as being directly influenced by Nyholm, despite the placement of this content in the passage. D is a misreading of information from the first of Nyholm's studies, an inquiry which did deal with the concept of "counter-illumination concealment" but is never clearly depicted as providing a definition of this concept.

6) CORRECT ANSWER: B
The word "released" refers to "energy" (line 60) which takes on specific forms as the result of a reaction and is released in a form of this sort. Energy could be produced or generated by a reaction, so that B is appropriate. A is wrongly negative (and indicates that something is left out), C refers to a human activity (NOT to energy), and D refers to a context of freedom that is inappropriate to the passage.

7) CORRECT ANSWER: D
The word "adhesive" is used in the context of a situation in which bacteria "attach" (line 81) to a squid. D raises the proper context of physical connection, while A best describes a liquid that becomes solid and B and C are positive value judgments, NOT neutral descriptions of a physical process.

8) CORRECT ANSWER: C
In lines 73-75, the author indicates that the bacteria described in the passage (which coexist with the squid being studied) produce light using a specific enzyme. This content thus traces light to the bacteria, NOT to the squid themselves without the bacteria, so that C is appropriate. A and B describe light production in general terms (not organisms, as required by the prompt), while D explains the bioluminescence observed in the experiment but does NOT clearly trace it to the bacteria as opposed to the squid.

9) CORRECT ANSWER: B
The authors use the relevant words to describe how the squid have developed to use bioluminescent bacteria for defensive purposes (a context indicated by lines 84-87), so that B is an appropriate choice. Eliminate A, because the relevant paragraph directly states that the squid are NOT conscious of how their survival mechanism arose. C raises a benefit (rapid development) that the largely positive final paragraph does not directly discuss, while D misconstrues the benefits that the bacteria impart to the squid as benefits that bacteria use for their OWN purposes.

10) CORRECT ANSWER: C
The table indicates that more than 700 types of fungi exhibit bioluminescence, so that C (which indicates that more than 2000 types of fungi could be part of this group) is an appropriate answer since the number of fungi does NOT have a defined upper limit. A directly contradicts the table's information on anglerfish, B directly contradicts the table's information that MORE THAN 70 squid ecotypes exhibit

bioluminescence, and D is contradicted by the table's similar "Primary Use" information for the lanternfish and the firefly.

11) CORRECT ANSWER: A
In lines 14-35, the authors of the passage call attention to defensive- and sustenance-based uses of bioluminescence such as confusing predators (eliminating B), camouflage (eliminating C), and attraction (eliminating D). Only mating is not mentioned, though this use is considered for the firefly and the lanternfish in the table; thus, A is the best answer.

Chapter 3.3 | School Start Times

1) CORRECT ANSWER: D
While the author argues that there are benefits for "later class start times" (lines 56-57), the author also concludes the passage by emphasizing that new or modified research should be undertaken "in the future." This content directly supports D, while A misstates the author's point that the research was confined to Singapore so far to wrongly indicate that the research CANNOT extend to the United States. B misstates the purpose of the passage (to outline a study and explain its importance, NOT to trace the effect of past studies in start times), while C neglects the topic of school start times altogether.

2) CORRECT ANSWER: D
The word "implications" refers to the impact of the "life-changing" effects that changing school start time could have. B ("decisions") is incorrect because it refers to the choice itself to change school start times rather than the effects of said choice. A ("consequences") merely refers to the effect of changing the school start time without considering how much of an impact it would have. C ("repercussions") has a negative connotation as it refers to an effect that is unintended and unwelcome. D ("significance") is correct because it speaks to the impact and gravity of the decision to change school start times.

3) CORRECT ANSWER: D
In lines 37-39, the author indicates that school times correlate with "levels of melatonin" for relatively large numbers of students; this information assumes consistent melatonin activity across students, as D properly indicates. A and C both refer to apparent outcomes of the study, not to PREMISES, while B wrongly indicates that one factor behind school start times is the MAIN factor, a point that is never in fact argued by the author.

4) CORRECT ANSWER: B
See above for analysis of the correct line reference. A indicates the difficulty of changing cultural norms but should NOT be taken as evidence for Question 3 B, which overstates the role of cultural norms by characterizing them as the "primary" factor in determining school start times. C calls attention to the broad implications of the study but does not provide specifics that would align with an answer to the previous question; D calls attention to an implication of the study, not a premise.

5) CORRECT ANSWER: B
The word "measured" refers to various effects that were linked to "adjusted start times" by researchers; these researchers gathered data from children, or observed the children after the start times had been adjusted. B is the best choice, while A and C both wrongly indicate that the researchers were judging or ranking the children (not gathering data). D calls attention to the act of thinking or rumination, not to gathering information as an active part of an experiment.

6) CORRECT ANSWER: B
In lines 57-61, the author notes that the researchers described in the passage determined a connection between circadian rhythms, recommended sleep hours, and well-being. This information directly supports B, while A mistakes the study's interest in well-being for a focus on the very different benefit of academic performance. C mistakes the emphasis on school start times for an emphasis on wake-up times and provides a more definitive recommended time than the passage in fact does; D references a premise of the study, NOT an idea confirmed by the outcomes of the study.

7) CORRECT ANSWER: D
The relevant lines explain that a perceived benefit (increased sleep time) decreased "10 months" after an experiment that enabled the benefit was begun; D similarly indicates a benefit that, though not reversed, diminishes over time. A and C both indicate improvement at a LATER stage, not a diminishing benefit. B describes a possible benefit that becomes "negligible," not a benefit that is clear though still strongly diminished, and thus does not provide an appropriately analogous situation.

8) CORRECT ANSWER: A
In lines 68-70, the author explains that the students considered in the study had "an earlier start-time than kids in the US have." This difference in timing indicates that the study of the student in Singapore may not be fully applicable to a scenario with clearly different timing; choose A as

appropriate. B refers to the amount of sleep attributed to the participants, NOT to the question of other countries. C (which does mention "other countries") and D provide suggestions for extending the research but do NOT note that the research may be inapplicable to specific situations as required by the prompt.

9) CORRECT ANSWER: A
The graphs indicate that pushing back the school start time caused the "More than 8 Hours" category to increase from 5% to 24%; this increase of 19 percentage points for a positive factor makes A an appropriate answer. The negative "Irritable and Annoyed" category saw a 1 percentage point increase (eliminating B), while the decreases for "Not Enough Sleep" (6 percentage points) and "Daytime Sleepiness" (5 percentage points) were much lower than the increase for "More than 8 Hours." C and D, respectively, can be eliminated based on this data.

10) CORRECT ANSWER: B
The graphs indicate that the negative "Irritable and Annoyed" category saw a 1 percentage point increase (26% to 27%); this information indicates worsening figures for this category and justifies B as representing the lowest benefit. A and D represent negative categories that decreased (and thus represent benefits), while C represents a positive category that increased (and thus also represents a benefit).

11) CORRECT ANSWER: C
The difference between passage's study and the study as depicted in figures 1 and 2 is that the passage study's school start time is adjusted from 7:30 AM to 8:15 AM, while the figures indicate an adjusted start time from 7:30 AM to 8:30 AM. This information would eliminate A and B because the adjusted time in figure 2 is not a "perfect simulation" of the adjusted time in the passage. D is incorrect because figure 1's start time (7:30 AM) is the same as in the passage's study (also 7:30 AM). Therefore, using the same information, C is the best answer because it correctly describes the difference in the adjusted start times per study.

Chapter 3.4 | Talent vs. Luck

1) CORRECT ANSWER: B
After explaining flaws in current attempts to explain success (lines 11-24), the author provides an overview of a study and concludes that "Talent and luck" (line 64) must be combined rather than isolated in order to ensure success. B properly calls attention to both skill and opportunity and thus fits the author's ideas, while A wrongly emphasizes luck OVER talent.

C distorts information from the passage (the author's critique of other explanations) to avoid the positive recommendation that the author in fact introduces. D wrongly introduces a tone of uncertainty when in fact the author provides clear ideas about the factors that relate to success.

2) CORRECT ANSWER: C
In lines 3-6, the author indicates that the "best idea" and "talent" do not necessarily lead to success; C indicates that "Talent" alone does not explain success and thus continues the author's discussion of the limitations of skills or aptitudes. Choose this answer, and eliminate A as a description of part of an experiment that does NOT clearly indicate that talent is problematic. B and D call attention to luck as important but do NOT directly address the role of talent as in C.

3) CORRECT ANSWER: A
In the second paragraph, the author calls attention to the "prevalent method" (line 11) of explaining success and explains the "inherent flaws" (line 13) in the current logic. This content supports A, while B distorts the author's actual intent (to explain ideas, not to SIMPLIFY an idea that is acknowledged as complex). C refers to later portions of the passage (since the study is ONLY explained in the paragraph that follows), while D mistakes the author's use of a personal hypothetical example (lines 19-24) for a personal or highly opinionated tone throughout the mostly explanatory and analytic paragraph.

4) CORRECT ANSWER: B
The word "internal" refers to factors related to "human nature" (line 17), particularly to the emotion- and memory-based factors explained by the author. B properly calls attention to what is felt or experienced by an individual, while A indicates a removal from group contexts, NOT impressions or emotions. C and D indicate factors that are automatic or pre-determined, NOT factors that relate to specific and distinct responses.

5) CORRECT ANSWER: B
In lines 65-68, the author explains that "combined" talent and luck would enable success for an individual who "took full advantage" of his or her opportunities. B properly reflects the use of talent in highly favorable circumstances; A (wealth) and C (passion) reference positive attributes or attainments but NOT talent specifically and are thus problematic. D references an employee's perception of luck in terms of superstition, not an ACTUAL lucky or fortunate circumstance, and is thus inappropriate to the ideas provided in the passage.

6) CORRECT ANSWER: C
See above for analysis of the correct line reference. A indicates a desired outcome (not the ACTUAL circumstances that would enable success). B calls attention to an experimental procedure (not to an outcome that indicates success), while D raises a possibility for enabling success (distributing funds equally) that is not raised in any answer to the previous question.

7) CORRECT ANSWER: B
The word "exploit" appears in the context of a finding that researchers could "use" (line 86) in monetary situations for positive outcomes; the finding would thus be put to practical use or applied. Choose B and eliminate both A and D as introducing inappropriate negatives. C seems to refer to the general monetary context but distorts the author's meaning, since success in research (NOT profit) is the author's focus in the relevant sentence.

8) CORRECT ANSWER: D
In lines 64-68, the author explains that "Talent and luck" must be present, along with the ability to take "full advantage" of opportunities, in order to enable success. This content supports D and can be used to ELIMINATE B as incorrect. A properly refers to talent but avoids the essential topic of luck, while C refers to a factor considered in the research described in the passage but omits the essential topic of talent.

9) CORRECT ANSWER: A
In lines 17-24, the author explains a "flaw" in human nature: the more successful a person is, the more that person is likely to remember events in a positive manner. The graph calls attention to this tendency, which the author does NOT see as a valid means of assessing success. A properly indicates that the author would be suspicious, while B would indicate that the author would argue entirely against the findings in the graph, rather than seeing the graph as representing an unreliable human tendency. C is contradicted by the author's skeptical tone, while D would criticize the graph itself as poorly constructed, NOT as presenting unreliable ideas.

10) CORRECT ANSWER: C
The graph presents retrospective data framing the relationship between success and memory of events (positive and negative). The graph concludes that more successful people remember a higher percentage of positive events while less successful people remember a higher percentage of negative events. C is the only answer choice that reflects this conclusion, indicating that a successful person would be more likely to

remember positive events leading to success rather than events that did not (negative events). The rest of the answer choices make no specific mention of memory. A points out that there are flaws in asking a successful person about how to be successful. B gives a general statement about replicating results. D examines whether talent or luck is a more important variable when determining success.

Chapter 3.5 | Climate Change

1) CORRECT ANSWER: D
The passage calls attention to alarming "recent data" (line 5) that are relevant to rising temperatures, then explains the detrimental "consequences" (lines 72-73) of such tendencies. This content supports D and can be used to eliminate A, since climate change is the ONLY threat that the author of the passage considers at length. B and C both distort the emphasis of the passage; while the possibility that climate change may not be a seen as a threat is referenced in the first paragraph, the passage as a WHOLE focuses on evidence that establishes the magnitude of the threat, NOT on recent points of debate.

2) CORRECT ANSWER: C
In lines 14-18, the author describes Gore's argument regarding the dangers of climate change as "compelling," so that C introduces an appropriate positive. A would wrongly indicate that the author is entertained by Gore's ideas or does not take such ideas seriously, while B (indicating inability to decide) is contradicted by the author's assertive positive tone. D would describe the author's response to the situation regarding climate change, NOT the author's response to Gore as a commentator.

3) CORRECT ANSWER: C
See above for analysis of the correct line reference. A and B indicate that Gore supports assertive action to address climate change but do NOT explain how the author feels about Gore's ideas. D presents facts relevant to Gore's book yet avoids any direct discussion of the author's sentiments regarding Gore.

4) CORRECT ANSWER: B
The word "recognize" refers to the damage inflicted on the environment, which is traced to ideas that are "assumed" (line 21) in a faulty manner. Here, "recognized" would refer to a more reliable or authoritative action, such as realizing or comprehending the damage. Choose B and eliminate A

and C as positives that would refer to people, NOT to a problem that must be analyzed. D references official or systematic acknowledgement, NOT understanding of the true scope of a problem.

5) CORRECT ANSWER: C
The word "alarming" refers to a situation that contrasts with a "safe" (line 32) condition, so that the word best indicates a dangerous or worrying situation. C is an effective answer, while A, B, and D all best refer to conflicts or dilemmas involving antagonistic individuals, NOT to a severe environmental problem.

6) CORRECT ANSWER: D
In lines 23-33 (the third paragraph), it is explained that the planet's CO_2 levels have been rising for decades and have surpassed the considered "safe" level (350 ppm). B is incorrect because the paragraph doesn't refer to temperature (only to CO_2 concentration) and thus a correlation cannot be inferred based on this text alone. A is incorrect because the paragraph never passes judgment on the most accurate way to measure CO_2 concentration or questions the accuracy of CO_2 level data. C is incorrect because it cannot be presumed that the planet has a maximum CO_2 level (a limit to how much CO_2 it can hold), only that there is a "safe" level of concentration as stated in the paragraph. D is correct as the paragraph states that in 1968 (post-industrial), the CO_2 level was 325 ppm, which is considered "safe" (below 350 ppm).

7) CORRECT ANSWER: B
In lines 86-87, the author (in the context of a larger discussion of second-order consequences) notes that one type of extreme weather event (flooding) has become significantly more frequent. This content supports B. A (oceans) references a first-order consequence, while C and D both provide misreadings of the evidence that justifies B; the author states that flooding has become more common in regions where flooding was once relatively uncommon, NOT that different regions are becoming dissimilar in weather patterns or that flooding is becoming prevalent in once-dry regions.

8) CORRECT ANSWER: D
See above for analysis of the correct line reference. A explains the water cycle disruption that results from ocean heating (itself a first-order consequence as described in line 63). B indicates the overall complexity of the consequences of climate change but does not call attention to

SPECIFIC consequences. C mentions dramatic rain patterns as a second-order consequence, but does not indicate whether the increase in such downpours is minor or "dramatic" in a manner that would justify Question 7 B.

9) CORRECT ANSWER: B
Al Gore's quotation ("predictions of our future can no longer be based on our past") serves as a warning to consider new events occurring in the world of climate and take them into account when deciding what to do about our environmental footprint. Thus, B is the best choice. A is positive and inconsistent with the grave seriousness of Gore's message. C is too negative and implies that Gore has a negative prediction for the future of the environment, which he does not. His quotation simply advises about precautions to take for the future and does not itself predict the future. D is incorrect as Gore is firm in his belief and doesn't seem to waver between sides or express uncertainty.

10) CORRECT ANSWER: C
The graph indicates that the last time the average global temperature briefly registered below 57.0 degrees was around 1980 and then continued a general uptrend. C is thus an effective answer. A, B, and D are incorrect because these choices indicate global temperatures ABOVE 57.0 degrees.

11) CORRECT ANSWER: A
As indicated in lines 23-33, the passage addresses the issue of CO2 ppm in the context of climate change, a problem that can be traced over time to current problems in the environment. Further assessment of CO2 levels would extend the author's discussion, so that A is an effective choice. B references extreme weather problems but raises a standard of assessment (loss of life) that the author avoids. C ("non-industrialized") and D ("before 1950") both neglect the author's emphasis on current conditions as they relate to worldwide activity that accounts for industrial countries.

Chapter 3.6 | Greenland Shark

1) CORRECT ANSWER: B
The author of Passage 1 notes that the tortoise described in the passage died at an "estimated age" (line 13); similarly, the Greenland shark described in the same passage has been "estimated" to be between 272 and 512 years old. Neither animal has a definitive age, so that B is appropriate. While the Greenland shark has presumably not been in captivity, it is unclear how much time ("most" or not) the tortoise has spent in captivity. Eliminate A as unsupported by the evidence given in the passage, and

eliminate C as raising a factor (extent of study) that is not discussed in terms of the tortoise. D is inaccurate because Passage 1 considers only the question of the "oldest living vertebrate" (line 18), NOT age comparisons for vertebrates and invertebrates.

2) CORRECT ANSWER: D
In lines 60-63, the author indicates that animals with "fast metabolisms and heart rates" tend to live shorter lives; thus, an especially long-lived animal should have a slow metabolism and a slow heart rate. D is thus the best choice, while A is contradicted by the passage. B and C call attention to one factor in each case for enabling a long life; neither answer presents BOTH of the factors that would enable an especially long life.

3) CORRECT ANSWER: D
See above for analysis of the correct line reference. A indicates the manner in which a single long-lived animal was studied rather than providing a general idea about lifespan. B references bodily processes related to lifespan but does NOT indicate what paces or configurations would connect to longer (or shorter) lifespans. C raises one factor (heart rate) that explains lifespan but does NOT reference metabolism as required by the previous question.

4) CORRECT ANSWER: B
The word "increased" refers to mileage that would "eventually" (line 60) wear down a tire; the mileage thus adds up or accumulates over time. B reflects the proper context of addition. A and D both wrongly criticize the mileage (which in fact is a necessary part of getting from place to place) as problematic or questionable. C wrongly indicates that the mileage becomes better over time, rather than having at least one negative effect (wearing down the tire).

5) CORRECT ANSWER: B
In lines 36-48, the author explains that carbon-14 dating and comparisons between cornea composition and body length are useful criteria in assessing the age of a Greenland shark. This information can be used to eliminate A and C as overturning findings presented in Passage 1, while the margin of error of over 200 years (lines 16-17) in assessing the age of a Greenland shark can be used to eliminate D. Only B is not in conflict with findings from the passage, since the author is concerned mainly with vertebrates and since even a 200 year-old invertebrate would not be older than the Greenland shark.

6) CORRECT ANSWER: C

The word "short" refers to the end of a spectrum represented by 272 years, with the other end represented by roughly 600 years (lines 78-85). Thus, the author is designating a low or (as commonly termed) "conservative" estimate. Choose C and eliminate A as designating a quick or dramatic event, NOT measurement related to centuries of time. B and D would both criticize the estimate as flawed, NOT call attention to the concept of a minimum, and should thus be eliminated.

7) CORRECT ANSWER: C

In the final paragraph of Passage 1, the author indicates that humans cannot "transpose" the abilities of the long-lived Greenland shark and most likely would not "be interested in switching lifespans" with this slow-moving shark despite the supposed attraction of longevity. This content suggests that humans cannot (in terms of lifespan) benefit from knowing that the Greenland shark is long-lived. C is appropriate, while A and B would wrongly indicate that the benefit is positively useful. D would best refer to information early in the passage (since humans are preoccupied with the idea of living forever), NOT to the more immediate discussion of a benefit that is questionable.

8) CORRECT ANSWER: A

While Passage 1 explains the discovery of a long-lived Greenland shark (lines 14-22), Passage 2 calls attention to humanity's "obsession" (lines 68 and 75) with longevity but indicates that the broad-based human desire to live for a long time will not be fulfilled by the discovery of a long-lived Greenland shark. A properly reflects this content. B and C distort some of the negative comments present in Passage 2; the author argues that the shark-related findings from Passage 1 are not applicable to human lifespans, NOT that the findings are unimportant (since the facts themselves are interesting) or that the data (as opposed to CONCLUSIONS drawn from the data are flawed. D misreads the unresolved matters from BOTH passages, since Passage 1 and Passage 2 both indicate that the age of the Greenland shark has not been definitively determined (rather than Passage 2 resolving this issue).

9) CORRECT ANSWER: C

While Passage 1 briefly mentions that the age of the newly-discovered Greenland shark has been publicized in *The New Yorker* (line 50), Passage 2 places more emphasis on publicity by analyzing how "newspaper articles" (line 87) have taken a high age estimate to intrigue readers who are naturally interested in longevity. This content supports C, while the author of Passage 2 argues that discoveries related to the shark are NOT medically applicable to humans (eliminating A). Only Passage 1 features discussion of historical events linked to the age of the shark (lines 32-35, eliminating B) or discussion of other sea creatures (lines 7-10, eliminating D).

10) CORRECT ANSWER: C
According to Passage 1, humans are determined to "appear and feel younger" (line 4); this content would align with the ideas set forward by the author of Passage 2, who notes that humans are obsessed with long life (lines 68-70) but notes that knowing about long-lived species will NOT enable humans to extend their lifespans (lines 96-107). This content supports C as appropriate. A, B, and D can all readily be eliminated because these answers assume that the author of Passage 2 would directly and fundamentally object to the ideas in Passage 1, which the author of Passage 2 in fact agrees with and builds upon.

11) CORRECT ANSWER: B
In lines 86-88, the author of Passage 2 indicates that "it doesn't seem plausible" for the Greeland shark to live for 600 years; the table places the age of the shark at roughly 512 years, a similarly high figure that the author could greet with skepticism. B thus calls attention to a species with an age estimate that may be suspiciously overstated. A calls attention to sea creatures that can live for over 200 years (which are referenced in the table) in terms of their VALIDATED lifespans; C and D reference the long-lived Greenland shark but do NOT reference its specific age in a manner that would allow assessment of the age provided in the table.

Chapter 3.7 | Drowsy Driving

1) CORRECT ANSWER: D
While the passage as a whole considers an experiment designed to assess drowsy driving behavior, the author notes that current technologies are flawed in their responses to the relevant dangers (lines 74-87) and that modifications to the new assessment model itself may be needed (lines 88-99). This information supports D, while A places too much emphasis on a single factor and neglects the author's focus on the need for further modifications. B (manufacturers) and C (accidents) emphasize details related to the discussion but OMIT key topics (the research inquiry in B, technology in C) of the passage.

2) CORRECT ANSWER: A
In lines 46-52, the author emphasizes that visual information linked to various factors was essential to the research described in the passage.

This content directly supports A, while B and C refer to background that might be useful in the design of a research inquiry, NOT to factors that are clearly designated as evidence by the author. D (indicating samples of common qualities for analysis) indicates a kind of activity that is NOT the same as testing participants for somewhat less predictable results.

3) CORRECT ANSWER: C
The word "premise" refers to assessment of "variables" (line 28) as a key feature in the design of an experiment; C thus refers to the fundamental format of an inquiry in an appropriate manner. A (indicating a goal), B (indicating a belief and suggesting uncertainty), and D (indicating performance of a task) refer to themes that may be relevant to experimentation generally but that do NOT reflect the context of overall design.

4) CORRECT ANSWER: C
In lines 70-71, the author indicates that "car input by itself" was problematic in terms of assessing drowsy driving behavior. C is the only answer that refers to car-related information on its own and is thus appropriate. A, B, and D all refer to factors that require assessment of the DRIVER's body (not the car alone) and thus would not logically refer to car input as an isolated factor.

5) CORRECT ANSWER: D
See above for analysis of the correct line reference. A refers to the activities of car manufacturers, NOT to a problem factor in assessing drowsy driving, while B refers to factors used to assess drowsy driving but does NOT indicate their accuracy. C explains the setup of an experiment designed to assess drowsy driving but, again, does not offer a clear statement in terms of which factors aligned with higher and lower accuracy.

6) CORRECT ANSWER: A
The word "alter" is used in the context of the effect of a "sudden burst" (lines 59-60) of traffic that would, after a period with no traffic, affect a driver's state of drowsiness. Thus, a sudden occurrence that would demand attention would act against or interrupt drowsiness. A is appropriate, while B, C, and D all indicate that the driver would remain drowsy in a different form or proportion, NOT that a stimulus would break through the drowsiness.

7) CORRECT ANSWER: B
In lines 77-80, the author indicates that technologies that could monitor drowsiness cannot effectively distinguish between the poor driving of a drowsy driver and that of a "distracted" one. B properly calls attention to the intrusion of other factors that do not clearly link to drowsiness. A, C, and D all focus on the design of the technology but do not reflect the author's actual criticism (which is based on outcomes, NOT vehicle choices), since the idea of one factor being mistaken for another is not present.

8) CORRECT ANSWER: C
See above for analysis of the correct line reference. A indicates that drowsy driving technologies are limited to high-end vehicles but should NOT be mistaken as evidence for Question 7 A, since the line reference critiques the technologies in terms of scarcity, NOT in terms of the very different problem of inaccuracy. B presents a feature of an experiment (not a criticism of the experiment), while D indicates that driving time cannot be used for assessment on its own, NOT that using driving time is itself problematic as falsely indicated in Question 7 D.

9) CORRECT ANSWER: B
In the relevant paragraph, the author assesses the "results" (line 74) of a study dedicated to drowsy driving and argues that current technology meant to measure drowsy driving may be problematic. Thus, B is an appropriate choice, while A neglects the fact that the author (rather than simply summarizing) is explaining how the study relates to current technologies. C wrongly criticizes the study itself, while D wrongly indicates that the study will be applied to real-world events, NOT that the study simply explains present problems.

10) CORRECT ANSWER: D
While the passage considers the problem of drowsy driving, the graph considers factors related to drowsiness WITHOUT clearly placing drowsiness in the context of driving. D properly indicates that the graph deals with a different main topic, while A and B wrongly indicate that the researchers mentioned in the passage would be interested in drowsiness OUTSIDE the context of driving. C is contradicted by the passage, which DOES feature the idea that physiological factors and drowsy driving are linked.

11) CORRECT ANSWER: C
In the graph, the category with the highest percentage is "Other," but it is not clear what individual factors account for the 26% measure for this category since "Other" is a blanket term that could cover one, a few, or a

very large number of factors. C properly indicates that the graph does not provide sufficient information for determining the highest measure. A, B, and D present factors that are NOT explicitly considered in the graph and that cannot be assumed to fall under "Other" without more evidence.

Chapter 3.8 | Pluto's Classification

1) CORRECT ANSWER: B
After explaining the change in Pluto's status, the author calls attention to the "differences of opinion" (line 16) among scientists as to whether Pluto should be considered a planet; experts such as Brown, Stern, and Tombaugh are considered in some detail. This content supports B, while the author's interest in the viewpoints of MULTIPLE specialists makes A problematic. C reflects the conflict between Tombaugh and Marsden but wrongly indicates that an entire scientific field (not just scientists whose views are seen as flawed) has suffered as a result of such conflict. D wrongly assumes that the author presents a definitive stance on the status of Pluto, when in fact the passage mainly functions to survey a debate that remains unresolved.

2) CORRECT ANSWER: D
Early in the passage, the author raises the issue of whether "scientists have an objective basis" (lines 15-16) for differences of opinion in classifying Pluto. Attempts to give certainty to the question through voting and through the development of criteria such as clearing the "neighborhood" (lines 44-45) indicate that D is an appropriate choice. A and C both neglect the fact that criteria OTHER than definitions (such as voting) were used in attempts to determine whether Pluto is a planet. B mistakes the desire of some scientists to change the status of Pluto for the topic of whether Pluto ITSELF will change in some physical way (a possibility that the author avoids analyzing).

3) CORRECT ANSWER: B
The relevant lines present the "three tests" (lines 2-3) that heavenly bodies must pass in order to be classified as planets; one of these, clearing the neighborhood, is objected to by Gerald van Belle in lines 58-60. B properly reflects this content, while A mistakes the idea that Pluto was discovered in 1930 (lines 22-23) for the idea that a definition of a "planet" appeared in the same year. C overstates the duration of the dispute over Pluto's status (since this debate mostly took place in a period of UNDER a century), while D wrongly assumes that the question of how to define a planet overall (NOT the question of whether Pluto in particular is a planet) is a point of intense contention among astronomers.

4) CORRECT ANSWER: B
The passage describes Marsden as part of an effort to undermine Pluto's planetary status based on the fact that Pluto did not "clear the neighborhood around its orbit" (lines 44-45); thus, Marsden would agree with the idea that a planet must "clear the neighborhood" in accordance with the IAU definition cited in lines 1-6. Choose B and eliminate A as representing an astronomer who discovered Pluto and who does NOT clearly disapprove of its planetary status. C represents a scientist who OBJECTS to the IAU definition (lines 58-60), while D represents a scientist who might be in favor of revising or expanding the definition (lines 88-90).

5) CORRECT ANSWER: A
The relevant words occur in the context of questions about the motives of scientists and thus indicate that "hard" or "objective" measures may NOT be present in considering planetary criteria. A properly reflects this questioning or skeptical tone, while B wrongly indicates that the author sees the objectivity of ideas about Pluto as definite when in fact the OPPOSITE could be true. C and D raise the possibility that the author is determining how or whether to use specialized language, when in fact the terms "hard science" and "objective basis" are relatively common and are used in the context of a debate that is meant to be understandable.

6) CORRECT ANSWER: C
The idea of "gravitational dominance" relies on a heavenly body having "no other bodies of similar size" (lines 47-48) under its influence, with only smaller bodies or satellites possibly present. C presents a scenario in which no bodies of any sort are present and thus fulfills the needed requirements, while A and B both indicate that LARGER bodies are present to dominate a smaller body. D is problematic because, while this answer describes a body with satellites that has left its orbit, the concept of gravitational dominance is understood in the context of an orbiting body ONLY (lines 44-45).

7) CORRECT ANSWER: A
The word "arbitrary" is used in the context of a scientific procedure based on "voting" (line 54) as opposed to unquestionable evidence; voting would naturally involve personal or subjective responses to an issue. A is thus the best answer, while B raises a context of lighthearted emotion and C raises a context of need or urgency, NOT a context of individual or personal response. D is contradicted by the passage, since voting WOULD be seen as a democratic process as compared to assessment of evidence by a few experts.

8) CORRECT ANSWER: D
While Marsden was notable for relying on a "vote to demote Pluto" (line 32), Brown described Pluto in terms of its properties as an "insignificant chunk of ice" (line 68). Both experts would object to the idea that Pluto is a planet, but would support their ideas using different standards. This content supports D and can be used to eliminate A (which attributes a positive stance to Brown). B and C both misread Brown's idea that Pluto is "insignificant" as an expression of indifference to the issue, NOT as part of an argument that Pluto should not be classified as a planet.

9) CORRECT ANSWER: D
The word "sufficient" refers to "alternative criteria" (line 83) offered and endorsed by an expert who seeks to classify Pluto; these criteria involve size and shape, or evidence that Pluto fits a standard. D reflects this context, while A raises the appropriate topic of "criteria" but indicates that new criteria are being added, not that preferable "alternative" criteria are being presented. B (which emphasizes visual imagery or verbal expression) and C (which emphasizes findings, NOT fundamental concepts) should be eliminated as introducing faulty contexts.

10) CORRECT ANSWER: C
While the passage cites a history of "differences of opinion" (line 16) in terms of the status of Pluto and indicates that scientists "agree to disagree" (line 88) on this issue, the graph provides ONE perspective indicating that Pluto is a dwarf planet. This information indicates an absence of consensus, so that C is the best answer and both A and B can be eliminated. D wrongly assumes that Pluto is of relatively little interest to scientists, when in fact the passage depicts Pluto as a source of ongoing debate.

11) CORRECT ANSWER: C
As indicated in the figure, Earth is smaller than Jupiter (in terms of miles measured), Kepler-22b (a multiple of Earth), Kepler-425b (a multiple of Earth), and HR2562b (a multiple of Jupiter). All other objects are smaller than Earth, so that exactly four objects are larger than Earth. Choose C and eliminate A and B as inaccurate. D would perhaps be appropriate if the question were about the planetary objects in an unclearly defined and vast region of the universe, NOT about the table which gives a set number of objects and facilitates a clear answer.

Chapter 3.9 | Diabetic Lifestyle

1) CORRECT ANSWER: D
In the passage, the author presents a study designed to investigate whether the website MyDoctorOnline.com "supported the needs of those who are diagnosed as pre-diabetic" (lines 16-17). The author then outlined possible improvements (lines 77-111) that would aid site users, so that D is the best answer. A neglects the fact that MyDoctorOnline.com is presented as flawed in some respects, NOT as positively "transformative." B neglects the essential topic of the website altogether, while C wrongly references multiple studies when the author was mostly interested in a SINGLE study conducted by Aimee Richardson.

2) CORRECT ANSWER: C
The relevant questions call attention to factors that people can perhaps "control" or "change"; the questions thus return to the topic of "advice" (line 6) mentioned earlier, with the specific intent of emphasizing that effectively addressing diabetes can be a challenge. Choose C and eliminate A as a distortion of the contents of the passage, since Richardson's study has not yet been introduced. B (diagnosis) and D (hypothesis) seem to reference elements of analyzing diabetes, but do not properly reference the context of advice and action that the questions are meant to address.

3) CORRECT ANSWER: B
The word "gaps" refers to an aspect of a website's "ability to fulfill" (line 18) the needs of patients; a study would naturally assess such gaps to identify strong and weak points. B properly calls attention to a negative factor that an assessment would address. A and D both call attention to PHYSICAL gaps and are thus out of context, while C indicates forgetfulness or irresponsibility and thus suggests inappropriate contexts as well.

4) CORRECT ANSWER: B
In lines 21-25, the author indicates that some website users had effectively "developed strategies" while users who fit a different profile were "overwhelmed"; this content indicates that the website may not serve all users equally well. B is appropriate, while A and C both wrongly criticize the study of the site, NOT the site itself. D calls attention to a problem with the site that the author (who is mostly interested in problems faced by people who HAVE reached the site) does not primarily consider.

5) CORRECT ANSWER: C
See above for analysis of the correct line reference. A and B explain the nature of Richardson's research, which considered user problems with an online resource, but do not explain EXACTLY what those problems were

as required by the previous question. D further explains Richardson's methods without addressing the specific drawbacks connected to the site itself.

6) CORRECT ANSWER: C
In explaining how Richardson designed the experiment so as not to "lead" a given subject to a given answer, the author indicates that Richardson used studies that were "either open-ended or exploratory" (lines 43-44); this content supports the idea of multiple methods in C as appropriate. A raises the idea of variation but in relation to the wrong topic (moderators, NOT tasks). B wrongly attributes a direct role to Richardson (who mostly collected data), while D raises a possibility that in fact COULD "lead" to specific answers through the manipulation of the subjects' emotions.

7) CORRECT ANSWER: C
The phrase "close-ended questions" is used in the context of a contrast with open-ended tasks that called upon subjects to "explore" (line 53) a site; the provided close-ended question (lines 57-58) instead required a single and direct answer from a list of options (lines 47-48). C reflects this content, while A assumes too much freedom in answering on the part of the participants. B and D are both contradicted by the options given (since answers extend beyond "yes" and "no" but ARE required) and should thus be eliminated.

8) CORRECT ANSWER: D
The author explains that close-ended tasks involve set answer choices from a provided list (lines 45-48), and D properly refers to the idea that pre-selected options have been given to participants. A and B both refer to forms of response that do NOT involve pre-set options (since the participants formulate their own answers rather than consulting a list), while C focuses on the themes of accuracy and expanded choices, NOT the idea of limiting possible choices to those provided on a list.

9) CORRECT ANSWER: A
According to the passage, Richardson conducted her study "using 3 different methodologies with five subjects" (lines 29-30); this format directly fits the ideas presented under a "case study design." Choose A and eliminate B (since no control group is present) and C (since the experiment assessed actual outcomes, NOT likelihood of an outcome) as raising design features that Richardson did not employ. D is incorrect because Richardson DID intervene by providing the subjects with tasks (lines 30-34) rather than observing the subjects as they would act without any sort of intervention.

10) CORRECT ANSWER: A
In lines 95-97, the author indicates that improved "organization of content" for quick access by patients was a desired change to the website; A indicates a change in organization that could result in greater efficiency for users. B and C call attention to the implementation of additional content, NOT to the reconfiguration of existing content. D refers to an element of Richardson's experiment (line 32), NOT a central element of the website itself, and thus raises an incorrect topic.

11) CORRECT ANSWER: D
See above for analysis of the correct line reference. A references a stage of Richardson's experiment, NOT a recommendation that resulted from the experiment. B indicates that recommendations were made without clearly specifying what the recommendations were. C indicates that the patients using the site did not find one of the site tools useful but does NOT provide a direct recommendation for improvement; this answer should not be taken as evidence for Question 10 B or Question 10 C, even though these answers seem to raise related topics.

Chapter 3.10 | Cooperative Economics

1) CORRECT ANSWER: B
After explaining ideas about the dynamics of sharing in the first paragraph, the author explains the details of a study that "utilized 44 male and 44 female Canadian undergraduate students" (lines 19-20) and outlines some of the implications (in terms of hierarchy and gender) of the findings of the study. This content is reflected in B, while A and D both avoid any direct mention of a research study and instead wrongly focus on smaller elements (real-life applications, specific factors) linked to the study. C wrongly assumes that the two studies were meant to be compared with one another, NOT that they tested different factors related to a single problem.

2) CORRECT ANSWER: A
The word "status" refers to a sharing scenario in which one person (as in real life) is a "superior" (line 14). A properly refers to essential positioning in terms of hierarchy. B raises a more specific monetary context that is flawed because it is unclear exactly HOW one person out-ranks another. C refers to physical state and D refers to respect; these words similarly distract from the idea of basic superiority to wrongly indicate how, exactly, two people are different.

3) CORRECT ANSWER: B
In lines 30-32, the author indicates that sharing with "more competent, lower-status" individuals is a likely scenario; B reflects both higher-to-lower sharing (CEO to employee) and highly positive performance. A refers to a reward that would be closer to lower-to-higher sharing, C does not raise the important issue of high performance, and D refers to high performance but NOT to hierarchical sharing.

4) CORRECT ANSWER: C
See above for analysis of the correct line reference. A indicates that lower-status individuals are not expected to share but does not indicate what kind of individuals (especially in terms of performance) ARE expected to share. B indicates a feature of experimental design (not an outcome that suggests a situation), while D refers to the second study considered in the passage, NOT to the first study as required by the previous question.

5) CORRECT ANSWER: A
The phrase "as a function of" is used to indicate that factors in an experiment (monetary rewards, competence and status) were linked in a clear manner as determined by researchers. A indicates that there was a meaningful correlation between readily assessed or measured qualities. B (sequence in time), C (disregard or contrast), and D (grouping or similarity) all raise contexts that do NOT simply indicate a correlation between factors.

6) CORRECT ANSWER: B
While the findings of the first study revealed a link between sharing and competence (lines 30-34), the findings of the second study revealed connections between gender, a factor NOT clearly considered in the first study, and sharing behavior (lines 43-47). This content supports B, while A refers to the PREMISES of the studies, not to FINDINGS. C is contradicted by the fact that competence for reward recipients was a consideration in both studies, while D similarly calls attention to the question of status, which was considered in BOTH studies as well.

7) CORRECT ANSWER: C
The author explains that "males share more than females" (line 67) because males form "large, stable groups of peers" (line 69) in which the involved males are regarded as equals. Women instead focus on "competition" (line 76) in group interaction, so that C is the best choice. A refers to a fact that may be explained by factors BEYOND the scope of the passage; historical disparities in status between men and women are not used by the author to explain the research. B and D both distort the actual

explanation in the passage to criticize women (who are mostly seen as competitive) and should be eliminated as inaccurate.

8) CORRECT ANSWER: D
In lines 87-89, the author indicates that people "report beliefs" that are "contradictory with their actions" in real life; in contrast to the experiment (which focused mainly on sharing actions), real-world scenarios may present a clear breakdown between different types of observations. D is thus appropriate, while A simply presents an experimental outcome, NOT a disparity. B calls attention to real-world implications but does NOT cite the possibility that the experimental findings and real-life observations will be different. C indicates that expanding the inquiry explained in the passage to real-life contexts may be useful but, again, does not address the idea of a disparity or difference.

9) CORRECT ANSWER: C
In figure 1, the second dark bar (low competence, low status) represents the lowest amount of money shared. Choose C as appropriate. A refers to the bar indicating the HIGHEST amount of money shared, while B and D both wrongly refer to high-status individuals.

10) CORRECT ANSWER: A
In figure 2, the first dark bar (high competence, low status) represents the highest amount of money shared. Choose A as appropriate. C refers to the bar indicating the LOWEST amount of money shared, while B and D both wrongly refer to high-status individuals.

Chapter Four

Questions 1-10 are based on the following passage and supplementary material.

4.1
Adapted from "Presence of Skeletal Banding in a Reef-Building Tropical Crustose Coralline Alga," a PLOS ONE article by Bonnie Lewis, Janice Lough, Merinda Nash, and Guillermo Diaz-Pulido, in which the authors build a new paradigm for determining the age of algae on the Great Barrier Reef's coral.

The Great Barrier Reef off the coast of Queensland, Australia is the world's largest coral reef and provides a home to billions of sea creatures. Sadly, since 1985, the reef has been slowly losing its mass. Although ships and human divers are part of the problem, a majority of its mass is lost due to the effect global warming has on sea water temperatures. When sea temperatures rise, organisms have difficulty maintaining the homeostasis that they developed through years of evolution, causing them to either adapt to these new conditions or die. In coral, specifically, global warming leads to bleaching, a phenomenon that leaves these organisms more prone to diseases. Once diseased, coral die off, and the species they had been both sheltering and providing nourishment for will subsequently either relocate to a new part of the reef or suffer the same fate.

As the ocean becomes warmer and more acidic from climate change, the need to find a way to learn more about these organisms has become paramount to saving the reef from a perilous future. In a study published in 2017, researchers sought to better understand algae and its relationship to the reef. Specifically, they investigated a method to determine the age of coralline algae called Porolithan Onkodes. This abundant organism provides calcium, thereby "calcifying," or attaching the coral together to build the reef—which stretches over 2700 kilometers. Indeed, calcium plays a major role in stabilizing the framework of the reef, thereby providing effective cover for the organisms that live there. The most similar comparison is a rainforest canopy, which provides its ecosystem with security and nourishment.

In the past, scientists haven't been able to study these algae as a result of turbulent reef conditions and the time it would take to complete such a feat. To combat such problems, the resourceful researchers broke up the study into 5 3-month periods (although five samples stayed the entire 15 months) and stabilized specimens on a PVC pipe filled with lead and secured to the reef. Prior to this, they had collected 20 samples of the specimen at the beginning of each 3-month period and dyed them with Alizarin Red, which would allow them to see the formation of bands over time. This banding is similar to tree rings because it reveals the organism's age—in trees, the correlation of rings to years is already known; in coralline algae, however, the correlation was, before this study, not known.

At the end of each 3-month period, the team analyzed the dye with microscopes to determine whether any bands had formed. In addition, they tracked the concentration of magnesium-calcite. What they found was that conceptacle bands, or specialized cavities in algae which contain reproductive organs, form once per year during summer. Furthermore, they found that magnesium-calcite is low in the winter and high in the summer, which correlates with the ability to form these bands during that period of time. Armed with this knowledge, the team believes that these bands are a useful proxy to determine the growth rate of the coral. Using the same logic, disruptions in the summer banding trend can help track what's going on with the environment. Researchers will now be able to tell when the climate has not allowed for bands to form, as a result of either extreme temperatures or high levels of acid, and hopefully implement an intervention to counter.

With temperatures continuing to fluctuate wildly, resulting in an ultimate net increase, hopefully this study provides insight into new ways to save the coral that has been sheltering marine life in the Great Barrier Reef for up to eight thousand years. The study's authors were optimistic that the study would "enable the development of metrics that can be used to track the impacts of climate stressors." Furthermore, if environmental scientists can predict temperatures and acid levels that will pose a threat to the reef, future techniques can hopefully be implemented in advance to protect the coralline algae from the subsequent negative effects. In years to come, the creatures living in this area won't be the only ones to be thankful: tourism at the reef is a multi-billion dollar industry, and the reef itself is one of the seven wonders of the world. Countless numbers of people who travel to the site every year will be especially appreciative.

Influence of Temperature and Acidity on MgCO3* Concentration

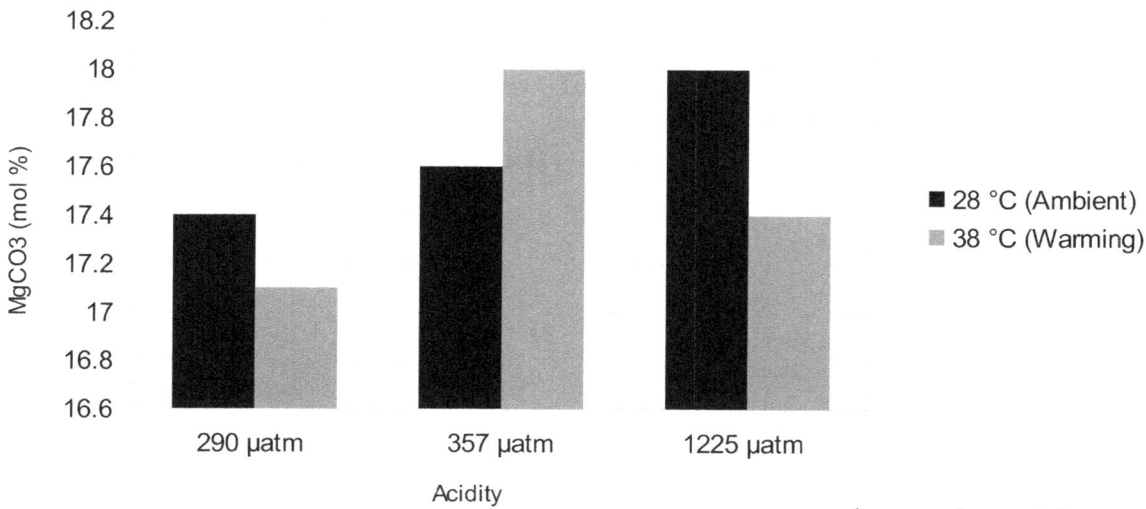

*magnesium-calcite

1

The passage is primarily concerned with

A) narrating the history of an aquatic community and the ecological crises it has encountered.
B) explaining the function of an organism and its significance in the surrounding environment.
C) identifying one cause of a phenomenon and showing how a relevant situation can be rectified.
D) describing the properties of an ecosystem and endorsing a major change.

2

The author indicates that the diminishment of coral reefs is concerning because

A) species that rely on coral reefs as shelter and a source of food are compromised by coral bleaching.
B) countries containing prominent coral reefs are dependent on tourism for economic stability.
C) coral reefs provide a stabilizing force which prevents ocean temperatures from extreme fluctuation.
D) scientists have not been able to pinpoint a source of damage to coral reefs and are therefore unable to stop further damage.

3

Which choice provides the best evidence for the answer to the previous question?

A) Lines 4-5 ("Sadly, since...mass")
B) Lines 8-12 ("When sea...die")
C) Lines 14-17 ("Once diseased...fate")
D) Lines 19-21 ("the need...future")

4

As used in line 27, "build" most nearly means

A) elevate.
B) constitute.
C) secure.
D) establish.

5

According to the passage, the researchers had not experimented on Porolithan Onkodesi because

A) they had not developed the technology that would allow them to study the algae up close.
B) they had dismissed the algae as an unimportant aspect of the reef's functioning.
C) the algae was found directly on the reefs, which would be damaged in the process.
D) environmental hazards and time constraints had made the algae difficult to study.

6

It can be inferred from the passage that the researchers are interested in Porolithan Onkodesi because

A) it maintains the structure of coral reefs through the process of calcification.
B) it provides the researchers with valuable information about the age of coral reefs.
C) it reveals an important connection between magnesium-calcite and coral reefs.
D) it presents a potential solution to extending the life of organisms in coral reefs.

7

Which choice provides the best evidence for the answer to the previous question?

A) Lines 28-31 ("Indeed, calcium...there")
B) Lines 45-49 ("This banding...known")
C) Lines 56-59 ("Furthermore, they...time")
D) Lines 59-62 ("Amed with...coral")

8

As used in line 44, "formation" most nearly means

A) evolution.
B) structure.
C) arrangement.
D) emergence.

9

It can be reasonably inferred from the passage and the figure that the ideal acidity for water in areas containing coral reefs is

A) 290 µatm.
B) 357 µatm.
C) 1225 µatm.
D) impossible to determine based on the information given.

10

The data in the figure offer an answer to which of the following questions raised in the passage?

A) Why are magnesium-calcite levels highest in the summer and lowest in the winter?
B) What effects do environmental disruptions like acidity and temperature have on magnesium-calcite levels?
C) Can coralline algae affect the acidity and temperature of the water where coral reefs reside?
D) How do fluctuations in magnesium-calcite concentrations affect the acidity of waters surrounding coral reefs?

Questions 1-11 are based on the following passage and supplementary material.

4.2
Adapted from a 2016 PLOS ONE journal article by Tao Yao, Stefan Treus, and B. Suresh Krishna titled "An Attention-Sensitive Memory Trace in Macaque MT Following Saccadic Eye Movements" in which the authors propose a method of bottom-up attentional processing in the visual system.

In 2016, German researchers sought to find out what neural mechanisms underlie the brain's response to moving targets. In everyday life, we experience the world as stable—even though the eye, head (brain), and body are constantly in motion—with the help of saccades coupled with some other, unknown phenomenon.

Saccades, or quick jumps that the eye makes between visual fixation points, have been extensively studied in previous research, but their role in stabilizing our world has never been fully understood. At this point, scientists know that when we look at something in our visual field, we don't stare directly at a point on the object; rather, we are constantly scanning (via saccades) over the entire visually-available area of the object—top to bottom and left to right—in order to get a complete picture into our field of view. On their own, these eye jumps would not seem sufficient to justify how we hold attention on one thing even in the midst of frequent retinal image displacements.

One theory that could explain why our world remains stable is that our brains "anticipate" the consequences of saccades, meaning that the information in our brain moves faster than the physical movement of our eyes. If true, this would mean that sight is experienced as "top-down," or internally guided based on prior knowledge, willful plans, or current goals, rather than "bottom-up," or constructed as you go, using no prior knowledge. If this is true, it would cause our brain to more quickly recognize information in the visual field as "whole pictures," rather than as broken-up into pieces.

This theory holds weight in the field of neuroscience for two reasons. The first is that the brain has a propensity for putting incomplete pictures together even in two-dimensional planes. The brain's need to do this is so that it can make sense of the world and make perceiving and understanding the world quicker and easier, therefore requiring fewer resources. The second reason is that the brain uses heuristics—or stereotypes based on previous experience that help us come to quick-and-easy solutions—to anticipate consequences based on environmental cues that much of the time we don't even realize are present. Both of these concepts help us to remain safe from dangerous situations and free from repeating events that had negative outcomes for us in the past.

Based on previous brain anticipatory behavior research, the study, conducted by Tao Yao, Stefan Treue, and B. Suresh Krishna, attempts to finally answer the question of exactly what mechanism our brain uses to prevent our field of view from becoming an unstable mess. In their research, the team's members employed electrical brain recording techniques, using Macaque monkeys as subjects. They first had the monkeys stare at a fixation point (usually a cross) in order to stabilize the eye and prevent saccadic movements. Once saccadic movements were fully repressed, activity in the brain was measured as a "baseline" of activity in order to later be compared to activity during saccades. Next, monkeys were trained to orient their field of vision to a "target" random dot pattern, or RDP, to stimulate a saccadic eye movement. At the same time as the target was presented, a distractor was presented, equidistant from the original fixation point but in the opposite visual field. The distractor would be used as a comparison when the team later analyzed the data. Again, activity in the brain, referred to as a "memory trace," was mapped via the electrical recording device.

Not surprisingly, the researchers found evidence of anticipatory activity in the brain. When the monkeys knew that they would soon be attending to an item in their left field of view (representing the aforementioned "target"), neurons corresponding to the left field of view in the brain fired more strongly than neurons corresponding to the right field of view (representing the aforementioned "distractor") fired. That the neurons in the target's direction experienced stronger stimulation implies that more neurons were recruited to attend to that field of vision. What's more impressive, though, is that the neurons fired prior to the saccade happening, meaning that the saccade itself didn't cause the activity—anticipation of focusing on a new target did.

Future research on this topic is needed, as the research team only had a combined 124 trials of data to examine, and the subjects were monkeys, not humans. The team indicates that they are optimistic about their results: "Our current results . . . resolve important issues concerning the . . . representation of visual stimuli." As more is understood about top-down versus

bottom-up processing in the visual system, scientists
will begin to fully understand the mechanisms behind
how we maintain a stable view of the world.

Strength of Neuron Activity for Macaque Monkey Experiment Subjects

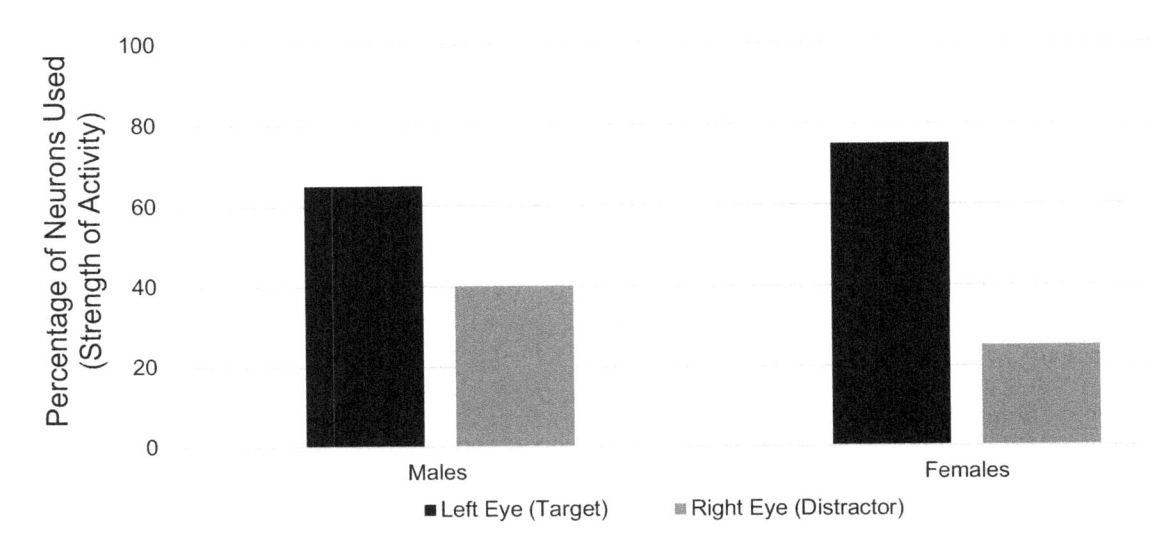

[Bar chart showing Percentage of Neurons Used (Strength of Activity) for Males and Females, comparing Left Eye (Target) and Right Eye (Distractor). Males: Left Eye ~65, Right Eye ~40. Females: Left Eye ~75, Right Eye ~25.]

1

The main purpose of the passage is to

A) survey a group of competing theories with the end goal of demonstrating how an experiment invalidated several of those theories.
B) explain the practical uses of a feature of human psychology that was not previously linked to a clear utilitarian function.
C) consider the theoretical explanations for a specific tendency in humans alongside an experiment that was designed to assess that tendency.
D) document a series of experimental procedures in a study of human perception in order to highlight a flaw in one of those procedures.

2

What purpose is served by the author's statement in lines 3-7 ("In everyday . . . phenomenon")?

A) To present technical information in a conversational and lightly humorous fashion
B) To relate a central topic of the passage to the reader's own experience
C) To summarize a central finding of the research described in the passage
D) To address a common fallacy regarding visual perception

3

Which of the following scenarios would reflect the use of saccades in making visual observations?

A) A student memorizes a list of terms by focusing on only a few items on the list at one time.
B) A student navigates an unfamiliar city by noticing prominent landmarks and using them as reference points.
C) A student comprehends a map of a continent by noting the individual areas where the continent is bounded by different bodies of water.
D) A student makes inferences about the size of a skyscraper by determining the building's number of floors from ground level.

4

As used in line 19, "justify" most nearly means

A) defend.
B) explain.
C) favor.
D) allow.

5

As described in the passage, the presence of a "top-down" model of sight can be explained by

A) the necessity of survival.
B) the brain's capacity to re-structure itself.
C) an aesthetic appreciation for unity.
D) a distrust of certain memories.

6

Which choice provides the best evidence for the answer to the previous question?

A) Lines 22-26 ("One theory . . . eyes")
B) Lines 30-33 ("If this . . . pieces")
C) Lines 35-37 ("The first . . . planes")
D) Lines 45-48 ("Both . . . past")

7

Which of the following quotations most effectively indicates that the experiment described in the passage supports the ideas about heuristics that are outlined by the author?

A) Lines 59-62 ("Once . . . saccades")
B) Lines 62-64 ("Next . . . movement")
C) Lines 80-82 ("That . . . vision")
D) Lines 82-86 ("What's . . . did")

8

As used in 74-75, "attending to" most nearly means

A) providing for.
B) focusing on.
C) operating alongside.
D) associating with.

9

Taken together, the information in the sixth paragraph (lines 72-86) and the data in the graph best support which of the following statements about Macque monkeys?

A) Male monkeys are more easily distracted than female monkeys are.
B) Female monkeys exhibit stronger anticipatory activity than male monkeys do.
C) Male monkeys are able to repress saccadic movements more efficiently than female monkeys are.
D) Female monkeys have greater eyesight than male monkeys do.

10

Which of the following best represents the percentage of neurons used by female macaque monkeys to attend to an item in their right field of vision?

A) 20%
B) 25%
C) 30%
D) 35%

11

The authors of the study mentioned in the passage (lines 49-51) would most likely regard the data presented in the graph as

A) identical to the results of their own study.
B) contradictory to the conclusions from their study.
C) supplemental to the findings of their own study.
D) inaccurate due to the method of data collection.

Questions 1-11 are based on the following passage and supplementary material.
4.3
The following passage is synthesized from the 2015 NIH article "How Taste Is Perceived in the Brain" by Harrison Wein and the 2013 NIH article "High Salt Detected by Sour and Bitter Taste Cells" by Miranda Hanson.

   Human beings and other mammals depend on their taste buds to guide their choice of foods. A sometimes overlooked sense, taste is an important contributor to our perception of the world. Crucially, foods that taste good to us stimulate the reward center in our brain, causing us to crave those foods. Conversely, if a food does not taste good, it stimulates an aversive pathway in the brain that causes long-term learned behavior—simply put, we don't want to eat, or even smell, that food ever again if it activates the severe end of the aversion spectrum. Scientists (and cooks) know that we are attracted to foods that are sweet, for instance, as these are usually high in energy and likely to activate the aforementioned reward pathway. A taste that is bitter, however, can warn of a potentially harmful substance. Another taste of particular interest to researchers is salt—which doesn't fit into any of the specific categories identified in taste buds.
   Linking salt to the bitter taste receptors, scientists have perhaps explained why human beings do not find high levels of salt appetizing. Most animals will consume salt up to a point, after which it becomes unappealing, making salt unique. Animals should want to consume salt: dietary salt, or sodium chloride (NaCl), is used by every cell in the body and is thought to be an essential ion. However, it does become harmful in excess—most likely indicating an evolutionary cause of its "unappealing in high quantities" property. Researchers have identified taste receptor cells that are able to detect low levels of sodium salts (necessary for a homeostasis in all cells throughout the body) through the epithelial sodium channel (ENaC), but cells responsible for aversion to high salt levels were unknown.
   Past studies show that bitter and sweet tastes are represented in several distinct areas, or "fields," of the taste cortex. Ryba and Zuker's teams recently explored whether activating such cortical fields in mice would evoke taste, even without the presence of an actual sweet or bitter compound. This idea is hardly new. For years, scientists have been activating neurons in the brain and evoking responses correlating with the activated area. Take, for example, the "music" processing center of the brain. If a neuron in that specific area is activated in a conscious human, the person will report having heard a sound even when none was present.
   In the taste study, they used a technique called optogenetics to selectively activate the bitter or sweet cortical fields. To implement optogenetics, you must first inject a virus that carries the gene for a specific light-sensitive protein into either the bitter field or the sweet field. Light can then activate the neurons that accept this virus and produce a protein in response. To activate the protein and stimulate the false "taste" sensation, the scientists implanted some customized optical fibers near the site of the injection.
   Once equipped with the light-sensitive optogenetic mechanism, the mice were given the option to choose one of two chambers. Entrance into one chamber would cause a stimulation in the "bitter" area of the brain, while entrance into the other would cause a stimulation in the "sweet" area. Mice naturally developed a preference for the chamber that was coupled with stimulation of the sweet cortical field area. As expected, mice whose bitter cortical field was activated when they choose that chamber learned to avoid it, quickly.
   Even when animals had no experience with bitter or sweet tastes, researchers could trigger behaviors corresponding to those tastes by activating cortical fields. This finding shows evidence of support for the view that one's sense of taste is hardwired into the brain. The way human beings think of taste is in the brain, as Zuker says: "dedicated taste receptors in the tongue detect sweet or bitter and so on, but it's the brain that affords meaning to these chemicals." The salt-related findings suggest that humans and other mammals have specialized salt receptor cells to make salt appealing. Bitter-tasting cells are activated by high salt concentrations, and our cells have evolved to help prevent consumption levels that could severely affect our health.

Chamber Preferences (Salty or Sweet) for 32 Mice

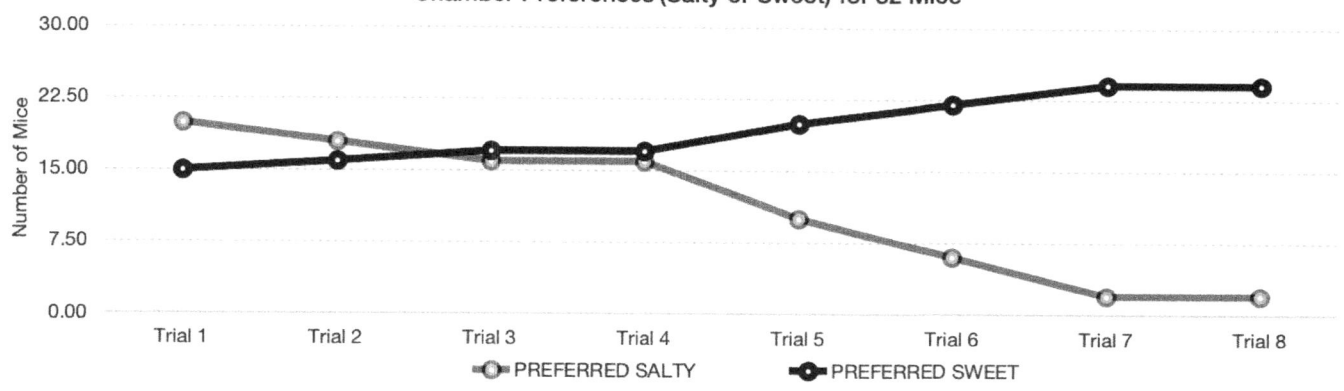

[Graph showing two lines across Trials 1-8: PREFERRED SALTY line starts around 20 and decreases to near 0; PREFERRED SWEET line starts at 15 and increases to about 23.]

1

According to the passage, how have scientists traditionally understood the body's responses to different tastes?

A) Eating habits are formed over time as the results of specific neurological reactions.
B) Specific food sources result in subconscious reactions that are still being classified.
C) Cells that react to specific foods take on the same structures in humans and in other mammals.
D) Dietary preferences began as survival mechanisms and gradually became the basis of cultural practices.

2

Which choice provides the best evidence for the answer to the previous question?

A) Lines 1-2 ("Human beings . . . foods")
B) Lines 6-11 ("Conversely . . . spectrum")
C) Lines 19-21 ("Linking . . . appetizing")
D) Lines 29-34 ("Researchers . . . unknown")

3

As used in lines 15 and 19, "bitter" most nearly means

A) resentful.
B) violent.
C) irritable.
D) harsh.

4

As described in the passage, salt is

A) identified as a specific category in taste buds.
B) generally unappealing if present in trace amounts.
C) supremely useful in different anatomical regions.
D) central to recent investigations of cell formation.

5

The author of the passage places the words "music" and "taste" in quotation marks in order to indicate that these terms

A) take different definitions in scientific and non-scientific contexts.
B) can describe occurrences that are to some extent simulated.
C) tend not to be explained in a precise or standardized manner.
D) are regarded by neurological researchers with healthy skepticism.

6

As used in line 50, "implement" most nearly means

A) certify.
B) craft.
C) enable.
D) enforce.

7

It can be reasonably concluded from the taste study that which of the following conditions must be fulfilled regarding the injected virus used in optogenetics?

A) Neurons must react to the virus without rejecting the virus itself from the body.
B) The virus must be able to survive prolonged exposure to intense light.
C) The final virus must itself be adapted from a non-fatal virus that occurs in nature.
D) Sweet and salty compounds cannot occur in high concentrations in the selected virus.

8

The author of the passage would agree that the areas of a mouse's brain that are linked to sweet tastes

A) are structured differently from the brain areas that are linked to salty tastes.
B) frequently share information with brain areas that are linked to visual perception.
C) can be activated in a manner that prompts and reinforces pleasing sensations.
D) may grow larger at the expense of brain areas that are linked to salty tastes.

9

Which choice provides the best evidence for the answer to the previous question?

A) Lines 58-60 ("Once . . . chambers")
B) Lines 60-63 ("Entrance . . . area")
C) Lines 63-66 ("Mice . . . area")
D) Lines 77-80 ("The salt-related . . . appealing")

10

Which of the following statements about taste preferences for mice is best supported by the graph?

A) Sweet tastes are more likely to repel than to attract a few mice in any test sample.
B) Mice can be trained to prefer salty tastes through a process of repeated exposure.
C) Salty substances are beneficial to mice but are seldom preferred to sweet tastes.
D) Mice do not uniformly prefer sweet tastes, even after repeated exposure to salt.

11

The author of the passage would argue that the information provided by the graph is

A) decidedly interesting, since it considers the experimental methods central to the passage.
B) generally useless, since it does not indicate how the recorded trends are linked to specific brain pathways.
C) somewhat informative, since it mostly indicates similar results to those of the research performed by Ryba and Zuker.
D) factually questionable, since it presents information that contradicts Ryba and Zuker's ideas about cell biology.

Questions 1-11 are based on the following passage and supplementary material.

4.4
The following passage is adapted from the 2010 *Atlantic* article "The End of Men" by Hanna Rosin.

After thousands of years, Hanna Rosin argues in a 2010 *Atlantic* article that "patriarchy is coming to an end." Once dominating economic territories,
Line men became the minority of the workforce in 2010,
5 for the very first time in US history. As proof that the shift is continuing, currently 40% of men and 60% women have or are obtaining a college degree. Furthermore, the shift towards women is prominent in middle management. According to the Bureau of Labor
10 Statistics, women now hold 51.4 percent of managerial and professional jobs—up from 26.1 percent in 1980. They make up 54 percent of all accountants and hold about half of all banking and insurance jobs. About a third of America's physicians are now women, as are
15 45 percent of associates in law firms—and both those percentages are rising fast. Is post-industrial, modern society better suited to women than to men, and what are the vast cultural consequences of this historically unprecedented role reversal?
20 In 1984, Roberta Steinbacher, a social psychologist, reported in a *People* magazine profile that "there's no question that there exists a universal preference for sons." Steinbacher lamented that women were becoming second-class citizens, while men
25 dominated. Fortunately, that trend appears to be no longer: directly in contrast today are data from sperm selection methods such as MicroSort, in FDA clinical trials, which show that requests for girls outweigh those for boys, at about 75 percent. It is possible
30 that the once-held preference for "first-born sons" is fading—and not only in the U.S. In countries from South Korea, India, and China, the preference for girls is gaining ground as well.
To attempt to understand the force behind this
35 phenomenon, post-Darwinians argue that skills such as communicating and thinking have become more important than stamina and physical strength in our post-industrial economy. In times when the majority of jobs required physical labor, it would have made
40 sense that men would dominate, but that is simply not the case any longer. Machines have taken over many of the hard-labor jobs, making way for women to no longer be thought of as "unsuited." In fact, since 2000, manufacturing has lost more than a third of its total
45 workforce, and has taken in few young workers. Even skilled jobs, such as for electricians, builders, or real estate agents, are scarce. Only two of 15 job categories predicted to grow by 2020 are dominated by men—computer engineer and janitor. Women get
50 all the others, creating an economy that is friendlier to women than to men.
As proof that the trend is sustainable, organizations like the Organization for Economic Cooperation and Development report that a country's
55 economic success is correlated to the power of women in their society, both economic and political power. In war-torn countries like Liberia and Rwanda, women are rising to leadership roles, becoming a "maternal rescue team" to their countries and
60 attempting to improve their fortunes. The more flexible and more nurturing behaviors associated with women are seen as more adaptive and better suited to successful fulfillment of social roles in today's world. In 2008, these "more-feminine" management
65 styles were quantified and researched. Using data from the top 1,500 US companies between 1992 and 2006, researchers at the University of Maryland and Columbia Business School found that women in top positions performed better. They cited skills such as
70 collaboration and creativity—as part of an innovation-intensive strategy—as especially strong contributors to such performance.
Even though the top tiers of US society remain male-dominated, Rosin describes this as what she
75 sees as the "last gasp of a dying age," with many powerful forces pushing for change. With this painful role reversal, male support groups are increasingly springing up in the America's rust belt and other similar places. Traditional family roles are being
80 turned upside-down, so some groups assist with lack of employment, while others teach relationship and social skills. Many of the men who wind up in these groups are casualties of the lack of manufacturing jobs—a true sign of the shifting times, as manufacturing jobs used
85 to be one of the most abundant sectors to turn to when in need of work.
Instead of being nostalgic for the past, society should embrace this change and figure out how to capitalize on it moving forward. As the perception of
90 the ideal business leader shifts, the old "command and control" model is seen as passé. Nowadays, leaders needs to channel their charisma, act like good coaches, and encourage hard work and creativity. Even such skills as reading body language and facial expression
95 have become important, as are "sensitive leadership" and social intelligence.

Figure 1

Percentages of U.S. Men and Women Relative to Education Level (2015)

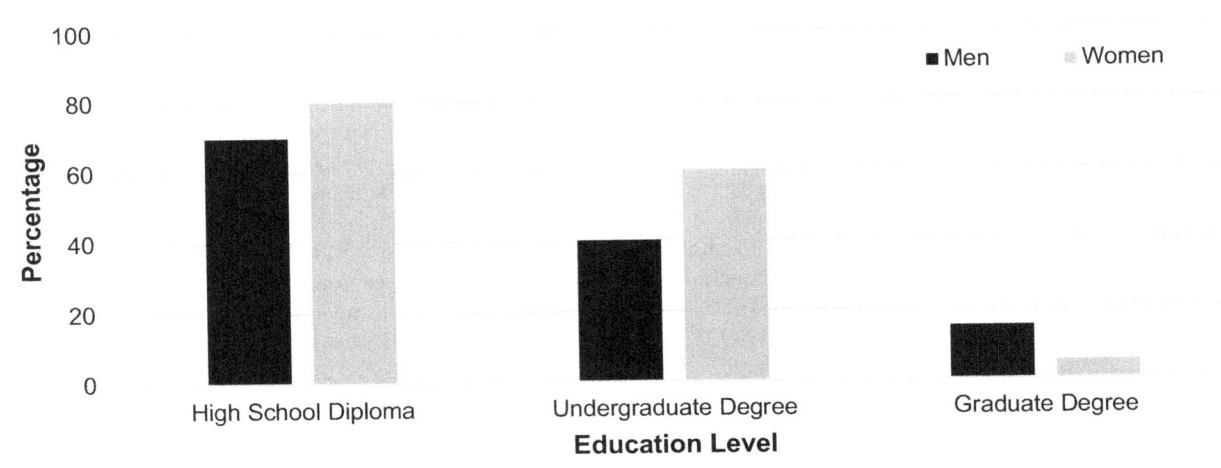

■ Men   ▪ Women

(Bar chart showing percentages by Education Level: High School Diploma — Men ~70%, Women ~80%; Undergraduate Degree — Men ~42%, Women ~62%; Graduate Degree — Men ~18%, Women ~8%)

Figure 2

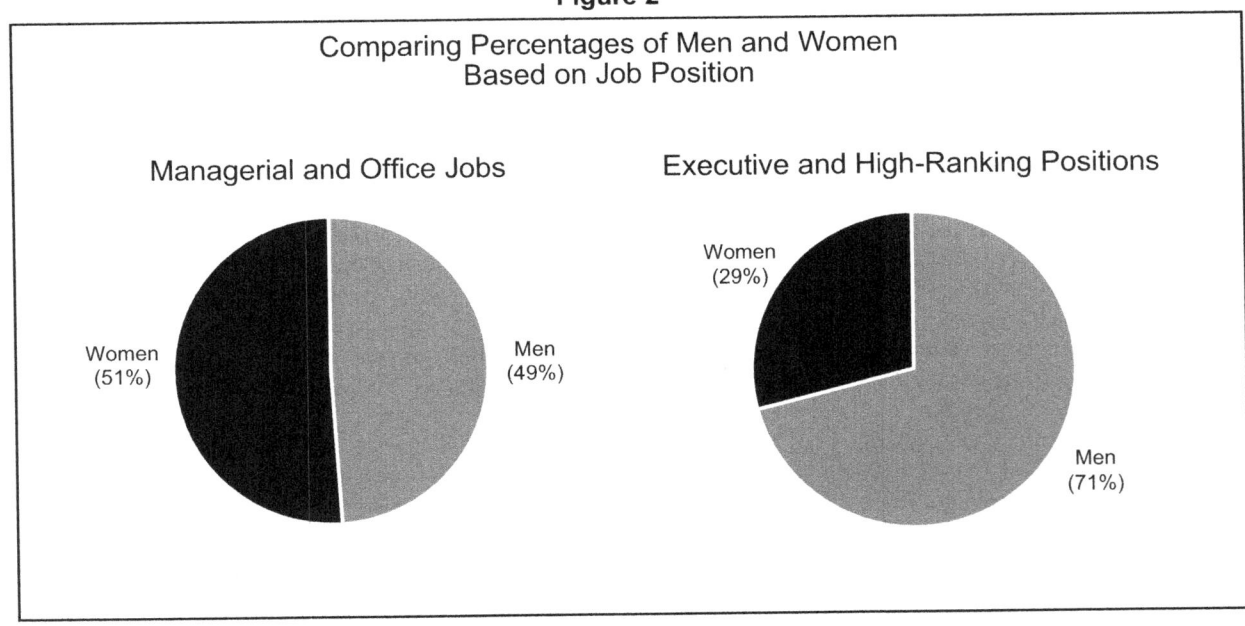

Comparing Percentages of Men and Women Based on Job Position

Managerial and Office Jobs
- Women (51%)
- Men (49%)

Executive and High-Ranking Positions
- Women (29%)
- Men (71%)

1

Throughout the passage, the author characterizes the modern United States economy as

A) troubling in the sense of alienation that it inspires in both men and women.
B) increasingly premised on time-saving and cost-efficient technology.
C) a model for the promotion of gender equality that other nations should follow.
D) notable for a shift away from manufacturing-based employment.

2

In order to argue that there has been a shift away from the social ideas cited by Steinbacher (line 20), the author of the passage presents

A) genetic analysis that reveals an unexpected preference.
B) a newly-acceptable ideological premise that was unfamiliar to Steinbacher.
C) a theory of technological development that contradicts Steinbacher's thesis.
D) information that indicates the presence of an international trend.

3

Which choice provides the best evidence for the answer to the previous question?

A) Lines 23-25 ("Steinbacher . . . dominated")
B) Lines 26-29 ("directly in . . . 75 percent")
C) Lines 31-33 ("In countries . . . as well")
D) Lines 38-41 ("In times . . . longer")

4

Which of the following pieces of information, if true, would offer the best support for the ideas endorsed by the Organization for Economic Cooperation and Development?

A) Structuring a company so that women perform at least 50% of all physical labor normally has a positive effect on workplace sentiment.
B) Large corporations with at least 50% of all leadership positions held by women tend to pay their executives relatively high salaries.
C) More than 50% of voters in countries with open elections see women as creative and compassionate leaders.
D) Democratic countries with 50% or more of all legislative seats held by women exhibit the most robust long-term economic growth.

5

Which choice indicates that the shift to an economic model that gives women new advantages may be problematic for men?

A) Lines 57-60 ("In war-torn . . . fortunes")
B) Lines 65-69 ("Using . . . better")
C) Lines 73-76 ("Even . . . change")
D) Lines 76-79 ("With this . . . place")

6

As used in line 61, "flexible" most nearly means

A) unpredictable.
B) accommodating.
C) multifaceted.
D) extensive.

7

As used in line 73, "top" most nearly means

A) least rudimentary.
B) most privileged.
C) least accessible.
D) most intimidating.

8

The final paragraph of the passage serves the function of

A) explaining how women excel in exhibiting leadership traits traditionally associated with men.
B) arguing that the qualities that enable women to succeed in business are applicable to a variety of other pursuits.
C) emphasizing the importance of qualities associated with women without mentioning women directly.
D) demonstrating that presumably feminine strengths such as compassion and communication are not in fact gender-specific.

9

Which of the following statements is logically supported by the educational statistics in figure 1?

A) The number of adults in the United States who hold high school diplomas has remained constant over time.
B) Only a small minority of the adults in the United States held graduate degrees in 2015.
C) The disparity between the number of women with undergraduate degrees and the number of men with undergraduate degrees will continue to increase.
D) Few people in the United States see graduate degrees as necessary for professional advancement.

10

The two charts presented in figure 2 offer information that most closely reflects the ideas and information attributed to

A) the Bureau of Labor Statistics (lines 9-10).
B) Microsort (line 27).
C) post-Darwinians (line 35).
D) the University of Maryland and Columbia Business School researchers (lines 67-68).

11

Do the data present in the figures support or undermine the arguments set forward by Hanna Rosin in the passage?

A) Support, because Rosin draws her own data from the years that are considered in the figures.
B) Support, because Rosin claims that men still dominate some of the positions of highest responsibility in the U.S. economy.
C) Undermine, because the charts indicate that men dominate skilled professions to an extent that contradicts Rosin's depiction of the job market.
D) Undermine, because Rosin argues that men have less interest in attaining advanced degrees than women do.

Questions 1-11 are based on the following passage and supplementary material.
4.5
The following passage is synthesized from Spiegel Online's "SPIEGEL Interview with Jerome Kagan" and Elsevier Journal's "Brain Imaging Reveals ADHD as a Collection of Different Disorders" by Rihannon Bugno.

In modern society, most persons have some knowledge of attention deficit/hyperactivity disorder (ADD/ADHD). It sprung into existence swiftly and quickly gained prevalence: the media has been reporting a sharp uptick in diagnoses over recent decades. However, Webb et al, authors of "Misdiagnosis and Dual Diagnoses of Gifted Children and Adults," suggest that the actual occurrence of AD(H)D is much lower than the rate of diagnosis. They also see a significant increase in stimulant medication prescriptions, such as Ritalin, to treat the condition. Misdiagnosis would be bad enough on its own—many physicians and psychologists are hesitant to diagnose children with psychological disorders at all—but combine being diagnosed improperly with taking potentially harmful drugs and you have a recipe for disaster. To protect kids from these issues in the future, we must come to a consensus as to whether the disorder exists and how exactly to determine that a diagnosis should be made.

Professor Jerome Kagan, a preeminent developmental psychologist, in a 2012 Der Spiegel interview, faults an eager pharmaceutical industry with selling the medications to treat what he describes as a sham illness: "it is an invention. Every child who's not doing well in school is sent to see a pediatrician, and the pediatrician says: 'It's ADHD; here's Ritalin.' In fact, 90 percent of these 5.4 million kids don't have an abnormal dopamine metabolism. The problem is, if a drug is available to doctors, they'll make the corresponding diagnosis."

Others besides Kagan question the AD(H)D diagnosis. Dr. Richard Saul, in a 2014 *Time* article, also says the condition does not exist as understood by the general public and defined in the DSM V. Saul says that, since 1937, doctors have been prescribing medications to cover up the symptoms. The DSM's definition and criteria have changed on several occasions since the diagnosis was first coined. He adds that the current criteria are so loose and variable that, at one time or another, the entire population of the US would meet the diagnostic requirements. He lists numerous alternative diagnoses that, under appropriate circumstances, would be a far better fit. He has found that his patients are either exhibiting "normal" behavior, or symptoms of what, after an extensive evaluation, turns out to be something other than AD(H)D.

On the other hand, health writer Eileen Bailey asserts that this phenomenon exists, observing that "in 2002, 75 scientists from around the world discussed the continuing inaccurate portrayal of AD(H)D and, in response, signed an AD(H)D International Consensus Statement." They asserted that there was "no question" that the disorder involved a deficiency in abilities that causes serious harm to those with the disorder.

As a whole, scientists appear divided as to whether AD(H)D exists, because the process of diagnosing is tricky. First, psychologists and physicians have to agree on a number of traits that represent the disorder; then, they need to determine which ones are crucial for the diagnosis, and what other criteria need to be present (length of time, severity of symptoms, effect on daily life); third, any underlying disorders that may mimic or cause AD(H)D need to be ruled out; lastly, and most difficult, it needs to be determined whether there is a biological component that can be traced to the disorder. If a biological marker can be pinpointed, diagnosing becomes much easier: in come neuroscientists, using those with the AD(H)D diagnosis as subjects, to try to determine which areas of the brain may be associated with this condition. As nothing has been found to solidify the existence of the disorder, arguments for and against its actual existence continue.

Four recent neuroscience studies attempted to identify and correlate brain-related phenomena to AD(H)D, purportedly, to support the existence of the disorder. Although the study wasn't particularly helpful in finding a brain-related AD(H)D marker, something interesting did come of the study: in reviewing the methods used in each of these studies, a pattern emerged. The subjects identified as having AD(H)D were presumed to have been diagnosed with the condition by a process consistent with the DSM V recommendations. It is unclear that any effort was made to explore how each initial diagnosis was made, or whether the diagnosis was in fact correct. In other words, these studies do not refute or confirm the AD(H)D diagnosis, but instead accept it as a given. If they want to have better success in defining the biological basis of the disorder, neuroscientists and others who wish to build a case to support the existence of AD(H)D must take steps to ensure that the DSM V criteria are properly applied. It is going to be impossible to determine whether there exists a correlation between any brain-related issue and AD(H)D, if they do not know that the diagnosis is accurate and the patient does, in fact, have AD(H)D.

Because of the exhaustive nature of the task of ruling out so many other possible causes, a correct diagnosis winds up being a challenge. Some experts say that it cannot be properly made after one 15-minute appointment with a general practitioner who looked at a questionnaire that was filled out by school staff and parents—which is what often happens.

Child AD(H)D Cases in the United States

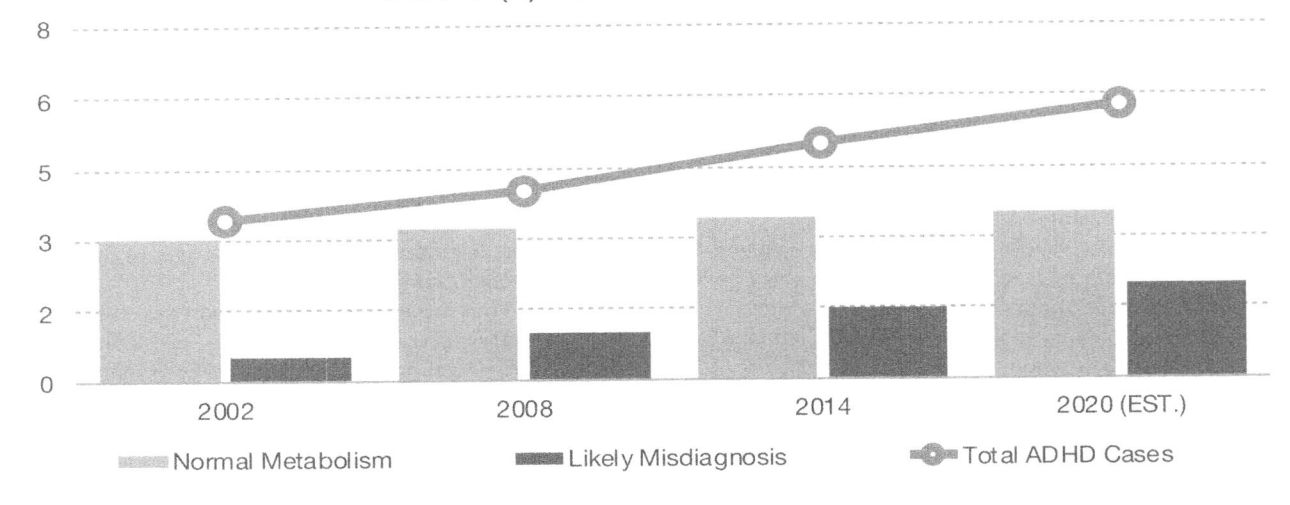

Year	Normal Metabolism	Likely Misdiagnosis	Total ADHD Cases
2002	3.0	0.7	3.7
2008	3.3	1.5	4.5
2014	3.7	2.2	5.5
2020 (EST.)	3.8	2.5	6.0

1

According to the passage, which of the following statements best describes the author's response to the possibility of ADD/ADHD misdiagnosis?

A) Irresponsibility on the part of schools and pediatricians should be proactively countered by more rigorous diagnosis.
B) Popular misconceptions about the disorders should be documented as a valuable first step towards new research.
C) Media outlets should revise their reporting procedures in order to provide more accurate coverage.
D) Practical measures should be taken to develop a widely sanctioned approach to this pressing dilemma.

2

Which choice provides the best evidence for the answer to the previous question?

A) Lines 3-6 ("It sprung . . . decades")
B) Lines 17-20 ("To protect . . . made")
C) Lines 25-27 ("Every . . . Ritalin")
D) Lines 32-33 ("Others . . . diagnosis")

3

On the basis of the information presented in the passage, Jerome Kagan would most likely characterize the "pediatrician" (lines 26-27) as

A) incapable of thinking critically about a common diagnosis.
B) deluded yet deeply concerned about children's well-being.
C) guided by typical yet regrettable treatment practices.
D) indifferent to a growing and alarming ethical problem.

4

As used in line 39, "coined" most nearly means

A) fabricated.
B) formulated.
C) brainstormed.
D) popularized.

5

The authors include the quotations from Eileen Bailey primarily to

A) submit expert testimony that undermines arguments proposed by those rejecting AD(H)D as a true illness.
B) introduce a counter-argument to those questioning the existence of AD(H)D.
C) provide a sense of balance and impartiality to prevent critics from contesting the fairness of Kagan's claims.
D) expand upon a line of reasoning that is close to the authors' own viewpoint.

6

As used in line 58, "divided" most nearly means

A) incapable of consensus.
B) unwilling to communicate.
C) accepting of discord.
D) afflicted with irresolution.

7

According to the passage, the debate over the existence of AD(H)D continues because

A) a definition of AD(H)D that is fully understood by only a few experts has remained in use.
B) psychologists and neuroscientists have resisted an interdisciplinary approach to diagnosis.
C) the DSM V recommendations encourage a method of diagnosis that has only seldom been changed.
D) researchers have not definitively linked the disorder to any precise areas of the brain.

8

Which choice provides the best evidence for the answer to the previous question?

A) Lines 67-68 ("it needs . . . disorder")
B) Lines 69-75 ("in come . . . continue")
C) Lines 83-87 ("The subjects . . . recommendations")
D) Lines 89-91 ("In other . . . given")

9

On the basis of the chart, which of the following statements can be inferred about ADHD misdiagnosis?

A) The number of cases of children who are likely to be misdiagnosed with AD(H)D is not expected to decrease beyond 2020.
B) None of the children who were apparently misdiagnosed with AD(H)D in 2020 exhibited abnormal metabolism.
C) Research performed in 2008 disproved the idea of a direct link between AD(H)D and abnormal metabolism.
D) Research performed in 2014 disproved the idea of a direct link between AD(H)D and abnormal metabolism.

10

If the overall trends illustrated in the chart continue over time, which of the following situations would be most likely in 2030 as compared to 2020?

A) A greater difference between total AD(H)D cases and the number of children with normal metabolism.
B) A consistent difference between total AD(H)D cases and the number of children with normal metabolism.
C) A greater difference between the number of misdiagnosed children and the number of children with normal metabolism.
D) A consistent difference between the number of misdiagnosed children and the number of children with normal metabolism.

11

The authors of the passage would regard the graph as a possible validation of

A) Webb and other specialists' idea that Ritalin is being prescribed to children who have been misdiagnosed with AD(H)D.
B) Jerome Kagan's idea that a substantial group of children has been misdiagnosed with AD(H)D.
C) Richard Saul's idea that doctors do not possess useful criteria for diagnosing AD(H)D.
D) Bailey's idea that AD(H)D is associated with serious impairments and deficiencies in children.

Questions 1-11 are based on the following passages and supplementary material.

4.6
Passage 1 is adapted from "There's No Place Like Home: Crown-of-Thorns Outbreaks in the Central Pacific Are Regionally Derived and Independent Events," a 2012 PLOS ONE journal article by Molly Timmers et al. Passage 2 is adapted from "Larval Starvation to Satiation: Influence of Nutrient Regime on the Success of Acanthaster planci," a 2015 PLOS ONE journal article by Kennedy Wolfe and a team of researchers at The University of Sydney in Sydney, Australia.

Passage 1

Coral reefs are known to be relatively delicate ecosystems. They need just the right ocean temperature, just the right amount of nutrients, and just the right populations of cohabiting species to sustain their existence. The primary threats to coral reefs today come from climate change in the forms of ocean acidification and warming, as well as worsening storms. Another threat, which has become more common, is the outbreak—or increased population—of a starfish called "Crown-of-Thorns" that attaches to coral and directly digests the tissue.

But is there an effective way to prevent Crown-of-Thorns outbreaks? No one is entirely sure what directly causes them, making prevention strategies difficult to come by. For many years, the foremost explanation for these outbreaks was the "larval dispersal hypothesis," which suggested that the starfish's larvae were carried on the strong, wide-ranging currents of the Pacific Ocean. This would mean that distant populations of Crown-of-Thorns starfish have genetic similarities, giving researchers a testable hypothesis to determine the accuracy of this theory.

Excited by this possibility, a group of researchers set out to determine exactly what sort of genetic similarities there could be between and among disparate populations. From 2005 to 2008, specimens were collected from the North Central, Northwest, and South Central Pacific—23 sites in all—which had both outbreak and non-outbreak populations. In all, the researchers obtained 656 specimens, including one which had been collected in 1982 in Hawai'i. The DNA of these samples was extracted and sequenced, and thereafter analyzed several ways: DNA was compared both between and within each region. For example, a specimen from the Northwest Pacific would be part of the regional group to be compared to those of the North and South Central regions, but that same specimen would also be compared to other North West specimens.

The team found that there were 341 haplotypes (DNA variations that are typically inherited as a set) that were specific to the regions of origin. Furthermore, significant variations were not found between outbreak and non-outbreak populations from the same area, and populations shared fewer and fewer similarities the more distant another population was. Taken together, these data led researchers to be fairly certain that genetic variations were due to local variations—not migration.

The findings on the genetic similarities and differences indicate that local environmental factors are behind the outbreaks. Several studies suggest that those local factors could involve a deluge of nutrients during the wet season, while other studies suggest that the declining populations of predators allow the starfish to multiply unchecked. Whatever the factor or combination of factors, the findings mean that management and prevention strategies should be tailored to local needs.

Passage 2

In January 2018, a new outbreak of the Crown-of-Thorns starfish on the Great Barrier Reef was reported by ABC News. Up until the last few decades, these outbreaks have occurred periodically, but now seem to to be increasing in frequency. According to the GBR Marine Park Authority, outbreaks last about 15 years. But what sustains these high population numbers? According to the "enhanced nutrient hypothesis," increased nutrients in areas with more starfish larvae increase the likelihood that the larvae will make it to a juvenile stage, and then to adulthood. Another, referred to as the "larval resilience hypothesis," holds that the larvae can survive just as well in low-nutrient, high-oxygen (oligotrophic) environments. However, neither hypothesis had been tested until the mid-2010s—several years after an outbreak was discovered on the Great Barrier Reef.

A team of scientists collected germ cells from adult starfish, created viable embryos, and raised the larvae in laboratory conditions. After approximately 48 hours, once they had digestive tracts, the larvae were divided into 5 groups, with 10 containers per group. Each group was fed a different microgram (or millionth of a gram, also symbolized as µg) level of tropical microalgae: Group 1 at a level of 0 µg, Group 2 at .01 µg, Group 3 at .1 µg, Group 4 at 1 µg, and Group 5 at 10 µg. The larvae were randomly sampled on certain days and photographed. From these photographs, the researchers measured length and width, and made note of any developmental abnormalities.

By day 18, those in Groups 1 and 2 were unable to "settle"—or cling to a larger, stable object—and exhibited stunted or more abnormal growth. Groups 3, 4, and 5 were the hardiest, but Group 4 showed the greatest gains. These findings suggest that an ideal level of nutrients, possibly provided by floods during a wet season, during the larval stage is a deciding factor in the success of these starfish to reach adulthood in large numbers.

The starfish can survive in an oligotrophic environment, but with just the right amount of nutrients, they truly thrive. However, as ocean acidification kills coral reefs, these starfish may not be as successful as this study suggests they could be. These findings must also be tested for populations that are farther off-coast, such as the population overtaking the Great Barrier Reef in early 2018.

Figure 1

Flooding in Australia (1985-2003)

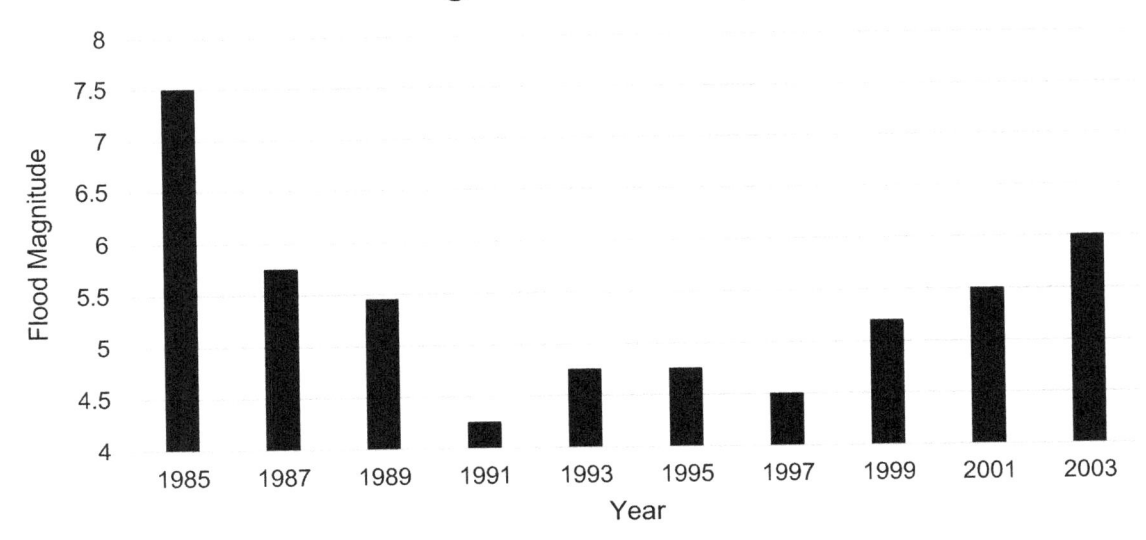

Figure 2

Crown of Thorns Starfish Population (1985-2003) Queensland, Australia

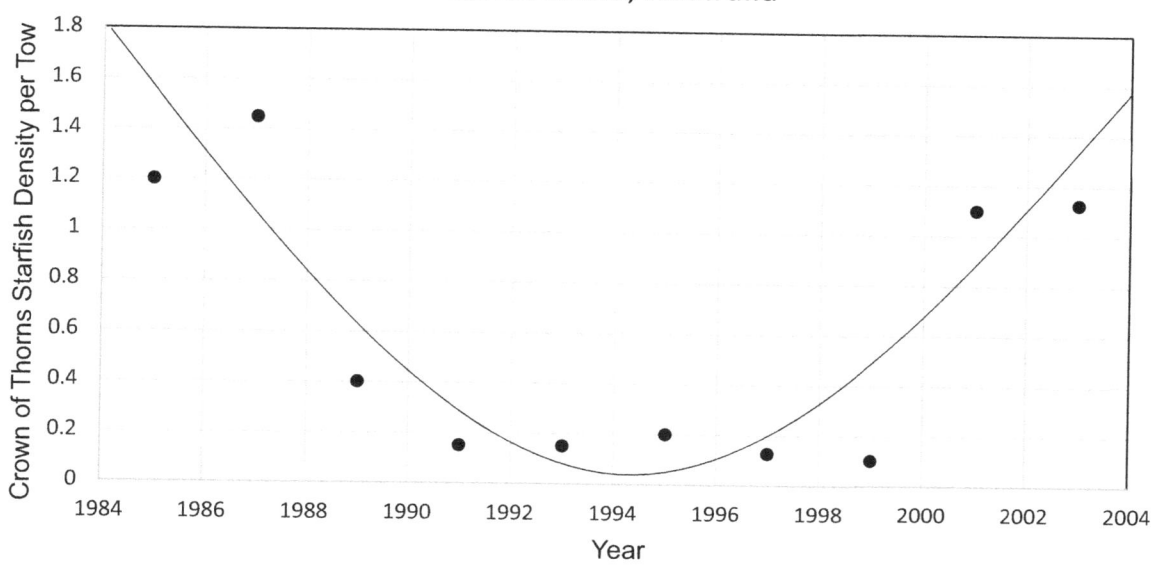

[Scatter plot with U-shaped trend line. X-axis: Year (1984-2004). Y-axis: Crown of Thorns Starfish Density per Tow (0 to 1.8). Data points approximately: 1985: 1.2; 1987: 1.45; 1989: 0.4; 1991: 0.15; 1993: 0.15; 1995: 0.2; 1997: 0.1; 1999: 0.05; 2001: 1.05; 2003: 1.1]

1

Passage 1 indicates that the "larval dispersion hypothesis" (line 16) is

A) increasingly credible on the basis of new research.
B) fundamentally similar to more accurate ideas.
C) well-formulated yet currently divisive.
D) not supported by the available data.

2

Which choice provides the best evidence for the answer to the previous question?

A) Lines 19-22 ("This . . . theory")
B) Lines 23-26 ("Excited . . . populations")
C) Lines 42-46 ("Furthermore . . . was")
D) Lines 52-56 ("Several . . . unchecked")

3

As used in line 18, "wide-ranging" most nearly means

A) strikingly versatile.
B) broadly circulating.
C) all-comprehending.
D) questionably defined.

4

As used in line 46, "distant" most nearly means

A) questionable.
B) hostile.
C) remote.
D) puzzling.

5

In Passage 2, the author refers to the "new outbreak" (line 60) as

A) an inspiration for the research documented in the passage.
B) a dramatic occurrence that changed a sensitive ecosystem.
C) a single event in a trend that has recently become evident.
D) an occasion that indicates some unexpected benefits of flooding.

6

The experimental findings discussed in Passage 2 would be most clearly contradicted by the idea that starfish

A) grow at roughly the same rate in the wild and in laboratory habitats that simulate natural conditions.
B) consume only a few species of microalgae as part of a diet that can incorporate other food sources.
C) develop normally even if their diet consists of only minuscule amounts of tropical microalgae.
D) mature rapidly over a relatively brief period and then abruptly cease to grow.

7

Which choice provides the best evidence for the answer to the previous question?

A) Lines 77-79 ("A team . . . conditions")
B) Lines 86-87 ("The larvae . . . photographed")
C) Lines 90-92 ("By day 18 . . . growth")
D) Lines 94-98 ("These . . . numbers")

8

Based on figure 1, which of the following years represents the strongest flood magnitude that occurred in Australia?

A) 1991
B) 1985
C) 2003
D) 1999

9

Which of the following is cited as a threat to coral reefs in both Passage 1 and Passage 2?

A) Rising global temperatures
B) Dwindling predator populations
C) Ocean acidification
D) Violent storms

10

In what respect does the research described in Passage 1 differ from the research described in Passage 2?

A) Passage 1 describes an attempt to substantiate a popular theory, while Passage 2 describes an experiment that revealed that same theory's flaws.
B) Passage 1 describes evaluation of specimens gathered from nature, while Passage 2 describes a laboratory study in which specimens were subjected to different conditions.
C) Passage 1 describes a study that relied on extensive fieldwork, while Passage 2 describes a study that was designed to respond to the ideas of non-experts.
D) Passage 1 describes a research project that became a source of controversy, while Passage 2 describes subsequent efforts to establish consensus.

11

Does the information present in both figures undermine or validate the ideas set forward in Passage 1 and Passage 2?

A) Validate, because both passages call attention to a possible link between flooding and the proliferation of starfish.
B) Validate, because both passages note considerable year-to-year fluctuations in flood volume.
C) Undermine, because neither passage calls attention to the destructive impacts of flooding.
D) Undermine, because neither passage explains exactly which nutrients flooding makes more accessible to starfish.

Questions 1-11 are based on the following passage and supplementary material.
4.7
The following passage is synthesized from the NIH article "Redefining Health and Well-being in Older Adults" by Carol Torgan and the NCBI article "Empirical Redefinition of Comprehensive Health and Well-being in the Older Adults of The United States" by M.K. McClintock, W. Dale, E.O. Laumann, and L. Waite.

Some think of health merely as the absence of disease, but it is more than that. Health means well-being, including social, psychological, and physical well-being. Unfortunately, many traditional models of health seem to focus on medical conditions, such as heart disease, cancer, and diabetes. The World Health Organization (WHO) has defined health as a "state of complete physical, mental and social well-being and not merely the absence of disease or infirmity." According to this definition, we should be evaluating health differently for a clearer picture of older adulthood. What's more, redefining and reevaluating health can allow for more accurate assumptions of lifespan, allowing doctors to predict how long patients will live with their current lifestyle or if they make lifestyle changes (for better or for worse).

At the University of Chicago, Dr. Martha McClintock and her team attempted to classify the health of senior citizens by using a comprehensive, longitudinal approach, supported by the National Institutes of Health's (NIH's) National Institute on Aging (NIA). They published their findings in 2016 in the Proceedings of the National Academy of Sciences. In McClintock's research study, more than 3,000 US adults from the ages of 57 to 85 were sampled and interviewed. The sample included US older adults who lived at home, no matter what their current health status was. Questionnaires covering 54 diverse health variables were administered. Five years later, the same participants were contacted again. They were either re-interviewed or noted for their inability to participate, due to either death or incapacity.

The researchers constructed two models. First was a traditional "medical model," using 19 of 54 variables from what is known as a data-driven latent class analysis (LCA) from the National Social Life, Health, and Aging Project (NSHAP). The variables included a variety of medical issues and organ functions, such as liver disease, kidney disease, diabetes, stroke, lung disease, cancer, and heart disease. A second model, a "comprehensive model," included 35 measures from the LCA. The redefined approach included variables covering aspects of well-being and health that were not present in the traditional model. The variables associated with the second model included frailty (such as urinary incontinence, anemia, bone fracture, and gait speed), sensory function (such as hearing, vision, and taste), psychological health (such as self-esteem, loneliness, depression, and stress), and health behaviors (such as smoking, drinking, and sleeping).

Not surprisingly, the comprehensive model gave a much better picture of health. About half of the people who were classified as healthy based on the medical model had a number of vulnerabilities that were identified by the comprehensive model. These vulnerabilities impacted the chances that they would become incapacitated or die within 5 years—something anyone would certainly want to know. Additionally, some of the people who had chronic disease had a number of strengths that allowed them to be reclassified as healthy under the comprehensive model. For instance, older adults who were clinically obese but were physically and mentally healthy in other respects actually had the lowest risk of dying or of becoming incapacitated.

An analysis of the entire comprehensive model of health and well-being showed several unique variables that were able to predict both incapacity and mortality. Strong markers for future health problems included having a broken bone any time after age 45, poor social engagement and sensory function, and poor mental health. In contrast, greater mobility generally was a predictor of well-being. Dr. Luigi Ferrucci, who is an NIH geriatrician overseeing aging and health research, says, "If I had to rank behaviors in terms of priority, I'd say that exercise is the most important thing associated with living longer and healthier. Exercise is especially important for lengthening active life expectancy, which is life without disease and without physical and mental/thinking disability."

Moreover, McClintock's researchers found that several specific medical diagnoses such as cancer and hypertension were not as important as mental health (loneliness), mobility, sensory function (hearing), and bone fractures, when it comes to defining vulnerable health classes. She says that "the new comprehensive model of health identifies constellations of health completely hidden by the medical model and reclassifies about half of the people seen as healthy as having significant vulnerabilities."

While the medical model puts ⅔ of US citizens into classes considered to be of robust health, the comprehensive model shows that ½ of the population belongs to less healthy classes, ones independently associated with higher mortality rates. These findings are consistent with research by other scientists at the NIA—and with the suggestions made by some parents who typically advise their children to stay away from bad habits, get plenty of sleep, exercise regularly, and eat well.

Today, persons born in the US can live to be about 79 years old, whereas a century ago, people could be expected to live only to age 54. In 2016, if you live to age 65, you're likely to live to age 85. Those who make it to age 85 are very likely to make it to age 92. For those people living past 65, it would be greatly beneficial to be able to advise them how to maximize their health during those years, and McClintock's redefinition of "health" certainly seems to be on the right track. The better factors that lead to good or bad health are understood, the better people can feel and live when they're older, and that's beneficial to everyone.

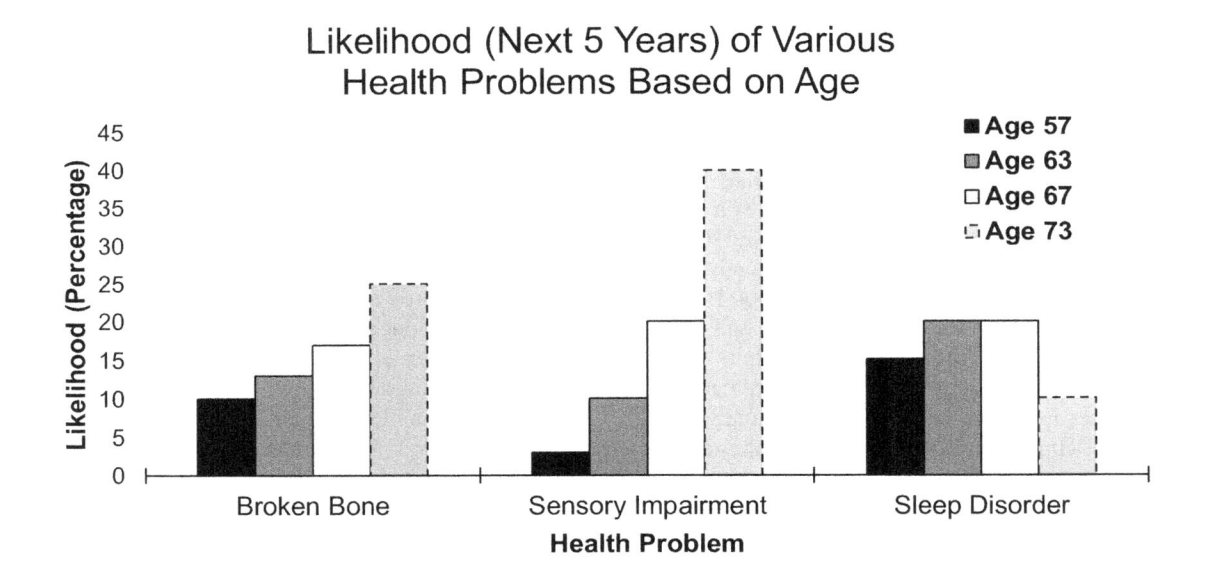

Likelihood (Next 5 Years) of Various Health Problems Based on Age

Health Problem	Age 57	Age 63	Age 67	Age 73
Broken Bone	10	13	17	25
Sensory Impairment	2	10	20	40
Sleep Disorder	15	20	20	10

1

The main purpose of the passage is to

A) provide support for the claim that health does not need to be redefined to fit today's standards.
B) describe the changes that can be made regarding the way that we define health to make old age more enjoyable.
C) detail the findings of one study that can revolutionize the future description of health for older individuals.
D) argue that one way to reduce the negative effects of risk factors is to incorporate exercise into daily life.

2

The second paragraph serves primarily to

A) present details of a study that is essential to understanding what it means to be healthy.
B) illustrate the daily duties of Dr. McClintock and her team at the University of Chicago.
C) demonstrate the types of articles published in the Proceedings of the National Academy of Sciences.
D) bring up an ongoing debate between proponents of the old and new classification systems of health.

3

According to the passage, the difference between the medical model and the comprehensive model is that

A) the medical model incorporates aspects such as psychological well-being, which the comprehensive model fails to acknowledge.
B) the medical model is a data-driven latent class analysis from the National Social Life, Health, and Aging Project.
C) the medical model primarily recognizes primarily disease and other ailments, while the comprehensive model includes well-being.
D) the comprehensive model focuses only on psychological health and healthy behaviors that are not assessed in the medical model.

4

Which of the following best characterizes the author's purpose in including the parenthetical information in lines 45-50?

A) To provide clarifying examples of the variables associated with the comprehensive model
B) To quantify aspects of the comprehensive model not associated with the medical model
C) To detail conditions that always lead to incapacitation or death within five years
D) To point out specific differences between the medical model and the comprehensive model

5

As used in line 44, "present" most nearly means

A) willing.
B) up-to-date.
C) incorporated.
D) in attendance.

6

Which choice best supports the idea that receiving a negative diagnosis does not definitely increase likelihood of mortality?

A) Lines 12-15 ("What's...lifestyle")
B) Lines 52-55 ("About...model")
C) Lines 56-57 ("These...years")
D) Lines 62-65 ("older...incapacitated")

7

As used in line 69, "markers for" most nearly means

A) ways to emphasize.
B) traits of.
C) demonstrations of.
D) signals of.

8

The passage suggests that a patient who experiences chronic disease would be able to increase his or her healthiness rating if he or she were to

A) become less mobile.
B) become more lonely.
C) improve sensory function.
D) improve hypertension.

9

It can be reasonably inferred that the author's primary purpose for including the comparison in lines 101-103 is to

A) indicate that healthcare has improved drastically within the past century, therefore increasing lifespan.
B) elucidate the benefits of increasing the scope of health to include factors outside of medical issues.
C) show how ineffective healthcare was before the study was conducted, thereby solidifying its necessity.
D) imply that healthcare was once much better than it is today and that more advancements are needed.

10

Based on the figure, which factor is least likely to be an indicator of future health problems?

A) Broken bone at age 57
B) Sensory impairment at age 57
C) Sleep disorder at age 57
D) Sleep disorder at age 73

11

Does the information in the figure support the claim in lines 103-105 ("if...92")?

A) Yes, because all the indicators directly correspond to the questionnaire used in the primary study.
B) Yes, because for a person with a broken bone at the age of 63, there is a low probability of future health problems.
C) No, because the chart only addresses probability of health problems based on three indicators.
D) No, because information provided in the chart directly contradicts the information in the passage.

Questions 1-11 are based on the following passage and supplementary material.
4.8
Adapted from a 2016 BBC Earth article titled "Why We Should Let Raging Wildfires Burn" by Claire Asher, a persuasive piece that investigates both how wildfires come about and how they can be stopped.

To those who don't know better, the image conjured of fall in California might be one of a peaceful and sunny day coupled with a calming breeze.
Line To those who have experienced the wrath of Santa Ana
5 winds during this season, however, the understanding is that it is no such thing. The Santa Ana winds are strong, extremely dry down-slope winds that originate inland and affect coastal Southern California and northern Baja California. They originate from cool
10 and dry high-pressure air masses in the Great Basin. These winds have been clocked at 150 mph, with some approximations showing even higher speeds. Add those gusts to a hot and dry climate, and you have discovered the recipe for wildfire season. Although wildfire season
15 has always been a blight to Californians, it's only getting worse thanks to the ever-growing effects of climate change. In December 2017, videos of infernos next to Californian cities went viral on social media, giving us evidence that a more vicious wildfire season
20 may become our new reality.

It's a given that we do our best to prepare for these intense fire seasons; however, forest management groups, industry groups, and political groups can't quite seem to agree on how exactly to
25 do so. At present, there are three choices: thin out the forests, conduct controlled burns, or let wildfires run their natural courses. Most people are (reasonably) suspicious of the last option, which leaves us with two different methods for managing fire by altering the
30 composition of the forest, known as fuel treatment. Now, how does it work?

Before the 1990s, there weren't really any published experiments comparing fuel treatments and their effects on a fire's behavior. A group of experts
35 changed that in 1995 by running such an experiment in a region of the western United States called the Sierra Nevada.

These experts chose a plot of mixed-conifer land that was 3000 meters by 9000 meters (only slightly
40 larger than the combined area of 3780 standard soccer fields), and was representative of the majority of the topography in the region. Their plan was to test 7 different methods of reducing or reconfiguring the fuel in forests. An 8th section of land was set aside as
45 a control group, where no treatment would be done. After the treatments, the team simulated wildfires in order to test which fuel treatment had been most effective.

The 7 treatments included prescribed burning,
50 pile-and-burn, and cut-and-scatter, in addition to four other methods that used canopy thinning (biomassing) alone or in combination with the first three treatments. In essence, the treatments either reduced the fuel in the space between the forest floor and the bottom
55 of the canopy, or moved the fuel closer to the forest floor so that the canopy would be less likely to catch fire. Additionally, two strips of land (one 90 meters wide and one 390 meters wide) that were free of most brush and trees over 3 meters tall were created in each
60 treatment area. These areas, called fuel breaks, would be used to determine which treatments were most likely to prevent a wildfire from crossing empty areas. The researchers then ignited fires on two different days with extremely dry and hot weather.

65 The results they found revealed a few patterns. In both scenarios, the land treated with prescribed burning experienced a fire that spread slower and was less intense than in any other area. Additionally, all four treatments that included biomassing saw the most
70 intense fires, and the two treatments incorporating cut-and-scatter had the fastest spreading fires. The treatments that used pile-and-burn and cut-and-scatter alone, as well as the control, had fire spreading into the canopy on the day with a more extreme temperature.
75 Moreover, on the same day every fire—except those in the areas treated with prescribed burning—created spot fires beyond the smaller fuel break, but none created spot fires beyond the larger break.

Although this experiment used predictive models
80 that assumed that the fuel was homogenous throughout each area and that the fires would not exhibit extreme behavior, it still produced a few important takeaways. The first, and perhaps most obvious, is that the fuel should be reduced or moved out of the canopy, or
85 both. The second is that prescribed burning shows the most promise as an effective fuel treatment to prevent wildfires from reaching their full potential. The third, and perhaps most important, is that combinations of fuel treatment and fuel breaks lead to the best results.

90 To many, it may seem frightening to literally fight fire with fire, but more and more people in fire-prone areas are gradually accepting this preventative measure. Public outreach and education are absolutely critical to implementing any of these land management
95 schemes. Changing public opinion must happen soon if we don't want the firestorms of December 2017 to become the new normal.

Relationship Between Fuel Targets and Fire Behavior

Fuel Targets	Examples	Prescription	Reasoning	Change in Fire Behavior
Surface Fuels	Live grass and brush, dead and downed wood	Prescribed burning, mechanical treatments	Remove, compact, or reduce continuity of surface fuels	Reduced spread rate and intensity
Ladder Fuels	small trees, brush, low limbs	Thinning, prescribed burning	decrease vertical continuity between surfaces and crown fuels	Reduced spread to crown fuels
Canopy Fuels	needles and small twigs in tree crowns	Thinning	reduce horizontal continuity	Limit spread of crown fires

Adapted from Chapter 9: *Landscape Fire Simulation and Fire Treatment Optimization* by Mark A. Finney

1

The primary purpose of the passage is to

A) explain the factors that can affect the intensity of a forest fire.
B) provide a brief overview of forest fires and their destructive behavior.
C) identify the various ways in which a forest fire can be extinguished.
D) determine the most effective method with which to minimize a forest fire.

2

As used in line 12, "approximations" most nearly means

A) guesses.
B) calculations.
C) estimates.
D) records.

3

As used in line 27, "natural" most nearly means

A) intended.
B) instinctive.
C) unimpeded.
D) predicted.

4

Which choice best describes the reason for the parenthetical statement in line 27?

A) It adds a lighthearted tone to an otherwise sobering topic.
B) It clarifies the reason that people are cautious about a method.
C) It shows that the author does not agree with a proposed choice.
D) It suggests that a possible solution is not worth considering.

5

The passage indicates that fuel treatments are primarily used to

A) prevent a forest's canopy from catching fire.
B) restrict a fire to the confines of a forest.
C) extinguish fires occurring in empty areas.
D) reduce the time in which a fire spreads.

6

Which choice provides the best evidence for the answer to the previous question?

A) Lines 27-30 ("Most people...treatment")
B) Lines 53-57 ("In essence...fire")
C) Lines 60-62 ("These areas...areas")
D) Lines 75-78 ("Moreover, on...break")

7

It can be reasonably inferred from the study described in the passage that prescribed burning can be effective because it

A) identified the variables that made forest fires most threatening to the environment.
B) altered the way that the wildfires began, thus creating a safer overall burn.
C) implemented fuel breaks, which helped to determine the most likely causes of burning.
D) revealed patterns that made treating wildfires easier to understand and control.

8

It can be reasonably inferred that the author describes a situation as "frightening" in line 90 because

A) a course of action is novel and as such might not work out as intended.
B) forest fires have consequences that laypersons are inclined to fear.
C) the general public is not educated enough to understand prescribed burning.
D) the nature of prescribed burning is paradoxical and as such difficult to support.

9

The last sentence of the passage serves mainly to

A) stress the importance of a course of action.
B) hint at a possible solution to a problem.
C) predict the consequences of a finding.
D) suggest that December 2017 had the worst fires on record.

10

According to the passage and the figure, which of the following fuel targets represents the "other" methods mentioned in line 52?

A) Surface
B) Ladder
C) Surface and canopy
D) Canopy and ladder

11

It can be reasonably inferred from the passage and the figure that the most effective fuel target was

A) surface.
B) ladder.
C) canopy.
D) none.

Questions 1-11 are based on the following passage.

4.9
Adapted from a 2016 *Atlantic* article, "How to Beat Dengue and Zika: Add a Microbe to Mosquitos," by Ed Yong, in which the author describes a novel and controversial solution to mosquito-borne viruses.

One of the signs—and certainly a downside—of warm weather is the presence of mosquitoes. Perhaps if all they did was bite, we would not mind. In many
Line countries around the world, however, a mosquito bite
5 can lead to a debilitating disease such as malaria, Dengue fever, or Zika.
These diseases are so serious because there are no cures for them: once someone contracts the disease, it must run its course. Even worse, as climate change
10 grows unchecked, so too do the epidemics spread by mosquitoes. Some experts have stated that in order to eliminate these diseases we should exterminate mosquitoes entirely. Others argue strongly against such measures. The consensus, though, is that basic
15 prevention is the most practical way to curb the spread of these mosquito-borne illnesses. There are simple solutions, such as insecticide and netting, and others that require more foresight, such as the introduction of dragonfly larvae into stagnant water, where they prey
20 on mosquito larvae. The best solution, however, may be found in the problem itself: mosquitoes.
To grasp how we might use mosquitoes to prevent the illnesses they carry, we must understand the mechanisms central to mosquitoes and infectious
25 diseases. The coexistence between the insect and the virus is called "symbiosis," a (typically) mutually beneficial interaction between two different organisms living in close physical association. In the symbiosis particular to the mosquito and the Dengue virus, the
30 virus spends critical stages of its life living inside the mosquito. One stage is reproduction, and the other is "travelling" to the salivary glands of its host, where the virus can be transmitted to a new host. The implication is that if the mosquito dies young, so does the virus.
35 Professor Scott O'Neill of Monash University found a way to use this to his advantage. He thought that if he introduced the bacterium *Wolbachia* into wild mosquitoes, he could effectively create an insect with a lifespan too short for the tastes of the Dengue virus.
40 *Wolbachia* is a bacterium found in most arthropods— it was last approximated to be in 60 percent of known species—that does not cause fatal harm to its hosts; nevertheless, it tampers with the reproductive mechanisms of its hosts, allowing them to reproduce
45 only with other infected individuals, and to produce offspring that are carriers as well.
O'Neill's team started with a type (or "strain") of *Wolbachia* called "popcorn," which was known to be an especially vicious infection in fruit flies; it could
50 cut the lifespan of its host in half. In order to ensure that this strain could be passed parent-to-offspring, the team spent years attempting to stably inject the popcorn *Wolbachia* into mosquito eggs. This was not accomplished until 2006, with the help of Conor
55 McMeniman, a molecular biologist at Johns Hopkins Bloomberg School of Public Health. The downside to this victory, though, was that the popcorn strain affected female mosquitoes in a such a way that if they did not die prematurely, they would likely be unable
60 to reproduce. Nevertheless, O'Neill was determined to see if *Wolbachia* could still combat Dengue inside a mosquito.
As it turned out, the bacterium could: according to researcher Elizabeth McGraw, who was also
65 instrumental to the breakthrough, *Wolbachia* consumes the very nutrients in the mosquito that would normally sustain the Dengue virus.
The team discovered this after injecting the virus into *Wolbachia*-infected mosquitoes. In nearly every
70 instance, the bacterium prevented the virus from gaining a foothold in the mosquito. The group quickly switched to a different strain of *Wolbachia*, and were able to test its transmission. They put *Wolbachia*-infected mosquitoes and uninfected mosquitoes
75 together in outdoor cages. After three generations, every mosquito carried *Wolbachia*.
Scott O'Neill's organization Eliminate Dengue did a trial run in two suburbs of Cairns, Australia in January 2011. With the approval of residents and local
80 authorities, the team released thousands of *Wolbachia*-infected mosquitoes over ten weeks. In the seven years since, the outbreak of Dengue has been drastically reduced, and the "Wolbachia blanket" (as field trial manager Geoff Wilson calls it) remains relatively
85 strong, only needing occasional reintroductions of the bacterium to the population.
Now called the World Mosquito Program (WMP), this organization operates in ten countries, according to its website. Its method is currently being applied
90 to Zika and Chikungunya, which are affected by *Wolbachia* the same way that Dengue is.
The potential impact on both world health and economy is enormous. Dengue fever alone can reach billions of dollars (US) in direct costs for prevention
95 and treatment across the world. Since the *Wolbachia*

method is self-sustaining, there may be very little cost for the treatment beyond initial investments. According to WMP, the cost of this measure will eventually be around $1 USD per person. Even better, because
100 *Wolbachia* is a living organism, it will likely grow and adapt to new environments. We may be looking at a future in which the major tropical diseases cast an insignificant shadow.

1

The main purpose of the passage is to

A) detail a new technique that could become revolutionary in an area of health and medicine.
B) introduce a professor who made an unexpected discovery regarding infectious diseases.
C) describe the methodology which makes mosquito control more effective now than in the past.
D) explore a recent development in disease control that can eliminate the threat of the Zika virus.

2

Which of the following was NOT mentioned in the passage as a possible solution for mosquito-borne diseases?

A) Introducing predatory species
B) Altering reproductive mechanisms
C) Infecting salivary glands
D) Using insect-repellent sprays

3

As used in line 10, "unchecked" most nearly means

A) unnoticed.
B) unstoppable.
C) rampantly.
D) spontaneously.

4

It can be reasonably inferred from the passage that the inclusion of the parenthetical statement in line 26 serves as

A) a way to imply that the relationship between mosquitoes and the Zika virus is not truly a symbiotic one.
B) an injection of sarcasm into a discussion of the idea that there could be any beneficial relationship with mosquitoes.
C) an acknowledgement of the fact that the author does not really know whether symbiosis plays a part.
D) a humorous digression from the serious tone that has prevailed until this point in the passage.

5

Which choice provides the best evidence to explain the reason that *Wolbachia* is effective at reducing transmission of viruses?

A) Lines 22-25 ("To grasp...disease")
B) Lines 35-36 ("Professor Scott...advantage")
C) Lines 36-39 ("He thought...virus")
D) Lines 40-43 ("*Wolbachia* is...hosts")

6

As used in line 39, "tastes" most nearly means

A) penchant.
B) appetite.
C) satisfaction.
D) liking.

7

Which of the following best represents the effect that O'Neill "thought" (line 36) would occur by following injection of *Wolbachia* into mosquitoes?

A) It will infect the mosquito's internal cells in a manner that makes it impossible for them to carry the disease.
B) It will cause the mosquito to become sick and die before it has a chance to contract a virus or infect humans.
C) It will limit the mosquito's reproduction to other carriers only and produce infected offspring with shorter lifespans.
D) It will prevent the mosquito from spreading the disease through its salivary glands.

8

It can be reasonably inferred from the passage that in order to determine the effectiveness of *Wolbachia* once it was injected into mosquitoes, the researchers

A) created a second strain called "popcorn," which would provide them with enough information to deem the experiment a success.
B) mated mosquitoes for three subsequent lifespans until they were assured that transmission of the bacterium persisted.
C) allowed the mosquitoes to reproduce with other infected mosquitoes over time to determine that they would not lose the bacterium.
D) tampered with the reproductive ability of mosquitoes in another manner that would act as a control to their experimental group.

9

Which choice provides the best evidence for the answer to the previous question?

A) Lines 44-46 ("allowing them...well")
B) Lines 50-53 ("In order...eggs")
C) Lines 65-67 ("*Wolbachia*...virus")
D) Lines 73-76 ("They put...*Wolbachia*")

10

The term "Wolbachia blanket" in line 83 most reasonably represents the area that

A) is covered by viruses that can be mitigated by *Wolbachia*.
B) Scott O'Neill's organization currently covers in Australia.
C) is considered to be dense with *Wolbachia*-infected mosquitoes.
D) has not yet been introduced to *Wolbachia*-infected mosquitoes.

11

In relation to the passage as a whole, the information in lines 93-95 serves what purpose?

A) It reinforces the need for innovative solutions like *Wolbachia*.
B) It states in detail exactly how much money virus prevention costs.
C) It is a reminder that diseases such as malaria are expensive.
D) It restates an idea about *Wolbachia* that was introduced earlier.

Questions 1-11 are based on the following passage and supplementary material.
4.10
Adapted from the 2018 *Popular Science* article "'Incredible Genes' Can Only Do so Much to Counteract an Unhealthy Lifestyle" by Claire Maldarelli, in which the author seeks to explain the role, or lack thereof, of genetic predeterminism in our lives.

The human body has around 25,000 genes, units of DNA that are passed down from parent to child via the X and Y chromosomes. Genes make up everything
Line in our body: our eye colors, skin colors, heights, and
5 even personalities. They do this by instructing proteins in the body to follow certain pathways. When enough proteins are sent down the same pathway, they amass to form organs, tissue, muscle, bone—in short, us.
   Knowing this, it's easy to believe that genes
10 control everything in our lives, including disease and affliction. But what if the role of genes is smaller than it appears? When it comes to our health, genes can only go so far. The decisions we make in our daily lives, such as diet, exercise, and other lifestyle
15 choices can impact the function of our genes. This was confirmed by a study published in the *New England Journal of Medicine*, which sought to challenge the definitiveness of risk for heart disease as determined by genes.
20   To assess an individual's risk for coronary artery disease, doctors usually take a few factors into consideration. High blood pressure, one of the major precursors to heart disease, is dictated by genetics in up to 70% of cases. This means that if an individual
25 is carrying the gene for high blood pressure, there is a 30-70% likelihood that that individual will develop high blood pressure at some point in his or her lifetime. Other factors, such as high levels of LDL (low-density lipoprotein, or "bad" cholesterol) and total cholesterol,
30 can also be influenced by genetics. In fact, at least a few dozen genes have been identified that contribute to one's proportion of LDL to HDL (high-density lipoprotein, or "good" cholesterol).
   In addition to genetic factors, there are several
35 lifestyle factors that can decrease one's risk of heart disease; four indicated by the American Heart Association to be significant are no current smoking, no obesity, physical activity at least once weekly, and a healthy diet pattern. These components of a healthy
40 lifestyle, in addition to the genetic factors mentioned above, were assessed for the study and used as predictors of coronary events.

The researchers used readily available data from three populations, tracking incidences of coronary
45 events (such as a heart attack or an ischemic stroke) over a twenty-year period. They sought to identify which combinations of lifestyle and genetics would correlate with higher occurrences of coronary events. They discovered that lifestyle choices have the
50 ability to undermine genetic predisposition. Among participants with a high genetic risk, a healthy lifestyle cut the frequency of coronary events by almost half, compared to those with a high genetic risk and an unhealthy lifestyle. The opposite was also proven to be
55 true: an unhealthy lifestyle can negate the benefits of "good" genes. Among participants with a low genetic risk, an unfavorable lifestyle almost doubled the rate of coronary events during the same time period.
   These results have major implications for
60 people who may feel resigned to their predetermined genetic code, as we now have definitive proof that lifestyle can be equally influential in preventing heart disease. This opens up the possibility of a change in the way we treat heart disease: focusing not on
65 treatment but on anticipation and prevention. The study's authors were optimistic about the possibility of developing a preventative strategy that can yield results for everyone, regardless of genetic risk profile. Amit Khera, of the Massachusetts General Hospital
70 Cardiology Division and one of the lead authors of the study, believes that even those at "high risk" can benefit from this alternative approach, targeting "intensive lifestyle modification to those at high genetic risk, with the expectation that disclosure of
75 genetic risk can motivate behavioral change."

Figure 1

Probability of Contracting Heart Disease over a 20-Year Period as a Factor of Lifestyle and Genetic Risk

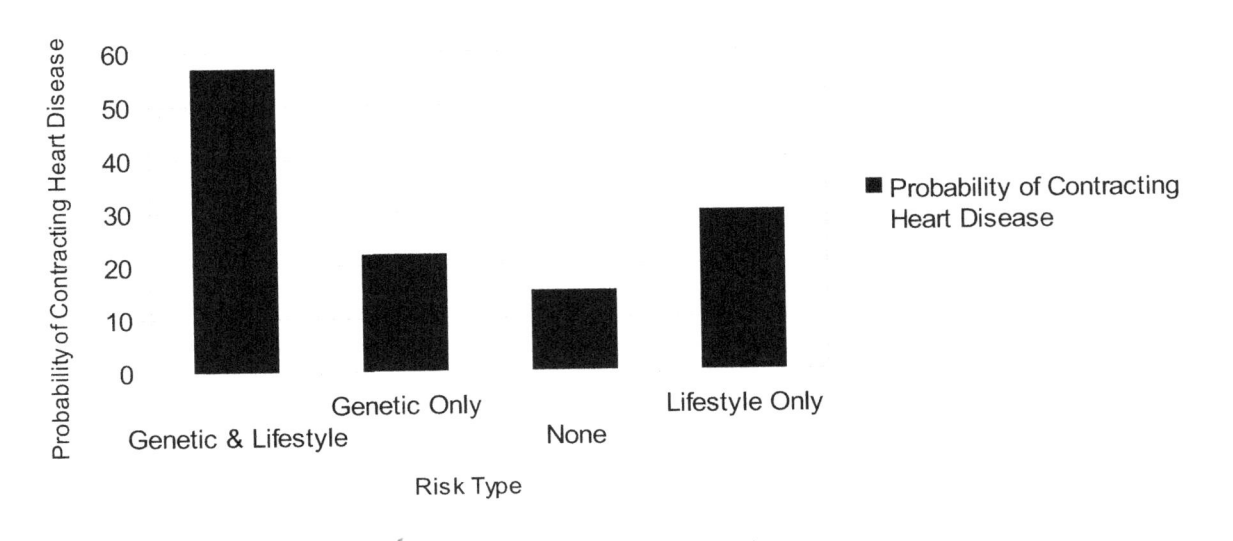

Figure 2

Percentage of the U.S. Population Falling into the Most Common Lifestyle Risks for Contracting Heart Disease

Lifestyle Risk	Percent Affected
Smoking	15.5
Obesity	33
Exercising less than once a week	80
Not eating vegetables	42.3

1

Which choice best describes the central claim of the passage?

A) Research shows that genes make up every aspect of us, physically and mentally, by programming proteins to follow certain pathways.
B) Research shows that high blood pressure and ratio of cholesterol are the most telling factors for heart disease and thus are what most concern doctors.
C) Research shows that for those with high genetic risk, a healthy lifestyle can be influential in treating heart disease.
D) Research shows that maintaining a healthy lifestyle is a good preventative strategy for heart disease regardless of genetic risk.

2

As used in line 20, "assess" most nearly means

A) verify.
B) examine.
C) gauge.
D) appraise.

3

According to the researchers, the results of the study offer hope to those with

A) an unhealthy proportion of LDL and HDL, which can only be caused by a combination of negative genetic and dietary factors.
B) significant lifestyle risks for high cholesterol because "good" genetics are influential at protecting against coronary events.
C) high genetic risk through a treatment that focuses on anticipating and preventing coronary events through a healthy lifestyle.
D) significant lifestyle risks as they can be motivated to undertake behavioral changes to protect their coronary health.

4

Which choice provides the best evidence for the answer to the previous question?

A) Lines 20-22 ("To assess...consideration")
B) Lines 22-27 ("High blood...lifetime")
C) Lines 35-37 ("In addition...disease")
D) Lines 59-65 ("These results...prevention")

5

Based on the information in the passage, how definite is the influence of genes?

A) The influence of genes is absolute because it controls important factors such as ratio of LDL and HDL or likelihood of exhibiting high blood pressure.
B) The influence of genes is not absolute because there are lifestyle factors that can undermine or negate the effects of genetic risk.
C) The influence of genes is absolute because genes are what we are made of and thus control our physical bodies and personalities.
D) The influence of genes is not absolute because genetic factors cannot control our health or the factors that doctors take into account.

6

According to the author, which of the following is an example of a lifestyle risk?

A) Eating fast food for every meal
B) Working in a high-risk profession
C) Trying to do dangerous stunts
D) Practicing unhygienic habits

7

The author makes which distinction in paragraph 3 (lines 20-42)?

A) The role that genetics plays in contracting heart disease is smaller than previously thought due to the influence of our daily lifestyles.
B) Research shows that unhealthy lifestyles can be harmful even to those who have low genetic risk for contracting heart disease.
C) Protein pathways are responsible for creating the parts of our body which cause most health risks, including heart disease.
D) Research shows that maintaining a healthy lifestyle is a good strategy, even for those with high risks, for preventing heart disease.

8

As used in line 68, "profile" most nearly means

A) outline.
B) description.
C) information.
D) record.

9

The researchers would most likely view the data in figure 1 with

A) strong agreement.
B) partial acceptance.
C) tempered disapproval.
D) complete disagreement.

10

Which lines provides the best evidence for the answer to the previous question?

A) Lines 43-46 ("The researchers...period")
B) Lines 46-48 ("They sought...events")
C) Lines 49-50 ("They discovered...predisposition")
D) Lines 50-54 ("Among participants...lifestyle")

11

According to figure 2, which lifestyle risk has the most influence on likelihood of contracting heart disease?

A) Regular smoking
B) Obesity
C) Infrequent exercise
D) Not eating vegetables

STOP

Answer Key: CHAPTER FOUR

SAT

4.01	4.02	4.03	4.04	4.05
1. B	1. C	1. A	1. D	1. D
2. A	2. B	2. B	2. D	2. B
3. C	3. C	3. D	3. C	3. C
4. C	4. B	4. C	4. D	4. B
5. D	5. A	5. B	5. D	5. B
6. B	6. D	6. C	6. B	6. A
7. B	7. D	7. A	7. B	7. D
8. D	8. B	8. C	8. C	8. B
9. D	9. B	9. C	9. B	9. A
10. B	10. B	10. D	10. A	10. A
	11. C	11. C	11. B	11. B

4.06	4.07	4.08	4.09	4.10
1. D	1. C	1. D	1. A	1. D
2. C	2. A	2. C	2. D	2. A
3. B	3. C	3. C	3. C	3. C
4. C	4. A	4. D	4. A	4. D
5. C	5. C	5. A	5. D	5. B
6. C	6. D	6. B	6. D	6. A
7. C	7. D	7. D	7. C	7. D
8. B	8. C	8. D	8. B	8. C
9. C	9. B	9. A	9. D	9. A
10. B	10. B	10. D	10. C	10. D
11. A	11. C	11. A	11. A	11. C

Answer Explanations

Chapter Four

Chapter 4.1 | Coralline Algae

1) CORRECT ANSWER: B
The passage is primarily concerned with a research project in which scientists "investigated a method to determine the age" of a species of coralline algae (lines 24-25) with the aim of using new information to protect a coral reef (lines 69-73). This content supports B and can be used to eliminate A and D, which both avoid discussion of the specific algae that interested the researchers. C does not reflect the fact that the scientists were interested in MULTIPLE factors in their study (calcium levels, age, and climate change) and should be eliminated for this reason.

2) CORRECT ANSWER: A
In lines 14-17, the author explains that the death of a region of a coral reef will negatively affect species that the area has "been both sheltering and providing nourishment for"; such species may relocate and may themselves die. A is the best choice, while B distorts content from later in the passage (tourists to coral reefs) to OVERSTATE the economic dependence of countries that feature coral reef tourism. C is inaccurate because changes in ocean temperature can harm coral reefs (instead of coral reefs THEMSELVES regulating ocean temperature), while D wrongly assumes that reef-related problems cannot be addressed when, in fact, scientists are working towards possible solutions.

3) CORRECT ANSWER: C
See above for analysis of the correct line reference. A explains that a coral reef faces a problematic situation but does not explain EXACTLY what (in the manner of C) the liabilities are. B provides a general principle applicable to organisms overall (NOT an outcome specific to coral reefs), while D indicates the importance of studying coral reefs to possibly prevent harm but does not provide a SPECIFIC cause for concern.

4) CORRECT ANSWER: C
The word "build" refers to the creation of a coral reef through a process of "attaching" (line 27) that uses connective calcium deposits. The calcium would thus secure the structure of the reef; choose C and eliminate A (which indicates lifting or glorifying action) as out of context. B would wrongly indicate that the calcium deposits are the ENTIRE material of the reef (rather than a connective material), while D would best refer to a process of founding or promoting among humans, NOT to the creation of a coral reef.

5) CORRECT ANSWER: D
The author indicates that researchers had not experimented on the relevant algae species on account of "turbulent reef conditions" (line 35) and the considerable "time it would take" (line 36) to carry out research. This content directly supports D, while the passage indicates that the researchers could address these challenges through scheduling and experimental design, NOT by developing new technology (eliminating A). Keep in mind that the algae IS seen as important to assessing environmental problems (eliminating B) and that the researchers are interested in preventing future environmental damage to reefs, NOT concerned that they will harm the reef themselves (eliminating C).

6) CORRECT ANSWER: B
In lines 45-49, the author explains that banding linked to coralline algae could potentially reveal an "organism's age"; such information would enable a better understanding of reef ecosystems. B properly reflects this content, while A and C refer to the calcium connected to reef formation but attribute the wrong goals (maintaining structure and explaining how calcium functions in reefs, NOT determining age) to the research inquiry. D distorts the content of the passage; Porolithan Onkodesi could help researchers to understand reef ecosystems, but this organism does not ITSELF provide a means of protecting reefs.

7) CORRECT ANSWER: B
See above for analysis of the correct line reference. A explains how Porolithan Onkodesi functions, NOT the specific interest of the researchers. C and D present outcomes and implications of the research considered in the passage, NOT a motive or source of interest as required by the previous question.

8) CORRECT ANSWER: D
The word "formation" refers to a property of bands as understood "over time" (line 45), so that "emergence" in D properly calls attention to

appearance in stages. Choose this answer and eliminate A as referencing difference over time but wrongly indicating IMPROVEMENT, not simply APPEARANCE. C and D both refer to physical objects but avoid the important theme of appearance over time.

9) CORRECT ANSWER: D
While the passage indicates that some "temperatures and acid levels" (lines 77-78) can threaten coral reefs, the author does not explain WHAT these dangerous measures are in terms of specific numbers. Thus, because neither the graph nor the passage indicates an ideal or safe acidity level in a clear manner, D is the best answer. A, B, and C all wrongly assume that information about an ideal level is directly stated in one of the sources.

10) CORRECT ANSWER: B
In the passage, researchers tracked the "concentration of magnesium-calcite" (line 53) in a coral reef ecosystem; the graph considers magnesium-calcite concentration at six different acidity and temperature measures, so that B is the best choice. Note that seasonal changes (eliminating A) and the role of coralline algae (eliminating C) are NOT explicitly considered in the graph. D is a misreading of the information in the graph, which considers the "Influence" of two factors on $MgCO_3$ concentration, NOT the converse influence of $MgCO_3$ concentration on acidity or temperature.

Chapter 4.2 | Saccadic Movements

1) CORRECT ANSWER: C
After explaining the issue of "the brain's response to moving targets" (lines 2-3) and a "theory (lines 22 and 34) that relates to this aspect of human behavior, the author presents a research study dedicated to finding the "mechanism" (line 52) that allows effective observation and response. C properly reflects this content, while A wrongly indicates that multiple theories (as opposed to one promising explanation) were considered for assessment. B misidentifies the response mechanism considered in the passage as lacking practical use (when in fact this mechanism is useful but requires EXPLANATION); D wrongly criticizes the study described in the passage, which was designed to provide a missing explanation but was not ITSELF clearly flawed.

2) CORRECT ANSWER: B
While the passage as a whole is dedicated to a scientific study of visual perception, the relevant lines explain what "we" humans see "In everyday

life." B properly indicates that the author is drawing a connection between the reader and the scientific content of the passage, while A mistakes the idea of relating the content to the reader for the idea of providing humor or amusement (a technique for creating an accessible conversation that is NOT here used). C is problematic because the specific research described in the passage has NOT yet been explained in detail and thus cannot be summarized, while D mistakes the idea of an "unknown phenomenon" for the very different negative idea of a flaw or "fallacy" in reasoning or belief.

3) CORRECT ANSWER: C
The passage defines saccades as "quick jumps that the eye makes between visual fixation points" (line 8-9) to form a total sense of visual information. C references a visual scenario that involves responses to some visual information to comprehend a whole; choose this answer and eliminate A (memorization) and B (navigation) as attributing the wrong purpose to the use of saccades (picturing a whole). D refers to a logical reasoning process that would help an individual to arrive at a measurement in terms of ONE property (height), NOT to the use of visual evidence to create a total image.

4) CORRECT ANSWER: B
The word "justify" refers to a factor that may or may not be "sufficient" (line 19) as it relates to a human response; the factor should help to indicate why the response occurs or should "explain" it. Choose B and eliminate A (context of argumentation) as inappropriate to linking different response occurrences. C and D both refer to positive reactions that one individual or group would have to another, NOT to the idea of a possible direct and logical link.

5) CORRECT ANSWER: A
In lines 45-48, the author explains that "concepts" such as stereotypes and cues can help people to "remain safe"; pre-formed and generalized ideas would logically be part of the top-down model. A properly links aspects of this model to safety and survival, while the sort of re-structuring mentioned in B may be closer to the bottom-up model that is the OPPOSITE of the top-down model. C reflects a part of the top down model (unity) but references the wrong goal (survival, NOT appreciation of visually beautiful or aesthetically pleasing properties); D introduces a seemingly appropriate negative (distrust) but relates this topic to memory, NOT to the actual negative of dangerous surroundings as mentioned in the passage.

6) CORRECT ANSWER: D
See above for analysis of the correct line reference. A and B explain how the top-down model of sight works but do NOT clearly indicate why this model is useful as the previous question requires. C indicate that the brain tends to order even incomplete information; this content does not suggest a clear benefit of the top-down model and should not be mistaken as justification for Question 5 C, which references forms that fit the very different theme of aesthetic pleasure or visual beauty.

7) CORRECT ANSWER: D
In lines 41-45, the author indicates that heuristics function to help humans "anticipate consequences"; lines 82-86 indicate that "anticipation" resulted in brain activity related to vision, so that D properly aligns with the author's ideas. A and B explain experimental procedures, not OUTCOMES that would support ideas about heuristics or that directly link to the idea of anticipation. C calls attention to neuron function, but does not address the nature of perceptions and predictions THEMSELVES in a manner that addresses the key ideas related to heuristics.

8) CORRECT ANSWER: B
The phrase "attending to" refers to the action of monkeys in terms of a "field of view" (line 75) where an item would appear; thus, the monkeys would observe the item or focus on it. B is appropriate, while A, C, and D all reference contexts that would indicate that the monkeys are collaborating with or interacting with the item, NOT that they are observing it.

9) CORRECT ANSWER: B
This question can be answered using information from the passage (specifically lines 72-86) and the graph itself. Lines 72-86 present information about how, in the study, anticipatory behavior causes Macaque monkeys to preemptively direct more neurons in their brain to attend to a target field of vision (left) than to a distractor field of vision (right). The graph shows female monkeys firing a greater percentage of neurons to a target field of vision than males fired. B is correct because it combines the context of anticipatory behavior and the trend depicted in the passage (females directing more neurons). A, C, and D provide the incorrect context (not anticipatory behavior) for the trends relevant the graph.

10) CORRECT ANSWER: B
This question can be answered by referring to the graph's "Right Eye Distractor" bar for the "Females" category. Using the scale, one can conclude that the bar lies above 20% (eliminating A) but below the

243

halfway point between 20% and 40% that indicates 30% (eliminating C and D). B is thus the most appropriate answer.

11) CORRECT ANSWER: C
The main conclusion based on the results of the study was that Macaque monkeys anticipated events visually by directing more neurons to a target field of vision (the left side) than to a distractor field of vision (the right side). B is incorrect because the graph actually supports the study's conclusion by showing monkeys using a higher percentage of neurons on target fields than distractor fields. A is incorrect because the graph's results include a separation between male and female monkeys, which differs from the setup of the study. D is incorrect the graph does not ever indicate how its data were collected. C is correct because it reflects how the graph adds on to the study's initial findings and conclusion.

Chapter 4.3 | Taste Perception

1) CORRECT ANSWER: A
In lines 6-11, the author links food preferences to brain activity that results in a specific "learned behavior"; this content supports A and makes a more uncertain answer such as B problematic, because the author is capable of clearly explaining the mechanism behind taste preferences. C mistakes the research described in the passage (which uses mice to investigate a human process) for a biological process that explains a response, while D raises the topic of cultural norms and thus departs from the passage's scientific emphasis.

2) CORRECT ANSWER: B
See above for analysis of the correct line reference. A explains that humans depend on their taste buds to assess foods but does not specifically explain HOW taste buds function in a manner that would relate to the previous question. C and D explain how humans respond to salt (NOT to tastes generally) and are thus too narrow to provide the broadly applicable view of taste responses required by the previous question.

3) CORRECT ANSWER: D
The word "bitter" refers to a taste that can warn of a "potentially harmful substance" (lines 15-16); to provide a clear warning of this sort, the taste would be strong and itself unpleasant. D provides the appropriate tone and meaning, while A and C reference traits appropriate to human personalities, not to tastes. B references dramatic or deadly movement and would thus be inappropriate to a description of a noticeable taste.

4) CORRECT ANSWER: C
The author explains that salt is used "by every cell in the body" (line 25) and thus indicates that salt serves a purpose for an organism's entire anatomy. This content supports A but should NOT be taken as evidence for D, since the role of salt as used by existing cells (NOT the role of salt in how cells are generated) is of interest to the author. A wrongly indicates that salt, which can be detected by the taste buds, is given a specialized category when in fact salt does not fit ANY category (lines 17-18). B mistakes the idea that salt can be unappealing in excess (lines 26-27) for the idea that salt is unappealing in trace amounts (when in fact it is harmless in moderation).

5) CORRECT ANSWER: B
In referencing "music" (line 43) and "taste" (line 56), the author explains that the activation of brain cells can lead to false sensations, so that the "music" or "taste" is not a fully valid perception of the outside world. B reflects this context of constructed experience, while the fact that "music" and "taste" are here understood in a SINGLE context as unreliable can be used to eliminate A as inaccurate. C and D wrongly indicate that the processes or broader concepts described in the passage are to some extent unreliable or flawed, when in fact the author uses the terms "music" and "taste" to help explain how a simulation can effectively be constructed.

6) CORRECT ANSWER: C
The word "implement" refers to how it is possible to "inject" (line 51) a virus in a manner that makes optogenetics possible; C properly calls attention to a context of practical procedures and outcomes that enable results. A wrongly refers to official qualifications, B wrongly indicates the ORIGINS of an idea (not the USE of an existing technique), and D wrongly indicates the exertion of power or dominance.

7) CORRECT ANSWER: A
In successful optogenetics, light must be used to "activate neurons that accept" (lines 53-54) a virus so that a response can be produced. A properly reflects this content, while B calls attention to key topics (the virus and light) but wrongly indicates that the use of light may threaten the virus. C and D offer conditions that surround the virus itself and that distort actual content from the passage, since the virus is non-fatal as modified (NOT as originally found in nature) and is linked to taste responses (but does NOT necessarily contain substances affiliated with specific tastes).

8) CORRECT ANSWER: C
In lines 63-66, the author explains that mice "naturally developed a preference" for a habit that stimulated a sweet taste sensation. C properly reflects the idea that the mice were guided to a specific taste preference, while A and D both focus on the physical properties of specific brain areas, not on how the brain areas FUNCTION in response to stimuli. B is problematic because, while visual perception can be helpful in finding food sources, the author is primarily concerned with the sense of taste on its own in the passage.

9) CORRECT ANSWER: C
See above for analysis of the correct line reference. A and B explain the structure of an experiment but do not present a FINDING related to sweet tastes in a manner that would be relevant to the previous question. D references a finding related to salty tastes but does NOT directly raise the topic of sweet tastes and thus avoids the topic required by the previous question.

10) CORRECT ANSWER: D
Although the graph indicates that a considerable number of mice developed a preference for sweet tastes by Trial 8, some mice STILL preferred salty tastes. Thus, the preference for sweet tastes was not absolute, so that D is the best answer. A (decreased preference numbers for sweet tastes) and B (increased preference numbers for salty tastes) indicate trends OPPOSITE to the overall trend indicated by the graph. C raises an issue (which tastes are beneficial to animals) that the graph does NOT consider in any direct way, despite the recorded preference for sweet tastes.

11) CORRECT ANSWER: C
In Ryba and Zuker's research, mice "developed a preference" (line 64) for sweet taste sensations; the graph reflects a movement towards this preference despite initially similar preferences for sweet and salty tastes. C is thus the best answer, while A is problematic because the graph itself does not clearly indicate whether methods from the passage (optogenetics in particular) were used to gather the data for the graph. B and D both wrongly indicate that the author of the passage would respond to the information in the graph in a negative manner.

Chapter 4.4 | End of Men

1) CORRECT ANSWER: D
In describing conditions in the United States, the author explains that the American economy has become "post-industrial" (lines 16 and 38) and that there has been a shift away from manufacturing jobs (lines 82-86); this content directly supports D as appropriate. A distorts the author's discussion of changed family roles to wrongly indicate that women (who are attaining new responsibilities) AND men are alienated. B wrongly places emphasis on the factors behind economic changes (when the passage is mostly concerned with gender roles), while C distorts the author's comparison between the U.S. and other countries (lines 29-34) to indicate that the U.S. is providing a guiding example, NOT simply exhibiting similar trends.

2) CORRECT ANSWER: D
In lines 31-33, the author cites a growing "preference for girls" in different countries; this trend would go AGAINST Steinbacher's idea that women "were becoming second-class citizens" (line 24). Choose D and eliminate A, since it is not clear that the "sperm selection methods" (lines 26-27) cited by the author actually involve genetic analysis. B and C both call attention to broad theoretical or argumentative constructs, when in fact the author opposes Steinbacher's ideas mostly by citing specific EVIDENCE.

3) CORRECT ANSWER: C
See above for analysis of the correct line reference. A explains Steinbacher's ideas but does NOT provide evidence or argumentation that goes against these ideas. B indicates a preference for girls but does NOT cite an international trend in a manner that would justify Question 2 D, while D cites the favorable employment conditions for women, a factor that Steinbacher does NOT explicitly consider and that is thus not clearly related to Steinbacher's main argument.

4) CORRECT ANSWER: D
According to the Organization for Economic Cooperation and Development, a country's economic success is correlated to "the power of women" (line 55) in that same country. D properly indicates that a society that places women in leadership positions in a considerable proportion experiences economic growth. Choose this answer and eliminate A as referencing labor by women, NOT an empowerment factor such as leadership or responsibility. B and C present situations in which women appear to be valued but do NOT, as required by the relevant content, link women's roles to overall economic prosperity.

5) CORRECT ANSWER: D
In lines 76-79, the author references a "painful role reversal" in which women are empowered and men feel alienated enough to form "support groups." D properly reflects a positive shift for women accompanied by a negative shift for men. A and B describe positive roles for women but NOT negative changes for men, while C actually indicates that men remain in power in some scenarios instead of primarily indicating that men may face disadvantages.

6) CORRECT ANSWER: B
The word "flexible" is used in the context of a discussion of behaviors that are seen as "adaptive and better suited" (line 62); B would properly indicate that the behaviors involve positive changes to accommodate new circumstances. A would wrongly criticize the behaviors as difficult to explain, while C (indicating variety) and D (indicating vast physical size or considerable scope) introduce faulty contexts despite introducing positive tones.

7) CORRECT ANSWER: B
The word "top" is used to describe specific "tiers of US society" (line 73) that are dominated by men; thus, B properly calls attention to the idea of a social level that is occupied by a powerful or privileged group. A raises the idea of whether the tiers are basic or complex (and thus departs from the appropriate context). C and D may seem to indicate that the "top" tiers are elevated, but raise illogical meanings (in C, since women CAN increasingly access the top tiers) and contexts (in D, since women are making progress and thus are most likely NOT intimidated).

8) CORRECT ANSWER: C
In the final paragraph of the passage, the author argues that society "should embrace" (line 88) the shift towards an economy that values communication skills attributed to women elsewhere in the passage (lines 69-72). Because the final paragraph does NOT mention women themselves but does mention their skills, C is an appropriate choice. A and D are problematic because the author argues that women are DIFFERENT from men in departing from skills premised on command-and-control; B wrongly shifts the author's discussion away from business-related skills, when in fact the final paragraph considers business EXCLUSIVELY and avoids the social topics that appear elsewhere in the passage.

9) CORRECT ANSWER: B
According to figure 1, just under 20% of U.S. men and well under 20% of U.S. women held graduate degrees in 2015, the year for all of the data provided in this figure. B is thus accurate, while A and C reference trends that would require consideration of MULTIPLE years in the figure. D offers information about how the public PERCEIVES graduate degrees, not about how many people have EARNED graduate degrees, and thus considers an issue beyond the true scope of the graph.

10) CORRECT ANSWER: A
The first chart indicates that women make up a slight majority of workers in "Managerial and Office Jobs," and this information aligns with the 51.4% measure provided by the Bureau of Labor Statistics in line 10. A is thus the best answer. Other answers consider groups or institutions primarily interested in family preferences (MicroSort, eliminating B) and job skills (post-Darwinians, eliminating C). While these answers consider the wrong factors for evaluation of Figure 2, D is relevant to "women in top positions" (lines 68-69) but does NOT provide a direct percentage measure in the manner of A.

11) CORRECT ANSWER: B
Although Rosin sees some "top tiers" (line 73) of the U.S. economy as dominated by men, Rosin also argues that this situation is changing and that women are taking on more formidable roles. The graphs indicate that men still dominate extremely high-level activities (graduate degrees and executive or high-ranking managerial positions) but that women are more prevalent in other areas. B reflects the fact that the graphs are in accordance with Rosin's ideas; A is problematic because the passage (despite explaining Rosin's ideas clearly) never explains the SOURCE of her information. C is problematic because Rosin DOES admit that men remain dominant in some respects, while D weighs in on an educational preference that Rosin (despite generally calling attention to progress for women) never specifically assesses.

Chapter 4.5 | Myth of ADD

1) CORRECT ANSWER: D
In lines 17-20, the author points out the necessity of determining "whether the disorder exists" and calls attention to the need for careful diagnosis; D properly reflects the author's desire to approach ADD/ADHD in a systematic manner. A distorts the author's point about misdiagnosis, which requires determination of whether ADD/ADHD in facts EXISTS rather than more diagnosis under the assumption that the disease is somehow

present. B and C focus on publicity related to the disease, when in fact the author is mostly concerned with methods of examination that would enable clearer and more widely accepted analysis REGARDLESS of the publicity that the disease receives.

2) CORRECT ANSWER: B
See above for analysis of the correct line reference. A addresses the history of ADD/ADHD but does NOT (as required by the previous question) present a clear recommendation from the author. C and D present facts that indicate that current approaches to ADD/ADHD diagnosis and treatment are problematic but do NOT, in the manner of B, provide a positive course of action supported by the author.

3) CORRECT ANSWER: C
While Kagan views ADD/ADHD as a "sham illness" (line 25), the pediatrician cited in the passage is described as treating the illness as valid and as prescribing medication for treatment. Kagan would naturally disagree with this approach, which is broadly applied to "Every child" (line 25) with school-related difficulties. C properly indicates a negative response, while A and B would criticize the pediatrician's intellect or powers of discernment, NOT the treatment practice itself. D would indicate that the pediatrician is consciously performing an unethical action without concern, when in fact the pediatrician is not making ANY moral considerations when diagnosing ADD/ADHD.

4) CORRECT ANSWER: B
The word "coined" refers to a "first" (line 39) activity in terms of designating or explaining ADD/ADHD; for a "definition and criteria" (line 38) to change over time, an initial definition of ADD/ADHD would need to be explained or formulated. B is thus appropriate, while A indicates a context of imagination or falsehood that is inappropriately negative. C (context of uncommitted thought) and D (context of publicity) also raise inappropriate contexts for the basic and initial presentation of an idea in medicine.

5) CORRECT ANSWER: B
The author presents Eileen Bailey as a writer who "asserts" (line 50) that ADD/ADHD exists and who cites debate around the "continuing inaccurate portrayal" (line 52) of the disease mostly to indicate its medical validity. This content supports B, while the fact that the author spends the passage presenting information, NOT arguing an independent viewpoint, can be used to eliminate A and D. Although the author is providing

different sides of a debate, C raises the idea that Kagan's claims will be called into question and thus distracts from the content of Bailey's testimony, which is central to the question.

6) CORRECT ANSWER: A
The word "divided" refers to "scientists" (line 57) who, in the context of the differing viewpoints on ADD/ADHD presented in the preceding paragraphs, have not reached consensus on the existence of ADD/ADHD. This information supports A, while B mistakes the idea of disagreement for the idea of a lack of communication (when in fact the scientists may be well aware of competing ideas). C wrongly indicates that the scientists accept a state of conflict (rather than desiring answers to issues surrounding ADD/ADHD). D inaccurately portrays the scientists as unable to make up their minds, when in fact DIFFERENT groups have formulated strong but conflicting opinions.

7) CORRECT ANSWER: D
In lines 69-75, the author indicates that determining "which areas of the brain" are linked to ADD/ADHD would resolve the issue of whether the disease exists; thus, because debate over the disease continues, it can be inferred that specific brain areas have not been found. D supports this content. A (defining the disease) and B (conflicting views from experts) appear to refer to points of contention from earlier in the passage that, while relevant to the examination of ADD/ADHD, do not THEMSELVES provide a primary or fundamental factor that explains why the debate continues. C is in fact contradicted by lines 37-39, which indicate several changes that surround the DSM V criteria.

8) CORRECT ANSWER: B
See above for analysis of the correct line reference. A indicates the necessity of tracing ADD/ADHD to a biological component, but does not explain that the component occurs SPECIFICALLY in the brain in a manner that would support Question 7 D. Both C and D indicate that ADD/ADHD is accepted as a valid diagnosis and thus reflect a potentially problematic situation; however, these answers do NOT indicate a specific fundamental factor that explains why ADD/ADHD remains a source of debate.

9) CORRECT ANSWER: A
For every year considered in the graph, the number of misdiagnosed cases (dark bar) increases from the previous year. This content supports A, which reflects the idea (present in the chart) that misdiagnosed cases will NOT decrease in 2020. B considers an overlap between two groups

(a possibility that the graph mostly avoids considering) and considers the 2020 data as measured from the past findings, NOT as estimated figures. C and D both reference research, when it is unclear how the graph on its own relates to any single research project, and should thus be eliminated as out of scope.

10) CORRECT ANSWER: A
The chart indicates increases over time for the "Total ADHD Cases" group and the "Likely Misdiagnosis" group, with the "Normal Metabolism" group remaining at a constant number. Thus, if the number of total cases rises while the number of children with normal metabolism remains constant beyond 2020, the difference between these two quantities will increase. A is thus the best answer, while the same line of reasoning CONTRADICTS B. Note also that the number of misdiagnosed children is lower than the number of children with normal metabolism BUT will rise over time; thus, the difference between these quantities will DECREASE, so that both C and D are incorrect.

11) CORRECT ANSWER: B
The only factors considered in the graph are the total number of ADD/ADHD cases, the number of children misdiagnosed with ADD/ADHD, and the number of children with normal metabolism. As of 2014, roughly 2 million children were most likely misdiagnosed (dark bar) with ADD/ADHD. This information supports B as accurate. Prescriptions (A), diagnosis criteria (C), and impairments (D) are topics related to the analysis present in the passage but are NOT directly considered in the graph; thus, all other answers should be eliminated.

Chapter 4.6 | Crown of Thorns

1) CORRECT ANSWER: D
In lines 42-46, the author of Passage 1 indicates that distant populations of starfish are dissimilar, thus presenting a contradiction of the larval dispersion hypothesis (which, on the basis of lines 19-22, indicates that distant starfish populations WILL exhibit similarities). D properly conveys a negative stance that contradicts the fundamentally positive statements in A and C. B misstates the author's analysis, which here features evaluation of the larval dispersion hypothesis on its OWN terms, not through comparison to other ideas.

2) CORRECT ANSWER: C
See above for analysis of the correct line reference. A explains what the larval dispersion hypothesis is but does not offer an assessment of the

validity of the hypothesis in a manner that would align with an answer to the previous question. B mentions the early stages of a research endeavor (NOT the hypothesis more specifically) and D mentions local factors that could influence starfish but does not focus on the necessary topic of group dispersion and similarity.

3) CORRECT ANSWER: B
The author describes the currents of the Pacific Ocean that carried larvae and created "distant populations" (line 19) as "wide-ranging," so that B properly indicates broad or extensive scope. A (versatile or multi-talented) and C (comprehension or understanding) present qualities of humans, NOT of currents, while D introduces an inappropriate negative.

4) CORRECT ANSWER: C
The word "distant" is used to describe specific starfish populations, which are analyzed in terms of how they differ from populations from "the same area" (line 44). Thus, the word should refer to a contrasting concept that would indicate that these other populations are far or physically "remote" from one another. Choose C and eliminate A, B, and D as words that introduce strong negative or critical tones and do NOT properly describe a situation of physical distance.

5) CORRECT ANSWER: C
The author of Passage 2 explains that outbreaks, of which the "new outbreak" is only one example, are "increasing in frequency" (line 64). This content directly supports C but renders A problematic, since the research described in the passage indeed deals with comparable outbreaks but is NOT mentioned until line 77 (so that, in this arrangement, it is not explicitly clear whether the outbreak inspired the research or not). B calls attention to the topic of changes and D calls attention to the topic of benefits, yet the first paragraph (which mostly notes a prevalent tendency and addresses theories) does not address either of these ideas at length.

6) CORRECT ANSWER: C
In lines 90-92, the author of Passage 2 explains that the nutrient-deprived starfish larvae exhibited relative weakness; the idea that nutrient intake does NOT inhibit development, as in C, contradicts this content. Other answers introduce factors that were not of primary interest to the researchers, such as the resemblance between a simulation and natural conditions (A), the scope of a starfish diet (B), and the total lifecycle of a starfish (D). Instead, the passage places emphasis on factors such as nutrient intake and reef acidification.

7) CORRECT ANSWER: C
See above for analysis of the correct line reference. A explains that the research team utilized starfish embryos in laboratory conditions, B explains laboratory procedures, and D explains that there may be an ideal level of nutrients for growing starfish. While some of these answers describe procedures (NOT findings that could be easily contradicted), D should not be mistaken as justification for Question 6 D, which discusses the growth rate (NOT the actual topic of nutrient intake) of starfish.

8) CORRECT ANSWER: B
This question can be answered by determining and comparing the flood magnitudes of each year listed in the answer choices to see which is the highest. The flood magnitudes of A (1991), B (1985), C (2003), and D (1999) are 4.25, 7.5, 5.5, and 5.25, respectively. Comparatively, B (1985) has the strongest flood magnitude of 7.5.

9) CORRECT ANSWER: C
Ocean acidification is mentioned as a threat to reefs in line 6 and in lines 101-102, so that C properly describes a point of similarity involving the two passages. A and D refer to factors mentioned early in Passage 1 but not at all in Passage 2, while B mentions a factor that is not of direct interest to either passage (even though a decrease in predator numbers may, in OTHER contexts, cause starfish to proliferate).

10) CORRECT ANSWER: B
While the research presented in Passage 1 involved the fieldwork collection of "specimens" (line 26), the research presented in Passage 2 involved observation of embryo development under "laboratory conditions" (line 79). This content supports B, while the fundamental differences in experimental design make the idea that both experiments responded to the same theory problematic (eliminating A). In fact, Passage 1 deals with starfish dispersion and Passage 2 deals with starfish development and sustenance. C wrongly raises the topic of non-experts despite the technical and laboratory-based focus of Passage 2, while D wrongly attributes a negative tone to the informative but not entirely conclusive research described in Passage 1.

11) CORRECT ANSWER: A
In its closing paragraphs, each passage links starfish nutrition and health to flooding, so that there is a meaningful correlation between starfish population and flood strength as indicated by the graphs. A reflects this content, while B raises an issue that is primarily addressed in Figure 1 but is avoided for the most part in the passages. C rightly indicates that

the passages are not primarily concerned with the destruction that results from flooding, while D indicates that Passage 1 avoids specific discussion of starfish nutrients. However, both of these answers should be eliminated as offering the wrong FUNDAMENTAL assessment of the relationship between the passages and the graphs.

Chapter 4.7 | Redefining Health

1) CORRECT ANSWER: C
After presenting the idea that "traditional models of health" (lines 4-5) may need to be reconsidered to account for new factors, the author explains how "Dr. Martha McClintock and her team" (lines 17-18) re-evaluated health in such a manner by accounting for disease alongside social and psychological factors. This evidence supports C and (since the author approves of the research team's work) directly contradicts A. B neglects the passage's emphasis on a single research study, while D focuses on a single factor (exercise) that is only one among many factors considered in the passage.

2) CORRECT ANSWER: A
In the relevant paragraph, the author explains how a specific group of researchers "attempted to classify the health of senior citizens" (lines 18-19) by obtaining information from questionnaires and interviews. This focus on procedural details supports A. B (the researchers and their institution) and B (National Academy of Sciences) both raise topics mentioned in the paragraph but wrongly neglect the focus on a single research experiment in favor of broader references to "daily duties" and articles in general, respectively. D references different perspectives that are mostly the concern of the PREVIOUS paragraph and also neglects the focus on research methods in the relevant paragraph.

3) CORRECT ANSWER: C
In lines 33-50, the difference between the two models is considered in detail. While the "medical model" deals mainly with disease-related factors, the "comprehensive model" considers daily activities, psychological states, and lifestyle choices. C reflects this contrast, while A is directly CONTRADICTED by the fact that the comprehensive model considers well-being in detail. B is problematic because BOTH models originate from criteria that can be traced to the National Social Life, Health, and Aging project, while D wrongly states that the comprehensive model and the medical model do not overlap when in fact the comprehensive model is an EXPANSION of the medical model that considers more factors.

4) CORRECT ANSWER: A
The parenthetical information lists the various items that are classified under comprehensive model categories such as "frailty," "sensory function," "psychological health," and "health behaviors." Thus, the details provide examples or illustrations, so that A is appropriate. B ("quantify") would be appropriate only if numbers or statistics (NOT categories) were present. C wrongly indicates that the conditions listed (which in some cases are negative) always lead to death and in doing so raises a topic that appears nowhere in the parenthetical phrases. D is problematic because the author has ALREADY established that the two models are different and is here instead focusing mainly on sub-categories for the medical model alone.

5) CORRECT ANSWER: C
The word "present" refers to aspects that the comprehensive model was notable for "covering" (line 43) and that the medical model was NOT known for "covering." Thus, a meaning indicating that the aspects were addressed or considered for study under a model would be appropriate. Choose C and eliminate A and D as choices that best describe the sentiments or actions of people, NOT the status of research factors. B introduces a theme (new or current) that does not directly fit the context of the sentence, which mostly addresses matters of experimental design and assessment.

6) CORRECT ANSWER: D
In lines 62-65, the author indicates that "clinically obese" adults experienced relatively low risk of dying, so that a negative diagnosis such as obesity is here NOT linked to death. D thus fits the requirements of the prompt. A mentions mortality but does not mention a negative diagnosis, B mentions the possibility of negative diagnosis but not the possibility of death, and C mentions a negative diagnosis that INCREASES the possibility of death.

7) CORRECT ANSWER: D
The phrase "markers for" refers to negative factors that are linked to "future health problems" (line 69). Thus, "markers" would be signs or signals that the problems could arise, so that D is an appropriate choice. A refers to expression or human action (NOT to a possible correlation of factors), B would best refer to human habits or characteristics, and C would refer to the act of proving a point step-by-step but NOT to fundamentally linked occurrences with the same accuracy.

8) CORRECT ANSWER: C
In lines 59-61, the author explains that people diagnosed with "chronic disease" could improve these health by emphasizing factors unique to the common model, one of which (on the basis of lines 44-50) would be "sensory function." This evidence supports C. A and B refer to NEGATIVE trends that would be considered under the comprehensive model. D references a chronic condition (line 83, NOT a positive health measure) that could not, as chronic, be removed.

9) CORRECT ANSWER: B
In the relevant lines, the author notes that life expectancy has risen to 79 (at present) from 54 (a century ago). This information sets up the approving discussion of redefining health to account for longer life expectancy and to "maximize" (line 107) health later in life. B is thus appropriate, while the author never directly explains what has CAUSED life expectancy to increase and focuses mainly on the repercussions of such an increase (thus eliminating A). C (wrongly negative towards earlier healthcare) and D (also wrongly negative towards the past and indicating further advancements) incorrectly draw focus away from the author's actual topic of healthcare at present and emphasize historical ideas that are not explicitly presented.

10) CORRECT ANSWER: B
The factor that indicates the LOWEST likelihood of future (next five years) health problems will have the lowest percent likelihood measure. B represents a small fraction of a likelihood of 13 and is thus the best answer. A and C cover the same age bracket (57 years) but provide significantly higher likelihoods. D covers a new age bracket that does not exceed a 13 percent likelihood, but still presents a higher likelihood than is offered in B.

11) CORRECT ANSWER: C
While the first chart considers three possible indicators of poor health, it is not clear that these are the ONLY factors considered in the relevant portion of the passage (which does not name specific factors at all and may thus present logical conclusions drawn from much more information). C is an appropriate choice, while A ("questionnaire") and B ("broken bone") reference factors that are NOT clearly mentioned in lines 103-105. D is problematic because the two sources of information do not address the same topic area and thus CANNOT contradict one another; while the chart considers ailments, lines 103-105 consider the very different issue of life expectancy.

Chapter 4.8 | Wildfires

1) CORRECT ANSWER: D
After describing the need to "do our best to prepare" (line 21) for intense fire seasons, the author provides an account of a research inquiry that indicated measures for possible "best results" (line 89) in addressing forest fire dangers. This emphasis on practical results supports D, while A and B both reference content essential for understanding forest fires but NOT the question of best outcomes that interests the author. C confuses the issue of managing a forest fire that is already burning (which interests the author) with the issue of extinguishing such a fire (a possibility that the author does not clearly raise).

2) CORRECT ANSWER: C
The word "approximations" is used in the context of the "clocked" (line 11) or measured speeds for winds; a context of observation and estimation in terms of figures would be appropriate. Choose C and eliminate A (which indicates too much uncertainty) and B (which indicates a systematic method, NOT a set of observations) as logically inappropriate despite seemingly similar contexts. D best refers to formal documents or physical sources of information, NOT to observed quantities.

3) CORRECT ANSWER: C
The word "natural" is used to describe a possibility that is contrasted with human methods for "managing fire" (line 29); thus a context of avoiding influence or intervention, as in C, is appropriate. A and D would both best refer to situations in which human intervention IS likely, while B refers to emotion or intuition in conscious individuals, NOT to a situation involving a forest fire.

4) CORRECT ANSWER: D
The parenthetical statement is used to help explain an "option" (line 28) that involves letting forest fires burn; this option is contrasted with options that seem more desirable from the perspective of managing a problem. D is thus the best choice, while A wrongly indicates that the parenthetical statement, which helps to EXPLAIN a serious topic, instead diverts from the author's discussion. B wrongly indicates that the author provides a line of argumentation or analysis, rather than a short note that captures an assessment of an attitude, while C wrongly mistakes the attitude of "Most people" (line 27) for the opinion of the author (who does NOT directly state her opinion) herself.

5) CORRECT ANSWER: A
In lines 53-57, the author indicates that fuel treatments were used to either reduce fuel amounts or to reposition fuel sources, all with the intention of making it likely that a forest canopy "would be less likely to catch fire." A properly reflects this content, while B and D refer to possible positive outcomes that are not EXPLICITLY linked to fuel treatments as a primary intention. C is logically flawed because fuel treatment, as a method, involves occupied spaces in which materials COULD catch fire but are meant to burn in a controlled manner.

6) CORRECT ANSWER: B
See above for analysis of the correct line reference. A introduces fuel treatment as a possible method of fire management but does not explain in detail how fuel treatment functions. C explains that fuel breaks are used to keep a fire from crossing empty areas (NOT that fires occur in empty areas, as wrongly indicated by Question 5 C), while D focuses primarily on comparative results linked to fuel breaks; neither such comparison nor fuel breaks themselves are directly referenced in any answer to the previous question.

7) CORRECT ANSWER: D
In the final stages of the passage, the author explains the physical "patterns" (line 65) linked to prescribed burning and indicates that the strategic use of fuel treatments and fuel breaks can help humans to "fight fire with fire" when wildfires break out. This content supports D, while A raises a threat (environmental harm) that the author (who is mostly concerned with the movement of fires) tends to avoid. B and C both call attention to the topic of the ORIGINS of fires, when in fact the author is more interested in how fires can be managed REGARDLESS of how they initially break out in forests.

8) CORRECT ANSWER: D
In explaining the "frightening" situation of fighting fire with fire, the author indicates that "Public outreach and education" (line 93) is needed; this information suggests that the proposed solution seems unusual and thus requires instruction to be implemented. Together with earlier content that indicates the fearsome nature of forest fires (lines 17-22), this content indicates that the author is suggesting a measure that would seem counterintuitive. D is thus appropriate, while A ("novel" or new and innovative) would wrongly indicate that the word "frightening" has a positive connotation. B refers to a possibly valid fact but does NOT directly reference prescribed burning or the reaction to it (since the actual topic of this answer is forest fire activity), while C wrongly criticizes the

general public (who may resist the author's ideas but COULD be educated or informed effectively).

9) CORRECT ANSWER: A
The last sentence references the deadly firestorms explained in lines 17-20 and indicates that a change of public opinion "must happen soon" in order to prevent future deadly events. This content indicates that urgency and activity are needed; A is appropriate. B wrongly refers to EARLIER content that explains the author's favored solution, and C wrongly indicates that the author is introducing new facts rather than simply urging a course of action. D rightly refers to the December 2017 fires but WRONGLY indicates a comparison involving other historical fires, which in fact are mentioned nowhere in the relevant sentence.

10) CORRECT ANSWER: D
The passage indicates that the "other" methods centered on "thinning" (line 51) with the intention of protecting the canopy by manipulating fuel (through either reduction or repositioning) to prevent fires from reaching the canopy. While the ladder method would keep low-originating fires from reaching the canopy, the canopy method would naturally protect the canopy itself; both methods, moreover, use thinning. D is the best choice, while A and C refer to the surface method, which ONLY controls ground-level burning. B only refers to one of the methods that would logically fit the passage's recommended measures for protecting the canopy.

11) CORRECT ANSWER: A
In lines 79-89, the author points out that "prescribed burning shows the most promise" as an effective means of addressing fires and that "fuel breaks" (or relatively open stretches of land) should be used with other forms of fuel treatment. Surface fuel targeting in A would involve both prescribed burning and the creation of fuel breaks through surface clearing, while B would involve prescribed burning but NOT (as opposed to thinning) the clearing of entire surface areas. C would not involve prescribed burning, and D can be eliminated as contradicted by evidence from the passage that decisively favors A.

Chapter 4.9 | Wolbachia

1) CORRECT ANSWER: A
The discussion in the passage centers on the experimental introduction of "the bacterium *Wolbachia* into wild mosquitoes" (lines 37-38); for the author, projects linked to this idea could lead to "a future in which the

major tropical diseases cast an insignificant shadow" (lines 102-103). A is thus an appropriate choice; B (which does not focus on practical applications) and D (which ONLY focuses on the Zika virus) are both too narrow in scope. C refers to the control of mosquito populations, NOT to mosquito populations as they relate to the core topic of disease, and should thus be eliminated.

2) CORRECT ANSWER: D
The author explains that introducing mosquito-targeting predators (lines 18-20, eliminating A), alteration of mosquito reproductive patterns (lines 44-46, eliminating B), and using a bacterium to target a virus that occupies the salivary glands of mosquitoes (lines 31-33, eliminating C) are all possible methods for dealing with mosquito-borne diseases. Only insect repellants (NOT to be confused with the "insecticides" that kill insects and that are mentioned in line 17) are not mentioned, so that D is appropriate.

3) CORRECT ANSWER: C
The word "unchecked" refers to climate change, which makes mosquito-borne diseases "Even worse" (line 9); a word that indicates that a problem is severe, growing, or "rampant" would be appropriate. Choose C and eliminate A (context of observation) and D (context of expression or inspiration) as irrelevant. B is logically incorrect because the passage indicates that corrective measures CAN be taken to stop the spread of disease; climate change itself is never described as an irreversible problem.

4) CORRECT ANSWER: A
The parenthetical statement occurs within a discussion of how a symbiotic relationship works; while most symbiotic relationships involve "close physical association" (line 28), the relationship between the Dengue virus and a mosquito can involve the migration of the virus (lines 32-33). Thus, this relationship is NOT fully symbiotic. A is appropriate, while B and D are both contradicted by the fact that the author is offering a formal and analytic discussion, NOT taking a strong emotional tone. C is a distortion of the content, since the author indicates that the mosquito and the virus exhibit a non-standard form of symbiosis but and is in command of this exceptional fact, NOT uncertain about it.

5) CORRECT ANSWER: D
In lines 40-43, the author indicates that *Wolbachia* is widespread and "does not cause fatal harm" to its hosts, while the lines that follow indicate that *Wolbachia* both shuts down virus transmission and, in allowing host survival, also allows reproduction. This content supports D as appropriate.

A describes a general mechanism behind mosquito-borne diseases (NOT *Wolbachia* specifically), while B and C present references to one specialist's ideas about why *Wolbachia* MIGHT be useful, not assertions that *Wolbachia* IS useful in reducing virus transmission.

6) CORRECT ANSWER: D
The word "tastes" is used in the context of a virus that must survive but cannot do so in an insect with "a lifespan too short" (line 39). This context of unfavorable conditions justifies D, since conditions are NOT favorable or to the metaphorical "liking" of the virus. A refers to a repeated or characteristic habit (NOT to favorable conditions), while B (actual food) and C (pleasing emotion) raise contexts that are inappropriate.

7) CORRECT ANSWER: C
According to the passage, O'Neill thought or assumed that he could create an insect with "a lifespan too short for the tastes of the Dengue virus" (line 39); this content, along with discussion of alterations to "reproductive mechanisms" (lines 43-44), supports C as appropriate. A and D properly refer to the idea of limiting the spread of the disease, but do not properly explain that O'Neill considered the lifespan of the carrier mosquito as a primary factor. B refers to the topic of the mosquito's lifespan but, by citing the production of infected offspring instead of offspring that CANNOT effectively carry the disease, references the wrong desired outcome.

8) CORRECT ANSWER: B
In lines 73-76, the author indicates that the researchers placed both infected and uninfected mosquitoes in "outdoor cages" to monitor the spread of *Wolbachia* within the mosquito population; all mosquitoes carried *Wolbachia* after "three generations." B properly reflects this setup and outcome, while A and D reference ideas (biological tampering) that PRECEDED the investigation of whether *Wolbachia*, once present, could effectively spread. C distorts the content of lines 73-76 to wrongly indicate that different infected populations, NOT an infected and an uninfected population, were placed in proximity.

9) CORRECT ANSWER: D
See above for analysis of the correct line reference. A refers to a fundamental trait of *Wolbachia*, NOT to a step in a research project as required by the previous question. B and C present information relevant to infecting individual mosquitoes with *Wolbachia*, not information about the effectiveness of *Wolbachia* AFTER injection as required by the previous question.

10) CORRECT ANSWER: C
The term "Wolbachia blanket" refers to an area that, over seven years, has been the site of the offspring of "thousands of *Wolbachia*-infested mosquitoes" (lines 80-81). This content supports C and can be used to eliminate D, since the *Wolbachia*-infested mosquitoes have ALREADY been introduced. A is problematic because a *Wolbachia*-mitigated virus, Dengue, has been "drastically reduced" (lines 82-83) in the region, evidence that indicates that the mitigating measures have ALREADY taken effect in some way. B distorts evidence from the passage; while Scott O'Neill was at one point active in the "Wolbachia blanket" area, it is not clear that he is active in this region any longer and it is possible that another observer (Geoff Wilson, line 84) has taken control.

11) CORRECT ANSWER: A
The relevant information in lines 93-95 calls attention to the considerable "direct costs" associated with Dengue, a dangerous virus that the author (in presenting the research involving *Wolbachia*) discusses in terms of a possible solution. A thus properly indicates that the author is underscoring a health problem that has been discussed in the context of a possible solution. B is overly specific (when in fact the author only mentions "billions" of U.S. dollars without providing an exact figure). C and D wrongly indicate that cost was a key topic earlier in the passage, when in fact the author mostly discussed the deadly nature of mosquito-borne diseases but NOT the finances related to these threats.

Chapter 4.10 | Incredible Genes

1) CORRECT ANSWER: D
In the passage, the author indicates that "genes can only go so far" (lines 12-13) in leading to proper health and goes on to explain the results of a study that cited an "unhealthy lifestyle" (line 54) as a contributor to heart disease. Thus, the author emphasizes that lifestyle choices play a role in preventing health liabilities; D is appropriate while A is CONTRADICTED by the idea that both genetic and lifestyle factors are influential. B emphasizes individual factors instead of presenting the BROADER assessment that is the author's true central claim, while C mistakes the actual topic of heart disease prevention for the different topic of treating heart disease once it has occurred.

2) CORRECT ANSWER: A
The word "assess" refers to the action that doctors take in terms of considering "factors" (line 21) related to heart disease. Thus, the doctors are attempting to figure out or verify whether or not heart disease is present; A is the best answer. B would relate to extended analysis over time, NOT to direct and known factors that can be readily evaluated; C (context of physical measurement) and D (context of evaluating or pricing an item) both raise faulty contexts.

3) CORRECT ANSWER: C
In lines 59-65, the author explains that people who "may feel resigned to their predetermined genetic code" can prevent heart disease by taking action in terms of lifestyle choices, as indicated by the study. C properly aligns with the idea that action can be taken to counter genetic risk of heart disease through lifestyle choices. A, B, and D all wrongly refer to individuals who may experience lifestyle-based risks, when in fact the study is most instrumental in offering hope to those who are at risk for genetic reasons.

4) CORRECT ANSWER: D
See above for analysis of the correct line reference. A indicates that doctors take multiple factors into consideration to assess heart disease risk, B explains a few of these factors, and C indicates that both genetic factors and lifestyle factors can relate to heart disease risk. While these answers do provide background information for the study explained in the passage, NONE of them designate a group that should feel hope in the manner of D.

5) CORRECT ANSWER: B
In lines 34-42, the author explains that both genetic factors and lifestyle factors can play a role in determining human health, specifically in connection to heart disease risk. This information supports B and can be used to eliminate both A and C, which wrongly indicate that lifestyle factors are insignificant. D wrongly indicates that genetic factors themselves are fundamentally insignificant and is thus contradicted by the passage.

6) CORRECT ANSWER: A
The author explains the factors that are "components of a healthy lifestyle" in lines 34-42; one of these components is a healthy diet pattern, so that an UNHEALTHY diet pattern as indicated in A would be a lifestyle risk. While B, C, and D do note possible dangers to an individual, none of these answers fit lifestyle factors that are explicitly given in the passage; eliminate these answers as out of scope.

7) CORRECT ANSWER: D
While the author calls attention to "a few factors" (line 21) that link to heart disease, the passage then provides lifestyle measures that can "decrease one's risk of heart disease" (lines 35-36) even when fundamental risks are present. This content supports D, while A overstates the significance of lifestyle choices, since the author indicates that both genetic and lifestyle factors are significant. B focuses on unhealthy choices (not the HEALTHY lifestyle recommendations that here interest the author), while C neglects the topic of lifestyle choices entirely.

8) CORRECT ANSWER: C
The word "profile" is used in reference to the "genetic risk" (line 68) associated with a given person. Thus, the level of genetic risk would be based on a single person's medical information, so that C is appropriate. A refers to a broad or provisional depiction, while B (written or spoken representation) and D (a physical document) both seem to refer to information of some sort but ultimately raise inappropriate contexts.

9) CORRECT ANSWER: A
The chart indicates, with the "None" category, that avoiding both genetic risk and lifestyle risk can most effectively decrease the probability of heart disease occurrence. Moreover, individuals who eliminate lifestyle risk are less likely to experience heart disease than are individuals with both genetic risk and lifestyle risk. This information aligns with the idea presented in lines 50-54, namely that eliminating lifestyle risk can lower the overall risk of heart disease. Choose A to reflect concordance and make sure not to choose B, since the line reference only addresses a detail similar to a detail from the graph but does NOT indicate that the researchers would be skeptical in other respects. Both C and D wrongly indicate that the researchers described in the passage would find the information present in the graph fundamentally problematic.

10) CORRECT ANSWER: D
See above for analysis of the correct line reference. A and B describe procedures and objectives, NOT findings or data that would align with (or contradict) results present in the graph. C indicates that lifestyle choices can be more significant than genetic profile; while these factors are indeed considered in the graph, the information in the graph does not clearly indicate that one set of factors is SUPERIOR to the other.

11) CORRECT ANSWER: C
According to figure 2, the most widespread lifestyle risk for the U.S. population is infrequent exercise at 80%. C reflects this high percentage, while A (15.5%), B (33%), and D (42.3%) all align with lower percentages.

Chapter Five

Questions 1-11 are based on the following passage and supplementary material.

5.1
Adapted from a 2013 Public Library of Science article by Miguel Onorato, Davide Proment, Gunther Clauss, and Marco Klein, "Rogue Waves: From Nonlinear Schrödinger Breather Solutions to Sea-Keeping Test," which seeks to dispel the notion that rogue waves exist only in stories, and to create a model to test and predict the effect of these waves on ships.

Ever since humanity took to the high seas, there have been tales of monstrous waves appearing out of nowhere; tales of towering walls of water that could
Line dwarf the Great Sphinx of Giza or rival the Colossus
5 of Rhodes. But with the rise in objectivity of science, many of these stories were cast into doubt, much like tales of Greek Gods and Goddesses. Most scientists and mathematicians studying the behavior of ocean waves did not think it possible that, even in severe
10 storms, there would ever be a wave taller than 15 meters. Throughout the 20th century, however, stories of these "rogue waves" persisted.

On the afternoon of December 31st, 1994, in the North Sea off of the coast of Norway, the Draupner
15 oil rig was subject to a barrage of hurricane-force winds and 12 meter waves. Around 3:00, all workers were told to remain inside for the worst of the storm. Later, when engineers were scrutinizing the logs of a wave-height detector, it was discovered that the rig
20 had actually been hit by a wave over 19 meters tall! They had just attained the world's first empirical, indisputable measurement of rogue waves.

A number of questions were immediately raised in the scientific community: how do we graph and predict
25 rogue waves? How common are they? And how do we make ships that can weather them?

The answer to the first question begins in 1983 with Howell Peregrine, then a mathematician at the University of Bristol, who developed a solution to
30 the nonlinear Schrödinger equation. The Schrödinger equation—derived in 1925 by Erwin Schrödinger—describes changes in systems of matter, such as molecules, atoms, and subatomic particles over a period of time. Its nonlinear variant is crucial to the
35 study of waves. Peregrine's solution (also called a breather or soliton) was unique in that it could describe a wave that seems to come from nowhere and to disappear just as quickly. The first study of the Peregrine breather in a water wave tank took place
40 in 2010, three years after Peregrine himself passed away. Shortly thereafter, in 2012, another group of researchers studied the Peregrine breather in a water wave tank at the Technical University of Berlin.

The latter group used a model of a chemical
45 tanker to determine whether it was possible to employ Peregrine breathers in studying the effects of rogue waves on a ship. A suspension system was used to keep the model in a fixed location in the wave tank, so that the waves would hit the bow (front) of the
50 model first. The model was also fitted with force transducers, which would measure the pressure on the model from the waves: two were put on either side of the deck, and one was placed underneath on the keel. The movements of the ship were tracked by an optical
55 system of four infrared cameras in a 7 by 10 meter frame, and by 9 strategically-placed wave gauges. Two water gauges were used to measure the effects of the waves on the bow, and were placed on the foredeck and weather deck. Once the model was in place, the
60 researchers generated several waves based on the Peregrine breather and recorded the impact on the ship.

The researchers found that the forces on the ship had effected major vertical bending moments (vbm). In order to understand vbm, picture a large sponge. If
65 it is bent in half, the top side will grow wider while the bottom side will grow proportionately narrower; the top side is in compression, and the bottom side is in tension. When a ship has an extreme bending moment near its mid-length, according to the Society of Naval
70 Architects and Marine Engineers, there are usually two outcomes: the ship will be in a sagging condition or in a hogging condition. The former happens when a wave trough (the "valley" between two waves) occurs at mid-length, and the latter occurs when a wave peak
75 occurs at mid-length. The chemical tanker's bending moment caused the ship to go through hogging and sagging conditions in rapid succession, but this did not cause the ship to go into structural failure.

These findings show that it is entirely possible
80 to use the Peregrine breather to study the impact of rogue waves on ships, and it opens up avenues to apply the findings to engineer ships. Indeed, recent years have seen a growth in the industry's interest in the problem of rogue waves—especially since it has been
85 discovered that they're fairly common. In addition, scientists have been working on building a world-wide network of buoys that could broadcast the presence of rogue waves to all nearby vessels. All of these efforts will be invaluable to finally conquering this monster of
90 the oceans.

Maximum Documented Wave Height (December 31, 1994)

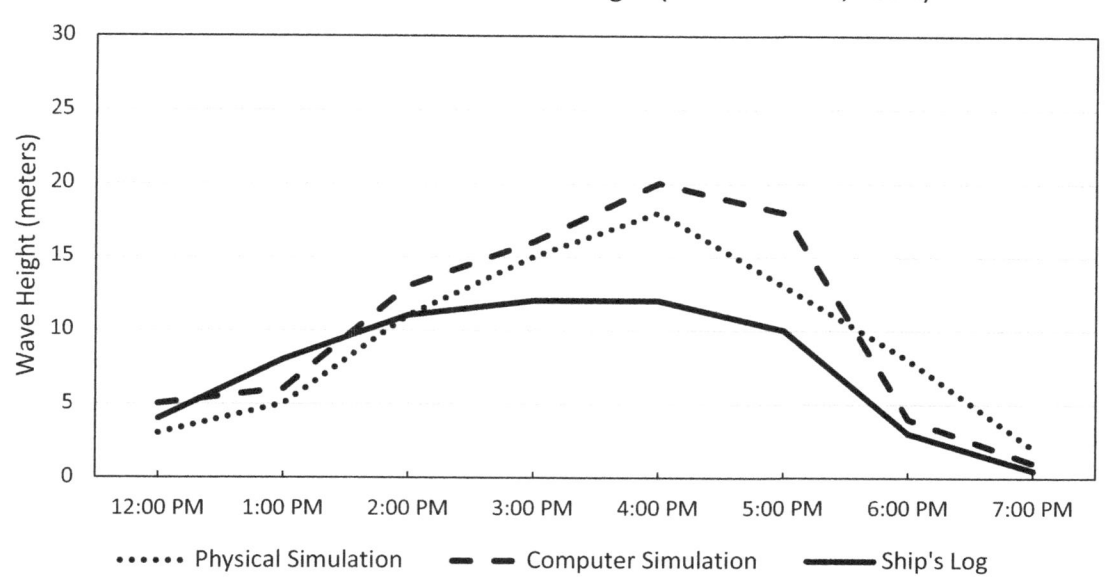

······ Physical Simulation   – – Computer Simulation   —— Ship's Log

1

The main purpose of the passage is to explain how

A) a misconception was overturned through conscientious fieldwork.
B) a theoretical conundrum led to an industrial application.
C) an extraordinary occurrence was illuminated by a research inquiry.
D) a bizarre event led to a revision of a popular mathematical model.

2

According to the passage, rogue waves were once assumed to be

A) a threat to human life that inspired various items of mythology.
B) of relatively little interest to physicists and mathematicians.
C) physically unlikely on the basis of modern scientific methods.
D) more prevalent but less dangerous than ancient sources indicated.

3

Which choice provides the best evidence for the answer to the previous question?

A) Lines 1-5 ("Ever . . . Rhodes")
B) Lines 7-10 ("Most . . . 15 meters")
C) Lines 11-12 ("Throughout . . . persisted")
D) Lines 23-26 ("A number . . . them?")

4

Which statement best characterizes the Schrodinger equation, as presented in the author's discussion?

A) It is normally only useful in describing small units of matter.
B) It provided one basis for studying the properties of rogue waves.
C) It has been modified as a result of inquiries surrounding rogue waves.
D) It was eventually replaced by the more complex equation developed by Peregrine.

5

As used in line 21, "empirical" most nearly means

A) pragmatic.
B) tested.
C) well-explained.
D) data-oriented.

6

As used in line 32, "describes" most nearly means

A) embellishes.
B) recounts.
C) illustrates.
D) fabricates.

7

Which of the following choices indicates that Peregrine breathers are fully applicable to the study of rogue waves?

A) Lines 41-43 ("Shortly . . . Berlin")
B) Lines 44-47 ("The latter . . . ship")
C) Lines 59-61 ("Once . . . ship")
D) Lines 79-82 ("These findings . . . ships")

8

The author urges readers to picture "a large sponge" (line 64) in order to

A) demonstrate how rogue waves themselves can expand and contract.
B) illustrate the reactions of a ship subjected to rogue wave impacts.
C) dramatize a process that only careful observers of data would normally discern.
D) continue an analogy suggested by the discussion of Peregrine's solution.

9

One possible outcome of the research described in the passage is the creation of

A) improved warning systems for rogue waves.
B) revised shipping routes that avoid areas where rogue waves are likely.
C) ships with thicker and lighter hulls.
D) shipboard devices that more accurately measure rogue wave heights.

10

Which of the following interval and measurement pairings represents the largest decrease in wave height?

A) Physical simulation, 5:00-6:00 PM
B) Computer simulation, 5:00-6:00 PM
C) Physical simulation, 6:00-7:00 PM
D) Computer simulation, 6:00-7:00 PM

11

In relation to the author's discussion in the passage, the graph primarily

A) indicates the accuracy of the wave height recorded in the Draupner ship's log.
B) demonstrates that computer simulations and physical simulations typically yield interchangeable results.
C) supports the idea that a firsthand record of a rogue wave may underestimate the wave's actual height.
D) implies that Peregrine's solution can be used to account for disparities between direct measurements and measurements extrapolated from models.

Questions 1-11 are based on the following passage and supplementary material.
5.2
Adapted from the book *In Pursuit of Memory: The Fight against Alzheimer's* by Joseph Jebelli. This book tackles the issue of preventing the cognitive disorder Alzheimer's once and for all through a new method called brain training.

Today, Alzheimer's disease threatens more people than cancer does, affecting potentially one in three people. Fortunately, "we are closer than ever to the abolition of Alzheimer's," says Joseph Jebelli, a researcher and author of *In Pursuit of Memory: The Fight Against Alzheimer's*. Jebelli contends that, far from being something to be feared, this illness is not only treatable, but also preventable. In his book, he discusses the preventive roles of stress reduction, diet, exercise, brain training, and sleep. He also highlights related experimental research, his own experience with Alzheimer's in his family, and his work as a neuroscientist.

The author shares the journey of his grandfather though progressive stages of the disease, noting his daily hikes in the foothills outside of northern Tehran, Iran. Jebelli observed that his grandfather was not a smoker, ate a healthy diet, and lived a mostly stress-free existence. Having inherited a fortune, his grandfather did not actually need to work. Looking at his grandfather and other individuals he had met, Jebelli sought to identify whether Alzheimer's is "an equal opportunity disease." While stress reduction, diet, exercise, brain training, and sleep all show preventive promise, brain training appears to be among the most interesting to emerge (although the author remains cautiously optimistic about preventive steps that anyone can take).

Jebelli became interested in the work of Ryuta Kawashima, who, in 2001, started researching the impact of video games on the human brain. Four years later, Kawashima created the *Nintendo Brain Training* game. In Japan, in nursing homes by the thousands, people began using this video game in an attempt to stave off dementia. Kawashima thinks his game works; it's in use by more than 30,000 people in Japan. Said Kawashima during a visit by Jebelli, "Patients who were doing nothing before, just sleeping and sitting in a wheelchair, were doing simple arithmetic problems."

Upon further discussion, it turns out that Kawashima indeed knows something about the neuroscience of the brain: the build-up of tau and beta-amyloid proteins, beginning at age forty, coincides with the onset of Alzheimer's symptoms. Therefore, brain training must start before that age.

Over 13,000 people were studied through research funded by the Alzheimer's Society in September 2009. In the study, subjects had to participate in the cognitive training for ten minutes a day, every weekday, for half a year. No improvement among those under age fifty was found with cognitive training. However, improvements with such activities as shopping, memorizing lists, and overseeing finances for those over sixty were found with such training. There are researchers who claim that the benefits can last as long as five years. Jebelli says that the jury is out on whether such training can prevent the onslaught of the illness, however.

In another study, 700 people over age 65 in the U.S. played checkers and cards as well as completed crossword puzzles and other puzzles; they were studied over a five-year period. The research suggested that the subjects were "47 percent less likely to develop Alzheimer's." Jebelli cites concerns about the study's small sample size, however.

At Tohoku University in Japan, Kawashima leads a group of forty neuroscientists in research funded by the game's profits. Simulating human conditions of deprivation and stimulation, researchers move mice between cages to mimic the experience of brain training. So far, the results show that the brains of old mice and genetically modified mice get bigger.

Says Kawashima, "We know that the prefrontal cortex is activated by brain training." This part of the brain is involved in decision-making, attention, and memory. It stands to reason that when we stimulate that part of the brain, its basic functions must improve.

One of the Tohoku researchers believes that the results they are seeing are due to a neuroscientific concept known as "brain reserve." The geriatric researcher James Mortimer came up with this concept decades ago, positing that each individual's brain has a set amount of resistance to mental decline, regardless of the amount of structure damage occurring. In what became known as the "Nun Study," Mortimer's co-researcher, D. A. Snowdon, was able to predict which nuns would develop Alzheimer's with 80 percent accuracy. Snowdon, believing that such brain reserves are developmental, suggested that the best thing parents can do for their children is to read to them.

Kawashima has concerns that any positive effects of brain training may be due to the Hawthorne effect: changes due to the fact that subjects know that they are being observed. These cautions should frame our understanding of any related research and results that attempt to correlate prevention of Alzheimer's with brain training. More research must be done to investigate the long term effects of brain training, and any other Alzheimer's research that shows promise, as the disease is as devastating to loved ones of people with Alzheimer's as it is to those suffering it themselves.

Results for Memorization and Problem-Solving Improvement Based on Brain-Training Video Game

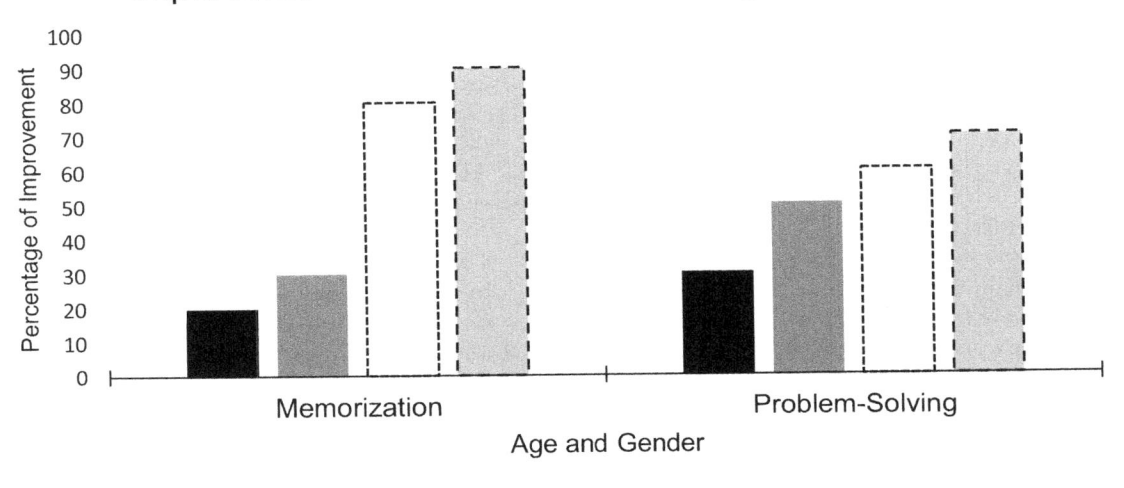

Category	40-59, Male	40-59, Female	60-79, Male	60-79, Female
Memorization	20	30	80	90
Problem-Solving	30	50	60	75

1

In the first paragraph, the author's use of the words "threatens" and "feared" primarily has the effect of

A) implying that past efforts to combat Alzheimer's disease have been ineffectual.
B) underscoring the fact that Alzheimer's disease is perceived as severely detrimental.
C) summarizing initial reactions that researchers such as Jebelli expect from non-experts.
D) suggesting the emotions of an individual who has been diagnosed with Alzheimer's.

2

According to the passage, Jebelli's research was inspired in part by

A) a longstanding interest in physical health.
B) questions related to social status.
C) the shortcomings of earlier investigations.
D) specific firsthand experiences.

3

Which choice provides the best evidence for the answer to the previous question?

A) Lines 6-8 ("Jebelli . . . preventable")
B) Lines 14-17 ("The author . . . Iran")
C) Lines 20-23 ("Looking . . . disease")
D) Lines 29-31 ("Jebelli . . . brain")

4

Which of the following facts would provide the best support regarding the "discussion" (line 40) about the effectiveness of brain training in fighting Alzheimer's?

A) The brain training game developed by Kawashima is currently being used by 17,000 people in South Korea.
B) Tau proteins play a more significant role in the onset of Alzheimer's symptoms than beta-amyloid proteins do.
C) Subjects who began brain training programs after the age of 45 did not show a meaningful increase in resistance to Alzheimer's disease.
D) Solving complex arithmetic problems is as effective as solving simple arithmetic problems in building up Alzheimer's resistance.

5

As used in line 39, "simple" most nearly means

A) elementary.
B) uninteresting.
C) forthright.
D) unvarying.

6

In what respect is the "research" mentioned in line 46 similar to the "study" mentioned in line 59?

A) Both projects utilized methods that appeared to contradict Kawashima's recommendations.
B) The two projects involved significant adjustments to the daily habits of participants
C) Jebelli has expressed that the results for both of these projects are inconclusive.
D) Cognitive improvements in both projects were limited to the youngest test subjects.

7

As used in line 70, "mimic" most nearly means

A) shadow.
B) resemble.
C) parody.
D) impersonate.

8

One issue that has not been fully resolved by current research on mental decline and brain training is whether

A) the psychological burden of Alzheimer's is more severe for those afflicted with the disease or for their loved ones.
B) the onset of Alzheimer's causes any redistribution of brain activity.
C) awareness of being monitored can affect a test subject's performance.
D) instances of Alzheimer's can be traced to genetic factors.

9

Which choice provides the best evidence for the answer to the previous question?

A) Lines 74-77 ("This part . . . improve")
B) Lines 88-90 ("Snowdon . . . them")
C) Lines 91-94 ("Kawashima . . . observed")
D) Lines 97-102 ("More . . . themselves")

10

Researchers from the 2009 Alzheimer's Society study would view the information in the graph with

A) complete acceptance; the results perfectly align with their own observations.
B) absolute rejection; the results are the complete opposite of what was observed in the 2009 study.
C) partial acceptance; the results differ from the 2009 study but support a broad trend seen in both studies.
D) an indeterminate sentiment because there is not enough information to answer the question.

11

Based on the figure, which individual would most likely gain the most overall improvement from the Brain-Training Video Game?

A) 68-year old female
B) 43-year old male
C) 65-year old male
D) 47-year old female

Questions 1-11 are based on the following passage and supplementary material.

5.3
The following passage is adapted from "Carbonado Diamond: A Review of Properties and Origin," a 2017 Gemological Institute of America article by Stephen E. Haggerty.

Kids should recognize the scale for assessing the hardness of different minerals, called the Mohs Hardness Scale. In elementary geology class, children will often be given a Mohs Hardness Kit and different minerals—from the softest, talc, to the hardest known, diamond—to test for "hardness." The rating of 10 for diamond has long been hailed as the top of the scale, until carbonados came in and challenged the rating. Whether made synthetically as nanocrystalline diamond aggregates, or in nature as carbonado, these substances and their extraordinary properties have forced scientists to extend the Mohs Hardness Scale to accommodate them. Some geologists have already assigned both nanocrystalline diamonds and carbonados a value greater than 10 or 11, extending the Mohs hardness scale to accommodate these newest, hardest substances.

Carbonado, a type of diamond, is actually harder than those that most people are familiar with and is only found in the Central African Republic and Brazil. Besides being porous and growing to large sizes—the largest carbonado is 3,167 carats—they are micro porphyritic, which means that they appear to be several small diamonds sintered together. Carbonados often have a patina (a film produced by oxidation), and display inclusions of metal alloys and highly reduced minerals. They are unique because they possess isotopically light carbon atoms as part of their composition, and several other unusual properties.

According to geologist Stephen E. Haggerty of the University of Massachusetts at Amherst, the carbonado's "toughness and tenacity, stemming from the random orientation of microdiamonds, are clearly superior to monocrystalline gem diamond, to the point that carbonado can only be cut by lasers." Haggerty performed extensive research of carbonado's physical and chemical properties, as reported in an article he published in 2014. There, he indicated that one of the carbonado samples he studied "is at the upper end of the hardness scale for natural diamonds, but we are confident that other carbonados will exceed this limit."

Because of the unusual characteristics of carbonados, scientists have formulated multiple theories as to their origin. The most prominent theory, perhaps the one that sparks the most debate within the scientific community, is whether or not these so-called Black Diamonds "came from outer space." According to a 1996 *New York Times* article, scientists have speculated that a combination of exploding stars, asteroid impacts, and natural radiation worked together to create these big diamonds. Specific theories of origin involve a variety of astronomical causes, including meteoric impacts, dwarf stars, or supernovas, often in combination with geological changes or actions.

Years ago, geologists just believed that these substances originated from a process similar to that of conventional diamonds, from crushing pressure and heat deep in the interior of the earth. Later, volcanic eruptions carried them up to the surface, long after they were formed. But in the 1980s, a team of researchers headed by physicist Luis W. Alvarez proposed a different theory: a large space rock had hit the earth, disrupting the climate and causing carbonados to be created. Further proving that these substances may not be Earth-like, unlike conventional diamonds, carbonados are slightly porous and opaque, and translucent rather than fully transparent. Says carbonado-expert Dr. Paul S. DeCarli, "They're better than regular diamonds because they don't cleave," but instead sheer off and sharpen.

However, scientists are not all convinced of this so-called "impact" theory. The unique polycrystalline structure of carbonados makes them impervious to implements such as diamond saws. After spending hours ruining several diamond saws in an attempt to examine the features of this mineral to support a cogent theory, carbonado researchers turned to another option: X-ray computed tomography. Via this method, pores in the carbonado diamonds were found which do not appear Earthly in origin. Researchers suggest that the origin of carbonados, when more fully understood, could offer explanations for sub-micron diamond growth and planetary evolution. Furthermore, because of their extreme toughness, carbonado-like diamond synthesis could provide a cheap, light-weight, and near indestructible material for industrial applications.

Although it's not quite clear which theory has the strongest backing—transported via meteorites or originating as earthly substances—carbonados are interesting and useful minerals, and their hardness has posed an interesting challenge for scientists who believed for years that a rating of 10 should be the absolute maximum for Mohs Hardness Scale. Although they are not beautiful like commercial diamonds, these diamonds are extremely rare and therefore can be quite pricey. Furthermore, they are so hard that they need to be cut by lasers, but this actually makes them an excellent substance to make cutting tools out of.

MOHS HARDNESS SCALE MEASUREMENTS FOR VARIOUS SUBSTANCES	
talc	1
gypsum	2
calcite	3
limestone	3.5
fluorite	4
slate	4.4
orthoclase	5
feldspar	6
sandstone	6.5
quartz	7
topaz	8
ruby	8.5
diamond	10
carbonado	10.4
nanocrystalline diamond	10.7

1

The main purpose of the passage is to

A) propose a few new practical and commercial uses for carbonados on the basis of recent commentary.
B) support a new line of analysis that could resolve a dispute among scientists.
C) demonstrate how researchers revised existing hardness criteria to accommodate carbonados.
D) explain the properties of carbonados and then outline a debate that surrounds these minerals.

2

As used in line 7, "hailed" most nearly means

A) sighted.
B) signaled.
C) acknowledged.
D) applauded.

3

In the second paragraph, the author characterizes carbonados as

A) relatively little-known.
B) physically unattractive.
C) surprisingly useful.
D) mysterious in composition.

4

As used in line 26, "display" most nearly means

A) depict.
B) define.
C) exhibit.
D) express.

5

Haggerty's description of the "toughness and tenacity" (line 32) of carbonados is best understood as

A) an instance of personification that makes a complex issue more accessible.
B) an expert opinion related to one of Haggerty's own research projects.
C) a direct response to a successful attempt to classify carbonados.
D) a broad statement that suggests the importance of future research on carbonados.

6

According to the passage, one important contrast between carbonados and softer diamonds is that

A) diamonds have never been traced to any specific extraterrestrial sources.
B) diamonds are capable of cutting substances that carbonados cannot cut.
C) carbonados cannot be cut with some of the devices that normally cut diamonds.
D) carbonados have fewer industrial uses than diamonds do on account of their opacity.

7

Which choice provides the best evidence for the answer to the previous question?

A) Lines 38-41 ("There . . . limit")
B) Lines 55-58 ("Years ago . . . earth")
C) Lines 64-67 ("Further . . . transparent")
D) Lines 72-74 ("The unique . . . saws")

8

The author of the passage indicates that the outer-space theory of how carbonados originated

A) is at present considered less convincing than earth-based theories of carbonado origin.
B) has been most effectively supported by details of the chemical composition of carbonados.
C) was formulated before the properties of carbonados were fully understood.
D) may involve sub-theories that assign different extraterrestrial sources to carbonados.

9

Which choice provides the best evidence for the answer to the previous question?

A) Lines 51-54 ("Specific . . . actions")
B) Lines 71-72 ("However . . . theory")
C) Lines 78-80 ("Via . . . origin")
D) Lines 87-93 ("Although . . . Mohs Hardness Scale")

10

Geologists have recently discovered a new mineral that is harder than fluorite but softer than topaz. According to the table, which of the following could NOT be the new mineral's Mohs hardness rating?

A) 4
B) 5
C) 6
D) 7

11

In relation to the passage, the table primarily provides

A) an overview of the process by which carbonados "challenged" (line 8) the top Mohs hardness rating.
B) an illustration of how scientists have succeeded in "extending the Mohs hardness scale" (lines 15-16).
C) an indication that carbonados are comparable to "several small diamonds sintered together" (line 24).
D) a suggestion that carbonados possess "unusual properties" (line 29).

Questions 1-11 are based on the following passage and supplementary material.

5.4
Based on a 2017 Nature Research Journal article, "Solutal Marangoni Flows of Miscible Liquids Drive Transport Without Surface Contamination" by Hyoungsoo Kim, Koen Muller, Orest Shardt, Shahriar Afkhami, and Howard Stone, this passage attempts to explain what the Marangoni effect is and how it can be used to aid in solving environmental problems.

Oil spills are a growing problem worldwide, and few good solutions currently exist to address them. They are an example of the omnipresent phenomenon
Line of the mixing and spreading of two or more liquids.
5 Other examples include ocean pollution; the brackish water of estuaries; processing of food, beverages and cosmetics; and polymer processing. Scientists have not been able to clearly describe how two miscible liquids mix and spread. Typically, since two liquids
10 will have two different surface tensions, the results are often counterintuitive: a liquid drop on a second liquid remains as a static lens for a period of time. In other words, it does not immediately spread and mix, but instead generates a "Marangoni-driven connective
15 flow." Often referred to as the "Marangoni effect," this phenomenon is the mass transfer along an interface between two fluids due to a surface tension gradient.

How would the process of cleaning up an oil spill be advanced if scientists understood these dynamics
20 better? Recently, a model has been developed that predicts the finite spreading time and the length scale, the convection flow speed, and the finite timescale. By establishing a model that describes the quasi-steady state for this flow, the researchers may enable surface
25 cleaning approaches without contaminating the water with spilled oil, as one of many applications.

An associate professor in the mathematics department of the New Jersey Institute of Technology, Shahriar Afkhami, can answer this question.
30 Professor Afkhami is currently heading a research team at NJIT that is working to make enhancements to a computational model that will help us better understand the Marangoni Effect. The computational model was initially developed by Ivana Seric, who is
35 one of his former Ph.D. students. The original research team, led by Princeton University's Professor Howard A. Stone, used advanced flow visualization techniques to capture and predict what happens when a single alcohol drop is placed on water, as well as a number
40 of Marangoni-driven factors that were not previously known, including spreading time, length scale, and surface mixing time.

The "tears of wine" that form along the rim of a wine glass may serve as an illustration of the
45 Marangoni effect, occurring when two miscible liquids with different surface tensions meet. The liquid with greater surface tension (water) pulls on the surrounding liquid with greater force than solutes, such as alcohol, that have lower surface tension. When "tears of wine"
50 are formed, the alcohol evaporates and lifts the wine up the glass. In the process, it raises the concentration of the water in the liquid, as well as the overall surface tension. When the material contracts, the liquid starts to pool on the glass walls as droplets. When they
55 become heavier than the force of the effect, they fall down into the wine.

In their research, Afkhami and the team focused on the spreading mechanisms and flows of a droplet that was fully soluble in a liquid bath. They collected
60 data such as finite diffusion times and length scales that occurred where the two liquids interface, and created videos that showed how the two materials mix together. The researchers were able to show how a drop of liquid that is deposited on another liquid
65 surface becomes like a static lens that does not mix and spread right away. At the same time, the situation generates a flow that would seem counterintuitive if the two liquids have different surface tensions.

The methods used to create and improve this
70 theoretical computational model are complex, involving filling a Petri dish with water, and varying the volume of the deposited drop, delivered by a syringe pump. Various physical properties of the water were measured, as well as for the deposited droplets
75 of isopropanol, ethanol, methanol, tert-butanol, and silicone oil. Scientists estimated the diffusion coefficient using a model. They also studied the effect of liquid bath viscosity, visualizing the flow pattern with hydrophobic polystyrene tracer particles and
80 making adjustments for side-view experiments. Top-view experiments involved a high-speed camera, and a second camera for side views. Physical properties and surface tension values were measured using a rheometer, a sandblasted cylinder system, and a scale.
85 The results suggest that even when a miscible solute causes a solutal Marangoni flow, it will mix with the bulk liquid and not significantly change the properties of the surface. Moreover, the solutal Marangoni flow is capable of delivering the materials
90 as well as cleaning the surface of the liquid without contaminating the surface. Through facilitating better understanding the dynamics of liquid-liquid flows, this

theoretical model can potentially enable an approach to cleaning surfaces, including oil spills, without
95 contaminating the surface of the water with additional chemicals.

Extent of the 2010 Deepwater Horizon Oil Spill

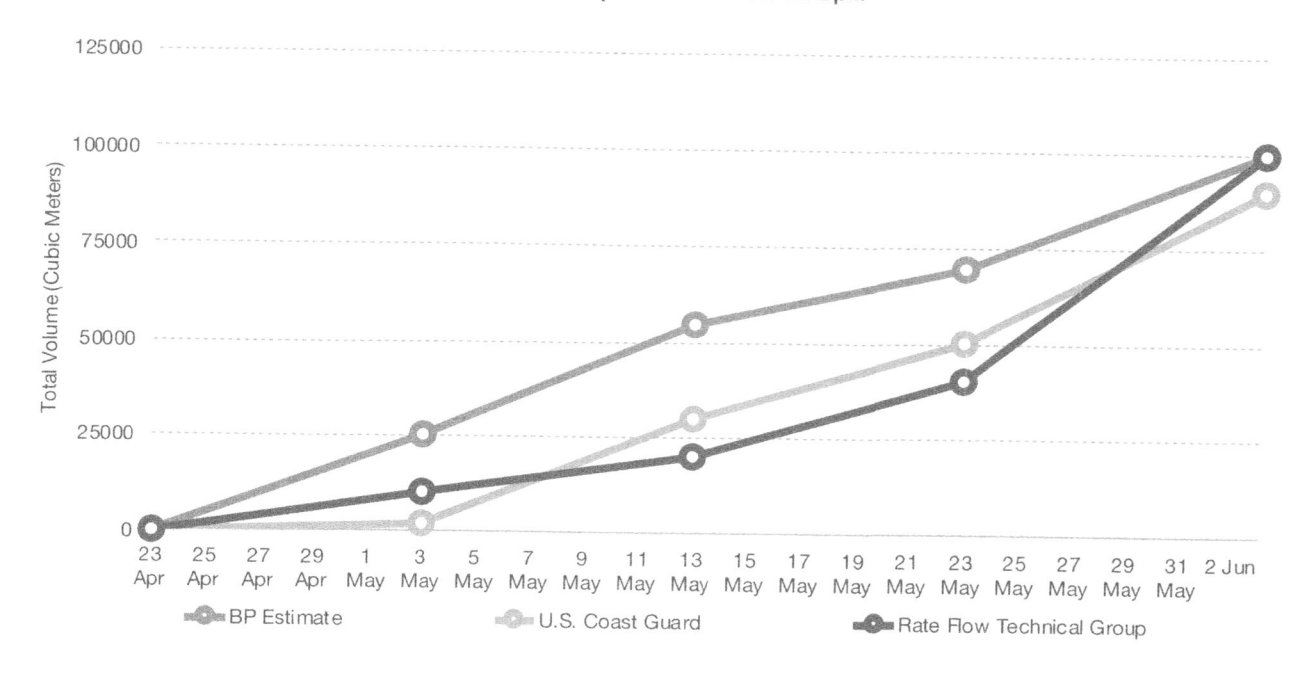

— BP Estimate   — U.S. Coast Guard   — Rate Flow Technical Group

1

The main purpose of the passage is to explain how

A) advances in modeling software have helped researchers to explain the Marangoni Effect.
B) a new mathematical model has helped ecological scientists to more accurately evaluate the extent of past oil spills.
C) an investigation into fluid dynamics may suggest a means of addressing problematic situations.
D) a revised understanding of the Marangoni effect helped researchers to repurpose a popular technology.

2

The author's purpose in listing multiple "examples" in lines 5-7 is to

A) suggest that everyday observations of the Marangoni Effect are of practical use to researchers.
B) highlight a limitation of physicists' current understanding of the dynamics of oil spills.
C) argue that the mixing and spreading of liquids is often a beneficial or at least harmless process.
D) indicate that a process central to the passage's discussion can be observed in contexts other than oil spills.

3

Which choice indicates that researchers have not yet fully explained the principles behind the Marangoni Effect?

A) Lines 9-11 ("Typically . . . counterintuitive")
B) Lines 15-17 ("Often . . . gradient")
C) Lines 30-33 ("Professor Afkhami . . . Marangoni Effect")
D) Lines 35-39 ("The original . . . water")

4

As used in line 12, "static" most nearly means

A) stiff.
B) stationary.
C) steadfast.
D) stolid.

5

The main purpose of the third paragraph (lines 27-42) is to

A) indicate shortcomings of existing explanations of the Marangoni effect.
B) explain the practical motivations behind the development of Afkhami's model.
C) suggest that a breakthrough was enabled by a radically interdisciplinary approach.
D) introduce an endeavor that the author later explains in considerable detail.

6

As used in line 50, "lifts" most nearly means

A) motivates.
B) energizes.
C) transports.
D) exalts.

7

In performing their research, Afkhami and the other scientists made use of

A) documentary footage of a process under investigation.
B) a controlled recreation of a household occurrence that is often overlooked.
C) data from less intensive research on the Marangoni effect.
D) both physical models and software-based visual simulations.

8

Which choice provides the best evidence for the answer to the previous question?

A) Lines 49-51 ("When . . . glass")
B) Lines 59-63 ("They collected . . . together")
C) Lines 66-68 ("At the . . . tensions")
D) Lines 69-73 ("The methods . . . syringe pump")

9

The final paragraph of the passage characterizes solutal Marangoni flow as

A) potentially useful in addressing a practical problem without introducing a new liability.
B) capable of dramatically altering liquid surface properties under a few specific circumstances.
C) seemingly ideal for addressing oil spill damage yet ultimately difficult to control.
D) still not understood in a manner that would indicate a real-world application.

10

According to the chart, on which of the following dates did the Rate Flow Technical Group report the extent of the Deepwater Horizon Oil Spill as less than both the BP estimate and the U.S. Coast Guard estimate?

A) April 23
B) May 3
C) May 23
D) June 2

11

A student claims that the graph offers support for Afkhami's findings regarding the Marangoni effect. On the basis of the passage, the student's claim is incorrect because

A) the flow rate model that was developed by Afkhami can only explain the activity of small amounts of liquid.
B) Afkhami's research was designed with the intention of challenging the measurements provided by BP.
C) the model that Afkhami used suggests that oil will normally spread over water at a constant rate.
D) Afkhami's findings are not explicitly connected to any of the three models considered in the graph.

Questions 1-11 are based on the following passage and supplementary material.

Adapted from a 2010 NCBI article, "Biofuels from algae: challenges and potential," by Michael Hannon and a team of researchers at The San Diego Center for Algal Biotechnology of UCLA.

Our global economy uses fossil fuels to function, including providing energy for transportation, heating, and lighting, but concerns about carbon emissions are driving the search for cleaner fuel alternatives.
[5] A growing number of renewable energy sources have long been seen as potential alternatives to non-renewable sources such as coal and petroleum. At the top of the list right now is a new sustainable, cost-effective option: algae. Liquid fuel produced by
[10] microalgae could have potential as a renewable energy source because it has high lipid content, grows quickly, and produces co-products and improved strains that can further its beneficial properties in the future—and it does not use arable land, meaning that won't take up
[15] any of that precious resource.

At this point, scientists are excited about the potential uses of this algae alternative, but they have much work ahead of them as several factors must be considered before algae can be determined to be a
[20] realistic alternative to fossil fuels. Biologists are in the process of defining the problems that stand in the way of making algae a viable alternative to fossil fuels, so that they can then determine the best methods to solve these problems—if they possess solutions that are
[25] worth pursuing.

The most glaring challenge is that clean fuels can command higher prices than their fossil-fuel counterparts. In 2009, it was estimated that algae-based fuel created with current technology could cost US
[30] $300-2600; in contrast, the cost for oil is $40-80 per barrel. Note, however, that, depending on the region, algae oil is estimated to cost as little as $84 per barrel, although that's still higher than the current steepest oil price point. At this point, it seems that the key to
[35] large-scale, lucrative algae production as a biofuel is finding the correct price point. While the final price per barrel of algae oil is challenging to estimate, costs can be decreased by improvements in engineering and use of a variety of system improvements.

[40] Beyond just cost issues, there are numerous challenges with production method and scale, as well as the process of extracting oil from algae. For algae to be produced efficiently and on a massive scale, engineering will have to be improved significantly
[45] to accommodate for controlling exposure to light and circulation of nutrients. In order to do so, engineers will have to create photobioreactors that are inexpensive and can be used in larger-scale efforts than are currently possible. The best solution may be that
[50] new species will have to be developed that can grow in open systems at low cost because the top three current methods for oil extraction are expensive but amenable to improvements.

Despite their setbacks, microalgal biofuels do
[55] have benefits. The fact that species can grow in many different types of aquatic environments, including saturated saline freshwater, means that the need to cultivate land is eliminated, possibly cutting farming costs. Furthermore, algae can grow very rapidly,
[60] sometimes doubling in as little as 6 hours. Lastly, every species produces oils that are rich in energy, some having as much as half of their mass stored as long-chain hydrocarbons. Such diversity gives researchers the chance to select from many production
[65] options—and if the aforementioned benefits weren't enough, they can be bioengineered for specific traits and co-products, providing endless possibilities in the future.

Maximum Costs (Per Barrel) for Algae Oil and Crude Oil

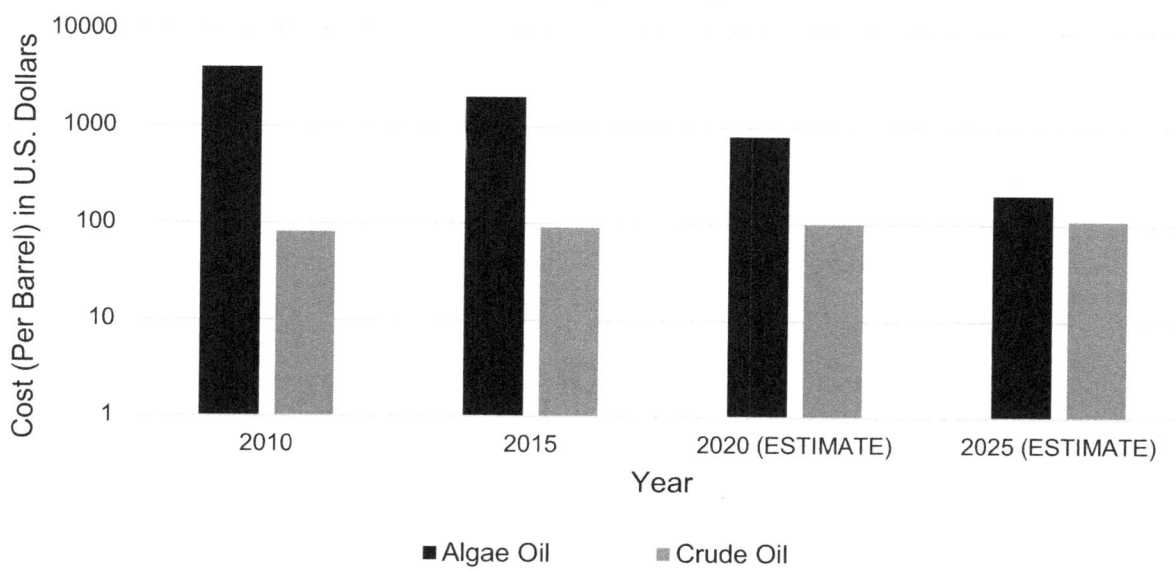

[Bar chart showing cost per barrel in U.S. Dollars (log scale from 1 to 10000) for Algae Oil and Crude Oil across years 2010, 2015, 2020 (ESTIMATE), and 2025 (ESTIMATE). Algae Oil costs decrease from about 4000 in 2010 to about 150 in 2025, while Crude Oil remains around 80-90 throughout.]

■ Algae Oil   ■ Crude Oil

1

The main purpose of the passage is to

A) urge a greater spirit of responsibility and efficiency in the development of energy sources.
B) refute a series of misconceptions that surround an exciting source of renewable energy.
C) examine an alternative fuel source that may be an asset despite current challenges.
D) offer an account of a research project that has met with unexpected success.

2

In lines 8-9, the author's characterization of algae as a "sustainable, cost-effective" option is best understood to mean that

A) algae may displace other renewable energy sources in the near future.
B) the possible usefulness of algae has already been acknowledged.
C) opposition to algae as a fuel source is disappearing.
D) the costs linked to algae are much lower than those linked to traditional fuels.

3

As used in line 25, "pursuing" most nearly means

A) following after.
B) implementing.
C) tracing.
D) meditating upon.

4

Which choice indicates that the main hindrance facing adoption of algae as a fuel source is NOT necessarily a matter of science?

A) Lines 5-7 ("A growing . . . petroleum")
B) Lines 16-20 ("At this . . . fossil fuels")
C) Lines 20-25 ("Biologists . . . pursuing")
D) Lines 26-28 ("The most . . . counterparts")

5

The author's analysis of the costs of oil and algae-based fuel primarily suggests that

A) algae-based fuels release significantly less pollution than fossil fuels release.
B) algae-based fuels release roughly the same amount of pollution over time that fossil fuels release.
C) the prices for algae-based fuel are often higher and have a relatively small range.
D) the prices for algae-based fuel are consistently higher and have a relatively large range.

6

One important effect of improving technology related to algae oil production would be

A) more sustainable farming of algae for uses other than oil.
B) the creation of devices that are also applicable to fossil fuels.
C) the development of algae species that require lower volumes of nutrients.
D) the ability to produce the oil at a lower price point.

7

Which choice provides the best evidence for the answer to the previous question?

A) Lines 42-46 ("For algae . . . nutrients")
B) Lines 49-53 ("The best . . . improvements")
C) Lines 59-60 ("Furthermore . . . hours")
D) Lines 63-65 ("Such diversity . . . options")

8

As used in line 63, "diversity" most nearly means

A) freedom from conformity.
B) a form of collaboration.
C) an array of options.
D) vibrancy of expression.

9

The main purpose of the final paragraph of the passage is to

A) list various factors that help to depict algae-related biofuels in an approving manner.
B) outline a few of the different research projects that have recently come to the author's attention.
C) offer an argument that overturns the author's earlier reservations about fuel costs.
D) suggest a compromise that will facilitate algae oil production.

10

The information presented in the graph suggests which of the following relationships between the maximum cost per barrel of algae oil and the maximum cost per barrel of crude oil?

A) Increased consumption of algae oil will lead to marginal increases in maximum price per barrel of crude oil.
B) These two quantities are both predicted to experience exponential changes over time.
C) The sum of these two quantities will most likely remain constant over time.
D) The difference between these two quantities is estimated to decrease over time.

11

Which of the following, according to the passage, would be responsible for the likely change over time in the maximum cost per barrel of algae oil?

A) Technological advancement
B) New consumer preferences
C) Government subsidies
D) Geopolitical competition

Questions 1-11 are based on the following passages and supplementary material.
5.6
Passage 1 is adapted from a 2015 NIH article titled "Ebola Vaccine Candidate Promising in Early Study." Passage 2 is adapted from a 2017 Journal of Nature article titled "Ebola Vaccine Approved for Use in Ongoing Outbreak" by Amy Maxmen.

Passage 1

The Ebola virus outbreak frightened millions of people when it began in 2014 in West Africa not only because of the virus itself, but also because it took a while to get it under control, as no licensed therapies or vaccines existed to help to prevent or control any future outbreaks. Finally, in 2015, a vaccine was developed and a subsequent early stage clinical trial was conducted by researchers at the Walter Reed Army Institute of Research (WRAIR) and the National Institutes of Health (NIH). The vaccine was called VSV-ZEBOV, which stands for vesicular stomatitis virus–Zaire Ebola virus, and it was comprised of a virus that mostly affected cows, but was genetically modified and attenuated for safety in human use. To make the vaccine effective, the researchers replaced the viral gene with a part of a gene obtained from a key protein that was contained in the Ebola virus' Zaire species. Because the vaccine does not contain the entire Ebola virus, it cannot cause the Ebola infection, making it a viable solution for a growing threat.

In the 2015 study, 26 subjects were enrolled as volunteers at the NIH Clinical Center, and 26 more at the WRAIR clinic. The experimental vaccine was administered at one of two dosage levels to 40 of the subjects, with the other 12 subjects receiving a placebo of saline solution. Drs. John H. Beigel and Richard T. Davey Jr. of the NIH's National Institute of Allergy and Infectious Diseases (NIAID) led the NIH trial. Drs. Stephen J. Thomas and Jason Regules led the WRAIR trial. Of the volunteers receiving the vaccine, most developed antibodies against the Ebola virus' Zaire species within two weeks of receiving the injection. Every subject developed antibodies within 28 days of receiving the injection, with higher immune responses observed among those receiving the higher dose of the vaccine. While volunteers tolerated this vaccine well, some experienced side effects. Among these were pain at the site of the injection and a transient fever that resolved itself with 12 to 36 hours after having received the vaccination. There was also an interesting positive side effect: many patients who reported having arthritis symptoms before the administration of the vaccine reported at the end of the study that those symptoms were gone.

Researcher Davey suggests that, based on their findings, the VSV-ZEBOV vaccine seems to be an excellent candidate that could be very useful in intervening when there is a future Ebola virus outbreak. Davey cited, "the prompt, dose-dependent production of high levels of antibodies following a single injection and the overall favorable safety profile of this vaccine" as factors in its favor.

Passage 2

To combat the growing Ebola crisis, researchers at the NIH and the Walter Reed Army Institute of Research developed a new vaccine called VSV-ZEBOV. Because of the success this drug was having in its trial stages, health experts from Liberia and Guinea campaigned to make the drug available for people in those countries who were suffering with the deadly disease. Once the vaccine reached the countries, volunteers began enrolling in a Phase 2/3 study in which one of two vaccines would be administered on an experimental basis, with VSV-ZEBOV being one of the two.

The study showed promising results, leading to a recommendation for a new, possibly safer, rVSV-ZEBOV vaccine in the DRC*. According to a related article published in the New England Journal of Medicine, "The vaccine candidate (rVSV-ZEBOV) is genetically engineered to replace the VSV glycoprotein with the glycoprotein from a Zaire strain of Ebola virus (ZEBOV)," to create the recombinant ("r") version. Recombinant vaccines take advantage of the ability of laboratory technology to cut and recombine DNA in a sequence that would not otherwise exist in nature. This is especially beneficial when a vaccine needs to utilise DNA sequences that could be harmful in their original state (i.e. a virus). According to the researchers who published their most recent findings in 2018, "the best estimate of the rVSV-ZEBOV vaccine efficacy is 100%." Merck made 300,000 doses of this vaccine available, as part of a 2016 agreement between the company and both the Vaccine Alliance and the international organization Gavi.

At this point, authorities are not sure whether it is economically viable to have the vaccine on standby for possible future Ebola outbreaks. The DRC began receiving reports of Ebola-like symptoms in April of 2017, and was able to confirm only two cases of Ebola. Dozens of additional suspected cases awaited diagnosis as of May 2017, but the World Health

Organization's (WHO's) assistant director-general of health systems and innovation, Marie-Paule Kieny, expressed concerns from her office and WHO's
[95] headquarters in Geneva, Switzerland about the 2017 outbreak. Does the small number of already confirmed cases justify the considerable logistical complexity and cost that come with deploying the vaccine? The WHO and Congolese authorities must address and factor in
[100] current uncertainties about the outbreak's magnitude in order to make a final decision about the vaccine's future.

*Democratic Republic of the Congo

Number of Test Subjects Who Developed Antibodies After Receiving Vaccination Types

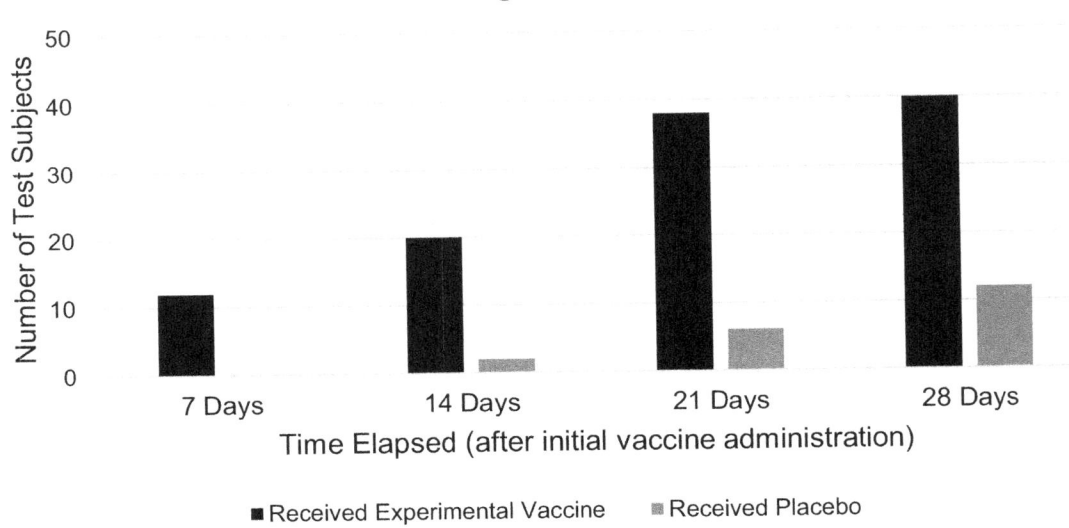

Time Elapsed	Received Experimental Vaccine	Received Placebo
7 Days	12	0
14 Days	21	3
21 Days	39	7
28 Days	42	14

1

The main purpose of Passage 1 is to describe

A) the successes and failures of a few related attempts to combat Ebola.
B) the process that led to the development of a new Ebola treatment.
C) the core concepts used by researchers responsible for developing vaccines.
D) the scope of an especially deadly recent outbreak of the Ebola virus.

2

In addressing the side effects of the VSV-ZEBOV vaccine, the authors of Passage 1 provide information on

A) the possibility of developing new therapies based on the vaccine's side effects.
B) the portion of test subjects that experienced a side effect of some form.
C) the specific symptoms of both positive and negative side effects.
D) the side effects first predicted by the researchers.

3

As used in line 38, "transient" most nearly means

A) unstable.
B) impermanent.
C) migratory.
D) insignificant.

4

As used in line 47, "candidate" most nearly means

A) competing claim.
B) prospective measure.
C) source of authority.
D) attempted rationale.

5

In relation to Passage 1, could the graph represent the results of the 2015 study described by the authors?

A) Yes, because the graph implies that the side effects of the vaccine were minimal for those subjects who were first to develop antibodies.
B) Yes, because the number of subjects who developed antibodies at 28 days is identical for the graph and the description of the 2015 study.
C) No, because the graph does not clearly indicate the side effects of the administered vaccine.
D) No, because the graph considers research that involved twice the number of participants in the 2015 study

6

Which choice most clearly indicates that the rVSV-ZEBOV vaccine may be preferable to the original VSV-ZEBOV vaccine?

A) Lines 60-64 ("Once . . . the two")
B) Lines 65-67 ("The study . . . the DRC")
C) Lines 67-73 ("According . . . version")
D) Lines 73-76 ("Recombinant . . . nature")

7

The situation as of May 2017, as described towards the end of Passage 2, can best be understood as one in which

A) the number of confirmed cases of Ebola was far exceeded by the available doses of rVSV-ZEBOV vaccine.
B) previous certainty about the efficacy of the rVSV-ZEBOV vaccine was complicated by the emergence of a resistant strain of Ebola.
C) theoretical models of the financial costs of deploying rVSV-ZEBOV were revised to account for new information.
D) authorities were inclined to limit production of the rVSV-ZEBOV vaccine in the face of a worldwide decline in cases of Ebola.

8

The question posed by the author of Passage 2 in lines 96-98 serves the purpose of

A) urging the reader to reflect on the high stakes involved in a public health crisis.
B) paraphrasing the ideas of Marie-Paule Kieny in an efficient manner.
C) comparing the outcomes desired by the WHO and by Congolese authorities.
D) weighing a situation that may call for action against a few practical challenges.

9

Which choice best describes the relationship between the two passages?

A) Passage 1 analyzes a series of public health problems that are presented in a more approachable and anecdotal manner in Passage 2.
B) Passage 1 explains the potentialities and drawbacks of a vaccine type that is more vocally endorsed in Passage 2.
C) Passage 1 discusses the development and testing of a vaccine type that is considered from the standpoint of deployment and treatment in Passage 2.
D) Passage 1 presents a hypothetical scenario that is considered in terms of its ethical significance in Passage 2.

10

The author of Passage 2 would regard the information about vaccine development in lines 14-20 ("To make . . . threat") of Passage 1 as

A) helpful in explaining the high efficacy of the rVSV-ZEBOV vaccine.
B) of little use to those who are trained to administer viable vaccines.
C) factually correct but at this point well-known to both researchers and the public.
D) closely aligned with her own understanding of the creation of useful vaccines.

11

Which choice provides the best evidence for the answer to the previous question?

A) Lines 53-56 ("To combat . . . VSV-ZEBOV")
B) Lines 76-78 ("This . . . virus")
C) Lines 78-81 ("According . . . 100%")
D) Lines 85-87 ("At this . . . outbreaks")

Questions 1-10 are based on the following passage and supplementary material.
5.7
Adapted from a BBC article on Africanized Bees called "Are Killer Africanized Bees Really That Dangerous?" by Henry Nicholls, investigating the root of our fear of this particular bee strain and whether there is evidence to substantiate our negative feelings towards such bees.

The common image we have of bees is polarized: on one hand, we see them as vital pollinators of many of the foods we know and love, including most fruits and vegetables. On the other hand, we avoid bees during spring and summer for fear of a painful (or worse, deadly) sting. This duality actually exists not because bees are both productive and predatory, but because there are two almost-identical subspecies of bees in North America: European bees and Africanized bees. Both groups pollinate plants and produce honey, but European bees are more docile, while Africanized bees are more hostile.

African bees had to adapt to the sub-Saharan African climate, surviving prolonged droughts and defending themselves against other insects and animals. Unlike their European counterparts, which became easy to handle as a result of their temperate climate, African bees became a highly defensive race, unsuitable for domestic use. Because of this, some experts have expressed wariness about the growing prevalence of Africanized bees, saying that their aggressiveness poses a threat to commercial U.S. beekeeping. Others suggest that hobbyists and commercial beekeepers should consider cross-breeding the two types of honeybees, making use of the most desirable traits of both the African and European breeds. But do the advantages outweigh the risks?

To understand the current proliferation of Africanized bees in North America today, we must look at the factors that brought them across the world in the first place. Africanized bees were first introduced to Brazil in the 1950s in an effort to increase honey production. Twenty-six swarms accidentally escaped quarantine in 1957, spreading throughout Central and South America, and arrived in the U.S. in 1985. Since then, Africanized bees have become the dominant type of honey bee for beekeeping in Central and South America.

The first Africanized bees in the U.S. were discovered in California, most likely having hitched a ride on a Venezuelan oil tanker. In order to survive the more moderate environment of the United States, African bees had to mate with European honey bees. Their offspring, *Apis mellifera*, were African-European hybrids and thrived in the Californian climate.

The major differences between Africanized honey bees and the European breeds are of temperament and hardiness. Africanized honey bees tend to swarm more and go farther. They are more likely to migrate as part of a seasonal response to a lowered food supply. They are also more likely to abscond: in times of stress, they leave the hive and relocate. They are more defensive when in a resting swarm than other types are. They guard their hive aggressively, protecting a larger alarm zone around the hive. They deploy in greater numbers for defense purposes and pursue perceived threats over much longer distances. All of these differences mean that Africanized bees are far more willing than European bees to go the extra mile (literally) for a pollination opportunity. As a result, they have become valuable among beekeepers for their prolific honey production, often as much as 100 kg (220 pounds) annually.

Worldwide, relatively stable geographic zones have emerged in which one of three situations exist: either African bees dominate, a mix of African and European is present, or only non-African bees are found. However, this has not come without problems: stinging incidents in Africanized bee areas are on the rise in such places as southern California. In response, some breeders have moved their operations to the harsher wintering locales of the northern Sierra Nevada and the southern Cascade ranges. These colder locales are unsuitable for and therefore off limits to the Africanized bees, resulting in a reduction in stinging incidents.

In instances when illnesses and mysterious maladies like colony collapse disorder (CCD) affect hives and honey production, beekeepers are understandably interested in the positive qualities associated with Africanized breeds. These economic factors are encouraging beekeepers to switch from the traditional bees of their ancestors to the more profitable Africanized honey bee.

The third option is to take advantage of the benefits of both breeds by purchasing a pre-fertilized (i.e., mated) European queen in areas where Africanized bees are well-established to maintain a hive's European genetics and behavior. Among other groups, hybridization may not even be needed: some beekeepers report that not all Africanized hives display the typical hyper-defensive behavior, showing that nurture might be prevailing over nature. The recent

95 successes reported among some breeders who have raised gentle Africanized bees indicate that this may indeed become our new reality.

Spread of Africanized Bees in the United States and South America during the 1900s

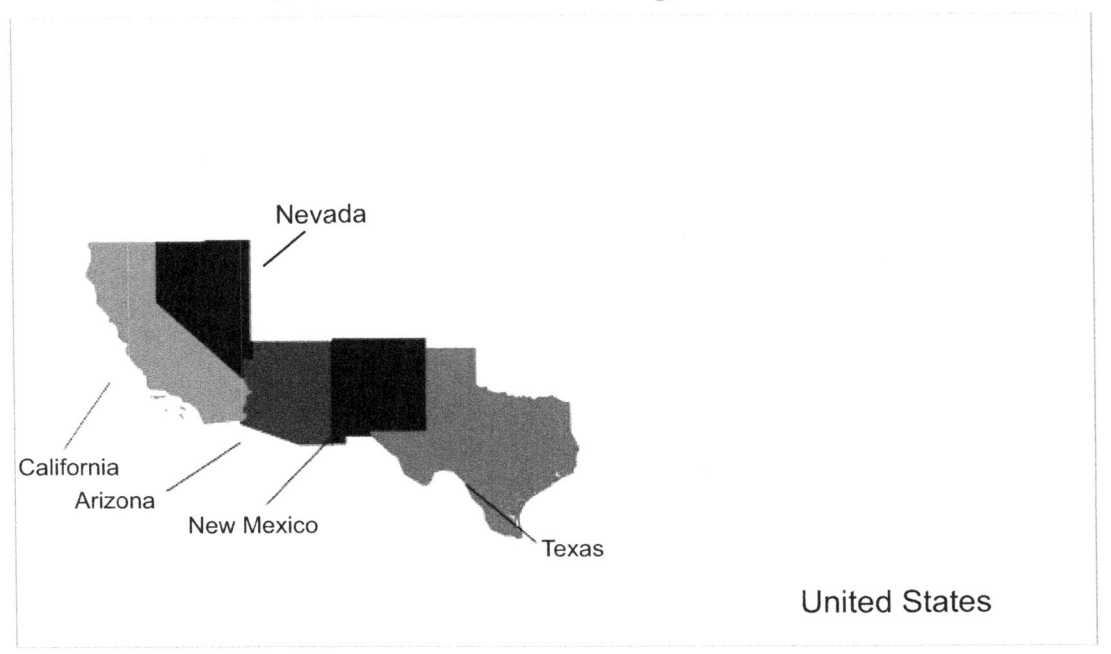

United States

LEGEND
- 1950's to 1960's
- 1970's to 1980's
- 1990's to 2000's

South America

1

What situation is most similar to the proliferation of Africanized bees in the United States?

A) An established company seizes an opportunity to expand and sets up franchises in multiple locations across the country.
B) A crop that is planted for its profitability eventually becomes an invasive species, disrupting other crops native to the area.
C) A group of people seeking employment relocates to another country where there are more opportunities.
D) A society conquers and colonizes an already-populated territory, forcing those native to the area to relocate.

2

As used in line 19, "domestic" most nearly means

A) civil.
B) commercial.
C) personal.
D) private.

3

The author indicates that Africanized bees first arrived to the Americas in what way?

A) They escaped from African countries that were trying to lower their bee populations.
B) They were imported to Brazil to stimulate the beekeeping and honey industries.
C) They migrated to California, where they crossbred with local bee species.
D) They were brought to the United States by Venezuelan smugglers.

4

Which choice provides the best evidence for the answer to the previous question?

A) Lines 23-25 ("Others suggest...honeybees")
B) Lines 31-33 ("Africanized bees...production")
C) Lines 33-35 ("Twenty-six swarms...1985")
D) Lines 39-41 ("The first...tanker")

5

As used in line 30, "factors" most nearly means

A) advantages.
B) variables.
C) influences.
D) circumstances.

6

What main effect do the words "deploy" (line 56) and "pursue" (line 57) have on the tone of the passage?

A) They contribute to a militaristic tone that highlights the aggressive temperament of Africanized bees.
B) They contribute to a strategic and technical tone that reveals the method behind Africanized bees' success.
C) They contribute to an antagonistic tone that depicts Africanized bees as a threat to other bee species.
D) They contribute to a formal and academic tone that emphasizes the significance of the bees' behavior.

7

Which of the following is NOT cited as a reason that farmers prefer European bees?

A) European bees are easy for beekeepers to manage.
B) European bees are less likely to sting humans.
C) European bees are able to survive in cold climates.
D) European bees are docile and gentle by nature.

8

Which choice provides the best evidence that farmers' concerns about Africanized bees may be somewhat overstated?

A) Lines 61-64 ("As a...annually")
B) Lines 74-77 ("These colder...incidents")
C) Lines 78-82 ("In instances...breeds")
D) Lines 90-94 ("Among other...nature")

9

According to the figure, Africanized bees could have arrived in Chile in what year?

A) 1953
B) 1967
C) 1988
D) 1992

10

Which of the following choices best identifies a point of disagreement between the figure and the passage?

A) The passage states that Africanized bees were first seen in South America, but the figure indicates that they were present in California before South America.

B) The passage indicates that Africanized bees have a relatively small presence in the United States, but the figure indicates that they are the dominant bee species in many states.

C) The passage implies that Africanized bees arrived in the United States in 1985, but the figure indicates that they could have been present in the United States as early as 1970.

D) The passage asserts that Africanized bees are the predominant species in Central and South America, but the figure indicates that their population is more highly concentrated in the United States.

11

Based on information from the passage and the figure, it can be reasonably inferred that throughout the 1990's in the U.S.

A) farmers began breeding Africanized bees in earnest, having realized the profits that these insects would bring to the honey businesses.

B) Africanized bees mated with European bees, allowing their offspring to survive colder areas like the northern Sierra Nevada.

C) average temperatures in the United States rose, allowing Africanized bees to inhabit areas that they normally would have avoided.

D) Africanized bees became less aggressive in temperament, leading to more beekeepers purchasing them for use in honey production.

Questions 1-11 are based on the following passage and supplementary material.

5.8
Adapted from a 2011 NIH article titled "Introduction to Behavioral Addictions," by Jon Grant, Marc Potenza, Aviv Weinstein, and David Gorelick in which the authors describe what behavioral addictions are and how to properly define and treat them.

    Psychologists have been conceptualizing behaviors like compulsive shopping, skin picking, excessive tanning, internet use, computer/video gaming, and others, in several different ways. Some suggest that these problems can be classified as a disorder of impulse control. Another conceptualization, which may not be mutually exclusive, suggests that such disorders are behavioral addictions. Behavioral addictions resemble substance addictions in several ways, including their natural history, prevalence and incidence among young adults and adolescents, and chronic relapsing course. Similarities in subjective craving, withdrawal, and intoxication are also observed, as is responsiveness to treatment. All together, these similarities definitely appear to indicate that behavioral addictions may be able to be classified and treated similarly to the way that well-known substance disorders are treated and classified.
    Limited data for compulsive buying, internet addiction, and video/computer game addiction exist—with data for pathological gambling being most extensive. Very little data for other behavioral addictions currently exist. These include excessive tanning, pathologic skin picking, love addiction, and sexual addiction. As of this writing, researchers have suggested that pathological gambling be treated as an addiction rather than an impulse control disorder in the DSM-V. They call for "substantial future research" that includes animal and human studies to address the lack of scientific research surrounding behavioral addictions, noting a lack of knowledge in the areas of treatment, neurobiology (including brain imagery), and genetics.
    Researchers Grant et al in 2011 examined and reported on the results of their review of the related literature in the American Journal of Drug and Alcohol Abuse, in an effort to compare behavioral addictions and psychoactive substance addictions. These researchers defined behavioral addictions as those associated with behaviors that "produce short-term reward that may engender persistent behavior, despite knowledge of adverse consequences, i.e., diminished control over the behavior." The common feature of such addictions is the inability to resist a temptation, drive, or impulse which is harmful to one's self or others. As with other behavioral addictions such as kleptomania and compulsive gambling, subjects report characteristic mood changes and symptoms of withdrawal. Because of this, personality may be a factor associated with behavioral addictions—some individuals reportedly are more impulsive and sensation-seeking, and less likely to avoid harm, according to several studies.
    Grant noted that psychosocial treatments may often be successful in addressing both substance abuse disorders and behavioral addictions. In his research, he reported that therapies such as cognitive behavioral therapy, motivational enhancement, and 12-step programs have been able to successfully treat behavioral addictions. He notes that interventions usually rely on a model to prevent relapse, including making lifestyle changes, coping with or avoiding high risk situations, and identifying abuse patterns. On the other hand, treatments typically include strategies for preventing exposure and response.
    It is interesting to note that no medications are currently approved to treat behavioral addictions, even though they share so many similarities with substance abuse disorders, which have pharmacological treatments. The authors, reviewing some of the medications used to treat substance abuse, propose that mu-opioid receptors, one of the four opioid receptors that exists in the human brain, play a similar role in both substance use disorders and behavioral addictions. A drug that targets those receptors, Topiramate, reportedly shows promise in treating compulsive skin picking, compulsive buying, and pathological gambling, and can reduce use of cocaine, cigarettes, and alcohol. This finding suggests that there may be a common neurobiological mechanism for both substance use disorders and behavioral addiction.
    There is growing evidence to suggest that these behavioral addictions are similar to substance addictions in many ways. While there are not sufficient data to warrant any new DSM-V Addiction and Related Disorders classifications, these authors call for additional research in this socially relevant field. They argue that if society is to prevent and treat such problems, we must properly categorize both behavioral addictions and impulse control disorders.

Percentage of People Successfully Treated for Behavioral Addiction through Various Treatments

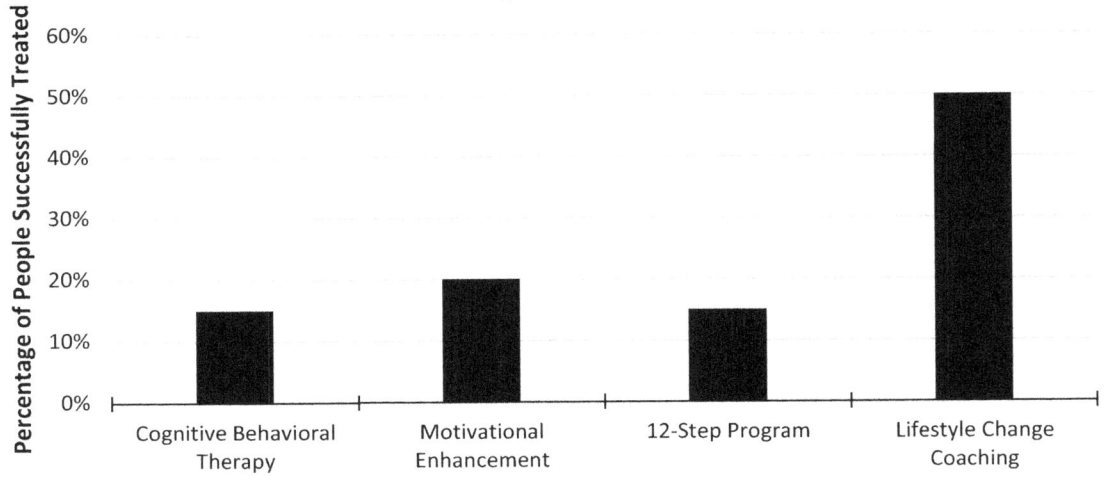

A bar chart shows the percentage of people successfully treated across four treatment types:
- Cognitive Behavioral Therapy: ~15%
- Motivational Enhancement: ~20%
- 12-Step Program: ~15%
- Lifestyle Change Coaching: ~50%

X-axis: Treatment Types
Y-axis: Percentage of People Successfully Treated (0% to 60%)

1

Which choice best describes the developmental structure of the passage?

A) The concepts behind a disorder are introduced, deficiencies in past research are noted, and an inquiry that may assist in treatment is then outlined.

B) The sides in a scientific debate are established, an experiment is explained in considerable detail, and a spirit of social engagement is then endorsed.

C) Competing definitions are presented, an effort to reconcile these definitions is then described, and the need for scientific consensus is then emphasized.

D) Findings from a recent set of experiments are outlined, the merits of the findings are explained, and an set of criticisms is then presented.

2

On the basis of ideas currently accepted by researchers, a person with a standard behavioral addiction normally exhibits

A) actions and compulsions that may endanger the physical safety of others.

B) an interest in self-expression that would be beneficial in a different context.

C) inability or unwillingness to consider long-term consequences.

D) the belief that the addictive behavior is in fact healthy.

3

Which choice provides the best evidence for the answer to the previous question?

A) Lines 12-14 ("Similarities . . . treatment")
B) Lines 14-18 ("All . . . classified")
C) Lines 39-43 ("These . . . behavior")
D) Lines 49-53 ("Because . . . studies")

4

As used in line 19, "Limited" most nearly means

A) Concise.
B) Isolated.
C) Simple.
D) Partial.

5

Within the passage, the authors develop their discussion of the work of Grant and others by

A) extending an analogy that can be traced back to the thesis of Grant's research.

B) paraphrasing Grant's ideas about the potential remedies for forms of addiction.

C) alluding to various credentials in a manner that indicates Grant's expertise.

D) presenting and assessing possible criticisms of Grant's research methods.

6

Which choice provides the best evidence for the answer to the previous question?

A) Lines 34-38 ("Researchers . . . substance addictions")
B) Lines 46-49 ("As . . . withdrawal")
C) Lines 54-56 ("Grant . . . addictions")
D) Lines 66-70 ("It is . . . treatments")

7

Which of the following would be logically expected as a strategy of "interventions" (line 60) that treat behavioral addictions?

A) A compulsive skin-picker enters a rehabilitation program following a nervous breakdown.
B) A woman diagnosed with internet addiction obtains a job that requires her to be online for most of the day.
C) A gambling addict makes a point of never driving past a casino that she had once visited on a weekly basis.
D) A consumer who is addicted to violent video games is ordered to take medication that calms her nerves.

8

As used in line 67, "approved" most nearly means

A) authorized.
B) rewarded.
C) praised.
D) conceded.

9

In the context of the passage, Topiramate is best understood as a drug that

A) has been shown to be highly effective in treating technology-based addictions.
B) is not clearly relevant to all forms of behavioral addiction mentioned by the authors.
C) will most likely undergo intense modifications before being approved for widespread use.
D) was developed following the discovery of a neurological link between behavioral addiction and substance abuse.

10

According to the graph, which of the following treatment types had the highest percentage of people successfully treated for behavioral addiction?

A) Lifestyle Change Coaching
B) 12-Step Program
C) Motivational Enhancement
D) Cognitive Behavioral Therapy

11

Do the data in the graph support the information regarding treatments for behavioral addictions in the fifth paragraph (lines 66-81)?

A) Yes, because Cognitive Behavioral Therapy typically includes exercises that treat substance abuse.
B) Yes, because Topiramate is often used as part of Motivational Enhancement.
C) No, because the data in the graph do not indicate any information regarding pharmacological treatment.
D) No, because the success of Lifestyle Change Coaching contradicts the validity of pharmacological treatment.

Questions 1-10 are based on the following passage.

Adapted from the 2018 PLOS article "Compositional Shifts in Root-Associated Bacterial and Archaeal Microbiota Track the Plant Life Cycle in Field-Grown Rice" by Joseph Edwards and a team of researchers at MIT.

When it comes to dieting, the ideal path towards the perfect body is marked by efficiency: dieters must cut fat and spur weight loss fast enough to give themselves the body they desire and before they give
[5] up out of frustration. One such method of obtaining a desirable body is through examination and subsequent alteration of "gut microbiota" (formerly known as "gut flora"). Gut microbiota is the name given to the microbe population—which includes tens of trillions
[10] of bacteria so diverse, they outnumber the diversity in human genes by 150 times—living in our intestines. It is known that these microbiota can predict things like malnourishment, obesity, and immune system functioning, making them a likely candidate to build
[15] a human diet around—one which would promote the production of beneficial microbiota while decreasing the production of those that would not be beneficial.

Change the conversation to plants, though, and the effect of microbiota is less well known. Scientists are
[20] well aware that bacterial communities exist within the roots of plants, and that they likely have an effect on the growth and health of the plant, but the specifics of those effects have remained elusive. Understanding the full effects of microbiota on plants could be critical to
[25] increasing the probability of planted seeds growing to full fruition, as well as keeping plant communities in at-risk areas (such as those subjected to long droughts) healthy. Furthermore, crops such as corn and rice are cornerstones of the diets of millions of people, and
[30] discovering the factor that increases the efficiency of their production could prove to be a literal lifesaver for malnourished populations across the world. Addressing this very issue, a recent study published in PLOS ONE Biology seeks to find out just what diverse microbiota
[35] exist in plant roots, and whether these bacteria can have an effect on plants similar to the one they have on humans.

In the study, the biologists investigated the microbiota of rice plants in California across three
[40] growing seasons, and in Alabama across one growing season. This setup allowed them to compare results, not only season to season, but also across regions with diverse climates. The researchers took DNA samples of the rice plants over time to study their genetic diversity
[45] through the duration of the plants' lifespans. These DNA data were then used to predict ages of plants in future studies. Next, they measured microbiota present in the roots of the plants over their lifespan for 84 days (the timespan it takes for the rice plant to flower). After
[50] collecting all their data, they set out to determine the outcome of the years-long study.

What the researchers found was telling: the chronological age of plants, as indicated by their DNA, directly correlated to the composition of their
[55] microbiota, but only through the 84-day window. Furthermore, the ebb and flow of specific types of microbiota were similar across all three growing seasons, as well as between the two sites. The researchers deduced from these results that the plant
[60] microbiota are greatly affected by anything that affects the plants' ability to grow until their flowering period. This is where drought comes into play. Drought is one of the most detrimental stressors during the life of a plant. As a result, plants that have been affected
[65] by drought should be expected to produce DNA of a plant that appears younger than its chronological age. This means that plants that experience drought are not being affected by the lack of rain alone—they're also negatively affected by the subsequent change in their
[70] gut bacteria, resulting in a less bountiful harvest for farmers.

Looking forward, the researchers are optimistic that root microbiota can be a boon to the agriculture industry. By understanding the mechanisms that
[75] underlie healthy plant growth via the nutrition a plant receives, future researchers will be able to effectively manipulate soil bacteria, therefore creating more robust, less stressed crops that fully mature even in below-optimal settings. For geographically drought-
[80] prone areas, this information provides confidence in the future of keeping residents well-fed, less susceptible to immune inflictions, and healthier.

1

The primary purpose of the passage is to
A) Clarify commonly misunderstood biological events.
B) Describe a method that can effectively solve a worldwide crisis.
C) Connect the findings of a study to potential benefits.
D) Outline the steps of a years-long agricultural experiment.

2

As used in line 12, "predict" most nearly means
A) estimate.
B) foretell.
C) develop.
D) prophesize.

3

According to the passage, what population would most benefit from the scientists' understanding of plant root microbiota?
A) A society that has instability in its reliance on exotic crops like dragonfruit and kumquat
B) A town that is experiencing extremely low rainfall due to climate change.
C) A family in the suburbs where grocery stores are miles away
D) Animals that live on farms known to be major agricultural centers

4

What effect does the sentence in lines 28-32 ("Furthermore . . . world") have on the discussion in the passage as a whole?
A) It provides information about the types of plants being used in the study.
B) It explains why the study is using plants to answer a question about humans.
C) It reinforces the reason that the relevant study will provide information valuable to humans.
D) It introduces the way in which the research team plans to carry out the research.

5

Which choice provides the best evidence that the researchers manipulated more than one factor in their study?
A) Lines 33-37 ("a recent...humans")
B) Lines 38-43 ("In the...climates")
C) Lines 43-45 ("The researchers...lifespans")
D) Lines 49-51 ("After...study")

6

The author indicates that the 84-day window was significant because
A) during that span plants are exhibiting the growth period most important to a crucial factor investigated in the study.
B) the research team had previously determined that this is the exact length of time that it takes for the plants in question to mature.
C) if plants do not mature before 84 days, they will have an abnormal rate of growth in their gut microbiota.
D) this is the time period when chronological age and DNA-age in the plants used in the study always sync.

7

Which plant population would have DNA that LEAST accurately represents its chronological age?
A) A flower past 84 days that has had no disturbances in its environment
B) A flower past 84 days that is currently experiencing an unexpected drought
C) A flower younger than 84 days that has been subjected to an abnormal dry period
D) A flower younger than 84 days that has had some ebb and flow in its microbiota

8

Which choice provides the best evidence for the answer to the previous question?
A) Lines 47-49 ("Next...flower")
B) Lines 52-55 ("What...window")
C) Lines 56-58 ("Furthermore...sites")
D) Lines 64-66 ("As a...age")

9

As used in line 78, "robust" most nearly means

A) powerful.
B) flavorful.
C) rich.
D) hardy.

10

The primary purpose of the final paragraph (lines 72-82) is to

A) outline what future research holds for the authors of the study.
B) detail the reason that the authors or the study are hopeful for the future.
C) deride possible outcomes that can result from further research on microbiota.
D) explain why the methodology of the study was so revolutionary.

Questions 1-11 are based on the following passage and supplementary material.
5.10
Adapted from a 2012 PLOS ONE journal article by a team of researchers at the British Columbia Center for Disease Prevention and Control Service, "Low 2012–13 Influenza Vaccine Effectiveness Associated with Mutation in the Egg-Adapted H3N2 Vaccine Strain, Not Antigenic Drift in Circulating Viruses"

January of 2018, the WHO* published a report on how well the annual flu vaccine in America was working during the 2017-2018 season to date. According to the report's findings, the season's flu [5] shot offered poor protection against the worst strain. The WHO is not sure what caused this alarming fact, but the organization has set out to determine how to prevent it from happening in the future. The first place to start is to evaluate the process that goes into [10] selecting what goes into the flu vaccine—a process that has led to a lot of uncertainty about how effective it may be in any given year.

The worldwide annual process of determining which flu strains to target begins with public health [15] agencies making an educated guess about which flu strain is going to circulate, based on clinical and laboratory studies, and surveillance. This prediction is made long before the flu season begins in the US, possibly a reason it has not had as much efficacy as [20] hoped. Soon after, the Food and Drug Administration makes the final determination of how to go about making the vaccines. Once the FDA determines what will go into it, the flu virus that will be used in the flu vaccine is grown in chicken eggs.

[25] Recently, scientists have pinpointed an issue with their standard approach that they believe is the cause of lowered rates of effectiveness with the resulting shot. These problems specifically relate to a strain of the virus known as H3N2, the same strain [30] that dominated the 2017-2018 season. They believe H3N2 coverage has lacked because "in the process of adapting the virus to grow in eggs... further changes to the [H3N2] virus [are introduced], which may impair the effectiveness of the vaccine." Apparently, [35] the H3N2 virus is mutating to adapt to the eggs, while the flu virus is growing to be used as a vaccine, and the result is a mismatch between the vaccine and the H3N2 strain. That doesn't mean one should forego the flu shot, say scientists, as the flu shot is about reducing, [40] not eliminating, a person's risk.

In order to determine just how much efficacy and protection against the flu has been lost, the Centers for Disease Control and Prevention released a recent Morbidity and Mortality Weekly Report that included [45] their study of the 2017-2018 flu season data. Typically, the effectiveness of the flu shot ranges between 50 and 60 percent. However, during years in which the circulating flu virus is the H3N2, that number drops drastically. Scientists tracked flu cases of 1,700 adults [50] and children in the US and learned that the flu shot was 36 percent effective, reducing someone's chances of getting ill with the flu and having to see a doctor by about one-third. Moreover, in 2017-2018, the vaccine was only 25 percent effective against this year's most [55] common strain of the flu. In Canada, an earlier report came up with similar findings, with the flu vaccine being only 17 percent effective against this strain.

Concurrently, a study of flu vaccine efficacy was conducted by Edward Belongia, epidemiologist at the [60] Marshfield Clinic Research Institute in Wisconsin. He found that, during H3N2 seasons, vaccines were 33 percent effective, corroborating data from the CDC. When influenza B seasons were compared, the effectiveness rate jumped to 54 percent, and 67 percent [65] during seasons of H1N1.

Some of the researchers who discovered this egg-related vaccine problem expect to find, in the future, other reasons that the annual flu vaccine underperforms. The production method that uses eggs [70] might not tell the entire story. For example it is thought that this virus strain mutates at a faster rate than other strains, making it more challenging to design a vaccine that matches what is circulating. The flu virus and scientists' response to it can be very complicated. [75] Pending the arrival of the long-awaited universal flu vaccine—a seemingly elusive dream of a vaccine that would offer protection from all flu viruses at once— it's important to understand how current production methods may cause the vaccine to be less effective [80] with certain strains.

*World Health Organization

Figure 1

Efficacy of the Flu Shot as a Factor of Age of Shot Recipient

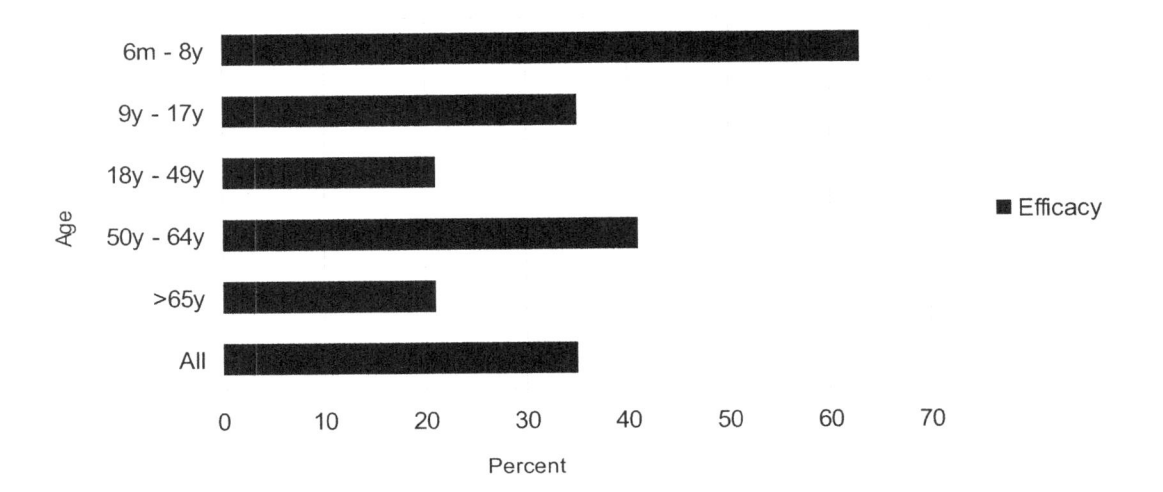

Age	Efficacy (%)
6m - 8y	~63
9y - 17y	~34
18y - 49y	~21
50y - 64y	~41
>65y	~21
All	~35

Figure 2

Percent Breakdown of the Most Common Flu Strains in the US

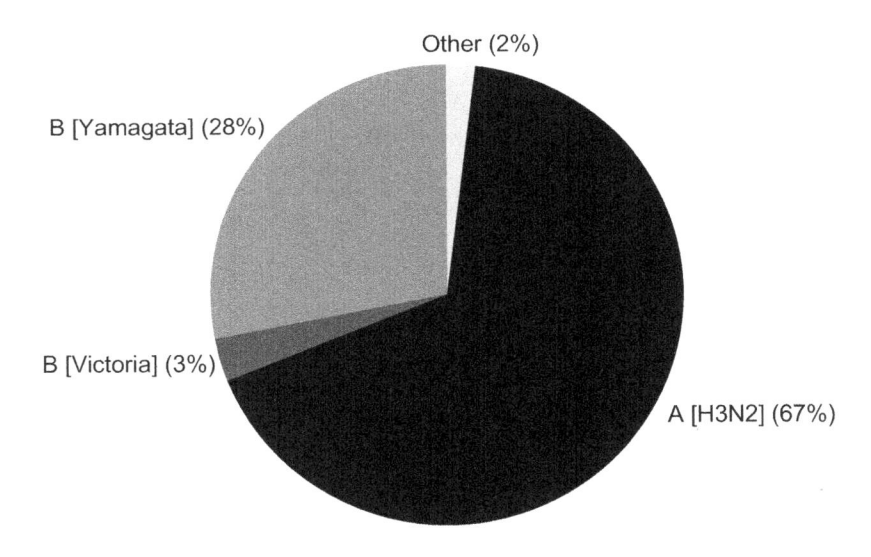

- A [H3N2] (67%)
- B [Yamagata] (28%)
- B [Victoria] (3%)
- Other (2%)

1

The main purpose of the passage is to

A) explain why current flu vaccines should be abandoned in favor of more innovative measures.
B) call attention to a feature of recent vaccines that has made fighting flu outbreaks more difficult.
C) argue that flu vaccination will remain problematic until a universal flu vaccine is successfully developed.
D) signal lapses in current knowledge of the H3N2 strain that make this version of influenza particularly threatening.

2

The information presented in the second paragraph of the passage (lines 13-24) primarily serves to

A) outline procedures that are followed on a regular basis.
B) highlight the interdisciplinary nature of vaccine production.
C) explain the flaws in a process that was once useful.
D) indicate why H3N2 can develop vaccine resistance.

3

As described in the passage, the H3N2 virus is notable for

A) its tendency to be confused with H1N1.
B) its dominance of multiple flu seasons.
C) its ability to escape detection by drastically altering its own form.
D) its resistance to measures that can counter other flu strains.

4

As used in line 40, "eliminating" most nearly means

A) redefining.
B) repudiating.
C) relinquishing.
D) removing.

5

Which choice provides the best support for the claims set forward in lines 38-40 ("That doesn't . . . risk")?

A) Lines 45-47 ("Typically . . . percent")
B) Lines 47-49 ("However . . . drastically")
C) Lines 69-70 ("The production . . . story")
D) Lines 73-74 ("The flu . . . complicated")

6

In assessing responsivity to the H3N2 virus, the researchers described in the passage made use of

A) projections of future flu shot effectiveness based on demographic data.
B) laboratory simulations that adjusted the vaccine production methods.
C) statistical evidence that spanned a few different age groups.
D) self-reporting from individuals who survived multiple flu outbreaks.

7

Which choice provides the best evidence for the answer to the previous question?

A) Lines 49-53 ("Scientists . . . one-third")
B) Lines 61-63 ("He found . . . CDC")
C) Lines 66-69 ("Some . . . underperforms")
D) Lines 75-80 ("Pending . . . strains")

8

As used in line 76, "elusive" most nearly means

A) unachievable.
B) undefinable.
C) underhanded.
D) uncompliant.

9

According to figure 1, which of the following age groups exhibited the highest flu shot efficacy over 8 years old?

A) 9-17 years
B) 18-49 years
C) 50-64 years
D) Over 65 years

10

In relation to the passage, figure 1 presents information that could

A) support the author's contention that some age groups are especially vulnerable to flu.
B) complicate the author's conclusion that some flu vaccines are more effective than others.
C) substantiate the author's idea that a universal flu vaccine would have immediate benefits.
D) contradict some of the author's claims about the typical efficacy of a flu shot.

11

Which information would be most helpful in relating the information about H3N2 in figure 2 to the information present in the passage?

A) The most common flu strain classified under the "Other" category in figure 2
B) The year or years of collection for the data in figure 2
C) The manner in which the data in figure 2 were collected
D) The number of fatalities from each flu strain considered in figure 2

STOP

Answer Key: CHAPTER FIVE

SAT

5.01	5.02	5.03	5.04	5.05
1. C	1. B	1. D	1. C	1. C
2. C	2. D	2. C	2. D	2. B
3. B	3. C	3. A	3. C	3. B
4. B	4. C	4. C	4. B	4. D
5. D	5. A	5. B	5. D	5. D
6. C	6. B	6. C	6. C	6. D
7. D	7. B	7. D	7. A	7. B
8. B	8. C	8. D	8. B	8. C
9. A	9. C	9. A	9. A	9. A
10. B	10. C	10. A	10. C	10. D
11. C	11. A	11. B	11. D	11. A

5.06	5.07	5.08	5.09	5.10
1. B	1. B	1. A	1. C	1. B
2. C	2. B	2. C	2. B	2. A
3. B	3. B	3. C	3. B	3. D
4. B	4. B	4. D	4. C	4. D
5. B	5. D	5. B	5. B	5. A
6. B	6. A	6. C	6. A	6. C
7. A	7. C	7. C	7. C	7. A
8. D	8. D	8. A	8. D	8. A
9. C	9. D	9. B	9. D	9. A
10. D	10. C	10. A	10. B	10. D
11. B	11. B	11. C		11. B

Answer Explanations

Chapter Five

Chapter 5.1 | Rogue Waves

1) CORRECT ANSWER: C
After providing an overview of rogue waves (lines 1-12) and describing one event linked to these extraordinarily large waves (lines 13-22), the author explains how researchers used "a model of a chemical tanker" (lines 44-45) to explore rogue wave dynamics. This content supports C, while A and D both wrongly indicate serious flaws in scientific ideas (NOT that scientists are performing experiments to uncover new information). B overstates a detail of the passage, the focus on POSSIBLE engineering solutions in lines 79-90, to wrongly indicate both that new applications have ALREADY taken place and that such applications are the central topic of the passage.

2) CORRECT ANSWER: C
In lines 7-11, the author notes that scientists "did not think it possible" for the properties of rogue waves to appear in actuality. This content supports C and can be used to eliminate B (since the passage indicates that scientists WERE interested in rogue waves but arrived at a negative assessment) and D (since scientists were suspicious of the reality of rogue waves and thus would not regard the waves as "prevalent"). A distorts content from lines 1-7, since here rogue waves are compared to items of mythology for the sake of explanation but are not cited as inspiring any portions of myths.

3) CORRECT ANSWER: B
See above for analysis of the correct line reference. A compares rogue waves to items of mythology but does NOT, as Question 2 A wrongly indicates, suggest that rogue waves inspired any elements of mythology. C mentions rogue waves but raises a topic (persisting tales) that does not align with any topics in the answers to the previous question, while D indicates that scientists were interested in rogue waves and can in fact be used to eliminate Question 2 B.

4) CORRECT ANSWER: B
In lines 30-38, the author explains that both the Schrodinger equation and Peregrine's solution could be used to study rogue waves; thus, the Schrodinger equation is not the only means of analyzing these waves, as indicated in B. Choose this answer and eliminate A as a misreading of a detail; according to the same lines, the Schrodinger equation CAN explain changes in small portions of matter yet may ALSO be used to explain larger units despite this focus. C and D both indicate that the Schrodinger equation was flawed or defective, NOT that it was one possibility for analysis when multiple were available, and should thus be eliminated.

5) CORRECT ANSWER: D
The word "empirical" is used in the context of an "indisputable measurement" (line 22) or a strong outcome involving data. D properly indicates this context, while A (context of practicality) and B (context of extensive procedures, NOT of a single effective observation) are problematic in topic despite introducing positive tones. C is illogical because the "measurement" prompted a number of questions (lines 23-26) and was thus not "well-explained" at first.

6) CORRECT ANSWER: C
The word "describes" refers to the relationship between an equation and "systems of matter" (line 32); an equation would, logically, show or illustrate how systems of matter operate. Choose C and eliminate A and D as indicating that the equation would exaggerate or overstate the operations of the systems, NOT show properties accurately. B refers to the action of a speaking person, not to the illustrative nature of an equation.

7) CORRECT ANSWER: D
In lines 79-82, the author directly states that "it is entirely possible" to use the Peregrine breather in the study of rogue waves; choose D as appropriate. A, B, and C describe early stages of an experiment that was designed to determine WHETHER the Peregrine breather might be applicable to rogue waves, rather than providing an assertion that the Peregrine breather is DEFINITELY applicable.

8) CORRECT ANSWER: B
The author introduces the image of a large sponge in order to help readers "to understand vbm" (line 64), the vertical bending movements of a ship affected by wave forces. B properly indicates this point of comparison, while A and D refer to waves but neglect the presence of a ship as required by the comparison. C judges the observers, rather than indicating that an image is being offered for the sake of comparison, and thus misdirects the

purpose of the "large sponge" reference.

9) CORRECT ANSWER: A
In lines 79-90, the author outlines possible applications of the research described in the passage; one practical use would be the creation of a network of buoys in order to "broadcast the presence of rogue waves." This content aligns with A, while B mentions a possible consequence of rogue wave monitoring but NOT a consequence that the passage explicitly considers. C distorts the author's broad idea that there might be new ways to "engineer" (line 82) ships to indicate a more specific solution than the author provides in terms of ship engineering. D refers to uncertainties about the activity of rogue waves raised early in the passage (lines 1-22), NOT to solutions to dangers as explained in the final stages of the passage.

10) CORRECT ANSWER: B
Between 5:00 and 6:00, the computer simulation exhibited a height decrease from just under 20 meters to just under 5 meters; the physical simulation also decreased in this interval, but did so by a lower difference. Thus, choose B and eliminate A as representing a smaller quantity. C and D both represent height differences of roughly 2 to 3 meters and thus indicate smaller differences than the roughly 15-meter measure indicated by B.

11) CORRECT ANSWER: C
In lines 13-22, the author explains that what were assumed by the members of the crew of a ship to be 12-meter waves were discovered to be 19-meter waves when analyzed using a "wave-height detector." Thus, direct records of waves may underestimate wave height, as further indicated by the fact that, according to the graph, BOTH a computer simulation and a physical simulation returned higher wave height measures than the ship's log did. C reflects this content, while A is CONTRADICTED by the disparities observed in both the graph and the passage. B is itself problematic because the graph exhibits a disparity between computer simulation and physical simulation measurements, while D introduces Peregrine's solution (which the graph never directly considers) to explain findings from the graph itself.

Chapter 5.2 | Preventing Alzheimer's

1) CORRECT ANSWER: B
In the first paragraph, the relevant words refer back to Alzheimer's disease, which the passage depicts as a debilitating condition that suggests

a need for preventative measures. B properly reflects this negative tone while accurately indicating the informative nature of the first paragraph. A criticizes measures to combat Alzheimer's (rather than depicting the disease ITSELF negatively), while C and D both wrongly focus on individuals other than the author, who is mostly discussing the nature of Alzheimer's.

2) CORRECT ANSWER: D
In lines 20-23, the author indicates that Jebelli was prompted to research Alzheimer's by the experiences of "his grandfather and other individuals he had met." This content aligns with D, while A and C indicate factors that could logically be considered by a researcher but not the SPECIFIC motive for Jebelli's research. B misconstrues the passage's topic of social habits in Alzheimer's research (or perhaps even the comfortable lifestyle of Jebelli's grandfather) as a direct explanation for Jebelli's inquiry.

3) CORRECT ANSWER: C
See above for analysis of the correct line reference. A references one of Jebelli's findings (NOT a factor that inspired his research), while B references Jebelli's grandfather without explaining the link between Jebelli's grandfather and Jebelli's research in the manner of C. Although D does explain that the work of another researcher interested Jebelli, the topic of existing interesting research does NOT align with an answer to the previous question.

4) CORRECT ANSWER: C
The relevant "discussion" entails the idea that "brain training must start" (lines 44-45) before the age of 40 for effective Alzheimer's disease prevention. C indicates that brain training begun by subjects after age 45 was ineffective and thus supports the ideas present in the passage. Note that the discussion surrounds a program operating in Japan (NOT South Korea, eliminating A) and based on simple arithmetic problems (NOT complex ones, eliminating D). While both of the proteins referenced in B are indeed mentioned in the passage as important factors, the author does not provide any analysis to indicate which protein is MORE significant, so that B is incorrect.

5) CORRECT ANSWER: A
The word "simple" refers to "arithmetic problems" (line 39) used as part of a game that was meant to address Alzheimer's disease. A would properly indicate that the problems (as features of a widely-applicable game) were somewhat basic or approachable. B would wrongly criticize the problems (which are meant to interest the people involved in the

game), while C would reference a positive personality trait (not a quality of math problems). D would illogically indicate that the problems, which occur in sets and are meant to keep users occupied, are all the same.

6) CORRECT ANSWER: B
While the "research" mentioned in lines 46-50 involved daily cognitive training over half a year, the "study" mentioned in lines 59-62 involved activities that took place over a five-year period. Thus, both endeavors involved significant changes to the activities of subjects; B is appropriate, while A is problematic because Kawashima would RECOMMEND changes in activity patterns to address Alzheimer's. C misconstrues Jebelli's concerns about the studies (limited applicability and size, NOT the idea that the studies have unclear or inconclusive results). D contradicts the findings of the "research" mentioned in lines 46-50, which mainly involved improvements for OLDER test subjects.

7) CORRECT ANSWER: B
The word "mimic" refers to the use of mice in research that would serve the purpose of "Simulating human conditions" (line 68); the experience of mice would thus approximate or resemble the experience of brain training in humans. B captures this meaning, while A and D wrongly indicate that the mice would be actively following or shadowing human models (NOT presenting comparable results). C would wrongly apply a negative tone to the inquiry involving the mice and should be eliminated for this reason.

8) CORRECT ANSWER: C
In lines 91-94, the author indicates that "the fact that subjects know that they are being observed" may make findings in terms of brain training problematic for the study of Alzheimer's. This content aligns with the idea of awareness in C, while A (psychological burden) and D (consideration of family members) present topics that relate to the author's discussion of the negative effects of Alzeheimer's but that are NOT directly cited as points of uncertainty. B wrongly distorts the passage's focus on using brain activity to combat Alzheimer's to focus on the very different possibility that Alzheimer's redistributes brain activity.

9) CORRECT ANSWER: C
See above for analysis of the correct line reference. A and B indicate that redistributed brain activity may offer a means of addressing Alzheimer's, NOT (as in Question 8 B) that Alzheimer's itself redistributes brain activity. D indicates that more research on brain training may be necessary but does not align with an answer to the previous question; the idea that different groups may be negatively affected by the disease (as indicated by

Question 8 A) is a point of CERTAINTY, so that this line reference raises the wrong topic.

10) CORRECT ANSWER: C
In lines 46-48, the author indicates that the 2009 Alzheimer's Society study revealed that, in terms of cognitive training, participants under 50 displayed no cognitive improvement while those over 60 did display cognitive improvements. The graphs would NOT support the idea that participants under 50 displayed no improvement (since all groups did improve) but would align with the idea of superior improvement for older participants that was also seen in the 2009 study. C properly reflects this relationship, while A overstates the extent of the agreement and B wrongly indicates that NO results are compatible. D is contradicted by the idea that the study and the graph consider similar age groups and similar factors, so that comparison of some sort is definitely possible.

11) CORRECT ANSWER: A
The figure indicates that female subjects between the ages of 60 and 79 displayed the greatest improvement in both "Memorization" and "Problem-Solving." A properly indicates a woman in this age range and is thus the correct answer. B and C both indicate male subjects (who underperformed the female subjects in the 60 to 79 group), while D indicates a female subject from the under-performing 40 to 59 age group.

Chapter 5.3 | Carbonados

1) CORRECT ANSWER: D
After explaining the Mohs Hardness Scale and some central properties of carbonados (lines 1-29), the author outlines a "debate" (line 45) surrounding the origins of carbonados and explains how these substances can be put to practical use. This content directly supports D as presenting the best overview of the passage. A (uses), B (dispute), and C (hardness measurement) all refer to DETAILS of the passage in isolation, not to the complete analysis that the author provides.

2) CORRECT ANSWER: C
The word "hailed" refers to the situation of diamond at the "top" (line 7) of a hardness scale; thus, diamond would represent a criterion in a broadly-applicable system of measurement. C properly indicates that diamond would be used or acknowledged in assessment. A and B both wrongly refer to visual properties or physical actions, while D indicates that diamond is being praised, NOT that it is simply recognized in a context of measurement.

3) CORRECT ANSWER: A
In the relevant paragraph, the author contrasts carbonados with substances that "most people are familiar with" (line 19) and calls attention to the "unusual properties" (line 29) of carbonados. This content directly supports A, while B introduces a negative judgment that is NOT supported by the author's neutral consideration of the physical properties (such as a patina) of carbonados. C offers a value judgment (surprising) that the passage does not support, since how well-known carbonados are (NOT whether they are seen as useless or not) is the author's focus. D is contradicted by the fact that the author clearly explains the composition of carbonados in the relevant paragraph.

4) CORRECT ANSWER: C
The word "display" refers to features that are "inclusions" (line 26) in the composition of carbonados. Carbonados naturally have or exhibit these properties, so that C is an appropriate choice. A, B, and D all refer to INTENTIONAL activities and are thus inappropriate to a description of minerals that do not have will or consciousness.

5) CORRECT ANSWER: B
The author explains that Haggarty "performed extensive research" (line 36) on the physical properties of carbonados, so that the relevant description of physical properties would link to Haggarty's own studies. B is thus appropriate, while A wrongly indicates that Haggarty's language (which is simply clear and direct) is meant to simplify an issue. C wrongly references EARLIER content in terms of carbonado classification, while D wrongly references the author's LATER discussion of debates and additional research surrounding carbonados.

6) CORRECT ANSWER: C
In lines 72-74, the author indicates that "diamond saws" cannot effectively cut carbonados, so that C properly captures a contrast presented in the passage. Choose this answer and eliminate A as referencing a debate (extraterrestrial origins) about carbonados that the passage does NOT clearly extend to diamonds. B is contradicted by the idea that carbonados are HARDER than diamonds, while D cites the opacity of carbonados as a problem when in fact the author mostly describes this trait a in neutral manner.

7) CORRECT ANSWER: D
See above for analysis of the correct line reference. A indicates that carbonados exceed diamonds in hardness but does NOT present a point of comparison that aligns with an answer to the previous question. B

and C reference ideas about the origins and properties of carbonados but should NOT be taken as evidence for Question 6 C, since the possibility of extraterrestrial DIAMONDS does not directly interest the author.

8) CORRECT ANSWER: D
In lines 51-54, the author notes that a "variety of astronomical causes" have been cited in connection to the origins of carbonados; D properly captures the idea of different explanations involving extraterrestrial origins. A (negative) and B (positive) assess the theories of origin linked to carbonados, when in fact the author notes that the theories of origin CONTINUE to inspire debate (lines 87-89). C distorts the passage's focus on carbonados as substances that continue to be investigated to present a timeline for investigation (theory formulated before understanding) that the passage does not support.

9) CORRECT ANSWER: A
See above for analysis of the correct line reference. B presents a point of dispute involving carbonados but should NOT be mistaken as evidence for Question 8 A, since the author is summarizing a debate but not taking a position. C provides possible evidence that carbonados originated in outer space but describes a finding, NOT a theory. D, like B, presents a point of dispute without situating the author as an advocate of a specific theory.

10) CORRECT ANSWER: A
According to the table, fluorite has a hardness rating of 4 and topaz has a hardness rating of 8. While a mineral harder than fluorite could fall within this range, such a mineral could NOT have the same rating as fluorite itself. Thus, A is the best answer, while B, C, and D should be eliminated as describing minerals that fall within the possible range.

11) CORRECT ANSWER: B
While the author explains that the Mohs Hardness Scale at one point functioned with a maximum rating of 10, the table indicates that the top rating now extends beyond 10 to account for substances harder than diamond. B effectively calls attention to the idea that the scale has been extended, while HOW the scale was changed is considered in the passage but NOT in the table itself. Eliminate A for this reason, then eliminate C and D as considering properties of carbonados other than hardness, which is the only property considered in the table.

Chapter 5.4 | Marangoni Effect

1) CORRECT ANSWER: C
After considering the challenges associated with "cleaning up an oil spill" (line 18), the author explains research involving a "computational model" (line 32) that could help to address this problem. C properly reflects this content and refers to the area of inquiry (fluid dynamics related to the Marangoni Effect) that the computational model considers. A wrongly avoids the oil spill topic entirely, while B refers to past oil spills, NOT to the possibility of more effectively cleaning up future oil spills. D wrongly indicates that technological adaptations have taken place as a result of the research described in the passage, NOT (as the author in fact explains) that the research is promising in its implications but has yet to be practically applied.

2) CORRECT ANSWER: D
The author's listing of "Other examples" is coordinated to follow a brief discussion of "Oil spills" (line 1) as instances of a notable behavior of liquids; the same behavior can be observed in the "Other examples." D properly reflects this content, while A is inappropriate because the author does not cite specific research or analyze the Marangoni Effect until LATER in the passage. B raises the topic of expert testimony (when in fact the author is providing examples without any such reference) and does so in an inappropriately critical manner. C is inaccurate because "pollution" (line 5) is one of the included examples and because whether the relevant behavior of liquids is mostly negative or positive is not directly considered. In fact, because pollution IS mentioned, such liquid behavior could normally be destructive.

3) CORRECT ANSWER: C
In lines 30-33, the author explains that a professor is "making enhancements" to a computational model that is devoted to the Marangoni Effect; because the model is NOT complete, it logically follows that the effect has not been fully or comprehensively explained. C is thus an effective choice, while A references fluid behavior and B references the Marangoni Effect WITHOUT indicating a clear limitation in understanding. D explains the nature of an inquiry related to the Marangoni Effect but does NOT, in the manner of C, indicate that the Marangoni Effect is not yet entirely understood.

4) CORRECT ANSWER: B
The word "static" is used to refer to a drop of liquid that "does not immediately spread and mix" (line 13); thus, the drop does not move. B

is an appropriate answer, while A would describe a solid or rigid form, NOT a drop of liquid. C (indicating determination or devotion) and D (indicating unwillingness to change) introduce personality traits that are naturally out of context.

5) CORRECT ANSWER: D
In the relevant paragraph, the author introduces the "research team" (lines 30-31) headed by Professor Afkhami and explains the team's research as it relates to the Marangoni Effect; later, the author provides additional detail (lines 57-84) regarding the experiment. D is thus accurate, while A applies a wrongly negative tone to a mostly explanatory paragraph. B focuses on an issue (practical motivations) raised ELSEWHERE in the discussions of possible cleanup applications of fluid dynamics research. C mistakes the collaborative approach to research outlined in the paragraph for an "interdisciplinary" approach that would draw on very different branches of knowledge, when in fact the involved experts were all working with fluid dynamics.

6) CORRECT ANSWER: C
The word "lifts" refers to a scenario in which liquid in a wineglass moves "up the glass" (line 51). C would best refer to a substance changing its placement. A and B both refer to strong or inspired emotions and are thus out of context, while D indicates glorification, a theme that is both overly positive and irrelevant to the basic movement of liquid.

7) CORRECT ANSWER: A
In lines 59-63, the author explains that a group of researchers in fluid dynamics "created videos" to document a physical process, so that A is an appropriate choice. B appears to focus on the modeling element of the research project described in the passage but introduces a negative ("often overlooked") that the author does not consider. C criticizes previous research as flawed (and thus distorts the passage's ACTUAL topic of finding new information about the Marangoni effect), while D mistakes the use of a "computational model" (line 32) as mentioned in the passage for the use of visual simulations using computer technology (which the author does not in fact consider).

8) CORRECT ANSWER: B
See above for analysis of the correct line reference. A explains the movement of liquid using an everyday example but should NOT (since no negative tone is present) be taken as evidence for Question 7 B. C and D explain how the researchers described in the passage investigated fluid dynamics using PHYSICAL situations and thus suggest that Question 7 D (which mentions software-based simulations) introduces a false topic.

9) CORRECT ANSWER: A
In discussing possibilities for cleaning oil spills, the author indicates that Marangoni-based methods can help in "delivering the materials as well as cleaning the surface" (lines 89-90) and can do so "without contaminating the surface" (line 91). This content directly supports A and can be used to eliminate C and D, which wrongly depict a Marangoni-based approach as fundamentally problematic or impractical. B is contradicted by the author's statement that the outlined method will "not significantly change the properties of the surface" (lines 87-88) of a given liquid.

10) CORRECT ANSWER: C
The question requires a day on which the figure reported by the Technical Flow Rate Group (darkest line) was the LOWEST figure given. C fulfills this requirement, while A gives a day on which all three figures were equal. B and D both give days on which the U.S. Coast Guard reported the lowest figure.

11) CORRECT ANSWER: D
The graph provides three models for the volume of an oil spill; although the passage does mention oil spills, none of the three models are explicitly mentioned in the context of the Marangoni Effect or of any of the passage's other core issues. Thus, the graph cannot be assessed in terms of the Marangoni Effect, which is a factor that it does not consider. D is the best answer, while other answers wrongly assume that the graph contradicts principles of fluid dynamics presented in the passage or that Afkhami was responding to a 2010 oil spill. Because no such points of connection are raised in the passage (which does not mention the 2010 oil spill) or in the graph (which does not mention any principles of fluid dynamics), A, B, and C should all be eliminated.

Chapter 5.5 | Algae Biofuels

1) CORRECT ANSWER: C
After explaining that algae-related fuel could be a "sustainable, cost-effective option" (lines 8-9), the author then outlines the "problems" (line 24) that the adoption of algae-based fuel faces. This content supports C, while A does not properly reflect the passage's focus on a single fuel source and B mistakes the author's actual consideration of possible problems for the correction of misconceptions (a negative that the author never mentions). D wrongly avoids any negative tone whatsoever, when in fact the author directly analyzes a variety of obstacles.

2) CORRECT ANSWER: B
The author's description of algae as sustainable and cost-effective is used to build upon the idea that algae is "At the top of the list" (line 8) of alternative fuel sources. Thus, algae ALREADY seems to hold some status as a promising energy source, so that B is appropriate. A indicates that other alternative fuel sources will disappear, NOT that algae is simply promising on its own. C raises the topic of public perception of controversy (which the author avoids), while D raises a topic that is only considered LATER in the passage (and is further contradicted by the fact that algae is more costly per barrel than oil).

3) CORRECT ANSWER: B
The word "pursuing" refers to "solutions" (line 24) that, for the author, may or may not be practical. B properly raises a context of putting into practice or implementing a solution, while A and C both refer to physical activities or movements, NOT to practicality. D raises a context of thought, not of potentially useful action, and is thus problematic.

4) CORRECT ANSWER: D
In lines 26-28, the author points out the "higher prices" of clean fuels relative to fossil fuels, thus indicating that economic factors (NOT purely scientific findings) may present a problem in terms of the adoption of algae-based fuel. D is thus appropriate. A calls attention to the potential of alternative fuels (NOT to a challenge), while B and C call attention to scientific problems (not to problems OTHER than scientific considerations) and thus do not align with the requirements of the prompt.

5) CORRECT ANSWER: D
In lines 28-34, the author indicates that oil may be a more cost-efficient fuel source than algae, because the lowest per barrel cost of algae is "still higher than the current steepest oil price point." This content, along with the considerable $300-$2600 range for expected algae oil production cited in the same lines, supports D and can be used to eliminate C as wrongly indicating a small price range. Because algae and oil are only compared in detail in terms of cost, NOT in terms of pollution, A and B are both out of scope (since it is possible, in contradiction of both answers, that algae would not produce any pollution whatsoever).

6) CORRECT ANSWER: D
In lines 49-53, the author indicates that technological advances in algae oil production could lead to "low cost" oil generation by new algae species. This content supports the emphasis on lower cost in D, while A and B wrongly shift focus away from algae oil production itself to consider SECONDARY benefits that do not clearly interest the author. C raises a

topic that appears to be supported by lines 49-53 (new species) but relates the development of such species to the wrong purpose (lowering nutrient volume, NOT the actual topic of improving prices).

7) CORRECT ANSWER: B
See above for analysis of the correct line reference. A raises the topic of nutrient regulation but NOT the topic of new species, and should not be confused as evidence for Question 6 C. C references a property of algae that is natural and that thus does not depend on "improving technology" as required by the previous question, while D raises a research-based benefit (diversity) that does not clearly align with an answer to the previous question.

8) CORRECT ANSWER: C
The word "diversity" refers to a situation in which many "options" (line 65) are available in algae production, so that C directly links to the content of the passage. A, B, and D all refer to positive traits attributed to groups of people, NOT to an experimental situation involving the use of algae, and are thus out of context.

9) CORRECT ANSWER: A
In the final paragraph, the author presents a variety of "benefits" (line 55) that can be connected to algae-related biofuels; some of the notable benefits relate to the adaptability, rapid growth, and diversity of algae species. This content supports A, while specific research (as opposed to broadly-applicable benefits) as mentioned in B is only considered EARLIER in the passage. C is problematic because the author, despite presenting benefits, still considers algae oil costs to be a problem and does NOT cite any specific benefit as directly overturning this liability. D mistakes the idea of presenting benefits after presenting liabilities for the idea of a compromise; the author does not at any point reference cooperation or negotiation in the manner that this idea requires.

10) CORRECT ANSWER: D
While the maximum cost per barrel for algae oil is estimated to decrease from over $1000 to closer to $1000 between 2010 and 2025, the maximum cost per barrel for crude oil is estimated to remain around $100 during the same period. The difference in costs for the two resources will thus decrease, so that D is the best answer. Keep in mind that the graph only measures prices, NOT total consumption (eliminating A) for the two resources. Note also that the price per barrel for crude oil is estimated to experience minimal changes (eliminating B) and that the price per barrel for algae oil will decrease (eliminating C).

11) CORRECT ANSWER: A
In lines 36-39, the author explains that "improvements in engineering" and other technology-based factors could lower the cost per barrel for algae oil. This content directly supports A as appropriate. B, C, and D all raise factors that, though perhaps broadly or vaguely related to the discussion of the global economy and consumer habits in lines 1-7, the author does NOT explicitly consider in terms of oil pricing.

Chapter 5.6 | Ebola Vaccine

1) CORRECT ANSWER: B
The author of Passage 1 describes the development of VSV-ZEBOV by documenting an "early stage clinical trial" (line 7) that took place in 2015. This content directly supports B, while A (more than one attempt or method) and C (concepts for vaccines overall) raise much broader topics and thus do not fit a discussion of a single vaccine used to combat Ebola. D describes the problem that VSV-ZEBOV was designed to combat but does NOT reference the vaccine itself.

2) CORRECT ANSWER: C
In lines 36-44, the author of Passage 1 explains that the administration of the VSV-ZEBOV vaccine was accompanied by both negative (pain, fever) and positive (disappearance of arthritis symptoms) side effects. This content directly supports C, while the focus on present observation ONLY can be used to eliminate A (which indicates future possibilities) and D (which indicates specific past predictions). B rightly indicates that side effects were present, but wrongly assumes that the author explains what portion of test subjects experienced such side effects when in fact no specific numbers are mentioned.

3) CORRECT ANSWER: B
The word "transient" refers to a fever that "resolved itself" (line 39) in a measurable period of hours; the fever was thus not permanent, so that B is an appropriate choice. A would indicate that the fever appeared irregularly, NOT that it appeared and subsequently disappeared. C would only be appropriate to the movements of people or animals, while D wrongly indicates that the fever (which could be a health liability and in any case WAS noticed) was unimportant or negligible.

4) CORRECT ANSWER: B
The word "candidate" refers to a vaccine that could be "very useful" (line 47) in addressing Ebola; B properly refers to the idea of a practical possibility indicated by the context. A, C, and D all refer to contexts

involving argumentation or discussion, NOT to the context of practical results that the author emphasizes.

5) CORRECT ANSWER: B
The author of Passage 1 explains that the 2015 study involved both a vaccine group and a placebo group (lines 23-26) and that 40 subjects developed antibodies within 28 days of vaccine injection (lines 33-36). B accurately indicates a similarity between these numbers and the numbers provided in the graph, while A is problematic because the graph does not address side effects in ANY manner. C presents accurate logic (that side effects are not considered) but offers the wrong fundamental assessment, while D is contradicted by the identical subject numbers for the graph and the study described in the passage.

6) CORRECT ANSWER: B
In lines 65-67, the author mentions the rVSV-ZEBOV vaccine as "possibly safer" than the VSV-ZEBOV vaccine, so that B reflects the contrast required by the prompt. A and C both call attention to the possibility of different vaccines but do not clearly indicate which one is PREFERABLE, while D provides a general advantage of recombinant vaccines but does NOT specifically state that this advantage could make the rVSV-ZEBOV vaccine superior to the VSV-ZEBOV vaccine.

7) CORRECT ANSWER: A
While the author indicates that 300,000 doses of rVSV-ZEBOV were made available (lines 81-84), as of May 2017 only two confirmed cases and "Dozens" (line 90) of suspected cases had been detected. Thus, the vaccine resources easily outnumbered the diagnosed cases by May 2017, so that A is the correct answer. B and C distort the idea that Ebola may be a future threat to wrongly indicate that new developments HAVE in fact taken place. D distorts the ideas of surplus resources and few Ebola cases to indicate that the vaccine has already minimized a threat in a manner that would definitely call for a new approach.

8) CORRECT ANSWER: D
The relevant question involves the issue of whether the small number of Ebola cases would "justify" (line 97) a complex and costly countermeasure; thus, the question involves consideration of practical circumstances for the best possible outcome. D reflects this content, while A wrongly describes a SMALL number of cases as a "public health crisis." B and C wrongly assume that the question is meant to reflect the viewpoint of a person or group OTHER than the author when in fact the author is here providing independent analysis.

9) CORRECT ANSWER: C
While Passage 1 is devoted to a "2015 study" (line 26) that entailed the testing of VSV-ZEBOV, Passage 2 considers the deployment of VSV-ZEBOV (lines 53-64) and the possible tactical uses of vaccines (lines 85-102). This content supports C, while the fact that BOTH passages are formal in tone and address serious public health issues can be used to eliminate A as inaccurate. B wrongly neglects the fact that Passage 2 presents an alternative to VSV-ZEBOV and notes the possible problems with vaccine deployment; D wrongly construes Passage 1, which mostly outlines an actual study, as hypothetical in nature.

10) CORRECT ANSWER: D
In lines 76-78, the author of Passage 2 explains that vaccines feature elements that "could be harmful in their original state"; the author of Passage 1 mentions similarly harmful virus elements in lines 14-20 and notes that a vaccine that utilizes such elements cannot cause "infection." Both authors agree that virus elements as used in vaccines are rendered harmless, so that D is the best answer. A mistakes general information used to explain viruses in Passage 1 for more specific information about a single vaccine that is ONLY mentioned in Passage 2, while B wrongly criticizes information from Passage 1 that the author of Passage 2 would find valid. C assumes agreement but wrongly focuses on the public response to information about viruses, NOT on the ideas of researchers or the ideas of the author of Passage 2.

11) CORRECT ANSWER: B
See above for analysis of the correct line reference. A mentions the development of VSV-ZEBOV but does not align with any of the more specific ideas about vaccine creation mentioned in lines 14-20 of Passage 1. C mentions a vaccine, rVSV-ZEBOV, that is NOT considered in Passage 1, while D raises a point of uncertainty related to addressing Ebola outbreaks but does not relate to the exact topic of engineering an Ebola vaccine.

Chapter 5.7 | Africanized Bees

1) CORRECT ANSWER: B
The author of the passage points out that Africanized bees are present in North America despite their origins on a different continent (lines 1-17) and calls attention to both the aggressive habits and the "growing prevalence" (line 21) of these insects. B properly references a situation involving commercial use and a need for control measures in terms of a

natural species. A and C both refer entirely to the actions of PEOPLE and avoid the theme of invasion or intrusion; D references a theme of invasion by people THEMSELVES, not a theme of organisms that are introduced by people invading an area.

2) CORRECT ANSWER: B
The word "domestic" refers to a use that is not possible in the case of "highly defensive" (line 18) Africanized bees, which are contrasted with bees that CAN be used for economic benefit by humans. Thus, "domestic" would refer to a desirable commercial factor that is no longer associated with Africanized bees. B is appropriate, while A refers to the demeanor or emotions of a polite person, NOT to a bee population. C and D both refer to the theme of individuality, not to the passage's key content of use and management of bees.

3) CORRECT ANSWER: B
In lines 31-33, the author explains that Africanized bees "were first introduced in Brazil" in an attempt to increase honey production; this content directly supports B as indicating the proper location and the economic intentions connected to Africanized bees. A and C both refer to ways in which the bees would SPREAD, not to the idea of how the bees first ARRIVED. D distorts a reference to a Venezuelan oil tanker (lines 39-41) that brought Africanized bees to California from elsewhere in the Americas but NOT to the Americas entirely.

4) CORRECT ANSWER: B
See above for analysis of the correct line reference. A presents a suggestion for managing bee populations, NOT a historical explanation of the movements of the Africanized bee population. C and D explain how the Africanized bees spread AFTER they arrived in the Americas, yet the previous question requires a reference to the arrival of the bees.

5) CORRECT ANSWER: D
The word "factors" is used in the context of bringing Africanized bees across the world "in the first place" (line 31); the author is thus explaining the original occurrences or historical circumstances linked to Africanized bees. D is appropriate, while A introduces an overly positive tone when in fact the introduction of the bees was somewhat problematic. B refers to uncertain or changing quantities (when in fact the history of the bees is well-known), while C references a theme of impact or change, NOT the idea of a set of historical events.

6) CORRECT ANSWER: A
The relevant words are used to describe Africanized bees, which behave "aggressively" (line 55) as explained in the relevant paragraph. Because the relevant words occur in phrases that build upon this characterization, A is the best choice. B and D both offer expressions of praise for the bees, which are mostly being described from a scientific and analytic perspective in terms of behavior, while C wrongly indicates that the author (who in fact notes that the bees can be problematic) strongly dislikes the bees themselves.

7) CORRECT ANSWER: C
While Africanized bees did evolve in a difficult climate that was by no means temperate (lines 13-16), the author does NOT argue that these bees cannot survive in climates that are different; in fact, the ability of the Africanized bees to spread indicates that the opposite may be true. C thus raises a faulty line of reasoning and is the correct answer. A, B, and D can be eliminated on the basis of lines 10-12 and lines 16-19, which indicate that European bees are less aggressive and thus less likely to sting than Africanized bees are.

8) CORRECT ANSWER: D
In lines 90-94, the author indicates that some Africanized bee groups do not display "the typical hyper-defensive behavior." Such behavior is construed as problematic for humans throughout the passage, and this indication that such behavior is not present among some Africanized bee groups indicates that human concerns may be overstated. D is appropriate, while A, B, and C all call attention to the positive qualities of Africanized bees WITHOUT clearly indicating that negative factors may be overstated.

9) CORRECT ANSWER: D
The map of South America indicates that Chile saw the arrival of Africanized bees in the 1990s or 2000s (darkest coloring), so that 1992 would properly fit the earlier of these time periods. Choose D and eliminate A, B, and C as referencing earlier decades that would be designated only by lighter colors.

10) CORRECT ANSWER: C
While the passage indicates that Africanized bees "arrived in the US in 1985" (line 35), the figure indicates that the bees could have reached California (intermediate coloring) at some point in the 1970s. C properly reflects this disparity, while A is CONTRADICTED by the fact that Africanized bees were found in some South American countries before the 1970s (lightest coloring) while NO coloring that indicates a presence

before the 1970s is present for the United States map. B (comparison of bee species) introduces a factor that the maps (which ONLY address Africanized bees) do not consider. D misstates the factors that the maps (which deal with date of introduction, NOT population or concentration) actually consider for Africanized bees.

11) CORRECT ANSWER: B
While the passage indicates that Africanized bees can mate with European bees (lines 41-44) but cannot in their original form survive cold locations in the United States (lines 71-76), the graph indicates that Africanized bees DID spread from California (relatively mild) to Nevada (relatively cold). Thus, to survive in the colder region, the Africanized bees were logically required to cross-breed with European bees. B reflects this content and reasoning, while A refers to some benefits of raising Africanized bees but does NOT clearly reference the geographic movements reflected in the U.S. map. C raises a factor (increasing temperature) that neither the passage nor the graph considers in terms of the spread of bee populations. D wrongly links an observed tendency (lines 91-94) in terms of lowered aggression to the theme of geographic spread; diminished aggression would explain why INDIVIDUAL farmers would find Africanized bees desirable but is not explicitly tied to the movement of Africanized bee populations.

Chapter 5.8 | Behavioral Addiction

1) CORRECT ANSWER: A
After explaining how "Psychologists have been conceptualizing" (line 1) behavioral disorders, the author explains the limited data and need for future research that surround these problems (lines 19-34). This content, along with the author's discussion of Grant's work on treatment methods (lines 54-65), supports A as the best answer. B confuses the absence of data with the idea of an active debate, while C neglects the topic of recent and potentially useful research that is central to the passage. D places too much focus on performed research, when in fact the author uses the early stages of the passage to explain concepts and note lapses in knowledge.

2) CORRECT ANSWER: C
In lines 39-43, the author explains that behavioral addiction involves the prioritization of "short-term reward" and the disregard of long-term consequences such as diminished control. This content supports C, while the author's focus on the psychological dangers faced by those with behavioral addictions (NOT the dangers to those around them) renders A

problematic. B and D distort the author's idea that behavioral addiction features negative outcomes that are disregarded; it does not follow from this idea that there are positive results or perceptions linked to behavioral addiction.

3) CORRECT ANSWER: C
See above for analysis of the correct line reference. A and B indicate that behavioral addictions are similar to other forms of addiction, an idea that is relevant to the required topic but does NOT align with any answer to the previous question. D notes a possible connection between behavioral addiction and personality, but the personality cited is NOT necessarily positive in a manner that would justify Question 2 B.

4) CORRECT ANSWER: D
The word "Limited" refers to the data for various behavioral addictions; overall, the author compares this already relatively scarce data to the "Very little data" (line 22) for other behavioral addictions. D properly indicates that the data are not complete or could be supplemented. A (short and direct expression), B (loneliness or removal), and C (straightforward or uncomplicated in nature) raise inappropriate contexts for a discussion of the level of data available in the study of behavioral problems.

5) CORRECT ANSWER: B
In lines 54-56, the authors explain an idea about the connections between disorders that "Grant noted"; this paragraph's focus on of Grant's ideas supports B as an appropriate choice. The same evidence should NOT be taken as support for A, since the authors deal with Grant's own comparison as paraphrased rather than extending the comparison through independent analysis. While Grant has surveyed the research of others (lines 34-38), Grant's OWN credentials are not clearly indicated in the passage (eliminating C). Moreover, while Grant's work is situated within a topic that has experienced data deficiencies (lines 19-25), the author does not actually criticize Grant's work itself as problematic (eliminating D).

6) CORRECT ANSWER: C
See above for analysis of the correct line reference. A explains how Grant and other researchers performed a study by surveying past findings but does not clearly align with an answer to the previous question. B and D refer to the topic of behavioral addiction but do NOT clearly explain methods specific to Grant's work and thus do not fit the requirements of the previous question.

7) CORRECT ANSWER: C
The "interventions" cited by the author involve measures that would cause subjects to address behavioral addictions by identifying risks and making lifestyle changes. C properly references a behavioral addiction that is managed through active and conscious risk avoidance. A and D both describe treatment methods for problems that have already reached a state of crisis, NOT conscious methods of managing risk and avoiding temptation. B would EXPOSE a person with a behavioral addiction to a source of risk and thus contradicts the methods explained in the passage.

8) CORRECT ANSWER: A
The word "approved" refers to the status of medications for behavioral addictions; no such medications are approved, yet there are "treatments" (line 70) for comparable substance abuse disorders. Thus, an "approved" treatment would be considered valid and would be put into effect. A is appropriate, while B and C would be more effectively used to indicate the strongly positive recognition of people for their accomplishments. D indicates acceptance or admission in terms of discussion, NOT use of a medication for treatment.

9) CORRECT ANSWER: B
In lines 75-79, the author explains that Topiramate can treat some behavioral addictions but does NOT mention behavioral addictions to technology (as designated in lines 1-4) in this context. Thus, Topiramate may not be relevant to all forms of behavioral addiction. This content supports B and can be used to eliminate A. Other answers distort the content of the passage, since Topiramate is not yet widely used for behavioral addiction treatment but will NOT necessarily undergo modifications (eliminating C) and since Topiramate can be used for various types of addiction treatment but was not clearly developed to treat behavioral addiction (eliminating D).

10) CORRECT ANSWER: A
While the graph indicates that Lifestyle Change Coaching led to a 50% success rate in treating behavioral addiction, all other treatment forms exhibited success rates of 20% or lower. Choose A to reflect this content, and eliminate B, C, and D as referencing methods with lower success rates than that of Lifestyle Change Coaching.

11) CORRECT ANSWER: C
While the relevant paragraph considers the possible use of "medications used to treat substance abuse" (line 71) in behavioral addiction treatment, the graph considers treatment methods that modify behavior but do NOT

clearly involve medication. C properly reflects a difference between the content of the relevant paragraph and the information in the graph, while A and B provide the wrong fundamental assessments while explaining details of treatment methods that (despite mentioning the methods themselves) the graph omits. D wrongly indicates that the author of the passage considers Lifestyle Change Coaching in the relevant paragraph, when in fact lifestyle changes are mentioned EARLIER in the passage and the relevant paragraph deals almost entirely with medication-based treatment.

Chapter 5.9 | Microbiome of Rice

1) CORRECT ANSWER: C
After providing background information on the role of microbiota for both plants and humans, the authors explain the procedures and results linked to "a recent study" (line 33) dedicated to the presence of microbiota in plant roots. The authors conclude the discussion by explaining how the research may link to beneficial effects for human society (lines 72-82), so that C is an appropriate answer. A mistakes the connection between different types of microbiota (human and plant) for a fundamental and more negative misunderstanding, while B is overly optimistic about the transformative potential of the study described in the passage. D neglects the emphasis on both background and benefits in presenting the study that interests the authors.

2) CORRECT ANSWER: B
The word "predict" refers to human properties linked to microbiota; these microbes can help humans to "build" (line 14) diets by arriving at useful conclusions. B, "foretell," properly indicates the action of drawing a conclusion from useful information. A best refers to specific quantities (NOT to more general traits or properties), C refers to a stage that would occur AFTER prediction, and D refers to a manner of indicating the future in a more mystical or spiritual manner.

3) CORRECT ANSWER: B
The research project described in the passage offers particular promise for "drought-prone areas" (lines 79-80), so that a population grappling with low rainfall would naturally benefit from the findings involved. Choose B as appropriate. A (instability) and C (distance from food sources) raise negatives that do not directly interest the authors (who mostly call attention to stress on plants due to resource shortages). D focuses on animals in a potentially prospering setting, when in fact humans facing disadvantages are the focus of the passage.

4) CORRECT ANSWER: C
The relevant sentence calls attention to important crops and indicates that more efficient production could benefit vast human populations. Shortly after, the authors place this sentence in the context of a recent study that could provide information to address the problems that have been raised (lines 32-37). C is thus an appropriate choice, while the fact that the procedural DETAILS of the relevant study (not a possible benefit) are only explained LATER can be used to eliminate A, B, and D, all of which assume that the relevant sentence itself presents such details.

5) CORRECT ANSWER: B
In lines 38-43, the author explains that the researchers gathered results both from "season to season" and across "regions with diverse climates." Thus, the references to the variation of both seasonal and geographic factors make B an appropriate choice. A provides the premises for the study but does NOT call attention to diversification of factors, while C and D explain how exactly the researchers conducted the study but PROCEED from B, which is the only answer to properly raise the theme of diverse factors as required by the prompt.

6) CORRECT ANSWER: A
In discussing the 84-day window, the authors explain that researchers monitored the flowering of rice plants in reference to microbiota composition (lines 47-55). This relationship between growth and microbiota (the key factor in the study) justifies A. Other answers distort this content: B is problematic because it is not clear whether the researchers themselves devised the 84-day window or relied on previous findings, while C mistakes the idea that chronological age and microbiota will have a limited correlation after 84 days for the idea that microbiota will develop abnormally after 84 days. D introduces a faulty relationship: DNA was used for assessment of chronological age, but stresses could cause the age determined by DNA evaluation to deviate from the plant's chronological age.

7) CORRECT ANSWER: C
In lines 64-66, the authors explain that drought can cause a disparity between a plant's chronological age and its age as indicated by DNA; this information occurs in the context of a discussion of plants within the initial 84-day interval for microbiota study. Together, this content supports C. Both A and B reference periods AFTER the 84-day stretch that the passage considers, while microbiota ebb and flow (lines 56-58) is described as a mostly common seasonal occurrence that does not generate an age disparity. Thus, eliminate D as a misreading of actual information from the passage.

8) CORRECT ANSWER: D
See above for analysis of the correct line reference. A explains an experimental procedure, NOT a result as required by the previous question. B indicates a correlation between age and microbiota when the previous question requires discussion of a disparity instead, while C calls attention to a similarity involving microbiota and avoids the question of chronological age in any clear manner.

9) CORRECT ANSWER: D
The word "robust" refers to crops that would be "less stressed" (line 78) and could survive in difficult conditions; thus, a context of durability or health is appropriate. D introduces an effective positive, while A would best refer to force or dominance, NOT to the question of survival. B and C both raise the context of taste, which is BROADLY relevant to a discussion of food but not to the specific sentence and the specific focus on survival conditions.

10) CORRECT ANSWER: B
In the final paragraph, the authors indicate that research described in the passage could offer "a boon" to the agriculture industry and "confidence" for residents of troubled areas. This optimistic tone supports B, while the focus on the results of the study (NOT on its authors themselves) should be used to eliminate A as inappropriate. C (future projects) and D (suggested comparison to other projects) both distract from the authors' focus on the future potential of the present project ALONE.

Chapter 5.10 | Flu Vaccine

1) CORRECT ANSWER: B
After providing an overview of current issues in flu vaccine science, the author of the passage calls attention to an issue that may be "the cause of lowered rates of effectiveness" (line 27) in flu vaccination. This content supports B and should NOT be mistaken as justification for A; the author does indicate that current vaccination is problematic but does NOT indicate that vaccination should be replaced with other medical methods entirely. C misstates the focus of the passage (current vaccines and the H3N2 strains, not a hypothetical universal vaccine), while D focuses too much on the H3N2 strain and neglects the broader content about flu vaccine development.

2) CORRECT ANSWER: A
The paragraph begins by mentioning "the worldwide annual process" (line 13) of devising a flu vaccine, then goes on to explain how this process proceeds until the final vaccine is ready. A is supported by this content. B introduces a theme ("interdisciplinary nature") that is nowhere precisely addressed in the paragraph's overview of a scientific process. C introduces a faulty negative tone and D introduces a topic, the H3N2 strain, that is only mentioned LATER in the passage.

3) CORRECT ANSWER: D
In lines 45-49, the author of the passage notes that flu shot effectiveness "drops drastically" when the H3N2 strain emerges, so that OTHER strains are by this same logic easier to fight with flu vaccines. D is thus appropriate, while H1N1 (line 65) is mentioned alongside H3N2 but NOT as a strain for which H3N2 is mistaken (eliminating A). Note that lines 25-40 call attention to the prevalence of H3N2 in one flu season (not to be mistaken for dominance of MULTIPLE seasons, eliminating B) and indicate that the strain is capable of adaptation (NOT of changing to the point that it cannot be detected, eliminating C).

4) CORRECT ANSWER: D
The word "eliminating" refers to a desired outcome in terms of addressing risk, but to one that is contrasted with the less thorough idea of "reducing" (line 39). D properly fits the idea of thoroughly counteracting risk. A (context of definition), B (context of personal or ideological rejection), and C (context of giving up an item or position) do not effectively refer to the context of addressing a health problem.

5) CORRECT ANSWER: A
Lines 38-40 indicate that a flu shot is valuable in eliminating risk but does not result in flawless disease resistance; lines 45-47 build on this idea by indicating that a flu shot has an imperfect but still useful effectiveness of over 50 percent. Choose A and eliminate B, which alludes to statistics but does not provide a specific number that would indicate that a flu shot is useful. C refers to flu shot production and D refers generally to the complications in responding to flu, so that neither choice offers supporting detail for the idea of flu shot effectiveness.

6) CORRECT ANSWER: C
In lines 49-53, the author explains that the researchers described in the passage "tracked flu cases" among adults and children in order to study H3N2. This content supports C and should NOT be mistaken as evidence for A (which mentions future projections, NOT case-by-case tracking) or

D (which mentions self-reporting, a testimony-based measure that should NOT be confused with the collection of data by researchers). B wrongly references content from elsewhere in the passage, since laboratory assessment of flu strains is performed to develop flu vaccines, but the author never traces such laboratory work to a study of the real-life impact of H3N2.

7) CORRECT ANSWER: A
See above for analysis of the correct line reference. B provides information about H3N2 but not a description of HOW the information was determined as demanded by the previous question. C deals with the underperformance of the annual flu vaccine and D deals with the difficult prospect of a universal flu vaccine; both of these answers stray from the topic of how H3N2 was studied.

8) CORRECT ANSWER: A
The word "elusive" refers to the "dream" (line 76) of creating the much-desired but (despite much research) still undeveloped universal flu vaccine. This dream is thus improbable or impossible at present, so that A is an appropriate choice. B (definition, a faulty context because the universal flu vaccine HAS been clearly explained), C (a negative indicating suspicious activity), and D (a negative indicating stubbornness) all raise inappropriate contexts.

9) CORRECT ANSWER: A
To meet the requirement of reflecting all age groups, the proposed experiment should feature an age group with a flu shot efficacy that is nearly equal to the efficacy for all age groups. Both "9-17 years" and "All" exhibit a roughly 35% efficacy. Choose A and eliminate B (lower than "All"), C (higher than "All"), and D (lower than "All").

10) CORRECT ANSWER: D
While the author of the passage indicates that a flu shot typically has an efficacy of 50-60%, figure 1 records an efficacy for all age groups of roughly 35%. These data contradict the data from the passage, so that D is appropriate. The author of the passage does not deal at length with different flu vaccine efficacies by age group, and at most notes that the research described in the passage considered a range of ages; thus, A wrongly references a factor that is considered in figure 1 but not in the passage. B (different vaccines) and C (universal vaccine) both consider factors mentioned in the passage but NOT addressed in the figure.

11) CORRECT ANSWER: B
While the passage focuses on H3N2 data from 2017-2018, the figure does not specify a range of years, so that such information (if present) would indicate how the figure is relevant to the passage. Choose B and eliminate A as an answer that deviates from the topic of H3N2 ITSELF to consider other strains. C raises an relatively minor factor, since how flu data is collected is of less importance than the issue of effectiveness by year is in assessing H3N2 (and since different methods of data collection may be equally reliable). D raises an issue that the passage, despite the focus on flu vaccine effectiveness, does not address in any detail.

Made in the USA
Middletown, DE
09 February 2020